The Foundations of Naval History

THE FOUNDATIONS
OF NAVAL HISTORY

*John Knox Laughton, the Royal Navy
and the Historical Profession*

Dr Andrew Lambert

CHATHAM PUBLISHING

LONDON

Copyright © Andrew Lambert 1998

First published in Great Britain in 1998 by Chatham Publishing,
61 Frith Street, London W1V 5TA

Chatham Publishing is an imprint of Gerald Duckworth & Co Ltd

British Library Cataloguing in Publication Data
A catalogue record for this book is available from the British Library

ISBN 1 86176 086 8

Typeset by Dorwyn Ltd, Rowlands Castle, Hants

Printed and bound in Great Britain by Bookcraft (Bath) Ltd

Contents

List of Plates

Foreword

It is with great pleasure that I take this opportunity to recall the invaluable and much appreciated assistance I have received from friends old and new in the course of researching and writing this book. I must begin by mentioning Don Schurman, to whom I owe the inestimable benefit of building on his pivotal chapter-length study of Laughton, the wider intellectual context he provided in *The Education of a Navy*, and opportunities to discuss Sir John more recently. Bryan Ranft, who followed Laughton's path from Greenwich to King's College, London, and did more than anyone to revive naval history in Britain, gave me an insight into the dynamics of these very different establishments. He has also suffered long enough to know the foibles of the author of this book far better than the author knows them himself. I fear he will not approve my use of the word 'doctrine', qualify it as I might, so I must apologise in advance. A number of friends and colleagues volunteered to read drafts of this book. I am proud to say no-one was 'pressed'. They all made important contributions to the development of the final version, ranging from specific expertise, through new material and advice, to that vital aid for every struggling author, the ability to stand back and take stock of the whole. In alphabetical order they were; John Beeler, Christopher Dandeker, Harry Dickinson, John Ferris, Robert Gardiner, Richard Harding, Sir Michael Howard, Derek Law, Christopher McKee, Sean McKnight, Julian Mannering, Robert Mullins, Bryan Ranft and Tony Sainsbury.

Long before this project had reached the stage at which readers were required I had already received assistance of great value. From the first serious stirrings of my interest in Sir John Knox Laughton, John Hattendorf has provided transcripts, photocopies, two important photographs, and the great benefit of his expertise on Mahan and Admiral Stephen B Luce USN. William Cogar provided an opportunity to present an earlier version of my thoughts to the Annapolis Naval History Conference in 1995, and published the results. Matt Uttley and Mike Smith, then of the Royal Naval College, Greenwich, allowed me to translate the lecture they wanted on the 'lessons of the Gulf War' into one on Greenwich and the development of doctrine in the Royal Navy only weeks before the College closed. Malcolm Walker invited me to write a brief life of Laughton the meteorologist, and aided my comprehension of an aspect of his life that I was otherwise ill-equipped to explain. Dan Baugh offered encouragement and the inestimable benefit of his insight. Peter Marshall recalled times past in the King's College History Department, and encouraged the project. The Department of Humanities Small Grant Fund supported a vital trip to Washington, which widened my research base and enabled me to discuss my work with a particularly well-informed audience.

In 1996 the Council of the Navy Records Society kindly invited me to take up Sir John's place as Secretary of the Society, and have been remarkably tolerant of my use of ancient precedents in Council meetings. Colin Matthew and Nicholas Rodger provided me with the priceless opportunity to re-examine the bulk of Laughton's nineteenth-century naval lives for the forthcoming *New Dictionary of National Biography*, while my good friend Roger Stearn kept the task within manageable bounds. Admiral Richard Hill, the long-serving editor of *The Naval Review*, provided transcripts and advice on the work of his predecessors. As Chairman of the Society for Nautical Research Admiral Hill provided leadership on another front that has been greatly appreciated. My colleagues and students have, for some years now, had Sir John glowering down on them from the wall, and have been remarkably understanding of this Victorian intellectual presence.

Among the archivists and assistants who made research for this book such a pleasure a special mention must be given to Clive Powell and Alan Giddings at the National Maritime Museum. They struggled against all manner of adversity to get the Laughton archive to my desk, located other collections and generally went above and beyond the call of duty. At King's College Patricia Methven and Kate O'Brien kindly explained the College Archives, located Laughton's official portrait, and supported this project. The staff of the Library of Congress Manuscript Room made my stay in Washington particularly productive. Andrew Tatham at the Royal Geographical Society unravelled the Society's minute books, Sir Clements Markham's notebooks and archive with great patience. In Cambridge the staff at Caius and at King's College uncovered further segments of the diffuse Laughton paper trail. At least they, like the Bodleian at Oxford, had the benefit of catalogued collections. In the University of London Paeleography Room the papers of Sir John Seeley and Albert Frederick Pollard required a more indulgent response to my enquiry. John Gardner supported my search for archival material on Philip Colomb, offered the hospitality of his home and provided a wealth of photocopies. At the Public Record Office William Seymour employed his unrivalled expertise to unravel a fascinating episode in Sir John's career. The staff at the British Library Manuscript Division maintained their reputation for providing an unsurpassed environment in which to conduct research. The Library of Reading University kindly sent me copies of the two Laughton items in the Longman archive. Picture research credits must go to Jonathan Coad, Alan McGowan for his help with the archives at the Greenwich College, and Peter Howard for translating old and indistinct images into a useable form. Without all of these people my attempt to understand Laughton's career would have been short, and this book could not have been written. Thank you.

The first, faltering version of my work was given to small group of colleagues at the Royal Military Academy, Sandhurst in 1990. I made many friends during my two years at Sandhurst. Late last year one of them, John Pimlott, was killed in tragic circumstances. John was the finest classroom teacher I have ever worked with, and an example to any academic. His capacity for hard work, taking pains, helping the ignorant and encouraging the able were legendary. It struck me very forcibly that the man I was writing about must have had a similar impact on his students and colleagues.

Despite the best efforts of my friends and colleagues the author has, as ever, followed his own inclinations, an approach which absolves them of any blame for what follows.

On a personal level Zohra, Tama-Sophie, my mother and father, and my wider family have all played a part. Their support is beyond price or understanding.

Andrew Lambert
Kew
St George's Day, 1998

Abbreviations used in the text

DNB	*Dictionary of National Biography*
DNI	Director of Naval Intelligence
EHR	*English Historical Review*
JNPA	Junior Naval Professional Association
NAM	National Army Museum
NID	Naval Intelligence Department
NMM	National Maritime Museum
NRS	Navy Records Society
RUSI	Royal United Services Institution

Introduction

Anyone writing a biographical study of a long-dead, largely forgotten historian has to face the obvious question, why? In the case of Professor Sir John Knox Laughton the answer is complex. Ten years ago I was trying to come to terms with the fact that naval history appeared to have no place in a British university or the higher education of officers in the Royal Navy. This reflection prompted two responses. The first led to a career as a motorcycle courier, the second laid the foundations of this book. If naval history was so unimportant I wanted to know why anyone had ever troubled themselves with the subject. In *The Education of a Navy* of 1965 Professor Schurman established that Laughton was the pioneer modern naval historian, arguing that he had provided the foundations for the development of modern naval thought. He, if anyone, held the key to my inquiry. While outlining my initial ideas I was fortunate to secure a Senior Lectureship at the Royal Military Academy, Sandhurst. The British Army, it appeared, had more use for a naval historian than the Royal Navy. Over the course of two rewarding years at Sandhurst I developed my ideas on service education, and when I joined the Department of War Studies at King's College, I was determined to revive Laughton's legacy as the key to a better understanding of the subject. Professor Schurman observed that it was the opportunity to teach naval history that inspired his study of the pioneer historians. There is no substitute for the regular, rigorous examination of ideas and arguments by students. My work has benefited greatly from the criticism of my undergraduate and postgraduate Option students taking 'Aspects of Naval History'. Their input has been complemented by the work of my research students, one of whom found that Sir John Knox Laughton occupied a prominent place in his own work. In order to teach any subject it is essential to master the principles upon which it is based. This problem confronted Laughton in the 1860s, and his response still informs the way in which we study the subject today. He knew that every subject has a history, and devoted much effort to the historiographical exposition that provided the starting point for his new endeavour. While the Ancient Greeks wrote naval history, and recognised the same dilemma of deciding whether it should be an educational tool or an accurate record of events in context, the decision to focus on Laughton was the right one. Understanding the work of the man who founded the modern discipline would provide an insight into more recent times.

This book began life as the Introduction to a reprint of Laughton's seminal articles, but the draft kept on growing. Visits to the Royal Military College, Kingston, Ontario, the United States Naval War College, the fortuitous discovery of Laughton's archive, a college-funded research trip to Washington and the support of a large number of colleagues, friends, archivists, librarians and other interested parties provided the raw material for a book. Then the new *Dictionary of National Biography* asked me to revise a large part of Laughton's work on nineteenth-century naval officers. When I finally admitted that I was writing a book a friend suggested that when historians reach a 'certain age' they turn to historiography. I was delighted to discover that he had a few years' head start on me, and repaid his wit by asking him to read the manuscript.

What follows is an attempt to explain the origins of modern naval history. It focuses on the core dilemma – how to balance the divergent strains of academic rigour and service education. Although Laughton worked inside the Royal Navy for thirty years, and the needs of the service remained paramount throughout his life, he did not sacrifice his critical faculty. Instead the Royal Navy accepted the educational value of his 'scientific' naval history, and it kept faith with him and his work as he developed an increasingly sophisticated methodology. Initially he worked alone, but after 1885 he adopted the best practice of his new colleagues, the professional historians, to draw them into the process. Laughton's work culminated when he founded the Navy Records Society in 1893, with his lifelong friend Admiral Sir Cyprian Bridge, the Director of Naval Intelligence, and effectively Chief of the Naval Staff. The two men created the Society as an unofficial historical branch for Bridge's Division. Yet they were careful to ensure that while they worked on subjects of interest to the contemporary Navy they employed the methodology of academic historians.

Sir John Knox Laughton was that rarest of creatures, an educator with the energy and the force of logic to persuade an armed force to accept the ideas he advocated, and follow him along new paths. In the process he developed naval history as a recognised branch of the new historical profession. Laughton was, by any standards, a remarkable man. He pioneered the modernisation of naval thought, developing naval history as the basis for a thorough study of tactics, strategy, leadership and service doctrine. His intellect spanned the century that separated Nelson from Fisher. His work was vital to the creation of the modern Royal Navy, and the United States' Navy, modernising the mental equipment of the world's most powerful navy, and helped to set the agenda for the task to be carried on across the Atlantic.

For too long historians addressing the Royal Navy in the period that separated the Crimean and First World Wars have perpetuated the myth that it was little more than a colonial gunboat force, commanded by hard-boiled seamen utterly devoid of brains and, with the exception of John Fisher, quite unable to face the challenge of the twentieth century. This is a grotesque parody. In reality the Royal Navy, the world's most powerful political instrument, was able to assimilate the impact of a near-permanent technological revolution on tactics, strategy and doctrine with far greater success than any other navy. It was served by an impressive group of intellectuals, among whom Laughton, Julian Corbett, Cyprian Bridge, Philip and John Colomb, Reginald Custance and Prince Louis of Battenberg are only a sample. These men worked closely with such pivotal figures as Astley Cooper Key, Geoffrey Thomas, Phipps Hornby, and John Fisher to create the modern service. Their contribution has been undervalued, largely because it relied on personal contact, influence and linkages, rather than official documents and new equipment. In essence the nineteenth-century Royal Navy was too professional a fighting force, and too important an element in national policy, for the stereotypes to be credible. At any time between 1815 and 1914 the Royal Navy was equal to the combined strength of any two other navies, the occasional public alarms about its state and condition being either political or service-driven attempts to improve funding or increase diplomatic influence.

Critics of the late nineteenth-century Royal Navy like to round off their condemnation by noting that even naval thought had to be imported from the United States. This book will demonstrate that the Royal Navy sustained a powerful intellectual community long before Alfred Thayer

✝ Mahan burst into prominence in 1890 and will show that Laughton's direct influence on Mahan was enormous.

As the pioneer of modern naval history, Laughton was the architect of a critical part of the pre-1914 Royal Navy's intellectual equipment. When he began work naval history was still in the age of chronicles and romance, but by the mid-1890s it had become a central element in the new English Historical profession, and the basis from which doctrine, tactics and policy were developed. In the process Laughton recruited Julian Corbett and inspired Alfred Mahan, the two men whose published output still dominates the literature on sea power and naval strategy. His methods and ideas moulded their development and informed their work. Laughton understood that history is both a process and a record, that it informs all other subjects, creates the base line from which they advance, and provides a running commentary on the progress of politics, ideas and technology. He also saw that naval history was only the examination of certain aspects of national and international history, the context in which

✝ MAHAN WAS PUSHING ON A DOOR WHICH WAS ALREADY AJAR

it had to be securely anchored, and that its importance came in the contribution it made to the understanding of those wider pictures.

This study is also a contribution to the better understanding of the Royal Navy that Laughton served, the historical profession he entered, and the links between them that he created. If we can fathom the motives and methods of this pioneer we will be better able to understand the disciplines we rely on to educate us for an uncertain future. The issue is timely, for as we enter the new century already fifty-five years distant from the last major war, there is a serious danger that we will repeat the mistakes of our ancestors. It was Laughton who reminded the Royal Navy that technical change was no reason to ignore the past, because the past was, and remains, the only real experience available to armed forces in time of peace: He sought the underlying principles of tactics, strategy, leadership and doctrine in the wisdom of the men who had given the service an unrivalled legacy of victory, seasoned with just enough disasters to avoid complacency. The folly of the Cold War obsession with contemporary relevance, to the exclusion of all else, should be obvious by now. This book was written in the belief that comprehension must be based on an understanding of basic principles, and the objects of those who developed the subject. In essence it asks why did John Knox Laughton devote the greater part of his professional and private lives to the development of naval history?

Ultimately this book is an attempt to show why naval history was created, and why it took the particular form that we still see today. In his lifetime Laughton found it hard to account for the astonishing ignorance of the naval past demonstrated by naval officers, statesmen, citizens and his fellow historians. He found it impossible to account for this collective, wilful neglect in a nation that owed Empire, power, trade and influence to its relationship with the sea. It would be pleasant to report that the situation has changed for the better in the intervening century, a century in which the ultimate value of the sea to Britain has been demonstrated with startling clarity, and yet wilful ignorance is more pervasive now than at any time in our history. There is not a single Professorial appointment in naval history in a British University and the Royal Navy is significantly less historically aware than it was when Laughton began his career. The history of Britain cannot be understood without constant reference to the sea, and the naval power of the British state. The best naval history makes those connections, for history is a single, seamless fabric.

CHAPTER 1

'A man of tact, skill and good humour': 1830-73

The career of any individual is shaped by heritage, education and experience.[1] John Laughton's formative years dominated his life, accounting for his formidable work ethic and his career choice, his ambition and his intellectual apparatus. Although born in Liverpool, on St George's Day (23 April) 1830, he claimed descent from the Orkney islands. Not only did he grow up in a major commercial port, but his father, James Laughton, a wine merchant, had served as a master mariner and privateer commander during the War of 1812.[2] James Laughton's Calvinist faith was reflected in the names chosen for his son. These paternal influences may explain Laughton's choice of career, and the depth of his commitment to the Royal Navy. His lifelong interest in irregular and auxiliary forms of naval power may also have its roots in his father's service, although they never discussed the subject. Of his mother, Ann, we know little. John was the second son, his brother James Brotherston, some ten years older, went to Australia in the mid-1840s, where he served as temporary headmaster of Sydney College, before returning to England. James published several sermons and four editions of a guide to the Isle of Man.[3] In his *Address to the Students of Sydney College* James Laughton observed 'Experience', says the proverb, 'teaches fools: but he is a wise man who learns from the experience of others'.[4] John Knox Laughton would make that proverb the motto of his career. He also had two sisters, Margaret and Ann.

---

1. Biographical details are drawn from Geoffrey Callender's uninspired article in *The Dictionary of National Biography*, Donald Schurman's *The Education of a Navy: The Development of British Naval Strategic Thought 1867-1914* (London 1965), Ch 5, Laughton's letter to the Council of King's College, London 6 July 1885, King's College London Archives (KCLA) KA/ILI L60 (Laughton File) and James Laughton's Will.
2. Williams, G, *The Liverpool Privateers* (London 1897), pp445-6. James Laughton worked for the ship-owners Brotherston and Begg, for one of whom he named his elder son.
3. Laughton, James Brotherston, *An Address to the students of Sydney College* Sydney NSW and *Johnson's historical, topographical and parochial illustrated guide to the Isle of Man* 1842, 1847, 1853, 1859.
4. *Address*, p8.

Closely connected with the sea, both by heredity and location, it is little wonder that John Laughton should have been drawn to a naval career, and followed his early interest in its history.[5] His father prospered in the wine trade, moving to the Isle of Man in the early 1840s, where John attended Forester's School between 1841 and 1843. In June 1843 the family returned to Liverpool, John spending the next two years at the prestigious Royal Institution School. Here he studied a modern, liberal curriculum which, although still dominated by the classics and maths, included modern history, French, German and scientific subjects.[6]

By the mid-1840s James Laughton was a wealthy man. He had retired from trade and moved his money into property. By 1849 he lived in a stylish Regency house at 75 Upper Parliament Street, owned another eight houses nearby in Falkner Square and entered himself in the Liverpool directory as a 'gentleman'.[7] Recognising that his son had above-average academic talent, probably on the advice of a graduate teacher at the Institution School, he used part of his income to send him to Cambridge. In 1846 John moved to study privately under the Reverend J L F Russell at Eversden in Cambridgeshire, preparatory to entering the University. This was a decisive step, removing him from the bustling commercial environment of Liverpool, dominated by shipping and trade, to the refined, cloistered community of an ancient university. Cambridge profoundly altered his outlook on life and gave his intellect a new form. There were many opportunities in Liverpool for a gifted mathematician with local connections, but they opened out into the fields of commerce, and the life of a Liverpool office. Although Laughton occasionally returned to Liverpool after 1846, he was no longer attuned to its dynamic, vibrant commercial culture.

John Knox Laughton was admitted as a pensioner at Caius College on 23 February 1848.[8] His father would have to find at least £60 a year, although the final figure often rose to £200, including £70 for a private tutor.[9] The degree required ten terms in residence, and most students also spent the long vacations in Cambridge. There were lectures for the

---

5. Laughton, J K, 'Wind Force, and How it is Measured. *Longman's Magazine* Vol 1 (April 1883), pp615-27 (p615).

6. Laughton-Mathews, V, *The Blue Tapestry: The Story of the WRNS* (London 1948), p23, Brown, A T, *Some Account of the Royal Institution School, Liverpool* (Cambridge 1924), pp26-7, 178, 385 and Laughton MSS, National Maritime Museum, London MS79/065.

7. *Grove's Liverpool Directory* 1823 (master mariner), 1825 (Wine & Spirit Merchant), 1827 as before but at a new address, and with separate business premises. James Laughton did not appear in the 1841 directory, the family then living on the Isle of Man. In 1849, he was listed as a 'gentleman', and remained under that heading in 1851 and 1857.

8. Venn, J A, *A Biographical Dictionary of Gonville and Caius College* (Cambridge 1898), Vol II, pp282-3.

9. The Cambridge University Calendar for the Year 1848, pp40-2, 211, 218.

Mathematics Tripos every day, and although Caius was one of the better colleges, no-one achieved a good degree without a private tutor. The principal recreations were walking and talking with fellow students.[10] As his father must have expected, Laughton was changed profoundly by his time at the University. As the son of a man who had prospered in trade Laughton was in a minority, only 6 per cent of his Cambridge contemporaries falling into this category. Most students had clerical or professional backgrounds, with a significant representation of the landed gentry. The cultural baggage Laughton brought from Liverpool must have been hastily abandoned, notably his father's Calvinism, which he had to abjure to enter the University, and any pride in his father's commercial achievements. The culture of the university, dominated by the Church of England and the service ethic, was antithetical to business. As a tutor pointedly declared in 1867, the education provided was 'not appropriate for a Liverpool Office'.[11] It provided the sons of business with a service/professional ethic that considered private profit a vulgar pursuit.[12] This experience may well have been critical, as Laughton devoted the rest of his life to the service of the Royal Navy.

With the new ethos came an impressive and equally influential intellectual training. The Cambridge Mathematical Tripos, as constituted in the early 1850s, was designed to test how hard the candidate had worked. There were more questions on the paper than could be effectively answered in the time available, yet every single one had to be attempted. The paper consisted of propositions and problems. The former, three-quarters of the work, could, with sufficient endeavour, be committed to memory and written out in haste, leaving enough time to complete the problems. The final examination, in early January, occupied 44½ hours, spread over eight days. Successful candidates were hard and fast workers, putting in 15 to 20 hours of preparation every day as the exam approached. This process 'stressed method, technique, precision, logic and rigour – and the method was transferable: the man who understood the principles of argument and knew how to derive generalisations from a body of factual material could teach himself any subject'.[13]

Laughton sat the Tripos in 1852, and graduated as a Wrangler, a First Class student. As three Caius men had graduated above him he was not eligible for a Fellowship at the College. Although this relative failure

---

10. Venn, J, *Early Collegiate Life* (Cambridge 1913). Venn was a near contemporary at Caius. Annan, N, *Leslie Stephen: The Godless Victorian* (London 1984), pp24-7 for an excellent description of the system.
11. Rothblatt, S, *The Revolution of the Dons: Cambridge and Society in Victorian England* (London 1968), pp65-8, 86, quote at p89.
12. Ibid, p93.
13. Ibid, p182.

closed the royal road to a University-based career in the Church, public schools, politics or a learned profession, the Tripos was the defining moment in Laughton's intellectual development. The emphasis on mastering the factual basis of a subject before progressing to problem-solving lay at the heart of his methodology, while his response to the workload, developing the ability to work rapidly and valuing accuracy above all else, determined his style. His mind retained the 'scientific' character it acquired at Cambridge for the rest of his life. The publication of the Northcote-Trevelyan Report in 1853, which emphasised competitive examinations and allowed entry to the Civil Service on merit, came too late for Laughton. Unlike the majority of his Cambridge contemporaries he lacked the patronage or family support to pursue the more obvious careers in the Church, the Civil Service or the University. Having failed to obtain a college fellowship, Laughton spent some time studying in Germany.[14] There is no indication that he considered returning to Liverpool. Instead he took one of the less obvious avenues open to him, joining the Royal Navy as a Naval Instructor in late 1853.

The role of the shipboard Instructors had been revised and upgraded by the Admiralty in 1836, preparatory to the closure of the Naval College at Portsmouth in 1837. The post was established with appropriate rates of pay, either as Instructor or Chaplain Instructor. Laughton's conscious decision to remain a pure Instructor involved some financial sacrifice. When the Admiralty introduced the rank of Naval Instructor it 'set out to recruit highly qualified university-trained teachers to replace the old Schoolmasters'.[15] Improved pay and conditions were offered, but the package was not particularly attractive, there were never more than fifteen graduates in service at any one time, and normally less than ten. There were far too few graduates to meet the needs of the service. Most Instructors were either chaplains who took additional pay, or non-graduates. This was unfortunate for the post required mathematical skill of a high order to teach navigation and other technical subjects. In 1853 Instructors were Ward Room Warrant Officers, wearing the same uniform as a Master, but without epaulettes. The pay was equivalent to other Warrant Officers, rising after ten years' service to parity with junior Lieutenants. In 1861 Naval Instructors became Commissioned Officers, an important improvement in their social standing, while their pay was restructured to advance alongside that of their naval contemporaries in 1864.[16] Despite

14. Bridge, C A G, 'Obituary' in *The Geographical Journal* Vol XLVI (1915), pp401-2. Unfortunately nothing more is known about this period.
15. Dickinson, H W, 'Educational Provision for Officers of the Royal Navy; 1857-77 (Unpub. Ph.D. London 1994), p70. I have benefited greatly from this important thesis, and from the advice of Dr Dickinson.
16. Ibid, p137.

this advance their role aboard ship required a constant compromise between the academic needs of their young charges, midshipmen wishing to
pass for lieutenant, and the requirements of a warship in commission,
where the commander would make a point of keeping the youngsters busy
with more practical tasks. As Laughton later observed, the inevitable clash
of priorities between the educator and the commander running the ship
required the Instructor to be a man of 'tact, skill and good humour'.[17]

Candidates for the service were taught and examined in mathematics,
algebra, geometry, trigonometry, astronomy, mechanics, hydrostatics and
the classics on board the Gunnery Training Ship HMS *Excellent*. The final
examination included navigation, the theory of projectiles as applied to
gunnery and navigational observations. French and drawing were useful
additional attainments. This curriculum posed few problems for Laughton. After qualifying he joined the 120-gun steam battleship HMS *Royal
George,* Captain Henry Codrington, on 27 December 1853. This was the
official date of his entry into the Royal Navy.[18] In March 1854 the *Royal
George* went to war as part of Vice-Admiral Sir Charles Napier's Baltic
Fleet. Although the Baltic Campaigns of 1854 and 1855 did not lead to
any major naval battles, and remain a largely neglected aspect of the
'Crimean' War, Laughton was present at several coastal engagements, and
the campaign culminated in the three-day bombardment of Sweaborg in
August 1855. These campaigns provided first-hand experience of sustained operations in a fleet of wooden sailing ships and also valuable
insight into the problems of alliance warfare. He soon realised that the
French Navy was Orleanist to the core, devoted to the exiled Prince de
Joinville and hostile to Louis Napoleon and his Empire.[19] That he secured
the favourable notice of his Captain, a boorish snob of limited abilities,
reflects well on his tact and discretion, while the fact that Laughton in
turn held Codrington in high regard says more about his relative youth.
His position and education brought him into contact with the ship's
senior officers, beginning a relationship with the service that would last
throughout a long life. The Instructor had to be responsive to the pattern

---

17. Navy Lists, various. Regulations for Naval Instructors. Lewis, M, *The Navy In Transition: A Social History, 1814-64* (London 1965), pp99-112, Lloyd, C, 'The Royal Naval
College at Greenwich and Portsmouth', *Mariner's Mirror* Vol 52 (1966), pp145-156. Laughton, evidence before the Shadwell Committee on Naval Education *Parliamentary Papers*
1870 XXV.
18. **Codrington,** Admiral of the Fleet Sir Henry John (1808-77), younger son of Admiral Sir
Edward, victor of Navarino. He never held a seagoing flag appointment. For the *Royal
George, Algiers* and *Trafalgar* see Lambert, A D, *Battleships in Transition: the Creation of
the Steam Battlefleet* (London 1984).
19. Laughton was greatly influenced by his early experience, and his early connections. His
Dictionary of National Biography entries on Napier and Henry Codrington reflect the
ignorant gossip that was common in 1854. See Lambert, A D, *The Crimean War: British
Grand Strategy against Russia (1853-56)* (Manchester 1990) for a modern assessment.

of life aboard ship, fitting his work around that daily combination of routines and sudden demands that characterise naval life. Laughton was, and remained, finely tuned to the needs of the service, developing his ideas to meet a perceived need.

By early 1856 Laughton's abilities had been recognised and he was appointed to the 84-gun sailing ship *Calcutta*, Captain William King-Hall, then fitting out at Devonport as flagship of the East Indies Squadron, commanded by Rear-Admiral Sir Michael Seymour.[20] Consequently Laughton served in the first three seasons of the Second China War. His gallantry at the bloody boat-action in Fatshan Creek was noticed in the London Gazette, he was one of the first to scale the walls of Canton and took part in the capture of the Taku Forts. He also earned highest praise as a teacher. Aboard the *Calcutta* he established connections that lasted his whole career, along with the particular type of credibility that is only ever accorded to service intellectuals who have seen action. Among the junior officers of the *Calcutta* were many who would rise to flag rank, including Lord Gillford, James Goodenough, Arthur Wilson, Edward Seymour, Richard Vesey Hamilton, William Kennedy, Harry Rawson, Michael Culme-Seymour and Thomas Sturges Jackson. Their success reflected many things, but more than one of them would look back with gratitude to 'the benefit of a first-rate naval instructor'.[21] This was no accident. Captain William King-Hall was noted for the care he took of his

---

20. **King-Hall**, Admiral Sir William (1816-86) C-in-C Nore 1877-79.

Seymour, Admiral Sir Michael (1802-87). Laughton considered Seymour one of the finest sea officers of the century, although China was his only fleet command. Laughton was appointed to the *Calcutta* on 4 March 1856 and joined on the 17th. Service Record ADM 196/78 & Log of HMS *Calcutta* 17.3.1856: ADM 53/6309.

21. Sturges-Jackson to the Council of King's College, London: KCLA KA/ILI L60. Seymour, E H, *My Naval Career and Travels* (London 1911), p67 quoted, with approval, in, Bradford, E E, *Admiral of the Fleet Sir A.K. Wilson* (London 1922), p17; King-Hall, L *Sea Saga* (London 1935), p224 and Rawson, G, *Life of Admiral Sir Harry Rawson* (London 1914), p18. Bonner-Smith, D, & Lumby, E W R *The Second China War, 1856-60* (London, Navy Records Society 1954). Clowes, W L *A History of the Royal Navy From the Earliest Times* (London 1903), Vol VII. *The Times* 25.4.1910 p6, 'Sir John Laughton and Naval History' a report on the celebration of his eightieth birthday.

Richard James Meade, Lord **Gillford**, eventually Admiral of the Fleet the 4th Earl of Clanwilliam (1832-1907).

Goodenough, Commodore James Graham (1830-75). Killed by a poisoned arrow on Santa Cruz Island. Perhaps the outstanding officer of his generation.

Wilson, Sir Arthur Knyvet Bt. VC (1842-1921). Outstanding fleet commander, Admiral of the Fleet and First Sea Lord 1910-11.

Seymour, Sir Edward Hobart (1840-1929). C-in-C China Station 1899-1902, during the 'Boxer Rebellion. Admiral of the Fleet.

Vesey-Hamilton, Admiral Sir Richard (1829-1912). First Sea Lord 1889-91.

Kennedy, Admiral Sir William Robert (1838-1916). C-in-C Indian Ocean.

Rawson, Sir Harry Holdsworth (1843-1910). Admiral and Colonial Governor.

Culme-Seymour, Sir Michael 3rd Bt.(1836-1920). Restored the morale of the Mediterranean Fleet after the loss of the *Victoria* in 1893.

Sturges-Jackson, Admiral Sir Thomas (1842-1934). C-in-C Devonport 1899-1902.

young charges, and having served in the Baltic in 1855 he probably selected Laughton on the basis of personal knowledge or recommendation. By the time the *Calcutta* arrived home Laughton had made a great name for himself, although he had spent most of the homeward voyage on the sick list.[22] As the majority of his fellow Instructors were poorly equipped for the professional side of their work, their teaching being considered more of a hindrance than a benefit for their young charges, it was little wonder that Laughton stood out.[23]

When the *Calcutta* paid off at Portsmouth in July 1859 Laughton was given six months' sick leave by Stonehouse Hospital.[24] He may have returned to Liverpool, to see his father for the last time, for James Laughton died on 5 December 1859 at 137 Upper Parliament Street. His extensive freehold and leasehold property in Liverpool was left to his wife, his daughters and if they died without issue, to his sons equally.[25] John would receive the freehold of a house in Falkner Square on the death of his mother. This formative but by now rather distant influence was replaced by a new source of inspiration and direction. On 7 February 1860 Laughton was appointed to the 90-gun steam battleship *Algiers* in the Channel Fleet, where he met Lieutenant Cyprian Bridge.[26] The two men served together for three years, and become lifelong friends. Bridge would be the most important influence on Laughton's career. Their first collaborative venture was to edit the ship's newspaper. Through their discussions Laughton recognised the need to study tactics, that history could provide lessons for the contemporary navy and that his own scientific training provided a critical intellectual advantage. Bridge's career demonstrated that the Victorian Navy was not anti-intellectual, although it did prefer its intellectuals to be discrete. In late 1860 the *Algiers* joined Vice-Admiral Sir William Fanshawe Martin's Mediterranean Fleet.[27] Here the two men watched 'Pincher' Martin transform an ill-found, mutinous collection of scratch-manned ships into a near-perfect fleet, conducting precise fleet manoeuvres in complete silence, something they would remember for the rest of their lives. During the Lebanese crisis of 1860-61 *Algiers* spent five months on the Syrian Coast, which provided opportunities for the officers to visit the Holy Land. Stimulated by the

---

22. Kennedy, W, *Hurrah for the Life of a Sailor* (London 1900), p116.
23. Dickinson, pp143-7.
24. Leave Granted 12 August 1859. Service Record ADM 196/78.
25. James Laughton's Will. Proved 18.4.1860. Laughton senior died on 5.12.1859. When he made his will in 1855 he owned 17-24 Falkner Square freehold, and 139 Upper Parliament Street leasehold.
26. **Bridge**, Admiral Sir Cyprian Arthur George (1839-1924). Director of Naval Intelligence, C-in-C Australia and China Stations.
27. **Martin**, Admiral Sir William (1801-95). First Sea Lord 1858-59, C-in-C Mediterranean 1860-63. A resolute Tory.

experience and anxious to understand what he had seen, probably to
explain the phenomena to his young charges, Laughton quickly filled
his cabin with books on the geography of Palestine, as Bridge was to
recall fifty years later. The habits of a lifetime were taking shape;
problems were encountered, learning amassed and answers developed.
After calling at Corfu and Naples, the *Algiers* paid off at Portsmouth in
December 1862.[28] Laughton spent three months ashore before returning
to the Mediterranean, where he joined HMS *Trafalgar*, another 90-gun
screw battleship. In February 1864 the *Trafalgar* returned home to pay
off and he took his last sea-going appointment, joining the new ironclad
Prince Consort, Captain George Willes, serving in the Channel Fleet.
Willes was an exceptional officer. In 1870 he was appointed effective
Chief of Staff at the Admiralty for the Franco-Prussian War
emergency.[29] He, like all Laughton's previous Captains, was highly
impressed by his Naval Instructor.

Laughton's selection for a shore post coincided with two major events
in his life. His mother died in April 1865 and the family home was sold in
May 1866. Laughton's share, along with the proceeds of the sale of his
house at 21 Falkner Square, may have enabled him to marry Isabella Carr
of Dunfermline. They probably met when the Channel Fleet visited the
Forth and staged a review in 1860. The *Algiers* was open to the public,
while many of her officers went ashore. Fifty years later Bridge still
recalled visiting Dunfermline Church.[30] By 1866 Laughton had earned a
formidable reputation as 'a careful, conscientious, efficient teacher'. He
was best Instructor in the service and Professor Main of the Royal Naval
College at Portsmouth was determined to 'ensure his being appointed to
fill the next vacancy'. As a Cambridge Wrangler Main would have appreciated Laughton's skill, even if he was no teacher himself.[31] This appointment elevated Laughton from a teacher of midshipmen to one of the
principal educators of the service, and he would need all his skill, tact and
dedication to meet the demands of his new position.

It has been customary to treat the mid-Victorian Royal Navy as little
more than a colonial police force, made up of worn-out small ships,
lacking the stimulus of a real rival, and irrelevant to the dramatic events of
the Unification of Germany. Such views reflect a paucity of research, and

---

28. Bridge, C A G, *Some Recollections* (London 1918), pp189-199. Laughton, J K, 'Thirty
Years Since', *St Andrew's Magazine* (May 1894), pp82-7, 98-102, and June 1894 pp128-136:
The Navy List various. Bridge to Laughton 14.3.1893. JKL MSS: JKL *DNB* article on W F
Martin.
29. **Willes,** Admiral Sir George Ommanney (1824-1901). C-in-C China 1881-84, Portsmouth 1885-88. *Report from the Select Committee of the House of Lords on the Board of
Admiralty 1871*, Willes evidence at pp117-124.
30. Bridge, p192.
31. Dickinson, pp158-60.

have been largely redressed by John Beeler's excellent study.[32] In 1866 the Royal Navy had just defeated Imperial France in a technological arms race of immense significance, decided by the superior financial resources and political commitment to naval mastery evinced by the British state. Naval power had played the critical role in the allied victory over Russia in the Crimean War, had recently deterred the United States, and was engaged around the world in the protection and furtherance of British aims. While the Navy was dominated by the need to assimilate new technology, it remained a battlefleet service. Most men served in large ironclads, in the Mediterranean and Channel Fleets, while the colonial conflicts were much more closely connected to the reality of nineteenth-century naval operations than critics of the 'gunboat' navy have realised. The gunboat was designed to bombard the French naval arsenal at Cherbourg, built to attack the Russian arsenal at Cronstadt, and used to open the rivers and ports of China to British trade. That they could also be employed against lesser states and slave traders was a testimony to the inherent flexibility of naval power. Most officers in the Navy of 1866 had seen active service in the Crimean or China Wars, or the Indian Mutiny. They were experts in coastal power projection, skills that were equally applicable against the forts of France, Russia, China and the United States, as well as the stockades of Malay pirates and Maori tribesmen. None of these men specialised in colonial service to the exclusion of battlefleet service, for it was the ambition of every officer to command one of the great fleets.

Laughton came ashore at a critical moment. With the end of the Anglo-French arms race, it was time to take stock of the ironclad revolution and integrate the new technology into the performance of old tasks, namely fleet battle, blockade, trade protection and coastal operations. This task, at all levels, would dominate Laughton's life. He was appointed Instructor at the Royal Naval College in July 1866.[33] The College provided practical in-service training for up to twenty-five officers between appointments. Although the principles of certain sciences were taught, notably the mathematics required to comprehend the theory of gunnery, this was only as an aid to the acquisition of professional skills.[34] The staff, under the Captain of the Gunnery Training Ship HMS *Excellent*, consisted of one professor, one instructor and an assistant for the observatory. The

---

32. Beeler, J F, *British Naval Policy in the Gladstone-Disraeli Era, 1866-80* (Stanford 1997).
33. Prof. Main to the Council of King's College London 3 July 1885. KCLA KA/IL L60. In 1885 Admiral Sir George Willes recalled that as Captain of the *Prince Consort*, he had given a positive reply to an Admiralty enquiry about Laughton's suitability for the appointment. *JRUSI* (1885) p933. He lived at Denton House, Victoria Street, Southsea.
34. Barnard, H, *Military Schools and Courses of Instruction in the Art and Science of War* (Washington 1872).

Captains between 1866 and 1873 were Astley Cooper Key to September 1866, then Arthur Hood until 1869 and Henry Boys. The First Gunnery Officer in 1868-69 was Lieutenant John Arbuthnot Fisher.[35] Although they were few in number, and worked in a draughty, cramped and evil-smelling building in the dockyard, the staff were talented. Laughton's main task, teaching maths to officers about to attend the gunnery course, put a premium on his expositional ability. Later Main would pay tribute to 'the assistance he gave me by his clear intellect and accurate knowledge'.[36]

However, Laughton did not rest on his pedagogical triumphs. His intellect, stimulated and trained at Cambridge, had been given direction by the experience of seamanship and war, and was now exposed to the brightest minds in the service. Among those to pass through *Excellent* at this time were old *Calcutta*'s Harry Rawson, Thomas Sturges-Jackson and Arthur Wilson, along with Gerard Noel, Hubert Grenfell, Lewis Beaumont and Reginald Custance.[37] Laughton wanted to contribute to the development of the service, and this shore posting was his opportunity.

Laughton was widely experienced in the relevant observational sciences of astronomy, meteorology and oceanography, becoming a fellow of the Royal Geographical, Royal Astronomical and Meteorological Societies. The close links between these bodies and the Royal Navy were emphasised when Laughton was elected a Fellow of the Royal Geographical Society (RGS) in January 1869. The statement that he was 'likely to become a useful and valuable fellow' was endorsed by two outstanding naval explorers, both recipients of the Society's Gold Medal, Captain Edward Inglefield and Rear-Admiral Richard Collinson.[38] Although initially hampered by his location at Portsmouth, Laughton was an active member,[39] and after the College moved to Greenwich he regularly

---

35. Wells, J, *Whaley: The Story of HMS Excellent 1830 to 1980* (Portsmouth 1980), pp213-4.

Key, Admiral Sir Astley Cooper (1821-88). First Sea Lord 1879-85. A long-term supporter of Laughton. Colomb, P, *Memoirs of Sir Astley Cooper Key* (London 1898).

Hood, Admiral Baron Hood of Avalon (1824-1901). First Sea Lord 1885-89.

Boys, Admiral Henry (1824-1904). Boys, W H, *Memoir of Admiral Henry Boys* (Privately printed Liverpool 1913).

Fisher, John Arbuthnot, later Admiral of the Fleet Lord (1841-1919). The dynamic, ruthless officer who revitalised the service before 1914.

36. Main to Kings 3 July 1885 KCLA KA/ILI L60. Dickinson pp243-5.

37. Noel, Admiral Sir Gerard Henry Uctred (1845-1918). Junior Naval Lord 1893-98, Second in Command, Mediterranean Fleet 1898-99.

Grenfell, Hubert Henry, Captain RN (1845–1906). Gunnery expert. Naval attaché in Europe 1877-1878. Retired 1887.

Beaumont, Admiral Sir Lewis Anthony (1847-1922). Director of Naval Intelligence, C-in-C Devonport 1905-08.

Custance Admiral Sir Reginald Neville (1847-1935). Director of Naval Intelligence 1899-1901, naval writer.

38. Certificate of Election 25.1.1869: Archives of the Royal Geographical Society. I am indebted to Dr Andrew Tatham for his help with the Archives of the Society.

39. Laughton to RGS 18.1.1871 & 28.5.1871: RGS Archives, Laughton File.

attended Society functions. The work as a scientist and observer established his intellectual standing. At the College his additional duties included teaching meteorology and marine surveying and as there were no suitable texts he wrote his own. The method he applied would become his trade mark, beginning work on meteorology in 1867 with a series of short articles in the relevant journals exploring the state of existing knowledge, mastering the theoretical and practical dimensions of the subject and exploiting his own journals for evidence, before developing a fully-rounded thesis. In preparing his book Laughton enlisted the help of two leading hydrographers, Captain Frederick Evans and Staff Commander Thomas Hull. That he began with a clear and well-made attack on the meteorological ideas of Captain Matthew Fontaine Maury USN, whose *Physical Geography of the Sea* was the recognised international authority, was bold, but typical. Laughton was not given to self-doubt, and convinced that his methods were correct he would take on anyone.[40] The final result of his work, the powerfully-argued book *Physical Geography in its relation to the Prevailing Winds and Currents*, was published by Potter, the Chart Seller to the Admiralty, in late 1870. A second edition was required in 1873.[41] The new quarterly journal *Naval Science* recognised the intellectual merit of his argument, and considered the lieutenants for whom it had been written were fortunate to have 'such a useful text book'. The book outlined the prevailing Hadley-Maury theory of the circulation of the atmosphere, and then dismissed it as unscientific and incompatible with known phenomena. Laughton developed his own system, based on the laws of the motion of fluids. *Naval Science* recommended all those interested should read the book for themselves.[42] The editor, Edward Reed, lately Chief Constructor of the Navy, and his collaborator and later co-editor, Joseph Woolley, lately Director of Naval Education and also a Cambridge Wrangler, knew Laughton and his work. They appreciated that he was one of the intellectuals attempting to revitalise naval education.

Although Laughton's concept that oceanic circulation was driven solely by the wind was, even as he wrote, being rendered obsolete by the theory of William Carpenter, the book attracted notice outside the service.[43] It was commended by Sir Roderick Murchison, President of the

---

40. Laughton, J K, 'An inquiry into the evidence on which the theory of the circulation of the atmosphere is based', *Philosophical Magazine* (1867), pp359-65.
Laughton, J K, also 'On the natural forces that produce the permanent and periodical winds', ibid, pp443-9. Laughton, J K, 'On Atmospheric Currents', *Symonds' Meteorological Magazine* (1870), pp158-60.
41. Laughton, J K, *Physical Geography in its Relation to the Prevailing Winds and Currents* (London 1870).
42. Reed, E J, *Naval Science: Number One* (London 1872), pp289-90.
43. Deacon, M, *Scientists and the Sea; 1650-1900* (London 1971), pp319-23.

RGS, at a meeting of the British Association in Liverpool in 1870, where Laughton read a paper on 'The Great Currents of the Atmosphere'.[44] Over the next year he took part in a wide-ranging debate on oceanic circulation, terming Carpenter's theory a 'crude speculation' which would mislead those lacking expertise. He also joined the discussion of Carpenter's paper 'The Gibraltar Current, the Gulf Stream, and the General Oceanic Circulation' at the RGS in January 1871.[45] His book also lead to a lifelong connection with the Meteorological Society, later the Royal Meteorological Society, of which he was elected a Fellow in February 1873, the same month the College opened at Greenwich. He served the Meteorological Society continuously until 1886, as a Councillor and as President in 1882-83.[46]

The methodology of Laughton's first book demonstrated the intellectual apparatus he used throughout his career. He began by establishing the definition of his subject: an attempt to explain the system of circulation of the atmosphere and the ocean. He then applied a scientific approach to the enquiry, building an impressive observational data base from which to develop a theory that would explain the phenomena, and then cross-checked his theory against real phenomena. His sources included American and French works of naval history, travel and physical geography, along with wind and current charts; his insights included lexicographical observations on the origins of the word 'typhoon'. Much of the preparatory work for this book had been conducted during his sea service. In the preface he declared:

> I have adopted a method which, though it differs essentially from that which has of late years been very generally followed, is, I would submit, both more exact and more scientific. I have endeavoured to explain the phenomena which are observed, rather than to observe phenomena in illustration of theoretical views. There is no more dangerous source of error in physical science than a strong conviction that certain phenomena must exist and a determination to find them. Difficult as it is to banish from the mind all preconceived ideas, and to inquire into things as they really are, not as they have been imagined to be, it is only by such a beginning that we can hope to arrive at knowledge and understanding of the truth.
>
> But the fact is, we are at all times in too great a hurry to generalise; we are too fond of repeating that Newton worked out the great idea of universal gravitation by generalising from the fall of an apple: perhaps he did; but we are not Newtons . . . Generalisation is necessary for scientific classifica-

OBVIOUS

---

44. Laughton, J K, 'On the Great Currents of the Atmosphere', *British Association Report* XL (1870), p170. Bridge, p401.
45. *Proceedings of the Royal Geographical Society* Vol XV (1871).
46. Unsigned Obituary Notice in *The Quarterly Journal of the Royal Meteorological Society* Vol 41 (1915), pp351-2. Lambert, A D, 'Portraits of Past Presidents: Sir John Knox Laughton', *Weather 1998*.

tion; it is necessary for a right understanding of the phenomena classified; it is necessary, if only as an aid to memory; but a hasty generalisation is, in all probability, a false one, and – founded on imperfect and incorrect data – leads to results on which no confidence whatever can be placed.

The work which I have undertaken would evidently not be complete without generalisation: without generalisation, it would have been imposs- ible for me to attempt anything like a systematic explanation of my subject, or to enter into the important question of cause: but to that generalisation I have been guided by thousands of independent and detailed observations, careless of any theory to which it and they might conduct me.

He concluded the preface by declaring that whatever the correctness of his argument;

there cannot, I conceive be any doubt as to the correctness of the method I have adopted. It is the method which has been adopted in every branch of science – except this – and often with the most astounding success: it is the method which has led to every advance in science during the last three hundred years.[47]

This remained Laughton's basic method of study throughout his career. It explained both the intellectual origins of his analytical processes, and the pitfalls he was anxious to avoid. The 'scientific' approach was, he be- lieved, equally applicable to all disciplines. When he turned to naval history this method determined the nature of his enquiries, and the prob- lems he hoped to solve.

Laughton's second book, *An Introduction to the Practical and The- oretical Study of Nautical Surveying* of 1872, although intellectually less ambitious, was more successful commercially. His object was to provide;

such a knowledge of principles, and to offer such guidance to practice, as will enable the young surveyor more readily to arrive at the end which he has in view – a mastery of the science; and as will enable others to appreciate more exactly and intelligently the results of the surveyor's work. It is, however, only as an **Introduction** that I offer it; and many problems of great interest and value, as well as the discussion of many refinements of correction and reduction, which, neat as they may be in theory, are of very little practical use, have been necessarily and purposely omitted.[48]

The journal *Engineering* was impressed by his efforts, and regretted the lack of an acknowledged textbook for the Navy. The reviewer suggested

---

47. *Physical Geography*, Preface ppiv-vi.
48. Laughton, J K, *An Introduction to the Practical and Theoretical Study of Nautical Surveying* (London 1872), ppv-vi. Second edition 1882, the book was still selling in the 1890s. Day, A, *The Admiralty Hydrographic Service: 1795-1919* (London 1967), p106.

that a committee of eminent surveyors, including Laughton, should be
assembled to produce a definitive text.[49]

The two scientific books indicated an active, under-employed and ambitious mind. Both were course texts at the Naval College, and significant
contributions to the intellectual life of the service. When he wrote them
Laughton had already begun work on naval historical subjects, both to
answer contemporary concerns and to increase his income. He began his
publishing career, aside from ships' newspapers, with a paper examining
the concept of 'The Sovereignty of the Seas' in the new, liberal *Fortnightly
Review*. Over the next sixty years he published numerous essays and
reviews covering every aspect of his career, from reflections on his sea-
time, through meteorology, surveying, exploration, current naval issues,
history, and above all, naval history. The essay form was critical to his
intellectual development; for as Walter Houghton observed of Matthew
Arnold: 'Plainly (his) creative mind was formed in the periodical mould
. . . he was a writer of periodical literature'.[50] His longer studies were
textbooks, collected essays or edited documents. One result of his vast
output was a style of writing that, as Don Schurman noted, revealed the
effect of 'a pen everlastingly on the march'.[51]

This aspect of Laughton's development reflected the mood of the time.
The growth of periodical literature defined the intellectual character of
nineteenth-century Britain, where the magazine was the main medium for
the exchange of ideas, exercising far more influence than books. This
reflected the omnivorous appetites of the Victorian era. Because most
journals were non-specialist, they provided a wide readership for authors
who wanted to influence 'public opinion'. The rise of a leisured middle
class, the fluid state of opinion on issues as disparate as religion, science,
politics and war, allied to increasing output of books, made the Review
the preferred intellectual entertainment. The reviewer's task was to educate, guiding those with limited time to the best new work, and sum-
marising everything of worth for those who would read nothing else. As
such they, rather than the authors' whose works they analysed, dominated the mass market for intellectual stimulation. As a consequence of
this exalted status, the regular contributors to the major titles included all
those who sought to lead or form society. Many reviewers found the
demolition of old myths a fruitful approach. Initially the journals, like the

49. *Monthly Register of the Junior Naval Professional Association* Vol 3 (20 June 1873), p38.
reproducing the review from *Engineering*.
50. Houghton, W E, 'Periodical Literature and the Articulate Classes' in Shattock, J and
Wolff, M (eds), *The Victorian Periodical Press: Samplings and Soundings* (Toronto 1982),
pp4-27, quote at p21. See also Tucker, A, 'Military' in Don Vann, J and Van Arsdel, R T
(eds), *Victorian Periodicals and Victorian Society* (Toronto 1994).
51. Schurman, *Education*, p84.

Whig *Edinburgh Review* and the Tory *Quarterly Review* were fiercely sectarian, publishing unsigned on the grounds that the opinions expressed represented editorial policy. This practice gradually died out, although the *Edinburgh Review* retained it until 1912. By contrast the Liberal *Fortnightly*, begun in 1865, was among the first to publish signed pieces.

At mid-century there was a wide range of periodicals, from the heavy-weight and authoritative quarterlies, through the more dynamic monthlies and fortnightlies to the all-but-ephemeral weeklies. The more frequently the journal appeared, the harder it had to work to survive, and the more likely it was to devote its budget to serialising a novel. Journals paid their contributors, and also provided an easier route into print for marginal subjects than books, where limited demand lead to high initial costs. For Laughton the shift toward the book as the primary means of exchanging naval information, both contemporary and historical, came too late to influence his career. Between 1889 and 1891 popular navalism created a market that would absorb any number of heavy, blue-bound memoirs and histories. The timing was perfect for Mahan. Before 1885 journals were the only opportunity Laughton had to develop his naval and historical ideas, and he used a wide range of them, from the august quarterlies, mainly but not exclusively the *Edinburgh Review*, to the specifically professional *Journal of the Royal United Services Institution* and *Colburn's United Service Magazine* through *Fraser's Magazine* and its successor *Longman's Magazine*, to the weekly *St Paul's Magazine*. He could also be found in *Brassey's Naval Annual*, *The Cornhill Magazine*, *The Army and Navy Gazette* and *The Athenaeum*.[52]

The review, short essay and textbook remained basic to Laughton's *oeuvre*. In the absence of a market, and lacking the time, or indeed the financial security, to devote a sustained effort to any particular subject, he never quite matured as an author of large-scale narrative and analytical studies. The essay remained more remunerative, and for Laughton developed into *Dictionary of National Biography* entries, introductions to Navy Records Society volumes, and contributions to part-works. With more time, and in a more encouraging environment, notably for naval books, he might have become a substantial author, but financial pressures, the state of the market and the sheer volume of his essay output barred his progress in this area.

While Laughton's development as an historian followed a similar pattern to his meteorological studies, the task came to dominate the rest of his life, reflecting the weak state of the subject. When he began work the existing works of naval history included some general studies and biographies, but there was nothing written to educate naval officers. The *genre*

---

52. See the Bibliography for his output.

was, with few exceptions, notably only for a lack of scholarly rigour, the provision of which was to be Laughton's contribution. His first essay addressed the basis of British naval mastery, examining the 1000-year-old claim to 'The Sovereignty of the Seas'. This, he argued, should 'be of interest to all Englishmen, though it is now only a memory of those past times when an unrestrained barter of cotton and sour wine was not supposed to be all that was necessary for the advantage and glory of our nation'. Clearly his liberalism was more Palmerstonian than Cobdenite. The paper defined the old claim, which had been limited to the narrow seas, and based on Norman jurisdiction of both shores of the channel. In developing this theme he imposed a sophisticated, and strikingly modern, tactical pattern on the Battle of Sluys in 1340. His explanation for the dropping of the claim to a Channel salute made Britain seem magnanimous and liberal in 1809, when her real motives had more to do with political and strategic reality.[53] The appearance of this piece in a mainstream review suggests that the subject was of interest, and that the author wanted to reach a wide public. In the following year he published a paper on the French Admiral Suffren for the more restricted audience of *Colburn's United Service Magazine*. This was his first contribution to the debate on naval tactics, the first stage in developing a new doctrine.[54] It concentrated on the tactical lessons of Suffren's Indian Ocean campaigns. Themes and examples deployed in these papers would remain central to his thinking.[55] Although a commendable effort, judged by contemporary standards, the paper on Suffren was more significant as part of the preparation for the *Essay on Naval Tactics* of 1873, than as an historical study in itself.

Laughton published his first thoughts on the role of history in service education, 'Sketches in Naval History', in 1870. The paper argued that 'what has happened, may happen again. It is this which constitutes the principal value of all historical enquiry'.[56] He advised his readers that many instructive passages were to be found in the more commonplace accounts of exploration and warfare, evidencing Thomas Cavendish's voyage, while Benbow's last fight showed the dangers of party and faction within a service where 'men as unyielding, but also as cross-grained as the oaks from which their ships were built, were numerous'.

53. Laughton, J K, 'The Sovereignty of the Seas', *The Fortnightly Magazine* Vol V (August 1866). Based on Harris Nicolas's *History of the Royal Navy* (1847) and Twiss, Sir Travers, *The Black Book of the Admiralty* (1857). See Rodger, N A M, *The Safeguard of the Sea: A Naval History of Britain*, Vol I (London 1997), pp78-9 for a modern discussion.
54. Doctrine, 'what is taught', is a modern shorthand for the core ideas and values of an armed service that inform the judgement of senior officers, and guide the execution of orders by junior officers. The term did not carry this meaning in Laughton's lifetime, but it has subsequently achieved such a wide currency that it will be used here.
55. 'Suffren' reprinted in Laughton, J K, *Studies in Naval History* (London 1885).
56. 'Sketches In Naval History', *St. Paul's Magazine* (October 1870), pp51-65.

The sanguinary combats of the First Dutch War in the Mediterranean demonstrated that legal niceties had been little observed, while the conduct of Lord Sandwich's brother Captain the Hon. William 'Mad' Montagu suggested that sanity had not always been a prerequisite for high command afloat. By contrast the treatment of female prisoners by Anson and Forbin provided examples of chivalry as elegant as any medieval chronicle. He cited Drake's execution of Thomas Doughty as an example of moral courage, the basis of leadership, and concluded with the thought that:

> Whether called on to quell a discontented spirit among his subordinates, or to order the movements of a fleet on the day of battle, the man who fears responsibility is unfit for command.[57]

Although Laughton's great work on naval history, to employ the subject on a wider canvas, began after he left Portsmouth, 'Sketches' revealed a well-informed, intelligent and enquiring understanding of the evidence, dominated by the search for relevance.

In addition to an ever-widening group of contacts within the Navy, Laughton's message reached further afield. The United States Navy was particularly interested in naval education. In September 1870 Laughton met Captain Stephen Luce USN at the Royal United Services Institute (RUSI). The two men shared a range of interests, from naval songs and navigation to strategy and tactics, but their discussions centred around the use of history in naval education.[58] It would hardly be an exaggeration to say that this meeting witnessed the foundation of modern naval strategic and historical studies in the Anglo-Saxon world. Their correspondence covered every aspect of naval service and education; from the finer points of galley tactics, through manning, steam tactics and the role of history. The most important aspect of this relationship was the exchange of ideas. Luce exploited Laughton's original intellectual contribution in his efforts to revitalise the United States Navy. In his practical measures, founding the Naval Institute, the Naval War College and spreading the message to the American public, he further exploited Laughton's works on tactics and history. Ultimately Luce would provide the inspiration and opportunity for Mahan's work, and the connection with Laughton that gave it form and substance. This second Anglo-American relationship, greater than the first, proved vital to the development of naval strategic and historical thought on both side so the Atlantic. Yet all that was a long way in the future. In 1870 Laughton had more pressing concerns; the College at Portsmouth was about to move.

---

57. Ibid, p65.
58. Information supplied by Professor John Hattendorf, United States' Naval War College. The first naval correspondence in Laughton's MSS is with Luce, dated 1875.

CHAPTER 2

The Naval University: 1873-85

_____ · _____

The closure of Greenwich Naval Hospital in 1869, combined with the idea of using the buildings for educational purposes, prompted a wide-ranging discussion on the way in which the existing system might be improved. The reforming Admiralty Board of Hugh Childers had already revised the system of cadet education when it addressed the higher education of the service. It was obvious that the Portsmouth College would require repair, increased staff and much improved scientific facilities.[1] By contrast, the palatial buildings of Greenwich, which date from the seventeenth century and remain one of the world's finest architectural compositions, were empty, having been vacated by the last naval pensioners in 1869. Greenwich had been completed as a naval hospital after the Battle of La Hogue in 1692, by a grateful monarch who preferred living at Hampton Court, where the river was cleaner. The question of what to do with these 'naval' buildings, a pressing political issue, would combine conveniently with the tide of reform at Whitehall.

An Admiralty Committee was appointed in January 1870, under Rear-Admiral Sir Charles Shadwell FRS (1814-86), another veteran of Fatshan Creek and the Second China War. Shadwell, a distinguished astronomer, was more of a scholar than a warrior by temperament, and John Fisher, who served under Shadwell in China, worshipped him.[2] Shadwell was instructed to consider whether the facilities for naval education were adequate, how officers should be examined, whether to base the College at Portsmouth or Greenwich and whether it would be useful to have facilities for officers to spend a limited number of terms at Cambridge. His Committee included Joseph Woolley, the Director of Naval Education, Captain A W A Hood, Director of Naval Ordnance and lately Captain of HMS _Excellent_, Alfred Barry, Principal of King's College, London and Spencer Butler, Secretary to the Greenwich Hospital Enquiry of 1860. The evidence gathered revealed a lamentable want of scientific knowledge in the officer corps, attributed to the early, brief

1. Dickinson, pp246-51.
2. Mackay, R F, _Fisher of Kilverstone_ (Oxford 1973), pp12-13.

education given to young officers in contrast to the later, longer and more thorough effort applied to the cadets of every other significant navy. The British system had the virtue of hardening the cadets up for sea service and instilling the military virtues of 'character and leadership'. If the early cadet entry was retained, then Shadwell came close to recommending a second tier of education for all officers, to prepare them for the later stages of their careers, rather than relying of the limited number of specialists and volunteers who had gone through the *Excellent* and Portsmouth. This quality of educational provision could not be achieved at sea.

In their report, published in July 1870, the Committee recommended modifications to the existing system of education, expanding the range of practical and related subjects provided to include languages, chemistry, metallurgy, geology, mineralogy, and naval tactics. There was no mention of the study of war at any level beyond tactics. The Committee stopped short of recommending that attendance on the one-year course be made compulsory. Laughton was interviewed, but he did not favour moving the College, and did not suggest that history should be part of the curriculum. However, the Shadwell Committee recommended that lectures on naval tactics be given at the College. On the basis of the expanded curriculum and enlarged, if still voluntary, student body, the civilians on the Committee favoured moving the College to Greenwich, which would be three times as expensive. The naval officers, to a man, preferred to stay at Portsmouth, where the education would be more 'practical'.[3]

Outside the Service, opinion largely favoured the move. *The Times* was not alone in suggesting that the magnificent buildings should be used for a naval 'University'. Even inside the service there were those in favour. In a paper that reflected his close friendship with Laughton, Cyprian Bridge argued that the new college would be a critical stage in the development of a naval staff, and it would also exploit the proximity of the world's leading naval engineering and shipbuilding firms, the Observatory and the academic strengths of the capital.[4] An enlarged college would improve the limited amount of worthwhile academic input available to officers during their careers.

However, such laudable aims had nothing to do with the final decision to move the college. The Member of Parliament for Greenwich was William Ewart Gladstone, the Liberal Prime Minister. His relationship with the constituency had always been difficult, particularly after the closure of the dockyards at Deptford and Woolwich and of the Hospital, and the complete closure of such a large source of local patronage would

3. Barnard, pp941-8. Dickinson, pp254-66.
4. Bridge, C A G, 'On the necessity of forming a Naval Staff, *Naval Science: Number One* (London 1872), pp9-14. Bridge and Vesey-Hamilton were among the handful of officers who favoured the move.

be disastrous. In a major speech at Greenwich on 28 October 1871 Gladstone promised new jobs at the hospital. On 30 January 1872 his diary included the laconic entry, 'Greenwich to be the centre of naval education'. In spite of the greatly increased cost, and his own ignorance of the requirements of service education, Gladstone had found a 'job' to secure his seat.[5] Even so he did not dare to face his constituents at the poll in 1873, when he took up the additional post of Chancellor of the Exchequer. Although he was re-elected in 1874, the honour was soured by the humiliation of coming in a distant second, behind Booth the gin distiller.[6] The close connection between the Prime Minister's standing in his constituency and the decision to move the College was well known. When Laughton gave a public progress report on the College in 1875, he acknowledged it as a fact.[7]

Once the Cabinet had agreed to move the College to Greenwich a second Committee assembled in 1872, under Admiral Sir John Walter Tarleton (1812-80), a Naval Lord, Joseph Woolley and Colonel Andrew Clarke RE, the Director of Naval Works, to consider the curriculum. They enlarged the vision of the Shadwell report to embrace the whole service, requiring more staff and educating more officers. Their report also called for thirty lectures on naval history, at a cost of £10 each. As Admiral Colomb was to lament, these were never found to be feasible, only six or eight were ever given in any one year, and the fee was halved.[8] The call for naval history, linked to the study of tactics, was not lost on Laughton. Thirty lectures at £10.00 would have been a 60 per cent increase in his salary, and even eight lectures at £5.00 offered a significant addition to the current figure £561.10.0 per annum.[9] Laughton, the only member of staff to transfer from Portsmouth, began work at Greenwich when the College opened in February 1873,[10] continuing to teach maths to the Lieutenants qualifying for the gunnery course. Apart from the Instructor on Fortification he was the sole member of staff on site for five months. Among the first students to pass through was Prince Louis of Battenberg. An outstanding Sub-lieutenant of 1874, Battenberg became a lifelong supporter of Laughton, and of the causes he advocated.[11]

---

5. Dickinson, pp267-84.

6. Morley, J, *Life of Gladstone* (London 1903), Vol II, p490.

7. Ibid, pp465-72. Matthew, H G C, *Gladstone 1809-74* (Oxford 1984), pp227-8. Laughton, J K, 'Scientific Instruction in the Navy' *JRUSI* Vol XIX (1875), p239.

8. Colomb, P, *Memoir of Sir Astley Cooper Key* (London 1898), pp391-404. Parliamentary Papers (1870) Vol XXV.

9. Admiralty to President of the College: 8.2.1873: ADM 203/1.

10. He was moved from the books of HMS *Excellent* to those of HMS *Fisgard* on 25 January 1873. Service Record ADM 196-81. He lived at No. 9 Gloucester Place while he worked at the College.

11. Laughton, J K, 'Scientific Instruction in the Navy' *JRUSI* (1875), pp217-41. Kerr, M, *Prince Louis of Battenberg* (London 1934), p34.

When the college was finally up to strength, Laughton, an 'Instructor in Pure and Applied Mathematics' became Head of Meteorology and Marine Surveying. The first three of his six lectures on 'Nautical Meteorology' were printed in *Naval Science*, making them accessible to the entire service, before the untimely demise of this promising, if alarming, technical journal.[12] The new College was on a far larger scale than Portsmouth, with a staff of five professors and eighteen instructors under a Director of Studies and the Admiral President. The greatest beneficiary of the move to Greenwich was Laughton, the new location giving him access to a wide range of service and academic contacts, both at the College and in the capital generally, that were vital to his development as an historian. As a recognised scientist and educator, and the senior Naval Instructor, Laughton became the semi-official College spokesman, providing a series of lectures at RUSI that ranged from College progress reports to discussions of major policy issues and raising the case for naval history. The attendance of the Admiral President, and other leading naval figures, lent official sanction to Laughton's opinions.

The Admiralty viewed the move to Greenwich as an opportunity 'to provide the most efficient means of higher education of Naval Officers adequate to the constantly increasing requirements of the Service', and 'the highest possible instruction in all branches of theoretical and scientific study bearing upon their profession', although this was not to prejudice 'the all-important practical training in active duties'.[13] The College became the point of contact between the officer corps and the scientists, through access to the academic resources of London, as well as an expanded dedicated staff. These last, most of whom were men of academic distinction and largely from Cambridge, were expected to further research into all aspects of science connected with the naval service. The selection of leading naval officers for the position of President reflected the navy's early interest. The first summoned to what the Admiralty termed 'the Naval University of Greenwich', was Rear-Admiral Sir Astley Cooper Key.[14] As Captain of HMS *Excellent* Key had been responsible for the Portsmouth College in the mid-1860s and was considered to be a 'scientific' officer. The courses of study proposed, and largely put into practice, were:

1. Pure mathematics, including geometry and calculus.
2. Applied mathematics, including mechanics, optics, and theories of light, electricity and magnetism.

---

12. Laughton, J K, 'Nautical Meteorology' Parts I, II & III in Reed, E (ed), *Naval Science*, Vol 3 & 4 (London 1874 & 1875), pp467-85, 108-113, 249-55, 348-58.
13. Dawson, C M, *The Story of Greenwich* (London 1977), p91 quoting the Admiralty Circular of 20 January 1873.
14. Admiralty to Key 17.12.1872: ADM 203/1.

3. Applied mechanics, theories of structures and machines.
4. Nautical astronomy, surveying, meteorology and chart drawing.
5. Experimental science, physics, chemistry and metallurgy.
6. Marine engineering.
7. Naval architecture.
8. Fortification, military drawing and naval artillery.
9. International and Maritime Law, law of evidence and naval courts martial.
10. Naval History and tactics, including naval signals and steam evolutions.
11. Modern languages.
12. Drawing.
13. Hygiene, naval and climactic.

The 1874 examination syllabus awarded marks for all subjects, to a maximum of 1500. Of these 500 were for algebra, geometry and trigonometry, and 400 for navigation and nautical astronomy. Laughton's two books were teaching texts.[15] This syllabus, with the exception of naval artillery, law of evidence and courts martial, was being taught by the end of the decade to a large, but amorphous, body of officers, many of whom were volunteers. The majority of those forced to attend were Acting Sub-Lieutenants who came for six months, along with Acting Assistant Engineers and volunteer Lieutenants. Within four years the total number attending the college at 1 January had dropped from 237 to 180. This reflected a fundamental flaw in the new educational edifice; it was never made a compulsory element in the naval career structure, and was not incorporated into the mainstream of service life. Doubtless the reasons for this was the same as is always advanced against intellectually stimulating studies that require time for reading and reflection, namely the lack of time in crowded career. Typically Admiral Sir Geoffrey Hornby, a man of ability and a supporter of the College, complained that there would not be enough lieutenants for sea service if they all took a one-year course ashore. The inanity of such arguments, which confused a fixed intake of cadets with a fluctuating demand for sea service, could hardly be exceeded. Any profession that does not make the time to contemplate the higher direction of its core activity is doomed to disappointment, at the very least.[16] This was a lesson Laughton would read to his students on more than one occasion.

At Portsmouth Laughton had developed his philosophy on the higher education of naval officers. As an educator and scientist he believed the

---

15. Admiralty Circular No.28 14.3.1874 ADM 203/1.
16. Soley, J R, *Report on Foreign Systems of Naval Education* (Washington, Government Printing Office 1880), pp49-55. A work drawing heavily on Laughton's 1875 *RUSI* Lecture.

only way to master a subject was to examine the principles upon which it was based. In his early career maths had served this function, being vital to an intelligent study of navigation, gunnery, engineering and surveying. When the new College and its 'scientific' curriculum were attacked by serving officers and naval writers, Laughton was called on to respond. In early 1875 he lectured on 'Scientific Instruction in the Navy' at RUSI, the preferred forum for College issues. That he began by stressing that education was no bar to practical application, leadership and courage was indicative of the nature of contemporary criticism. He argued that superior education would enable officers to expand on the success of the past. Laughton stressed that the object of naval education was both to impart knowledge, and to develop the power of self-education, which was vital if officers were going to acquire more knowledge throughout their careers, contrasting this with mere training. He believed mathematics was the only sure basis for the particular skills required by naval officers, and the exact and accurate intellect they would need. With his friend from HMS *Calcutta* Lord Gillford, a Junior Naval Lord, he began a long-term attack on the Cadet Training Ship HMS *Britannia*. It was widely acknowledged that *Britannia* relied on cramming an over-ambitious, largely maths-based syllabus into young boys, leaving little or no permanent understanding. Consequently, the work at Greenwich had to begin by repeating what had been taught prematurely and badly at *Britannia*.[17] While Laughton admitted that half the 33 hours spent in the class room each week were devoted to maths, he stressed that there were other courses running, although many of them required a significant maths input. He lamented the under-developed state of the Surveying Course demonstrated by his friend Staff Commander Hull, and that it had not yet been 'found advisable or practicable to introduce' Naval History. More significantly he lamented the failure of the new college to attract the large number of volunteer Captains and Commanders who had been such a feature of the Portsmouth College, attributing this to the 'bad press' the college had received, and the unjustified belief that it only taught maths.[18] The Admiralty responded to the ongoing public debate by summoning another Committee. In September 1876 the Reverend Osborne Gordon was directed to report on the courses, staff and examinations at the College. Gordon's report recognised that much of the Sub-Lieutenants' course was a repetition of the *Britannia* syllabus, and therefore a waste of effort. Furthermore many candidates needed to hire a private tutor

---

17. Pack, S W C, *Britannia at Dartmouth* (London 1966). Laughton, J K, 'Scientific Instruction in the Royal Navy' *JRUSI* Vol XIX (1875), pp217-41.
18. Wolley, writing in *Naval Science* disputed Laughton's argument on this point, but did not care to publish under his own name. 'Naval Education' Vol IV, pp328-9.

to meet the standards required. He advised a wider course of study, including history, and attempting to improve the status of the College.[19]

Little in the Gordon report would have surprised Laughton. He continued to press for improved mathematical education, calling for the abolition of the *Britannia* in favour of leaving boys at school until the age of 16 or 17, when they could be examined to a reasonable standard. He knew the whole purpose of the Sub-Lieutenants' course at Greenwich, which dominated the College, was to ensure that young officers had absorbed the material that had been rammed down their throats at *Britannia*. The American naval educator Professor James Russell Soley, in his Official Report on Foreign Systems of Naval Education, which largely followed Laughton's work on the British system, considered that the *Britannia* syllabus was 'hopelessly beyond the young student's reach'. They only began to comprehend the meaning of the 'mass of undigested facts and principles, crammed for the immediate purpose of passing an examination' when they arrived at Greenwich, after five years' sea-service, an experience ruined for many by the incubus of examinations.[20] Nor did the damage end there. Afloat, officers of intelligence and discernment, notably Laughton's friends Captain James Goodenough and Commander Cyprian Bridge, recognised that the nature of the modern naval officer was being warped by an undue reliance on examinations in mathematics and related subjects as the guide to future merit. In a lecture at the RUSI in March 1871, Goodenough had called for cadets to enter at 15 with certificates from good schools, and then spend two years studying a combined theory and practice course. The examination for the rank of midshipman would be taken in their 17th year, followed by another year of sea-service, practical gunnery training and related work. After one year in regular service they would be examined for Sub-Lieutenant.[21] In 1877 Bridge, who believed his own career had fatally stalled at the rank of Commander during a disheartening term aboard HMS *Audacious*, flagship of the China Station, condemned the whole system, and in particular the reliance on mathematics. In a letter of uncommon power, he tore into a system that produced 'exam' lieutenants, officers who he found to be useless on board ship.[22] Similar opinions were expressed in the House of Commons by Sir Thomas, later Lord, Brassey, the Liberal naval spokesman, backed up by his accustomed battery of selected expert testimony. Brassey considered modern languages deserved greater attention.

The Second President of the College, Admiral Sir Edward Fanshawe

---

19. Dickinson, pp295-307.
20. Soley, p90.
21. Barnard, pp947-8.
22. Bridge to Laughton 1.2.1877 from HMS *Audacious* at Hong Kong. JKL MSS NMM. Laughton was so struck by Bridge's argument that he kept this section of the letter.

1876-78, took seriously the criticism that unreasonably high standards caused the loss of the good practical men. But he was satisfied that the standard for the course, as opposed to that required for the 'first class certificate' that dominated the lives of the 'exam' Sub-Lieutenants aboard Bridge's ship, enabled any officer who possessed sufficient determination to pass. He recommended that the overall direction of naval education be centralised, under the Admiral President, to ensure closer links with HMS *Britannia*.[23] Woolley had retired as Director of Naval Education in 1874, and the post had been scrapped, leaving the relationship between Greenwich and Dartmouth in chaos.[24] While John Jellicoe, who passed Greenwich with three 'firsts' in 1879, made his mark under this system, he was an unusually talented mathematician.[25] Such exceptions did not invalidate Laughton's criticism. The next time he lectured on the Greenwich syllabus at the RUSI, in 1882, Fanshawe took the chair, and supported him wholeheartedly.

Laughton's second lecture was by way of a progress report. It reflected the 'practical' opinions of Laughton's friends, but retained his faith in mathematics. He observed that the failure to adopt an adequate history course reflected the view that history was not a 'scientific' subject, as defined in the original Admiralty Circular of January 1873. This document was the basis of his 'Scientific Study of Naval History', both in nomenclature and methodology: naval history had to be 'scientific' if it was going to be brought into the Greenwich curriculum. His wider conclusions reflected his educational understanding. As *Britannia* had an unwholesome, narrowing effect on the intellect of the boys, it should be closed. Teaching everything by example and rule of thumb methods denied them an opportunity to comprehend the principles on which the subjects were based. This time he was able to refer to Professor Soley's Report, which largely reflected his own 1875 lecture, saying that 'first class men' depended on private tutors, of whom there were many around the College.[26] After an unusually wide-ranging and well-informed discussion, involving Fanshawe, Lieutenant Campbell, and his friend Gerard Noel, Laughton concluded with his best Nelson example, the 'Trafalgar Memorandum'. An educated officer, he argued, would understand his admiral's battle plan, and would not have to fall back on simply placing his ship close alongside that of the enemy.[27] The message was repeated

23. Brassey, Sir T, *The British Navy: its Strength, Resources and Administration. Volume IV. Dockyards, Reserves, Training, Pensions* (London 1883), pp530-566.
24. I am indebted to Dr Dickinson for this point.
25. Bacon, R, *The Life of John Rushworth, Earl Jellicoe* (London 1936), pp41-2 for a defence of the 'three one's' men.
26. Laughton, J K, 'On the Several European systems of Naval Education', *JRUSI* (1881), pp108-29 and reprinted as a pamphlet.
27. Laughton, J K, 'Naval Education', *JRUSI* (1882), pp339-368 esp. p349.

sixty years later by Admiral Richmond.[28] Laughton recognised that the purpose of a superior historical education was to inculcate leadership and develop doctrine.

Laughton was not alone in his efforts to develop a sound basis for naval thought. In the mid-1860s three distinct strands of intellectual activity were in progress, inspired by the challenge of steam, armour and the ram. Although these strands were initially distinct, if not isolated, it was soon obvious that they offered mutual support, and would be developed into the basis for modern naval doctrine. The work of Sir John Colomb (1838-1909), beginning with his 1867 pamphlet, *The Protection of our Commerce and Distribution of our Naval Forces Considered*, developed a basic strategy for Imperial Defence from an analysis of contemporary statistics. Colomb argued that Britain had a unique global position, based on naval power, and that the connections, sea communications, that enabled the structure to function, were the vulnerable points. The key to their protection lay in the global chain of bases, from which the Navy could operate. The soundness of this basic concept was weakened by his preference for coast defence vessels and local forts to protect these bases, and a complete lack of historical awarness.[29] This weakness, which reflected and reinforced the contemporary notion that the past had become irrelevant, accounted for the flaws in Colomb's thought, as well as the remarkable, precocious coherence of his argument. For the next forty years Colomb pursued his theme, which grew to encompass Imperial Unity, with a remorseless determination. After he married a wealthy widow in 1866, acquiring an estate in Ireland, he resigned his commission and devoted himself to imperial defence.[30] Colomb's ideas were important, Schurman and Ranft having demonstrated that they were a major element in the process of creating the strategic ideas that dominated the Navy in the early years of the twentieth century.[31] That process required Colomb's theories to be cross-checked against the experience of the past – an area in which the work of his elder brother played a major role.

Vice-Admiral Philip Colomb (1831-1900) began his work on naval doctrine at the opposite end of the spectrum to his brother.[32] During a leisurely five-year term as Flag Lieutenant at Devonport (1857-62) he developed a system of light and sound signals, based on the Morse code,

28. Richmond, H, *Naval Training* (Oxford 1933).
29. Schurman, p24.
30. D'Egville, H, *Imperial Defence and Closer Union* (London 1913), a resume of Colomb's ideas and essays. Schurman, pp16-34.
31. Ranft, B M, 'The protection of British seaborne trade and the development of systematic planning for war, 1860-1905', in Ranft, B M (ed), *Technical Change and British Naval Policy 1860-1939* (London 1977).
32. Schurman, pp34-59. For a discussion of how this process worked in the late 1880s see Chapter 4.

allowing ships to communicate at night, which he had encountered at Keyham during the laying of the first Atlantic cable.[33] Once his system had been officially recognised, in 1865, he was invited to revise the Signal Book. The object was to create a signal book suitable for the ironclad Navy, which required new or clarified terminology and new tactical forms.[34] Colomb's work was dominated by the need for comprehension, clarity and ease of use. He wanted to produce a signal book that could be used effectively. The work of French, Russian and British writers was considered, but the basic ideas came from Admiral Sir William Martin's work. While he examined the older signal books, Colomb's work, like that of his brother, was not historically informed. He would develop the historical side of his work in the late 1880s, under Laughton's guidance. History would be the critical instrument for the development of the work done by the Colomb brothers, and the integration of their two distinct strands of thought into a modern naval doctrine. From the mid-1860s Laughton had recognised that the only secure base for analysis was the record of past experience. In time he would create that base, providing the factual foundations to underpin and enhance the theoretical work of the Colombs.

In contrast to the limited, if significant, work of the mid-1860s, the early 1870s witnessed the brief flowering of a naval intellectual movement. A significant group of relatively junior officers were inspired by the Franco-Prussian War to press for a more systematic, intellectual and professional approach to the development and transmission of service doctrine, the education of officers and the conduct of operations. Arguing that they were now living in a 'scientific age', the supporters of this movement produced two lasting memorials to their efforts, a discussion forum and a quarterly journal. Although neither survived the decade they were critical to the development of Laughton's thinking, and the establishment of his reputation.

Laughton's interest in naval tactics, apparent before 1870, reflected the mood within his immediate circle, which was mostly composed of officers attending the Portsmouth College and HMS *Excellent*. In January 1872 this mood coalesced into the 'Junior Naval Professional Association' (JNPA), largely through the efforts of Lieutenant Hubert Grenfell, a friend and colleague of Laughton, who had qualified on board *Excellent* in 1871, and returned as First Gunnery Officer in 1873.[35] The JNPA was intended to provide 'opportunities of instruction and information to junior officers of the Royal Naval, Royal Marine, and Royal Naval Reserve services, on all questions of professional and scientific interest',

---

33. Pasley, L, *Admiral Sir T S Pasley* (London 1900), p245.
34. Autobiographical Notes – Vice-Admiral Philip Colomb. MS in private hands.
35. Wells, J, *Whaley*, pp218 & 215.

and to benefit from 'discussion and the conflict of opinion' on professional subjects. In short, it was a debating society, to meet at all naval ports. Initially the new body had the sanction of the Liberal Board of Admiralty, although this was a temporary advantage. Membership was limited to lieutenants and their juniors, although senior officers, Army officers and civilians could be elected as honorary members. In the first year seventy-eight members joined, including Lord Charles Beresford (1846-1919) and Gerard Noel. The Association published a monthly digest of naval information between April 1872 and July 1874 and papers presented to meetings. Laughton lectured at Portsmouth on 'The Austrian Arctic Expedition', and 'On Land and Sea Breezes'.[36] Although membership reached 300 in 1874, the loss of Admiralty support, the hostility of the incoming Tory ministry and the difficulties of sustaining a society led by junior officers who spent most of their careers afloat, saw the JNPA die away. Looking back with the hindsight of fifty years, Admiral William Henderson, the long-serving editor of *The Naval Review*, founded in 1913, and a founder member of the JNPA, considered it a precursor of the Naval Society, a forum where the free exchange of ideas could help to form sound doctrine.[37]

Laughton's paper 'Land and Sea Breezes' and Bridge's 'Fleet Tactics', delivered at Plymouth, were singled out for praise by Edward Reed in his contribution to the intellectual revival, *Naval Science*.[38] This quarterly, which began as a 'puffing advertisement' for Reed, improved over time, but was never commercially viable.[39] Reed set out to produce a high-quality journal dealing with all the scientific aspects of the naval service, from ship design to the theory of weather. His claim that the tone would be didactic, rather than polemical, must have been hard to swallow at the Admiralty. He praised the formation of the JNPA, even if he was disappointed by its early productions, and expected much from Greenwich even before it had opened. Unfortunately his journal was pitched at a level that interested its editor more than the majority of his intended audience, including too many complex, theoretical papers which required a high level of competence in mathematics, and were too far removed from the practical concerns of officers in mid-career. Bringing in Joseph

---

36. *Monthly Register of the Junior Naval Professional Association* Vol 1 (20.5.1872), p15, Vol 3 (20.6.1872), p38.
37. Henderson, Adm. W. 'The Naval Society and Review and an Historical Abstract of other service periodicals', *The Naval Review* (1922), pp386-402, esp. p390. I am indebted to Admiral R. Hill, for this reference and other materials relating to the *Naval Review*.
38. Reed, Sir E (ed), *Naval Science* Vol II (London 1873), p540. Laughton's paper was considered to be the best in the volume, Bridge's was equally prominent in the sister publication at Plymouth.
39. *Monthly Register of the Junior Naval Professional Association* Vol I (20.5.1872), p15, reprinting an editorial from *The Portsmouth Times*.

Woolley as co-editor in 1874 did little to improve matters. When Reed entered Parliament he wound up the journal, which had lasted only four years. Although both the JNPA and *Naval Science* proved short-lived they had given Laughton opportunities to publish. When they collapsed he transferred his work to other journals. After publishing some contributions unsigned, notably a characteristic effort on 'The Definitions of Nautical Astronomy', *Naval Science* published his Greenwich meteorology lectures under his own name, a sure sign of official approval. The failure of the naval intellectual movement reflected the lack of interest at the senior level, symbolised by the abolition of the post of Director of Naval Education, which left the two educational establishments without co-ordination. Most flag officers had opposed the move to Greenwich, rejected the idea of entering cadets at school-leaving age, and favoured leaving the *Britannia* onboard ship, where they could inculcate older, simpler values.[40]

The case for history as the basis for the study of tactics had been accepted by the Tarleton Committee, inspiring Laughton's groundbreaking papers on tactics and history of 1873 and 1874. Laughton had proved his capacity as a professional educator and possessed the skill to develop the new subject. However, the dominant theme at this stage was the development of contemporary naval tactics, a subject required under the new syllabus, and it was only through this link that naval history could be introduced. In his early discussions with Bridge, Laughton recognised that history would supply the evidence he required to teach tactics. In this he was repeating the approach adopted in his scientific books. His first efforts were a necessary stage in a self-devised learning process, developing his approach to the use of history in naval education. The more he became aware of the materials available, and the illustration they could provide, the more he became convinced that history was critical. At the same time he was well aware that the existing system of naval education was narrowly conceived and unnecessarily pragmatic.

The ambition and ability that enabled Laughton to master and publish on scientific subjects while working at Portsmouth was applied to naval tactics. His method reflected the critical value of mathematical training in 'cultivating . . . an exact and accurate tone of thought'.[41] This approach had served him well as a practical scientist, and would be developed as the study of history came to be more important than the tactical problems it had been deployed to solve. It was this basic methodology that set Laughton apart from the other historians, tactical theorists and strategists of his generation. He was never satisfied with the vague, romantic and often

---

40. I am indebted to Dr. Dickinson for advice on this issue.
41. Laughton, J K, 'Scientific Instruction in the Navy', *JRUSI* (1875), pp217-41 at p223.

non-existent 'evidence' deployed in their work. He can be distinguished from Mahan by the relative importance the two men placed on accurate scholarship and the 'lessons of history'. While Laughton, the historian, sought material which would allow him to examine the strategic issues and develop his understanding, Mahan, the strategist, selected his evidence to support a pre-determined thesis on the significance of 'Sea Power'.

The basis of naval tactical thought had been thrown into confusion by the advent of the steam battleship in the early 1850s. Hitherto steamships had been auxiliaries for sailing fleets: now they were the dominant instrument. In the aftermath of the Crimean War the French Navy made significant progress in the theoretical and practical development of steam tactics, which had inspired General Sir Howard Douglas, the leading authority on naval gunnery and Lord Palmerston's preferred source of defence advice, to produce *Naval Warfare under Steam* in 1858. Douglas hoped that steam would introduce more precision into manoeuvres.[42] While his system was over-ambitious it led Palmerston to insist that the Admiralty send an Admiral to command in the Mediterranean who would devote his attention to this subject.[43] The officer selected, Sir William Fanshawe Martin, had already produced his *Observations on Steam Tactics and Rowing Boat Evolutions* in 1858. During his three-year term in command (1860-63), part of which Laughton and Bridge observed from on board HMS *Algiers*, Martin introduced the fleet to steam manoeuvres. In 1863 he summed up his experience in *Observations of the Scheme for Screw Ship Evolutions*, sharing Douglas's view that the old line-ahead should be replaced with oblique or line-abreast formations. These would provide better opportunities for mutual support, the use of the ram and the development of axial firepower.[44] The vital distinction between evolutions, the system of drill designed to develop ship-handling skills and effective co-ordination, and tactics, the control of fleets and squadrons in battle, needs to be stressed. Logical thinkers, notably Bridge, recognised the distinction, and stressed the importance of conducting realistic tactical exercises.[45] However, as most contemporary officers realised, these could only be conducted *after* the fleet had been drilled up to a high *and common* standard of ship-handling in close company. It was to this end that Martin, and his successors, notably Sir Geoffrey Hornby, spent so long working up their fleets in 'goose-step' evolutions. Both men recognised that such skills, as part of a sound

WITH

---

42. Douglas, Sir H, *Naval Warfare under Steam* (London 1858), pvii.
43. Palmerston (Prime Minister) to the Duke of Somerset (First Lord of the Admiralty), 8.5.1860 Somerset MSS Buckingham Record Office 1392 M/L19/60.
44. Sandler, S, *The Emergence of the Modern Capital Ship*. (London 1979), pp119-22. Gordon, A, *The Rules of the Game: Jutland and British Naval Command* (London 1996), pp182-4.
45. Bridge, C A G, 'Fleet Evolutions and Naval Tactics', *JRUSI* (1873), pp227-43.

doctrine, were the foundations on which victories would be built, not the method that would secure them.

In the early 1870s the debate on the tactics, and even the ships, of the future was in a state of confusion. The dramatic impact of new technology in the Russian and American wars, together with the apparent success of the ram at Lissa, left naval officers without a firm doctrinal basis from which to prepare for the next war. While some favoured improved signalling systems, others recognised the limits of control in battle, and preferred simple systems relying on delegation of authority and initiative. Among the best-informed, and most influential voices in the contemporary tactical debate were those of French officers, who often combined technical data and historical examples. Laughton was familiar with the work of the leading French authorities, notably Xavier Raymond, Baron Grivel, Admiral Bouët-Willaumez and Admiral Jurien de la Gravière. Laughton joined the debate, in response to a specific stimulus.[46]

In March 1873 the JNPA put up a 50-guinea prize for the best study of 'The Manoeuvres and System of Tactics which fleets of ships of modern construction should adopt to develop the powers of the Ram, Heavy Artillery, Torpedoes etc. in an action on the open sea'. Essays were submitted unsigned. The competition was taken seriously at the highest level, being judged by three leading Admirals, Sir Alexander Milne, Sir Alfred Ryder and Sir Astley Cooper Key.[47] The prize was won by Laughton's friend Gerard Noel, but Laughton's 20,000 word *Essay on Naval Tactics* was placed second and the judges noted that it 'contains much valuable material, and indicates considerable care and research in the composition'.[48] The three best essays were published in 1873. Laughton's object had been was to produce a, 'scientific study [we will see later what he meant by this expression], of Naval Tactics'. He used history to demonstrate that the results of the fleet actions of 1794-1805 were quite anomalous, reflecting ill-trained French and Spanish crews rather than any peculiar skill on the part of the Royal Navy. Furthermore some eighteenth-century 'victories' were in effect strategic defeats, because the enemy achieved his object by avoiding decisive action. For this he blamed the rigidity of the Fighting Instructions, conceived during the Dutch

---

46. For French tactical thinking and thinkers at this period see: Hamilton, C I, *The Anglo-French Naval Rivalry 1840-1870* (Oxford 1993), Ch4. Roberts, S (ed. Ropp, T), *The Development of a Modern Navy: French Naval Policy 1817-1904* (Annapolis 1987). Brassey, Vol IV, pp464-87. Battesti, M, *Le marine de Napoléon III* (Paris 1997), Vol II, pp673-701. Sandler, Ch5 analyses the debate in Britain.
47. **Milne**, Admiral of the Fleet Sir Alexander (1806-96). First Naval Lord 1866-68, 1872-76, C-in-C North America 1860-64 Channel, C-in-C Mediterranean 1869-70. An officer of great ability.
   Ryder, Admiral Sir Alfred Phillipps (1820-88). C-in-C China 1875-78, C-in-C Portsmouth 1879-82.
48. *Monthly Register* Vol II (20.3.1873) and Vol III (20.2.1874) p21 for the result.

Wars, which were entirely inappropriate to the different strategic conditions of the French Wars. He argued that the basic principle of success in
naval combat was concentration of force against a portion of the enemy
fleet. Suffren had employed these tactics, but his superior skill had been
negated by the discipline and courage of the British fleet under Sir Edward
Hughes. By contrast Nelson's crushing victories reflected concentration of
force and superior personnel. However, he believed superior personnel
would count for little if a heavy shell burst in the battery of an ironclad, and
any future advantage would have to come from superior tactics. Therefore,
he argued tactics should be studied at a theoretical level, with all sides equal
in point of ability. For such an approach he required fixed data.[49] This
could only be provided by a suitably 'scientific' base.

Laughton began by examining the manoeuvring powers of ships,
stressing the need for homogeneity and the importance of superior
powers of turning, especially for ramming. For squadrons he contended
that the ideal tactical unit, for ease of signalling, was the homogeneous
three-ship *peleton*. This was the conclusion of Bouët-Willaumez's 1865
paper on ironclad tactics, and was widely accepted in Britain, not least by
Bridge and Admiral Ryder. Laughton stressed that the squadron, rather
than the ship, was the basic building block of a fleet, as it had been since
the time of the Armada. Three-ship units could more easily learn to
combine than a larger group. He stressed that tactics was a system of
attack and defence, as distinct from evolutions, which were a form of
exercise. Although this critical distinction has never been set out with
such clarity, Laughton's work has been ignored in the twentieth century,
leaving armchair admirals to argue that the complex *evolutions* of the
Signal Book were intended for use in combat. Tactics and strategy were
also distinguished, strategy being defined as movements relating to the
conduct of the campaign, as distinct from those relating to the battle.
Laughton argued that the strategic objects of the Admirals would deter-
mine whether they fought, and the tactics they would employ. He believed that blockade and the defence of trade were the usual occasions for
battle. Furthermore Admirals normally had a choice of whether to fight,
and, if brought to battle, how to fight and when to break off. This was the
most important point raised by the paper. It placed Laughton, writing
almost twenty years before Mahan, on an altogether more sophisticated
analytic plane. He demonstrated that strategic plans had to be developed
that would *force* a reluctant enemy to fight, because only then would
skilful opponents, like the French, be brought to battle. He closed by
stressing the need for practice, determination and experience, in contrast

---

49. Laughton, J K, *Essay on Naval Tactics* (Portsmouth 1873); normally bound with Noel,
G H U (ed), *Gun, Ram and Torpedo* (Portsmouth 1873). See Gordon, A, pp206-7 for an
assessment.

to romantic notions of 'heaven-born inspiration' commonly substituted for thought and analysis.

Writing in the *Edinburgh Review* Bridge compared his friend to the famous French theorist Père Hoste; both men were mathematicians teaching navies, both codified tactical thought. He also drew attention to the logical structure and superior style of the paper:

> the literary merits of Mr Laughton's contribution, already known as a forcible and elegant writer, are particularly high. His work abounds in historical allusion and historical parallel. Even when he deals with the mathematical questions which happen to arise, he does so in a manner by no means likely to prove repulsive to an ordinary reader.[50]

Although *Naval Science* recognised that Noel's was the best essay, it gave Laughton great credit for his 'thoughtful and altogether excellent' effort to understand the lessons of the past, 'with the view of making them our assistants, either as guides or warnings'. Such work would require 'deep search' because previous generations had not made the sort of methodical records that would be of immediate use and consequently most tactical history was 'rubbish'. There was a way to rectify this weakness. The reviewer declared; 'We should like to see Mr. Laughton take the matter up, and work out the historical problem from those hidden records which are so difficult to collect'. However, he would need the co-operation of a serving officer, as his tactical ideas were 'nearly as theoretical as some of his continental contemporaries'.[51] Rarely can the man and his life's work have been so succinctly outlined.

This important paper was influential on both sides of the Atlantic. Captain Stephen Luce USN and Sir Thomas Brassey were notable disciples.[52] Laughton was the only British 'civilian' authority cited in Brassey's monumental compilation *The British Navy* of 1882.[53] The central theme, the importance of concentration of force in combat, historically demonstrated, was accepted by a number of important British officers, notably Key and Philip Colomb. Key, a personal friend and patron of Laughton's from the early days at Greenwich, had used him as the academic spokesman for College policy at the RUSI. He also allowed him to publish his lectures in *Naval Science* and supported his attempt to provide

---

50. 'Ocean Warfare', *The Edinburgh Review* (July 1874), pp1-31 at p25.
51. *Naval Science: Number Three* (London 1874), pp426-7.
52. Hayes, J and Hattendorf, J, *The Writings of Stephen B Luce* (Newport 1975), pp71. Luce's paper 'Tactics and History: On the Study of Naval History (Grand tactics)' of 1887 were largely based on Laughton's papers of 1873 and 1874. See also Luce/Laughton Correspondence.
53. **Brassey**, Thomas, First Earl (1836-1918), was the leading Liberal naval spokesman. His monumental compilation was given a favourable reception in the *Edinburgh Review* by Laughton. It remains invaluable as an introduction to contemporary naval thinking, provided the strongly 'liberal' character of the selection is recognised.

history lectures. Later, while First Sea Lord, he made a major contribution to Laughton's historical work. Colomb, a prominent writer on naval tactics, gradually moved toward Laughton's historical method. Laughton's essay was republished twelve years later. It was as close to a tactical text book as the Royal Navy was prepared to go.

Through his work on tactics, Laughton had recognised that what the Royal Navy needed was not a new set of rigid 'Fighting Instructions' but a new doctrine for the ironclad era. He also recognised that this need, for understanding and principles, could only be met by an accurate study of the past. Whereas maths was the basis of junior-level service training, he believed that history would support the education of the service mind. By 1874 Laughton was ready to present his views to a high-ranking professional audience, and for all the feigned diffidence with which he opened his seminal paper 'The Scientific Study of Naval History', at the RUSI on 22 June 1874, he expected a positive hearing.[54] The paper was an extended argument for a Naval History course at Greenwich.

Recognising that history would never secure an important place in the Greenwich curriculum until it was recognised as 'scientific' Laughton began by stressing that what little history the average naval officer knew was romantic, inaccurate and useless. He went on;

> I also find that an idea that the history of the past contains no practical lessons for the future, and is therefore a useless branch of scholarship daily gathers strength; and is, indeed, put prominently forward by those whose opinions on purely technical questions have a just claim to our respect.

By contrast, he argued, naval history should be studied thoroughly, because it 'contained lessons of the gravest meaning'. Laughton's naval history examined the way in which fleets had been collected and manned, the course of events leading to victories and defeats, and the principles of tactics. The results of such study would be the development of a coherent written doctrine, to the lasting benefit of the service and the serving officer. This history-based approach was in stark contrast to the technological obsessions that dominated contemporary naval thought and remain a powerful influence. As a 'sales pitch' for an new, and apparently irrelevant, subject, Laughton's paper can be accused of over-ambition, but it was not without intellectual force and a strong, coherent theme. As a service 'insider' he called for a conservative approach to the ideas and institutions of the Navy, as befitted the critical instrument of national policy. Much of the paper was devoted to exploding old myths and misunderstandings about the nature of naval power, re-using material

---

54. Laughton, J K, 'The Scientific Study of Naval History', *JRUSI* Vol XVIII (1874), pp508-27.

from the 1866 paper 'The Sovereignty of the Seas'. This was critical. He had to clear the ground of the accumulated rubbish of half a century, and dig down to sound historical foundations, before building a new, structured doctrine. He repeated the basic point of the tactics paper, itself the product of historical scholarship, that it was unwise to look back to the victories won by haphazardly raised fleets of ill-assorted craft, or to the era of Nelson, when the enemy was in a state of confusion. Rather, it was necessary to study naval history to prepare officers to meet equally well-educated opponents. This was the function of doctrine. While Laughton never used the word 'doctrine', which had a far narrower meaning in the 1870s, his work had a width of purpose that can only be effectively covered by this modern shorthand. This marked an enhanced role for history in his thinking, even in comparison with the tactical paper of the previous year. Significantly Key, the Admiral President, and Admiral Ryder, supported him from the audience. Key explained the meaning of 'scientific' to a sceptical audience, and repeated Laughton's tactical ideas, while Ryder demonstrated that other navies were taking history far more seriously. The Chairman, Vice-Admiral Nicholson, urged Key to ensure that the College provided students with enough time to study history.[55] Key and his successors failed to meet this request, relying on Laughton to provide a few lectures was a poor substitute for a proper course of instruction.

When Laughton used the noun 'science', or the adjective 'scientific', he wished to convey a specific meaning, a meaning sufficiently distant from modern usage as to require elucidation.

> Science is knowledge; accurate and exact knowledge, as distinguished from loose, vague, and empirical; and in this, the true sense of the word, history may be studied scientifically just as well as anything else. If the genesis of a plant or the habits of an insect are things worthy so to be studied, how much more are the words, and deeds, and destinies of our noblest and greatest men; and with a Navy such as ours, possessing such a history, it is a matter of very sad reproach that so few of our Officers are really well informed concerning it. I should be ashamed to guess at the very small percentage of officers on the active list who could correctly and intelligently discuss even the leading events of our annals; such say as the battles of Barfleur, or Quiberon Bay, or the First of June; Rodney's campaign in the West Indies, or Sir Edward Hughes' East Indian campaign; Keppel's action off Ushant in 1778, or d'Orvilliers' cruise in the Channel in 1779.[56]

This positivist approach dominated his work before 1885, when he served the Navy, and was never entirely abandoned. He went on to set out what history could be used for:

---

55. **Nicholson,** Vice-Admiral Sir Frederick William Erskine (1815-99), another veteran of the Second China War.
56. Laughton, J K, 'Scientific Education in the Navy', *JRUSI* (1875), pp233-4.

A great deal has been said at different times about the study of tactics, but the scientific study of history is the study of tactics; it is a great deal more; it is the study of strategy, of organisation, and of discipline, and it is the only sound basis of that study.[57]

The impact of the lecture was immediate. In a long and wholly positive report *The Broad Arrow* recognised the problems of historical knowledge in a scientific age, but saw in this lecture a way forward:

> what is really wanted is to stifle the notion that naval history is merely a record of battles and a tale of blood. Naval history, like all other history, tells us the history of a nation in one of its several branches of activity. Through the tangled thread which envelopes the story of our Navy's life for centuries we can, by careful study and scientific analysis, trace the meaning of disaster and the cause of success; and out of this analysis we shall find it possible to weave, not with probable, but possible certainty, where the path of success may be found; and in this history we shall find a fair guide not only in the actual matter of fighting, but in any other matters intimately affecting the welfare of the Navy. Mr Laughton's paper deserves profound thought; not only because it is a faithful and able effort to expose fallacies, and lead us to appreciate what is the truth in our naval traditions, but because he shows the way to a study which to every naval officer cannot fail to be interesting, and to give him the highest views and wishes to maintain the welfare of the Royal Navy. Our only suggestion is that, in a series of lectures or a book, Mr. Laughton should elaborate what he has so skilfully touched on in his paper; for he has not only the keen perception necessary for such a task, but, what is far rarer, the actual knowledge.[58]

This review demonstrated that there was a wider audience for Laughton's work, and must have encouraged him to persevere. In Germany a similar pioneering approach was being applied to military history by another de-mythologising historian of war, Hans Delbrück. He began work in the late 1870s, but spent his career in almost permanent intellectual warfare with the Great German General Staff over the nature of Frederician strategy. The contrast with Laughton's development of his message within the establishment, and his success in securing a hearing, should be of interest to all defence intellectuals, and particularly to those who work in service education.[59]

In June 1875 Laughton submitted a detailed proposal for a course of ten lectures to the President of the College, Admiral Key. As this would require an addition to his salary it was, inevitably, referred to the Treasury, which just as predictably refused to sanction the change. The

---

57. Ibid.
58. *Monthly Register* Vol III (20.7.1874), pp115-6 from *The Broad Arrow*. The degree of intellectual sympathy shown in this review suggests that may have been written by Bridge.
59. Bucholz, A, *Delbrück and the German Military Establishment* (Iowa 1985).

Admiralty agreed to add a paltry £31.10.0 to his salary for taking on this important task.[60] The sum could only have been derived by paying 3 guineas each for ten lectures. Laughton was far from happy with this mean-minded response, and would have refused the offer had the task not been cut back to a course of six lectures a year. However, he was determined that the new President, Vice-Admiral Sir Edward Fanshawe, should recognise that this was a very poor substitute for a longer course that would provide a core programme and new lectures every year. He hoped the course would expand to meet his ten lecture outline, although he would have to begin with six. These were:

I   Ancient and Medieval war with galleys, in the Mediterranean; down to the battle of Lepanto.
II   The origin and early organisation of western navies; and the history of medieval war in western seas; down to the death of Queen Elizabeth.
III The development of navies in Europe during the 17th century; including the wars between England, Holland, France and Spain: down to the Treaty of Utrecht.
IV   The wars of the 18th century, down to 1780.
V   The War of American Independence, with more especial reference to the year 1782.
VI   From the Peace of 1783 to the present time: including the War of the French Revolution.

To these I would wish to add, as occasional lectures:

A.   Actions between frigates, single ships or small squadrons.
B.   Strategical value of cruising against the enemy's commerce.[61]

This basic programme could be expanded into a course of ten lectures, which would more nearly meet the needs of the College, and the service, to which he saw the course being directed. It would also require expanded research and an increase in the lecturer's salary. Fanshawe and the Director of Studies, Professor Thomas Archer Hirst, were content to begin with the six-lecture programme, and despite their references to increasing the course later, it remained stuck at six for the next fifteen years.[62] However, Laughton had won an important victory. His scientific reputation and standing in the service had persuaded the Admiralty and the College that history was sufficiently 'scientific' to be included in the syllabus. To meet their concerns he would have to establish new standards for naval history and to persuade practical men that history was the only true basis for naval doctrine.[63] He delivered this message in

---

60. Admiralty to President of RNC 24.2.1876: ADM 203/1.
61. Laughton to Fanshawe 13.3.1876: ADM 203/1.
62. Hirst marginalia on above. Ibid.
63. Laughton, J K, 'The Study of Naval History', *JRUSI* (1896) pp800-8.

the Greenwich lectures, which began in 1876, and reached a wider constituency in article form, both for professional and public periodicals. Advanced notices for the Greenwich lectures were posted at the service clubs in London, making them available to a significant proportion of the officer corps over the next ten years.[64] Laughton, who knew his audience well, deployed his ideas in short, detailed, self-contained sections. This paralleled the delivery of other types of information in the naval academic syllabus. He was an excellent lecturer. Admiral Fanshawe remarked:

> I was very favourably impressed by the learning and diligence with which he had collected materials and the skill and ability with which he deduced just conclusions from the data thus collected.

One of Laughton's students demonstrated a wider awareness of the impact of his work:

> Before Mr Laughton devoted himself to the study of the subject, naval history existed in two forms; fairly accurate but decidedly meagre accounts of actions at sea; and thrilling, but somewhat mendacious narratives apparently written with the view of propagating a belief in the inherent superiority as seamen of Englishmen over foreigners. Mr Laughton has succeed in giving us history, worthy of the name. Hitherto the results of his labours have only appeared in the form of lectures and occasional papers, but it is the hope of the service that before long these fragments may be welded together and may be published in a complete form.[65]

The 'service' referred to was not the relatively small constituency of naval officers who had actually heard the lectures, but the entire officer corps, who had access to the published versions. Laughton's work was accepted, understood and encouraged. Although history would define his career after 1885 it was only one aspect of Laughton's work for the Navy; it cannot be seen in isolation from his work on contemporary subjects, for John Knox Laughton was first and foremost a servant of the Royal Navy. When the first naval intellectual movement collapsed, in 1875-76, he used his position, experience and contacts to begin the process all over again. This time he would avoid the twin pitfalls of over-ambition and official displeasure by starting at the bottom, and working inside the system. His first career, as a naval technical educator, had reached a plateau. In the next phase he attempted to bring the level of historical understanding up to the same level.

WHAT DOES THIS MEAN?

---

64. Soley, pp58-9.
65. Admiral Sir E G Fanshawe to Council of King's College, London, June 1885. Captain Thomas Sturges-Jackson to same, 30 June 1885; KCLA KA/ILI L60.

CHAPTER 3

'The Scientific Study of Naval History': 1875-85

—————— · ——————

Between 1875 and 1885 naval history dominated Laughton's intellectual life. After devoting the second half of the 1870s to consolidating his original concept in small-scale studies, largely based on secondary literature and logic, he gained fresh insight and impetus from new materials in the early 1880s. At the same time the purpose of the exercise expanded, from the development of service doctrine, primarily as the basis for modern tactical thought, to the role of the Navy in national policy. In the process he acquired another expertise, in the field of modern history, and established himself as a major contributor to mainstream journals. Although modern history was only one of the many areas in which he worked, it proved critical to the completion of his work for the Navy.

By 1875 Laughton had settled into the new routine at Greenwich, specialising in Meteorology and Surveying, subjects for which he had written the recommended texts. The College had not lived up to the fondest hope of 1870, and would never become a 'Naval University', despite an enlarged staff, easy access to the centres of academic and service intellectual life that London offered, and an expanded syllabus. It had little to offer the higher branches of the service, being more of a technical finishing school for junior officers than a preparation for command, reflecting the careless attitude of the Liberal Admiralty down to 1874, and the outright hostility of their Tory successors. John Jellicoe, who took first-class certificates in all three branches of theoretical knowledge, recalled with pleasure the teaching of the Mathematics Professor Carlton Lambert in 1878-80, but he was unusual.[1] Another able student, George Ballard, who took the six-month Sub-Lieutenants' course in 1882, was not over-enamoured of mathematics. He never believed that it was 'necessary to be a good mathematician to be a good officer'. He described the course as:

—————————————

1. Bacon, R H, *The Life of John Rushworth, Earl Jellicoe* (London 1936), p47.

merely a condensed repetition of the instruction in mathematics, navigation and theoretical subjects which we had undergone during the previous six years, ever since joining the *Britannia*, the only additional subject being lectures on winds and currents and a more advanced stage in physics and 'steam'.[2]

Although Ballard appears to have missed the history course, which was only run once a year, Laughton still made an impression on him. What little intellectual impetus was provided for potential flag officers came from Laughton's infrequent lectures on tactics and history. That he was able to give them at all reflected the high regard in which he was held by the first two Presidents.

Laughton's scientific output was limited. Between 1875 and 1885 he produced a children's geography text, dedicated to his own children, and five journal articles on weather analysis and forecasting.[3] He would produce little more written work in these fields, beyond a pair of reviews in 1895 and 1905.[4] His contribution to these subjects was now more practical, as a Councillor, Secretary, Vice-President and President of the Meteorological Society. His scholarly output for the Society was reflected in his 1882 Presidential Address 'Historical Sketch of Anemometry and Anemometers'.[5] During his Presidency the Society stabilised its finances by doubling the subscription, and received the Queen's recognition as 'Royal'.[6] The more prestigious Royal Geographical Society invited Laughton onto its Council in 1880, which he attended regularly until the end of his term in 1884. He also served on a variety of sub-committees connected with the library, publication, scientific purposes and maps.[7] Committed to maintaining the link between the Society and the Service Laughton nominated officers at Greenwich. However, when he accepted a seat on the Council he made it clear to the Secretary, Clements Markham, that for him 'all matters connected with naval history and archaeology have an especial interest'.[8]

---

2. Ballard, Admiral Sir G, 'Admiral Ballard's Memoirs; Part Four', *The Mariner's Mirror* Vol 62 (1976), pp249-50.
3. Laughton, J K, *At Home and Abroad; or First Lessons in Geography* (London 1878); 'Changes of Climate', in *British Quarterly Review* (1 October 1876). 'Weather Forecasting', *Fraser's Magazine* (June 1878), pp671-92; 'The Law of Storms', *Nautical Magazine* Vol XLIX (1880); 'Our Winter Storms' *Fraser's Magazine* (June 1881), pp758-70; 'Wind Force and How it is Measured', *Longman's Magazine* Vol 1 (April 1883), pp615-27.
4. 'Weather Prevision' *The Edinburgh Review* (April 1895), pp514-36.
'Typhoons and Cyclones' *The Edinburgh Review* (January 1905).
5. Laughton, J K, 'Historical Sketch of Anemometry and Anemometers' *Quarterly Journal of the Royal Meteorological Society* (1882), pp162-4.
6. Obituary, *Journal of the Royal Meteorological Society* (1915), pp351-2.
7. Council Minutes of the Royal Geographical Society: RGS.
8. Laughton to Markham (as Secretary of the RGS) 3.3.1880 & 28.4.1880 (quote): RGS Archive, Laughton File.

This emphasis reflected a major shift in his ambitions. He was now attempting to master naval history, 'with a view of bringing out a History of our Navy that may have some pretensions to accuracy and exactness'.[9] He also began a forty-year career as an *Edinburgh* reviewer in 1875. His introduction to this august journal was almost certainly provided by Bridge, who had been writing for Henry Reeve (1813-95), the editor of the *Edinburgh Review* since 1872. Laughton's relationship with Reeve can be implied from the fact that he wrote Reeve's biography.[10] Reeve, a man of great ability, had a wealth of contacts in the highest sections of British and French Society, yet remained almost anonymous. He combined a post in the Privy Council Office with a literary career, initially as a translator, then as the leader writer on European affairs for *The Times*, and finally as editor of the *Edinburgh Review*. A genuine, if Whiggish, Liberal, and a follower of Lord Palmerston, Reeve cared nothing for the opinions of the masses, preferring to influence the leaders of society through personal contact and fine writing. He found Gladstone's later career, culminating in the Irish Home Rule question, insufferable, seceding from the mainstream of the Liberal Party for the Liberal Unionist camp. Because articles appeared unsigned, Reeve approved them all.[11] He was a major influence on Laughton, and there are close similarities in their outlook, attitude and assessment of popular politics.[12] Reeve had been among the first to attempt an analysis of the influence of seapower, after the astonishing success of Palmerston's brief Syrian Campaign in 1840, and Allied strategy in the Crimean War.[13] This insight lead him to encourage naval articles.

Typically, Laughton's career as an *Edinburgh* reviewer began in a narrow field of expertise, building on the Arctic paper presented to the JNPA, before broadening into the leading contributor on naval history and policy, and a major writer on modern history.[14] His first article, in April 1875, dealt with recent Arctic exploration, and was followed by

---

9. Laughton to Leslie Stephen 10.11.1882: Sidney Lee MSS Bodleian Library, Oxford.
10. Bridge to Laughton 21.4.1896 JKL MS. Laughton, J K, *Memoirs of Henry Reeve* (London 1898), 2 vols. One interesting feature of the book is Laughton's complete exclusion of himself, to the extent of leaving his name off the cover! Rutger's University Library, United States confirms there is no Laughton material in the Reeve's archive.
11. Lecky, W E H, 'Henry Reeve, C.B., F.S.A., D.C.L.'; *Historical and Political Essays* (London 1910), pp221-6. A brilliant summary from a master of the historian's art.
12. Clive, J, 'The *Edinburgh Review*: The Life and Death of a Periodical,' in Briggs, A (ed), *Essays in the History of Publishing: in celebration of the 250th anniversary of the House of Longman 1724-1974* (London 1974), pp115-140. Although this practice ended in 1912, as part of general 'modernisation' Laughton's last contribution, which appeared amidst a number of signed pieces, went through the press unsigned. Clearly he found the reviewer's anonymity useful.
13. Laughton, J K, *Memoirs of the Life of Henry Reeve* (London 1898), Vol 2, pp375-6.
14. See the bibliography for details of these reviews.

another in 1877. While he recognised the scientific value of the expeditions, and accepted Clements Markham's view that they were 'greater tests of courage and endurance than the perils of naval war', he doubted the wisdom of further attempts. His scientific expertise provided a critical approach to what were largely narrative accounts. He would have known the leading figures in British arctic exploration at this time, Captain Albert Markham and his cousin Clements, Secretary of the Royal Geographical Society, and singled them out for special praise.[15] Yet he also saw other, wider, lessons. The success of the recent Austrian expedition may 'temper our maritime pride, and force from us the admission that our sailors have no exclusive right in those qualities which deserve, if not win, success'.[16] Laughton's other *Edinburgh Review* reflections on contemporary, or near-contemporary naval subjects before 1885 will be considered in the next chapter.

More significant for the future was a review of the biography of Charles Kingsley in April 1877. Laughton concentrated on Kingsley's term as Regius Professor of History at Cambridge, and his philosophy of history. He believed Kingsley's popularity was based on his charming manner, rather than any intellectual power, as he was neither an 'exact scholar', nor equipped for 'the stern work of a historian'. Consequently his inaugural lecture, 'The Limits of Exact Science as applied to History', may have been intended to be humorous, but Laughton was hardly the man to acknowledge the need for a light touch in education, at any level. Instead he concentrated on Kingsley's intellectual legacy. He believed that his scholarly output would prove ephemeral because it was too obviously present-minded.[17] Present-minded intellectual lightweights with a pleasing style would be a major problem for the 'stern' and 'exact' Laughton.[18] Others felt the edge of his finely honed mind. He considered the Scottish historian John Burton's *History of the Reign of Queen Anne* so badly proportioned as to be merely the study of some key issues. It lacked any sense of chronology, and the dates and the details of naval actions were unreliable.[19] The latest edition of Pepys' diary received a mixed reception. Laughton was pleased to see that 'lewd passages' had

---

15. **Markham**, Admiral Sir Albert Hastings (1841-1918). A noted Arctic explorer, but generally held responsible for the *Victoria* disaster. See Gordon, A, *The Rules of the Game* (London 1996).
16. 'Arctic Exploration' and 'New Arctic Lands', *The Edinburgh Review* (April 1875), pp447-81; and (January 1877), pp155-69 quotes from p169 and 156.
17. 'Charles Kingsley', *The Edinburgh Review* (April 1877), pp415-46: quote at p435.
18. See JKL to Leonard G Carr Laughton 21.12.1897 where he complains of David Hannay's *A Short History of the Royal Navy:* 'the man writes well – if only he would stick to facts and curb his imagination'. Other names to conjure with are those of Browning, Badham and Montgomery; even 'respectable' journalists like Clowes and H W Wilson were taken to task.
19. 'Queen Anne', *The Edinburgh Review* (April 1880), pp512-47.

+ HE WASN'T CALLED 'KNOX' FOR NOTHING!

+

been left out, but deprecated the omission of the daily routine of the office in a work that was vital to students of naval history. He also pointed out that the Admiralty offices at Somerset House had been moved 'to a cluster of typhoidal dens in Spring Gardens' in 1869.[20] George Otto Trevelyan earned unstinted praise for his *Early History of Charles James Fox*, his style being compared to that of his uncle, Thomas Babington Macaulay. This book exercised a considerable influence on Laughton's already 'Whiggish' view that eighteenth-century government was weak and corrupt, and provided the basis for his lifelong, unquestioning vilification of Lord Sandwich.[21] His linguistic attainments led to reviews of the long-running series of French histories based on the papers of the Duc de Broglie, works on Swedish and Dutch subjects, and studies of both Napoleons. Although he considered the reign of Napoleon III too recent for 'history, properly so-called', the conduct of his wars had already provided valuable lessons. 'For naval, and still more for military officers, the strategical or tactical results of these have already afforded, and will long continue to afford, matter for earnest professional study'. The man and his English hagiographers were dismissed with contempt.[22]

Laughton's first review of naval books, headed by William Schaw Lindsay's *History of Merchant Shipping*, began by considering the state of the market for such texts.

> It might fairly be supposed that to a people whose wealth and power are peculiarly derived from the sea, the history of navigation would have a very marked interest, and that works treating of the origin or development of naval energy and maritime enterprise would be eagerly sought after. That this is not altogether the case is very evident from the rapidity with which recent books on these subjects, and on naval history and biography, have found their way into the trade list of 'remainders', to be sold for anything they will fetch, sometimes for prices little above their value as waste paper. And yet no-one whose studies have led him to examine carefully into this class of literature can wonder at it; for sailors are, in the natural course of things, men of action, and their writings are too often in a style which few care to read; whilst on the other hand, the difficulties and technicalities which stand in the way of an outsider, render it almost impossible for such a one to write honestly and faithfully on a subject with which he is not familiar. It is thus that several of our best known naval works are either clumsy records, destitute alike of literary skill and critical judgement, or are the productions of facile pens in the hands of professed bookmakers. . .

STILL
TRUE !

20. 'Diary and Correspondence of Samuel Pepys', *The Edinburgh Review* (July 1880), pp223-57.
21. 'The Early History of Charles James Fox', *The Edinburgh Review* (October 1880), pp540-77. This theme recurs whenever the period is discussed in any of his work. See Rodger, N A M, *The Insatiable Earl: A Life of John Montagu, 4th Earl of Sandwich* (London 1993), esp. pp160-64 for a corrective to the final version of Laughton's attack, contained in his edition of *Letters of Lord Barham*, 3 vols (London 1906-10).
22. 'The Bonapartes', *The Edinburgh Review* (January 1882), pp221-56, quote at p256.

These last he particularly reviled. Regrettably, while Lindsay was a seaman, and wrote well, his account frequently wandered off into naval archaeology, and ignored many of the best authorities. Consequently Laughton devoted much of his review to integrating the other major title in the review, Sir Travers Twiss's *The Black Book of the Admiralty*, with his own impressive knowledge of the secondary literature to reconstruct the early history of British navigation. He used this to distinguish between Britain's power and independence in earlier times, based on naval strength, and her present unrivalled luxury and wealth, based on commerce and manufactures. The former reflected, 'the enterprise, the vigour and the steadfastness of her sons', not cold commercial calculation.[23] The only large-scale work of naval history he had an opportunity to discuss in this period was Low's *History of the Indian Navy*, a work marred by a want of literary skill, over-earnest argument and excessive detail.[24]

These reviews revealed much of Laughton's attitude to his new subject. He had identified the weaknesses of the existing canon, and took particular delight in trenchant criticism of absurdity, notably the common habit of attributing undue significance to old maritime graffito. He considered naval history could only be mastered by those who combined the historian's dedication to accurate, scholarly study with the experienced eye of a seafarer. That he possessed the skill, character and sea-sense to meet these exacting demands he had no doubt, but he was in no haste to enter so unpromising a market. Having devoted a considerable effort to mastering the literature, he was not impressed by what he had found. He would retain an historiographical emphasis to the end.[25] Believing that the 'scientific' method, which he had used in *Physical Geography*, was the basis for the analysis of *any* subject, he carried over the methodology into naval history. His basic need remained that of a practising lecturer in a largely pragmatic environment, whose object was to produce further 'approved texts' for the College. The task was complicated by the lack of any suitable model, let alone an existing canon. If he was going to do the job properly he would have to define the subject.

When Laughton began work naval history was a particularly unprepossessing field. As popular literature it lacked the ready appeal of a recent major war; the critical role of the Navy in the 'Crimean' War had passed unnoticed, for want of significant bloodletting, in contrast to the drama provided by a brave but amateur army. Even Nelson, the definitive

23. 'Lindsay's Merchant Shipping', *The Edinburgh Review* (April 1876), pp420-55, quote pp420 and 455.
24. 'Indian Navy', *The Edinburgh Review* (October 1878), pp343-79. The tedium is relieved by the knowledge that the original sources are no longer extant.
25. Laughton, J K, 'Historians and Naval History' in Corbett, J S (ed), *Naval and Military Essays* (Cambridge 1913), pp3-22.

'naval hero' was far from popular in a society that found a growing sense
of its own moral rectitude, combined with increasing historical and technical distance, made him seem at once distasteful and irrelevant. Within
the Navy steam, rifled guns, armour and torpedoes were now the royal
road to promotion. This fact was already evident in the career of Laughton's patron Key, and proved critical to his protégé John Fisher.[26] In
consequence Laughton's task was doubly difficult, as he had to return
naval history to the centre-ground both of naval education and popular
culture. To succeed he had to make the subject relevant, and there was
precious little to build on.

One of the basic problems for naval history, then and now, has been
the lack of critical mass. In consequence the subject has limped along with
a combination of old and new works, each reflecting the anxieties of the
age in which they were written in their themes, narrative drive, selection
and omission of evidence. Reliance on secondary sources from various
eras has denied naval thinkers the materials to create a successful and
durable overview. It was not accidental that the most important criticism
that Laughton would make of Mahan in 1890 was that the materials
required to build such a broad structure did not exist. Laughton
addressed the weaknesses of the genre in a manner that was typical of the
man: he tried to deal with as much of the subject as he could, to draw in
evidence from the wider field of history and involve other scholars who
would help to advance the subject on a broad front.

In as much as there was an accepted English 'naval history' in 1875 it
comprised two recognised classics and a variety of antiquarian,
hagiographic and speculative works. William James's five, later six volume
The Naval History of Great Britain, published in 1822-24 covered the
eventful years between 1793 and 1820.[27] It is customary to complain,
following Laughton, that James's work was strictly confined to events at
sea, totally ignored national history, strategy and even the significance of
the events being discussed. In fact James stressed that he was writing 'a
narrative of the different naval actions fought between Great Britain and
her enemies since the declaration of War by France in 1793'.[28] He was
well aware of the difference between history and narrative, and made it
clear that he was compiling the latter. He stressed that his work was based
on a wealth of first-hand contemporary information, sources such as log
books and letters, which he considered more reliable than later official

---

26. Mackay, R F, *Fisher of Kilverstone* (Oxford 1973), pp37-40 et seq. for the role of Key in
Fisher's career.
27. James, W, *The Naval History of Great Britain from the Declaration of War by France in
1793 to the Accession of George IV* (London 1822-24) 5 vols. More commonly found in 6
vols, continued by other hands to include events up to Navarin. Laughton 'Historians',
(1913) pp19-20.
28. James, Vol 1 Second Edn. pxxiii.

publications.[29] Although his work was rarely analytical, and gave way all too readily to a xenophobic Tory bias, particularly when dealing with Americans, it has stood the test of time as a work of reference. In addition James, for all the apparent simplicity of his narrative, had a powerful agenda. In 1827 he presented a copy of the second edition to the Prime Minister, George Canning, and linked his work to the menacing tone recently adopted by the American President. James wanted to reverse the fallacious opinion, based on widely-circulated American claims, that they had won the War of 1812. Having been detained in the United States during the war, he had reason to doubt the veracity of the claim, and his first books, on the War of 1812, had begun the process of countering 'Yankee' propaganda, a task for which bald factual narrative was a more effective weapon than any work that presumed to attempt more. The Admiralty certainly approved of James's work, and made a large purchase. In writing to Canning James was seeking a wider circulation for his ideas; Canning, a skilled strategist and a calculating player of the diplomatic game, could make good use of the material.[30] But within a year both men were dead, leaving James's narrative shorn of its purpose.

At the other extreme to James's bald blow-by-blow account lay the work of Sir Nicholas Harris Nicolas (1799-1848). Nicolas, a naval lieutenant of 1815, saw no service afloat after 1816 and took up a legal career at the Inner Temple, being called to the bar in 1825. In the interval he had married a descendant of an Elizabethan Privy Councillor, and began his literary career with a biography of his wife's ancestor. As his legal career was restricted to claims of peerage in the House of Lords Nicolas had ample opportunity to pursue his literary interests. His output of legal, antiquarian, biographical and edited material over a period of 26 years was a monument to his 'almost unparalleled industry'. Despite the lack of any formal education after the age of eight, Nicolas had the judgement to master his material, and a clear, if not always easy, writing style. Once committed to research he became a powerful critic of the existing Records Office and its publication programme, leading to a major overhaul of the system.[31] Between 1844 and 1846 he produced a seven-volume edition of *Nelson's Dispatches*,[32] and then began work on *A History of the Royal Navy from the Earliest Times to the Wars of the French Revolution*, deliberately setting out to cover the ground left by James, and to address

29. Ibid, pxxvii.
30. See Laughton's *DNB* entry on Henry Ducie Chads for his assessment of James's hostility to Americans. Stapleton, E J, *Some Official Correspondence of George Canning; 1820-1827* (London 1887), Vol 2, pp340-6.
31. 'Sir N H Nicolas', *The Gentleman's Magazine* (October 1848), pp425-29, includes a lengthy bibliography.
32. Nicolas, Sir N H (ed), *The Dispatches and Letters of Vice Admiral Lord Viscount Nelson* (London 1844-46) 7 Vols. Reprinted by Chatham Publishing 1997-98.

the 'extraordinary neglect' of naval history in Britain.[33] His intention was to supplant the old chronicle-based action narratives with a fully-rounded history of the growth and management of the service, providing both 'Civil History' and 'Military History'. His scope was as wide as that of his predecessors had been narrow; he covered trade, ship design, manning, pay, prize-money, discipline, dockyards, lighthouses, pilotage, maritime law, the claim to 'The Sovereignty of the Seas' and brief lives of leading figures.[34] The evidence would be drawn from the Public Record Office, where he was both a regular researcher and a close friend of the Assistant Keeper Sir Thomas Duffus Hardy.[35] Nicolas was rigorous in assessing the veracity of source material relying only on those that 'were *contemporary* with the events which they relate'. He defended his approach in typically combative terms that Laughton would approve:

> To superficial or impatient readers many of the minute facts may appear tedious and unimportant; but such details as are indispensible for a thorough knowledge of any particular department of History.[36]

Furthermore he refused to 'colour any fact with the view of gratifying the national pride; his only desire is to seek the truth'.[37] When Nicolas died in August 1848, he had only carried the narrative as far as the French wars of Henry V. When William Laird Clowes launched his *The Royal Navy: A History from the Earliest Times to the Present* in 1897 he paid Nicolas the highest of back-handed compliments, describing his book as, 'a brilliant failure', estimating that he would have required at least fifteen, and possibly twenty, further large volumes to complete a book on the scale of the first two.[38] While the market may well have baulked at such bulk, Nicolas was perfectly capable of producing it, and was writing on commission. Hubris almost caught up with Clowes, who seriously misjudged the scale of his own naval history.[39]

Laughton's intellectual and methodological debt to Nicolas was immense. He must have acquired and read Nicolas's works at an early stage in his naval career, which would explain his wide-ranging interest in the pre-fifteenth century navy, the awareness of Britain's neglect of her naval past, the importance of examining the subject with the widest perspective,

---

33. Nicolas, Sir N H, *A History of the Royal Navy from the earliest times to the Wars of the French Revolution* (London 1847), Vol I, pvii.
34. Ibid, pix.
35. Cantwell, J D, *The Public Record Office: 1838-1958* (London HMSO 1991), pp233.
36. Nicolas, *History*, Vol I, pxi.
37. Ibid, pxii.
38. Clowes, W L, *The Royal Navy: A History from the Earliest Times to the Present* (London 1897), Vol I, pviii.
39. Lambert, A D, 'Reflections of a History of the Royal Navy', *The Naval Review* (1997), pp393-9.

and of avoiding nationalistic bias. At the end of his own career Laughton paid Nicolas a most handsome tribute. While he doubted if the project could have been completed, for want of financial support, even if Nicolas had lived, and considered it more a history of the navy than naval history; 'it is incomparably the best naval history that we have. It must serve as a foundation for future writers; but it is not easy reading'.[40] In a very literal sense Laughton used Nicolas's two major texts as the 'foundation' of his own naval writing. Initially he quarried materials from them for his early studies, then he used the *Royal Navy* as the base line from which to begin fresh research. It was no accident that he chose the Elizabethan era for his first effort at sustained archival work; later he would use his influence to encourage other scholars to work on periods that fell between Nicolas and James. Of the existing accounts that touched on the period between 1422 and 1793 Laughton had little to say. The general histories were noted only for their ignorance of nautical affairs and the short measure they gave to the Navy, with the noteworthy exception of Ranke's work. When he came to naval works there were few that warranted any attention, and with most of them this took the form of an intellectual health warning.[41] Although the weakness of the literature would initially hamper Laughton's efforts to create a historical basis for contemporary doctrine, it did provide him with a *tabula rasa* on which to develop the subject along the lines that he wished it to follow. Despite the importance of Nicolas's work it was Laughton who gave the critical impulse to the direction and development of the subject, and as such Laughton can rightly be called the father of modern naval history.

In order to use history to develop naval thinking, Laughton exploited the entire history of naval activity. In the absence of a large English naval literature he spread his net widely, hauling in and examining any naval literature as he developed his understanding. This eclectic policy was reflected in the published output of his 'scientific' phase, between 1875 and 1885. Although some of his lectures covered long periods the bulk of his output consisted of relatively small-scale studies, covering the widest range of naval subjects in an essentially didactic manner. Naval history was being used to teach the Navy about tactics, strategy and policy. Although a few pieces along these lines would appear after 1885, when he entered his second career, they properly belong to the earlier period. The 'scientific' essays dealt with ancient warfare, the Venetian navy, John Paul Jones, English privateers and the Austrian Admiral Tegetthoff, but they were dominated by French subjects. During this period French historical, tactical and strategic literature provided a basic building block for his

---

40. Laughton, J K, 'Historians and Naval History' in Corbett, J S (ed), *Naval and Military Essays* (Cambridge 1913), pp21-2.
41. Ibid.

intellectual development. This was not accidental, as France was the only other significant naval power of the era, and possessed a rather more impressive naval literature than Britain. With the French naval challenge of 1858-65 still fresh in the memory Laughton introduced his students to the tactical ideas of Grivel and Bouët-Willaumez, Xavier Raymond's strategic studies and the historical work of Chevalier and Admiral de la Graviere.[42]

Having accepted the challenge of providing tactical and historical lectures at Greenwich, Laughton set out his manifesto in the 'Scientific Study' paper of 1874. As a positivist he used the term 'scientific' to mean, 'accurate and exact knowledge'.[43] History should be studied accurately because 'it contained lessons of the gravest meaning'.[44] His long-term aim, to create a coherent, written doctrine, could only be met by developing the subject until it possessed a critical mass of material. To begin with he had to rely on the 'case study' method, examining specific subjects in lectures and articles which illuminated the particular point that he wished his audience to address. He combined wide research in secondary sources, in all relevant languages, with localised enquiries and personal contacts. His critical method was comparative, applying a considerable knowledge of naval history and modern naval affairs, together with his own rigorous logic, to the available materials. From this he would deduce his conclusions as to merits of the sources, and develop the 'lesson' he wanted his audience to consider. Much of his work involved 'demythologising' the past. This aspect of his work, finding educational value in the exposure of absurdity, error and bias, can be compared with that of his near contemporary Delbrück. Laughton knew that his naval audience would expect him to develop his argument in a clear, concise and accurate fashion. That he met their requirements is beyond doubt.[45]

Laughton's College lectures were published. Each had been written around a specific theme, be it contemporary tactics and command, in the case of Tegetthoff, or trade defence, naval policy, irregular adjuncts to national naval power and the impact of loss of command of the sea. Although the establishment of a specific requirement for history at Greenwich was the critical impulse behind the 'Scientific Study', Laughton had already developed a strong interest in the educational uses of the subject. In his first published work, he had made a significant point about the navies of Britain and France.

---

42. For an excellent summary of French literature at this period, see Hamilton, C I, *Anglo-French Naval Rivalry 1840-1870* (Oxford 1993), Ch.4, and Battesti, Vol II, pp273-302.
43. Laughton, J K, 'Scientific Instruction in the Navy', *JRUSI* Vol XIX (1875), pp233-4.
44. Laughton, J K, 'The Scientific Study of Naval History', *JRUSI* Vol XVIII (1875), pp508-27.
45. Fanshawe to Council of King's College, London June 1885: KCLA KA I/LI L60.

The one great difference between them was, and still is, the difference in the natural tastes of the people. In England the navy is a direct consequence of a seafaring disposition, heightened to a necessity of self-preservation by commercial aptitude. In France, on the contrary, the navy appears only as an exotic, which indeed a careful cultivation can bring to a certain growth, but which withers away when deprived of the sheltering warmth of a strong government.[46]

This distinction, probably developed from the work of Xavier Raymond, dominated his assessment of the importance of the Royal Navy, and gave his analysis of French policy and strategy a particular 'offensive' emphasis. It was because the French Navy had been built and rebuilt as a direct challenge to Britain that French naval history required study. His Suffren article, which was linked to his study of tactics, established the French admiral's superior conception of theatre strategy while taking the opportunity to reduce the more absurd claims of nationalistic French historians. As he observed, with characteristic humour, Suffren's status at home owed more to the inadequacy of his contemporaries than his own success, for he won no sea battles. That he might have been more successful with adequate support from his captains gave his career a serious import for British naval officers. It taught them to treat their enemies as their equals, or, in some aspects, their betters.[47] The career of Colbert demonstrated how a powerful navy could be rapidly created in an autocratic state, but it also revealed that the application of money and power would not meet all requirements. In Colbert's case he discovered evidence of inexperience in shipbuilding, and something more significant:

Colbert, whilst able to build and equip ships in a manner equal to those of any country in Europe, was not able to improvise, in a similar way, a race of men who could be compared with the sailors of Holland.[48]

This approach was developed in a study of Abraham Du Quense, which assessed the long-term effects of the different origins of the British and French navies. The argument that the French were better educated, but less practical, was supported by his own observations in 1854-55. He compared the relative standards of seamanship, cleanliness and linguistic aptitude of the two fleets, and concluded that while the French spoke their ally's language better, the English ships were cleaner and better handled.[49]

46. Laughton, J K, 'The Sovereignty of the Seas', *The Fortnightly Review* Vol V (August 1866), pp718-33 at p728.
47. Laughton J K, 'Suffren', *United Service Magazine* (May and June 1867), reprinted in *Studies in Naval History* (London 1887): henceforth *Studies*.
48. 'Colbert', *St Paul's Magazine* (December 1868), pp342-57, reprinted in *Studies* quote at p53.
49. 'DuQuense: The French Navy in the Seventeenth Century', *Fraser's Magazine* (November 1874), pp638-53, reprinted in *Studies*.

By 1874 Laughton was planning a naval history textbook, to follow his earlier efforts on meteorology and surveying. He produced a series of essays which 'endeavoured, however feebly, to carry out my idea of The Scientific Study of Naval History', to be published as a book.[50] The details were probably agreed at this time with Longman's.[51] Publishing books in article form first was a common, and financially attractive, option in the 1870s and 1880s. After 1874 almost all the 'Scientific' papers appeared in Longman's *Fraser's Magazine*, which had been edited by the Tory historian James Anthony Froude until June 1874, when he handed over to the Irish poet William Allingham.[52] Each essay examined a specific issue on which Laughton believed the Royal Navy needed to be better informed. The basic method was to use the existing secondary literature to develop a narrative, but to apply a critical approach and, after 1879, exploit the Admiralty archive to resolve doubtful points. The essays, written over a period of sixteen years, reflect Laughton's growing powers as an historian and a strategist. The first essay, on Suffren, set out the method, applied a critical faculty to the question of what constitutes victory, and the value of tactical skill. Those on Colbert and Du Quense of 1868 and 1874 were less ambitious, being little more than critical narratives. It is no coincidence that the earliest correspondence preserved by Laughton dates from 1875. His status within the service was rising, and he recognised that the letters he received would be useful. Correspondence had become a critical part of his research.

In a trilogy of papers discussing French privateering, he examined the nature of the threat that would be posed by a resumption of this form of warfare. The problems would be greater now, because Britain imported basic foodstuffs, not just luxury goods. He argued that armed merchant ships had never been capable of effective self-defence, and that some system was required. Convoy, although then largely out of favour, was the only system mentioned. The privateer studies began with a paper on the French commander François Thurot, a case study in the level of defence required by commercial harbours.[53] After criticising French doctrine, which avoided decisive action in favour of pursuing strategic

50. Laughton to Captain Stephen Luce USN 10.8.1875 Luce Papers: Library of Congress.
51. The contract for 1000 copies of the book is dated 21.8.1885, but this is hardly conclusive as to the commencement of the project, in view of the long relationship between the parties. Longmans & Laughton Contract 21.8.1885. LONGMANS II 233/104 Longmans Coll. University of Reading.
52. Dunn, W H, *James Anthony Froude: A Biography 1857-1894* (Oxford 1963), pp329, 350. Warner, A, *William Allingham* (Cambridge 1975). When *Fraser's* ceased publication the last 'Studies' article appeared in *Colburn's United Service Magazine*, rather than *Fraser's* direct replacement, *Longman's Magazine*, which carried one of his last papers on weather in the first volume, 'Wind Force and How it is measured', *Longmans'* Vol I (April 1883).
53. John Allan, Solicitor of Banff, Scotland, to Laughton 21.12.1876 JKL MS. Allan had agreed to consult the local archives for evidence of Thurot's activities.

advantage, thereby leaving their fleets and squadrons exposed to the danger of tactical defeat, he concluded that Thurot's career 'seems to me to show that a naval force, however numerous and active, is not in itself sufficient to protect our commerce from loss, our coasts from insult and our towns from pillage'.[54] Thurot's failure reflected bad weather, bad luck, lack of seamen and subordination to the army: 'But it is not wise always to trust our safety, our prestige, or our honour either to the caprice of the weather or to the presumed incapacity of a possible enemy'.[55] He concluded that a minimum standard of local coast defence was essential.

Laughton's examination of the life of John Paul Jones covered similar ground, but dealt with a more successful enemy, a renegade Scotsman who, 'sold his birthright for a mess of pottage'. Laughton observed that recent French pamphlets advocating attacks on undefended seaports provided a good reason to be prepared; it is 'from the story of the past, that we ought to be armed against the indefinite possibilities of the future'.[56] A study of Jean Bart addressed the dangers of a closed officer corps. As the son of a privateer captain he recognised that irregular forces had provided valuable auxiliaries to national maritime power, and wondered whether they should be brought into regular service in wartime. Under the terms of the Declaration of Paris of 1856 privateering had been abolished, depriving the state of the opportunity to exploit the experience of modern merchant skippers. In contrast to British practice in the last 200 years the French had employed privateers to command regular warships, and even admitted them to the officer corps at a rank reflecting their age and ability. In reviewing the literature of the most famous privateer, Laughton exploited his access to the Admiralty archives to demonstrate that French histories contained numerous absurdities and distortions, many of which he characterised as 'Jacobin' attempts to make an impetuous, unthinking hero out of a skilful and cunning privateer.[57] The attempt had far more to do with the worship of his humble origins, than any understanding of the nature of the privateers business. For the French the myth of Jean Bart the *sans culotte* had become more important than the reality.[58] When he turned to Duguay-Trouin he found a similar case, although the man's

---

54. 'Thurot', *Fraser's Magazine* (January 1878), pp1-88. Reprinted in *Studies*. Quote at p361, see Young, G V C and Foster, C, *Captain Francois Thurot* (Stockholm 1986) for a modern study. Although occasionally critical of Laughton's views the book is not persuasive.
55. *Studies*, p362.
56. 'Paul Jones: The Pirate', *Fraser's Magazine* (April 1878), pp501-22. Reprinted in *Studies*, quote at p411.
57. For a more sophisticated discussion of the political role of history in France since the Revolution see Gildea, R, *The Past in French History* (New Haven 1994). Although the literature Laughton was addressing was relatively simple, and the bias blatant, his analysis remains significant.
58. 'Jean Bart', *Fraser's Magazine* (March 1882), pp343-60. Reprinted in *Studies*.

own memoirs were honest, and far less bombastic than the common run of English accounts. Laughton concluded that Duguay deserved his fame, as the only bright chapter in the otherwise unrelieved gloom that fell over French affairs at sea between 1692 and 1713. He also observed that, even now, it was possible for exceptional individuals to get into the French officer corps from outside the regular career structure, but not the British.[59]

This case had already been driven home by studies of two remarkable English privateers of the eighteenth century, Fortunatus Wright and George Walker. He emphasised that their greatest services had come, not at the apogee of British maritime power, but in those periods of weakness and uncertainty, the War of the Austrian Succession and the American War, when the regular forces had not acquired that degree of superiority that would drive the enemies trade from the sea. It was just such a situation that Laughton wanted his audience to contemplate.

> It is scarcely to be doubted that, when we are engaged in a European war, our enemy will endeavour to attack us, to injure us, by 'cruisers', such as a few years ago Russia openly proclaimed her intention of fitting out; and the defensive measures adopted by our own admiralty, the instructions under which merchant steamers are built and surveyed, leave as little room to doubt that we should at least follow suit. Between such cruisers and the privateers of old there would be little effective difference.[60]

Laughton advocated a return to the old practice which provided a recognised entry into the Royal Navy for merchant officers. This would re-establish the links that had bound the two sea-services together in the days of Britain's rise to greatness, provide the war reserve of junior officers that was so hard and so expensive to maintain in peacetime, and avoid the need for a bloated list of junior officers in the event of war. He supported the noted ship-owner and Liberal MP Sir Donald Currie's call for an official link between the sea services, to provide Britain with an unrivalled reservoir of naval strength.[61]

The nature of the 'cruiser' threat in the next war, a minor theme in the first five privateer essays, dominated the final instalment. Convinced the ban on privateering set out in the Declaration of Paris of 1856 would be abrogated or ignored in wartime, Laughton wanted his audience to be prepared. Contemporary wisdom was that the mercantile convoy would no longer serve, but what were the alternatives? The option of mercantile self-defence was exploded by examining the career of Robert Surcouf, the last

---

59. 'Du Guay-Trouin', *Fraser's Magazine* (April 1882), pp498-518. Reprinted in *Studies*.
60. 'Fortunatus Wright', *Fraser's Magazine* (October 1881), pp462-78. See *Studies*, quote p195. The reference is to the Russian war scare of 1878.
61. 'George Walker', *Fraser's Magazine* (November 1881), pp589-623. See *Studies*, pp249-51.

great French privateer. Laughton emphasised Surcouf's professionalism. Once again popular French histories made him into an unthinking fire-eater; had this been his character his career must have been short and ended aboard a British prison hulk. Only by recognising the skill and resource of opponents like Surcouf could the Royal Navy prepare for the threat to trade in the next war 'and the trade that will be aimed at . . . will be not the wealth of the east, but the everyday necessities of English life – the corn, the beef, the mutton'. If the Navy proved incapable of defending this vital trade the effect would be rapidly felt by the government of the day.[62]

The immediate political impact of England losing command of the sea was illustrated in his essay on Jean de Vienne, the French admiral who turned the tide in the Hundred Years War. In a piece developed for Lecture II of the Greenwich programme Laughton attributed superior strategic insight to the French King, Charles V, and blamed Edward III for over-taxing his maritime resources. French ascendancy at sea resulted in the loss of England's French provinces, ravaging attacks on the English coast, and the Peasants' Revolt. Laughton argued that it was the realisation, after the sack of Gravesend, that the oppressive taxes were being misspent, rather than the taxes themselves, that was the direct cause of the Revolt. Unable to account for the inability of the French to press their advantage with an invasion, which modern scholars would attribute to limited aims and weak logistics, Laughton rationalised medieval warfare by suggesting the French had over-concentrated and become too complex. The belated English revival at sea he attributed to the removal of foreign privileges and the introduction of protectionist legislation.[63] His own politics were already moving to the right.

Only one paper addressed a contemporary subject, the battle of Lissa of 1866. Laughton began his study of the only fleet action between ironclads by showing how the Austrian Admiral Tegetthoff had prepared himself, throughout his career, for the decisive moment. In this way the essay addressed the critical role of history in the higher education of the Navy.

> There is a certain tendency in the minds of those who are most earnest in the cause of naval education to confuse the means with the end, and to imagine that all that is wanted is a competent knowledge of such sciences as mathematics, physics, geography, astronomy, navigation even, or pilotage, gunnery or naval architecture. In reality, and so far as the duties of a naval officer are concerned, all these are but branches, however important, each in its different degree, of that one science, the art of war, which it is the business of his life to practise.

---

62. 'Robert Surcouf', *United Service Magazine* (February and March 1883). *Studies* quote at p457.
63. 'Jean de Vienne. A Chapter from the Naval History of the Fourteenth Century', *United Service Magazine* (October 1880). *Studies*, see pp23-4. This paper was largely re-used in the draft chapter of Laughton's incomplete 1913 naval history textbook.

The details of this art could be acquired by instruction, but the ability to use them, as required of captains and Admirals, necessitated a different approach.

> Where the official instruction ends, the higher education really begins. From that time it is the man's own experience, and reading, and thought, and judgement, which must fit him for the requirements of higher rank.

In the absence of personal experience, 'the wise man will learn from the experience of others'. This method could be applied to seamanship and navigation,

> so also will he learn the art of commanding ships or fleets from the history of his great predecessors.... But this is a higher and graver study than all that has gone before.

For, unlike navigation and astronomy;

> the science of war is not one of mere rule and precedent, for changing conditions change almost every detail, and that too in a manner which it is often impossible to foresee.
>   The commanding officer who hopes to win, not merely to tumble into distinction, must therefore be prepared beforehand for every eventuality. The knowledge of what has happened already will not only teach him by precedent; so far as that is possible, it is easy, and within the compass of everyday abilities; it will also suggest to him things that have never yet been done; things in the planning of which he may rise to the height of genius, in the executing of which he may rise to the height of grandeur.

This was the role of doctrine. It was because history, and only history, could contribute hard evidence to this process that it was 'a study of real and technical importance'.[64] In the absence of personal experience the only way to learn the business of modern war was to profit from the experience of others, both in earlier ages, and other navies. Only by such preparation could commanders master the art of leadership, prepare themselves for the changing conditions of the next war and develop the capacity to think at a higher level. This approach placed Laughton in the exalted company of the great strategic thinkers. Research for this paper took him to German and Italian sources, led to a correspondence with the Chief Constructor of the Danish Navy on the ships present at the battle of Heligoland, and with his friend and fellow Greenwich lecturer William White on ships used at Lissa.[65]

---

64. 'Tegetthoff: Experiences of Steam and Armour', in *Fraser's Magazine* (June 1878), pp671-92. *Studies*, quote at pp148-50.
65. J C Tuxen, Danish Navy, to Laughton 4.5.1878; White to Laughton 8 & 16.5.1878: JKL MS. Manning, F, *The Life of Sir William White* (London 1923), pp59-76. White had also taught Tuxen at Greenwich, ibid, pp357-8, 379.

In 1875 Laughton produced 'The Venetian Navy in the Sixteenth Century' as a study in the interdependence of commerce and national greatness.

> How the might of Venice steadily declined with the decline of her commerce is well known; and the conviction forces itself on us that were our commerce and manufactures similarly to decline, the imitation might extend beyond the days of prosperity, even to those of ruin.

However, he considered it no part of the historian's business to peer into the future, a task he was happy to leave to statesmen and politicians. His own 'more modest task' was 'to examine into the realities of the past'.[66] He noted that 'the superiority of work done in Government yards, by Government workmen under efficient Government superintendence, has been abundantly proved over and over again, not only in our own country, but in France'.[67] This particular thrust was aimed more at the last Liberal government than the incumbent Tory ministry. His observations on the campaign of Lepanto, the apogee of Venetian naval power, were suggestive. The loss of Cyprus was due to the ambition of Spain in Italy, which paralysed the actions of Venice in 1570, allowing an inferior Turkish fleet to blockade the Cypriot ports. Again, it was not, as the Spaniards argued, the weakness of the Venetian navy that caused the delays before Lepanto, but Spanish policy. Such examples of the deflection of strategy by politics would dominate the work of Julian Corbett after 1900. The decline of the Venetian navy was, Laughton argued, due to the general decay of the state, not to any defect of the service, the perfection of which he had established.

The remainder of Lecture I, on Ancient Warfare, was not published until 1889, although it had been written in the 1870s. The paper appeared after Lord Brassey had suggested that this was one period of history that naval officers might know in sufficient detail to derive some benefit from the 'historical lessons'.[68] It demonstrated Laughton's willingness to act as a conduit for new material to enter the naval mainstream. He applied his linguistic abilities, and acquired some new intellectual connections, to produce a paper that outlined the naval history of the ancient world for the naval officer. Stephen Luce sent a paper on ancient naval warfare, which Laughton shared with Edmond Warre, the Eton Tutor, Oxford rowing blue and noted authority on ancient galleys.[69] Warre corrected

---

66. 'The Venetian Navy in the Sixteenth Century', *Fraser's Magazine* (October 1875), pp483-500 at p483. This essay was not reprinted in the collected edition.
67. Ibid, p485.
68. Brassey, Lord, *The British Navy* (London 1882), Vol IV, p531.
69. **Warre**, Edmond, (1837-1920). Later Headmaster and Provost of Eton. Warre to Laughton 3 & 18.8.1877, regarding Luce's 'Fleets of the World', *United States Naval Institute Proceedings*, Vol III (1874), pp5-24. JKL MS.

Laughton's assumption that the ancients had no effective signalling system, and tried to interest him in his own code, which was based on ancient practice. In the debate on the range and speed of galleys under oar Luce and Laughton considered Warre's figures excessive for such strenuous activity in a hot climate.[70] That Warre was correct revealed the limits of their amateur efforts. The paper eventually appeared in an early number of the revived *Colburn's United Service Magazine*, having lain on the shelf for some time. The purpose was clear:

> it is purely as an essay on the primeval development of naval strategy and tactics that I venture on a brief and necessarily imperfect sketch of this very early naval history.

In tactical terms he linked ancient tactics, based on ramming, with those of the early steam fleets. Greatly attracted by the image of the Athenian navy being created by Themistocles, he described it as the first truly professional navy because it had not developed out of existing seafaring activity. He attributed Athenian success to professional rowers, high standards of drill and a recognition that the ship was the weapon, not a mere fighting-platform.[71] Salamis, he argued, demonstrated that, even then, 'science could overcome brute force'.[72] The importance of tactical skill, based on a professional navy, was the major theme of both papers. The second opened with the Carthaginian Wars, and he stressed that, while the Carthaginians were a maritime people, they were no more *naval* than the land-bound Romans. They did not possess the naval skills of the Athenians. Although they were better seamen than their adversaries, this resulted in an unhealthy overconfidence in the early encounters. As a result they adopted ' "go at 'em" tactics which have been described as the epitome of the whole science of naval war: they saw their enemy, they went at 'em and they got very thoroughly beaten'. The Romans won because they possessed superior military skills, and developed a system to recreate their favoured environment at sea.[73]

Laughton did not develop the striking parallel between these conflicts and the Anglo-Dutch wars of the seventeenth century. After deprecating the growth in size of warships in the late Republican period, because with a peculiar logic he seemed to reserve for this particular contemporary question, however highly they may have been thought of at the time, 'we

70. Laughton to Luce 6.1.1878 Luce MS Library of Congress.
71. 'Early Developments of Naval Warfare: Part One', *Colburn's United Service Magazine* (September 1889), pp523-37, quotes at p523.
72. Ibid, p529.
73. 'Early Developments of Naval Warfare: Part Two', *Colburn's United Service Magazine* (October 1889), pp683-99; quote at p686.

may doubt whether they were really as effective as smaller ships'.[74] This, at least, reflected Laughton's interests at the time of publication. This was the last paper of the 'scientific' phase. By the time it appeared the text-book had already been published.

The 'scientific' phase culminated in the publication of *Studies in Naval History* in 1887. The book was dismissed by Donald Schurman as 'a collection of previously printed articles that devoted sympathetic atten-tion to some prominent French naval personalities'.[75] However, in a study that deals with the development of doctrine and historical method, the educational thrust and analytical power of Laughton's textbook re-quires more analysis. Laughton claimed that the articles had been written as 'a contribution to the earnest study of naval policy, strategy, or tactics', with a view to republication in book form.[76] His intentions were well known in the Navy. The service was being educated, whether at Green-wich, or in the wider field, and had no trouble recognising the merit and the import of Laughton's message. His lectures and articles were a funda-mental challenge to the complacent assumption of British pre-eminence at sea that modern writers have assumed were held by the Royal Navy of Laughton's day. That they were understood, accepted and encouraged demonstrates that the assumption is misplaced. This ground-breaking book enabled history to become a fundamental part of the naval intellec-tual renaissance. It remained a key text, requiring a second edition in 1896. Montagu Burrows, the ex-Naval Captain and Chichele Professor of Modern History at Oxford, recognised the naval educational thrust of the text, the originality of the method, and the 'exceptional' quality of the essay on Tegettoff.[77] Laughton sent copies to his most important col-leagues. Cyprian Bridge was 'very grateful' and only regretted the absence of 'The Sovereignty of the Seas'.[78] Stephen Luce was 'very glad' to receive his copy, combining his thanks with a copy of a paper 'containing liberal quotations from your articles' and an early notice of the United States Naval War College that he had been instrumental in establishing.[79] Laughton's ideas and arguments were a critical part of Luce's intellectual armoury during this critical stage in American naval development. By the time Luce wrote Laughton had moved on.

Studies in Naval History was a new type of naval history, written to educate the Royal Navy. It grappled with hard lessons and spent much

75. Schurman, D, *The Education of a Navy: The Development of British Naval Strategic Thought 1867-1914* (London 1965), p90.
76. *Studies:* Preface.
77. Burrows, M, *The English Historical Review* (1888), pp592-5.
78. Bridge to Laughton 5.10.1887 JKL MS.
79. Luce to Laughton 22.12.1887 JKL MS. Luce, SB, 'Tactics and History', *USNIP* Vol XIII No 2 (1887), pp175-201 reprinted in Hayes and Hattendorf, pp69-97.

effort to consider the strategy and actions of the 'enemy', France, which, by no coincidence at all, happened to be the only contemporary naval rival. It was the very antithesis of the narrow, one-sided and simplistic 'drum and trumpet' chronicles that comprised the standard texts when Laughton began his work. The lectures and articles on which the book had been based were well received by the Royal Navy, the target audience, but the method was limited, and once he had realised the wealth of material available in the archive Laughton shifted to a more ambitious approach which reflected the new 'professional' standards of academic history.

Through his correspondence with Luce and Warre Laughton developed a particular interest in flags, both for signalling and as national or divisional symbols. One of the six boxes that make up his archive contains letters, pamphlets, sketches and drawings relating to flags. In 1880 he wrote a major article on the subject, and MacMillan's agreed to publish a proposed book-length version in 1895.[80] Although Laughton never delivered a manuscript, being too busy with the Navy Records Society and his *Memoir of Henry Reeve*, he continued to collect material. Mahan described the English flags on Dutch tombs while at the Hague Peace Conference and provided details of the American flag.[81] Laughton saw flags and battle honours as a major elements in the creation and maintenance of naval tradition. He considered the widespread ignorance of history displayed by the contemporary navy to be a shocking waste of resources that could be used to built the *esprit de corps* of ships and fleets. He called for each ship to be provided with a flag, bearing the battle honours won by its predecessors, after the manner of Regimental colours. As early as 1870 he had written 'the *Dreadnought* – a brave old name that has long been one of the glories of our navy'.[82] Later he would deprecate the opportunistic naming of ships, giving *Victor Emmanuel*, *Sultan* and *Shah* as recent examples of names without tradition or meaning for the service. He did not doubt that names mattered:

> in this very materialistic age we are too apt to overlook the force of sentiment and to measure the strength of a fleet by its iron or coal, or big guns. It was none of these that brought past honour to our flag, and for myself, I believe they will play but a secondary part in upholding it.[83]

He applied the same rationale to trophy flags, and was annoyed to discover that a large number of flags taken at Camperdown and St Vincent, which had been laid up at St Paul's Cathedral in December 1797 had been

---

80. 'The Heraldry of the Sea:- Ensigns, Colours and Flags', *JRUSI* (1880), pp116-148. MacMillan to Laughton 15.4.1895.
81. Mahan to Laughton 17 & 21.6.1899, 4.7.1899 & 28.8.1900.
82. 'Sketches in Naval History', *St Paul's Magazine* (October 1870), p53.
83. 'Heraldry', pp147-8.

lost, probably discarded like so much old lumber.[84] The Dean simply did not understand the significance of the flags. When he attended the Dutch Naval exhibition at the Hague in 1900 he was pleased to see a Spanish 'streamer' from the Armada prize *San Mateo*, and devoted a few pages to the subject of Spanish flags.[85]

In 1890 Captain Lord Walter Kerr invited him to write the commissioning book for the new ironclad *Trafalgar*, a task for which he was ideally qualified by his expertise on Nelson, and service aboard a previous *Trafalgar*.[86] By this time the quarterdeck of new ships was fast becoming a 'shrine', marked with the dates of battles in which previous ships of that name had featured. A commissioning book enlarged on the historical significance of the ship's name. Well-chosen names joined battle honours and flags as standard elements in the maintenance and transmission of service tradition. This awareness of the past was vital for a service that had fought its last major battle, as Laughton never tired of reminding it, against particularly poor opposition in 1805. When he had first gone afloat he served in ships designed and built in Nelson's time, under an Admiral who joined the navy in 1798. By 1900 every aspect of the naval service had changed, and only a handful of senior officers remained who had served in the 1850s, and of these the most significant, John Fisher, was widely regarded as anti-history. While Fisher and Laughton were never close, Fisher possessed an intelligent understanding of history, was particularly well informed on Nelson and proud to record that he had been nominated for the service by Sir William Parker, the last of Nelson's captains. His famous aphorism that history was 'the record of exploded ideas', reflected the use the 'Syndicate of Discontent', inspired by Reginald Custance, made of history to attack his policy as First Sea Lord.[87]

Despite his reverence for naval tradition Laughton remained a critical scholar. If the Navy went to war in 1914 simplistically anticipating a second Trafalgar it was not for the want of warning from Laughton, and Corbett. Here, as ever, he had tried to educate the service by offering an accurate understanding of the past. Sadly his message was widely ignored, in favour of the romantic haze he so loathed.[88] He was simply unable to compete

---

84. Clucus (Dean of St. Paul's) to Laughton 15 & 30.6. 1887: JKL MS.

85. Laughton, J K, 'The Naval Exhibition at the Hague', *The Monthly Review* (November 1900), pp67-82, at pp71-2.

86. **Kerr**, Admiral of the Fleet Lord Walter Talbot (1839-1927). C-in-C Channel 1895-97 First Sea Lord 1899-1904. The first Catholic to hold such high posts in the Service since James, Duke of York. Laughton, J K, *The Story of Trafalgar* (Portsmouth 1890) 40pp.

87. Mackay, R F, *Fisher of Kilverstone* (Oxford 1973), pp4-5. Hamilton, W M, *The Nation and the Navy: Methods and Organisation of British Navalist Propaganda, 1889-1914* (London 1986), p194.

88. Breemer, J. 'The Burden of Trafalgar: Decisive Battle and Naval Strategic expectations on the Eve of World War One', *Journal of Strategic Studies* Vol 17 No 1 (March 1994), pp33-62.

with the sheer scale of output of the numerous naval 'penny-a-liners', and even reputable newspaper writers, who pushed the dangerous delusion of inevitable and overwhelming victory. It was for this reason that he was anxious to recruit fellow labourers to support his cause.

Although Laughton's study of flags and signals, closely linked to the tactical questions of the 1860s and 1870s, was never completed, it took on a new life in the work of William Perrin, the Admiralty Librarian, and Julian Corbett.[89] It was one of many themes and subjects that Laughton would open, and happily pass on to others for completion having recognised, at an early stage, that the task of writing reliable naval history on the scale required for naval education and doctrine development was beyond the efforts of any one man. Therefore he was happy to help others with his own ideas, research notes and contacts. Laughton had recognised the scale of his self-imposed task when he gained access to the Admiralty archive at the Public Record Office.

Having realised from his investigation of the unfortunate case of Lieutenant Baker-Phillips, one of Bridge's ancestors who had been executed for cowardice, that the Public Record Office was the key to accurate scholarship, Laughton spent the latter part of the 1870s trying to gain unrestricted access to the Admiralty papers.[90] At the time these could only be consulted with the consent of the Board, to answer specific queries. His efforts were initially rebuffed, then obstructed and finally, in 1879 grudgingly conceded on a personal basis, for material from before 1792. Even this concession required the intervention of his friend Admiral Key, the First Sea Lord. Key was the most important naval officer in Laughton's life between 1873 and 1885. Access was granted in recognition of a lifetime of service to the Navy, the doctrinal purpose of his endeavour and an awareness that he was a historian *for* the Navy. Six years later Laughton had opened this treasure house to all reputable scholars. He knew that it would require the efforts of many men to interpret the material. In 1886 general access, if only down to 1792, was finally granted. This was critical, enabling naval history to move into the academic mainstream, and this, in turn, ensured that it could meet the Navy's needs.[91] However, this apparent success contained the seeds of a doctrinal disaster. By restricting access to pre-1800 material the Admiralty deprived the first generation of historian/strategists of the opportunity to work on the most

---

89. Perrin, W G, *British Flags: their early history, and their development at sea; with an account of the origin of the flag as a national device* (Cambridge 1922). Corbett, J S (ed), *Fighting Instructions 1530-1816* (London NRS 1905), and *Signals and Instructions 1776-1794* (London NRS 1909).

90. Laughton, J K, 'The Study of Naval History', *JRUSI* (1896), pp800-01. Bridge to Laughton 20.12.1886: JKL MS. The case had been under discussion for some time.

91. Cantwell, J D, *The Public Record Office: 1838-1958* (London HMSO 1991), pp106, 159-60, 197, 330.

relevant, and least understood, period of British naval history, the years after Trafalgar. Only belatedly, in the middle of the First World War, did Corbett begin to sense just how much had been lost through the failure to study the Crimean War.[92] Only in 1929 were the records of the nineteenth century opened to scholars, and even then the cut-off date was 1885.[93] By that stage more recent events were the focus of naval interest. The damage has still to be rectified. Although the documents have been released, much of the naval history of the nineteenth century remains *terra incognita*.

At a personal level Laughton found the Record Office a congenial place to work. Hubert Hall, head of the Government Search Room during the 1890s, became a close friend and was a constant source of information. He was also Editorial Director of the Royal Historical Society from 1891 to 1938.[94] Other senior members of the Office, including the Deputy Keeper, supported Laughton's work, even if they occasionally found his interventions troublesome.[95] The Record Office was central to Laughton's academic life after 1885. For all the treasures it housed the fact that it was only five minutes walk from King's College made it uniquely accessible. Here he conducted research and met fellow scholars.[96] Initially Laughton used the Record Office to cross-check the French histories for his 'scientific' essays, but over time it became the key to all his work. But Laughton had one last 'scientific' project to complete before this phase of his career was complete. He would produce another College textbook, a fully-rounded study of a single career, to serve as the basis for the higher education of all naval officers.

In 1881 a new President was appointed to Greenwich. Vice-Admiral Sir Geoffrey Thomas Phipps Hornby (1825-95) was the outstanding senior officer of his day. In a forty-year career he had seen much service, exploiting the twin patronage tracks of having an Admiral and Sea Lord for a father, and a three-times Prime Minister for an uncle, to reach the head of his profession relatively early. Once there he displayed uncommon ability, real insight, and outstanding leadership. Known throughout the service as 'Uncle Geoff', Hornby was the acknowledged master of fleet tactics, both the evolutionary *exercises* used to teach the finer points of ship-handling, and the simpler combinations required for the most effective use of naval forces *in battle*. He was, and would remain for the rest of

92. Corbett, J S, 'The Revival of Naval History', *The Contemporary Review* (1916), and 'Napoleon and the British Navy after Trafalgar' *The Quarterly Review* (1922), pp238-55.
93. Cantwell, p404.
94. Humphreys, R A, *The Royal Historical Society 1868-1968* (London 1969), p69.
95. Cantwell, pp329 (Hall), 348, 394. Laughton letter to *The Times* 'National Records' 17.5.1910 p4. Scargill-Bird to Laughton 27.5.1910: JKL MS.
96. Laughton to Corbett 28.11.1893. Corbett MS Box 14.

his life, the personal embodiment of the Navy.[97] Hornby arrived at Greenwich fresh from a famous term as Commander-in-Chief in the Mediterranean, where his abilities had been tested to the full. His reputation was unrivalled. Although he only stayed at the College for a year Hornby was an active President, taking particular interest in the higher aspects of naval education. He attended Laughton's history lectures, and provided his own course on tactics. This led to an important meeting of minds on the core issues of tactics and command, and the two men became close friends.[98] Hornby replaced Key as the most important naval officer in Laughton's world, a development paralleled in the career of another dynamic figure of the era, John Arbuthnot Fisher.[99] In both cases Hornby was seen as the greater man, and the more certain source of influence, even if Laughton's motives were less cynical than Fisher's. Hornby and Laughton agreed with the Admiralty view that no formal tactical education should be given, so as to avoid the 'mischief' that would result from the official adoption of any particular system. Hornby stated:

> It is often asked, what is to be our fighting formation in future ? None has been prescribed: it is to be hoped that none will be prescribed. To prescribe any would be exceedingly foolish and in a high degree presumptuous. Foolish; for all our past history shows us the evil of having a prescribed formation for fighting in ; it needed the genius of a Nelson to disentangle us from the mess. Foolish; for, unless perhaps the state of his enemy's bunkers, there are few things an admiral would give more to know beforehand than the formation in which his enemy was going to fight. Presumptuous; because in the present day, we have no business to speak with authority.[100]

Instead naval history would provide the basis for a new doctrine. It was this need, as developed in discussions with Hornby, that resulted in the publication of Laughton's *Letters and Dispatches of Horatio, Viscount Nelson* in 1886. Laughton re-edited and condensed Harris Nicolas's seven volume edition, to make it easier for naval officers to own and use. The work was dedicated to Hornby, while the introduction demolished the myth that Nelson's tactical ideas could be summed up in Lord Cochrane's phrase, 'never mind manoeuvres, always go at them'.[101] It

97. Egerton, M, *Admiral of the Fleet Sir Geoffrey Phipps Hornby* (London 1896), a daughter's dutiful memorial. Gordon, A, *The Rules of the Game: Jutland and British Naval Command* (London 1996) provides a fresh perspective. See pp184-9. However, there is a pressing need for a modern biography of Hornby. The neglect of this central figure is one of the greatest weaknesses of most existing studies of the Victorian Navy.
98. Egerton, pp331-7, 339.
99. Mackay, R F, *Fisher of Kilverstone*, pp177-81.
100. Laughton, J K, 'Naval Warfare', *The Edinburgh Review* (July 1885), pp234-64, at p238.
101. Laughton, J K, *Letters and Dispatches of Horatio, Viscount Nelson* (London 1886), ppvii-xx. Corbett's handling of the 'Trafalgar Memorandum' in 1905 was strikingly similar.

also attacked the idea that any modern battle would rapidly degenerate into a *melee*, put forward by Admiral Sir George Elliot.[102] For Laughton, and Hornby, the *melee* was the negation of skill erected into a system. Only through control could real victories, victories as complete as Trafalgar, be won. It is worth stressing that the contribution of Greenwich to this work was personal, not structural. Neither Hornby nor Laughton were tasked with doctrine development.

The Nelson volume completed Laughton's tactical studies. He remained convinced that a decisive concentration of force remained the pinnacle of naval tactical thought. Where Nelson contributed a fresh insight was in stressing the importance of command style. The basis of his tactical system lay in taking his captains into his confidence. Having explained his concept Nelson then provided the a basic level of performance for those less inspired, or less able: 'in case signals can neither be seen or perfectly understood, no captain can do *very wrong* if he places his ship alongside that of an enemy'.[103] It should be recalled that at Trafalgar Nelson made no attempt to signal once the fleets were in action. His approach, which would be termed mission-analysis, or *auftragstaktik* today, remained the most effective form of fleet tactical control while fleets relied on battlefield-obscuring black powder artillery. It could only be used by fleets in first-class fighting order, *and* acting offensively. For Laughton Nelson completed the development of sailing ship tactics, his transcendent abilities enabling him to reach a new level of comprehension and exposition.

In order to use Nelson to teach these timeless lessons Laughton had to present the Admiral as a man who could be admired in the round, his character free from the aspersions of earlier generations. When Philip Colomb reviewed the book in the *Edinburgh Review* he stressed the degree to which Southey was responsible for the hostile view of Nelson's conduct at Naples, and blamed him for the widespread currency of such opinions. By addressing the various aspects of the hostile version, Laughton had done excellent service, and his success would, by implication, make his interpretation of Nelson the tactician that much more effective for the Navy.[104] Laughton made Nelson *the* naval exemplar, stressing his supreme professionalism, his mastery of tactics and strategy, his inspirational leadership and humanity. These sublime aspects of the profession could best be understood by a close study of the greatest admiral of all. Nelson would remain at the core of Laughton's work and, through his

---

102. 'Naval Warfare', pp239-40.
103. Ibid, Nelson Memorandum 9.10.1805 p422. My emphasis.
104. Colomb, P, (unsigned) review in *The Edinburgh Review* (October 1886), pp542-75. The copy in Laughton's pamphlet collection in the Naval Historical Branch Library has Colomb's signature.

example, came to dominate the work of other scholars, and other navies. He told one correspondent: 'the fact that it [the book] has induced you to examine Nelson's letters . . . is a complete and satisfactory justification, if I had felt that I needed one'.[105] At the same time he made a conscious identification between Nelson and Hornby, the modern officer who most closely matched his supreme talents. Curiously enough Hornby was not entirely convinced of Nelson's pre-eminence. When Mahan asked him who he placed second among the British Admirals he replied; ' "St. Vincent, if second". I gathered that he thought Nelson erratic'.[106] The book rounded off Laughton's work to create a new kind of history to serve naval education and tactical thought, it established him as an authority on Nelson and completed the 'scientific' phase of his career. Before it appeared his life had been profoundly altered. In the early 1880s his wife died, leaving him with a son and three daughters all under the age of sixteen. Then at the end of 1884 he received notice that his naval career had run its course.

---

105. Laughton to Oscar Browning 28.5.1886. Oscar Browning MS King's College, Cambridge: OB i/a.
106. Mahan to Laughton 14.8.1895 JKL MS.

CHAPTER 4

'Retired Pay £400 per annum': Charting a New Course, 1885-90

·

In 1885, with over thirty years service behind him, Laughton left the Naval College. The reason for the sudden end to an important career lay in the flawed origins of the College. All courses beyond that for Acting Sub-Lieutenants remained entirely voluntary, and from the late 1870s the number of volunteers at Greenwich fell off so rapidly that it seemed that the staff outnumbered the students![1] Rather than make the College central to the naval officer's career structure and increase the number of junior officers in the service so that the College could act as significant career stage, the Admiralty decided to reduce the teaching establishment. The President, Vice-Admiral William Luard, recommended that a Naval and Mathematical Instructor and an Instructor in Mathematics should be reduced, following the decision taken in 1877 to replace Naval Instructors with civilian Professors. The Admiralty concurred, and Laughton was informed by the Admiral, in person, on 27 December 1884 that he would lose his post, effective from Easter 1885. He would then be placed on half pay, unless he was re-deployed afloat, despite 'Their Lordships satisfaction with and approval of his past services'.[2] Significantly he remained Lecturer in Naval History, a position worth up to £50 a year, and held this post until 1887, when he was replaced by Philip Colomb. In 1885 Laughton was entitled to the maximum Greenwich Hospital pension for a Naval Instructor without Holy Orders of £400, a useful sum, but not equal to his current salary of £653. This may have influenced his decision to retire. On 23 April 1885, his 55th birthday, he was formally retired, at his own request.[3] In calculating his final settlement the pensions branch noted his service afloat, the continuing use of his textbooks, that he had four dependant children aged between 10 and 16, no private income and, critically, that there was 'Nothing against him'. It helped that he was recommended for the pension by Key, the First Sea Lord. His pension file

---

1. Collister, P, *The Sullivans and the Slave Trade* (London 1980), p175.
2. Admiralty to the President of the College, 23.12.1884 ADM 203/4.
3. Service Record ADM 196/81. Salary Book, Royal Naval College, p23.

was closed with the singularly inappropriate statement; 'Retired Pay £400 per annum'.[4] Laughton's selection for retirement was no reflection on his competence.[5] It was a realistic and fair decision under the existing rules. He would have to retire when he reached 60, and may have already been thinking about what to do in 1890! With the benefit of hindsight it is possible to see his thirty years of naval service as little more than an apprenticeship for what was to come.

In May 1885 Samuel Rawson Gardiner, Professor of Modern History at King's College, London, resigned his appointment, having received a fellowship at Oxford. The College advertised the post in late June, with a salary of £50 per annum, and an additional 18/- (90 pence) per term for each matriculated student. The conditions were hardly onerous. The Professor lectured from 1.15 to 2.30pm on Tuesday and Friday for three terms, totalling thirty-three weeks per annum. Retirement was fixed at 65, although it could be postponed annually at the request of Council. Probably forewarned by his friend Gardiner, Laughton applied, advising the College that he wished to retain the history post at Greenwich, a small commitment of six lectures a year that would not interfere with the professorship.[6] He was supported by testimonials from friends, colleagues, pupils and, essentially, a clergyman, including Henry Reeve, editor of the *Edinburgh Review*, his local Vicar, the Directors of Studies from Portsmouth and Greenwich, Admiral Fanshawe, the second President at Greenwich, and his pupil from the *Calcutta*, and later Portsmouth, Captain Thomas Sturges Jackson. An additional, unsolicited, testimonial was provided by Key, the First Sea Lord, who made the time to write during the Penjdeh Crisis and the painful process of leaving office. Laughton's other senior supporter, Hornby, was then at sea with the projected Baltic Fleet. Reeve broke the anonymity of the *Edinburgh Review* to reveal that Laughton had written eleven unsigned articles in past six years, which would 'have justly obtained for him a considerable reputation as an historical writer', had they appeared under his name. He stressed that these were general historical articles, chiefly dealing with 'the 17th & 18th centuries, with which Mr. Laughton is perfectly acquainted'. This was the pay-off for the sustained hard work of the past decade, spent mastering 'Modern' European History. Neither Reeve not Laughton mentioned the articles on Arctic Exploration and naval policy. Professor Thomas Archer Hirst, Director of Studies at Greenwich for the first ten

---

4. ADM 6/446 f8. *The Navy List*, various dates: regulations for Naval Instructors. Laughton, J K, 'Naval Armaments', *The Edinburgh Review* (April 1894), pp474-5 on the shortage of junior officers.
5. Vice-Admiral Luard, President of the College, to Laughton 27.12.1884. KCLA KA/ILI L60.
6. Laughton to King's College, 6.7.1885: The File on Laughton's Appointment, KCLA KA/ILI L60, contains the advertisement, together with his application and the testimonials.

years of the College, reported that his lectures on naval history, 'were highly appreciated by the naval officers who attended them'. All spoke of his skill and patience as a teacher. Sturges-Jackson also solicited the vote of the Dean of Wells, an influential member of the College Council, describing Laughton as: 'a man of great powers and untiring research'.[7] On 10 July the Council elected Laughton to the position on the verbal recommendation of the Search Committee. There is no record of the number or quality of any other applicants.[8] The appointment reflected Laughton's stature as a 'Victorian Intellectual'. A true polymath, he relied as much on proven capacity as a teacher as subject expertise, although he was careful to stress his general historical knowledge.

The move to King's should not be seen as a promotion, or even a sideways step into academic life. It was an opportunity to prolong his career and increase his income. Together with other literary work the post amounted, in the Navy's terms to 'a doubtful £160 a year'.[9] He needed the money. On 1 July 1886 he married his second wife, Maria Josepha de los Angeles di Alberti of Cadiz.[10] He already had four children under the age of twenty and there would be five more. At the same time he moved from Greenwich to 130 Sinclair Road, West Kensington. From there the growing family moved to Catesby House, Manor Road, Barnet in mid-1891.

Laughton quickly adopted his new title for publications, along with 'Lecturer on Naval History at the Royal Naval College'.[11] However, King's College London, as it existed in 1885, should not be confused with the world-famous institution it had become a century later. In 1885, noted its official historian,

King's College was not a public institution. It was an Anglican Seminary, established by churchmen for ecclesiastical purposes. It was dominated by bishops and the nominees of bishops, and it was pledged by its constitution to the maintenance of the doctrines and duties of Christianity as taught by the Church of England.[12]

---

7. Sturges-Jackson to Mrs Spink 1.7.1885, in Dean of Wells to College Secretary 8.7.1885 KA/IC/L59.
8. Laughton File, Letters to King's College; Reeve 3.7.1885; Lambert 1.7.1885; Main 3.7.1885; Archer Hirst 1.7.1885; Fanshawe undated; Sturges-Jackson 30.6.1885; Key 6.7.1885. Laughton to College Secretary 11.7.1885: KA/IC/L59.
9. ADM 6/446 p8.
10. Service Record ADM 196/81.
11. Laughton used many variations of his three main claims to distinction, Naval Instructor, Fellow of Gonville and Caius, and Professor of Modern History, branching off into 'author of . . .' for boy's stories. He was always 'RN'.
12. Hearnshaw, F J C, The Centenary History of King's College, London: 1828-1928 (London 1929). Quote at p381. Hearnshaw was Laughton's colleague and successor as Professor of Modern History. His slight, and slighting, references to Laughton leave the impression of a man embittered by being long denied the higher position by a durable and determined senior. Curiously he ended his own career writing a popular work of naval history!

As a denominational establishment, King's applied religious tests to both staff and students, excluding all those who did not subscribe to the Anglican creed. Evidently Laughton had not returned to the Calvinist faith of this father, which he had abjured to enter Cambridge. The religious tests were only abolished in 1903, when severe financial problems forced the College to seek government funds that were only available to non-denominational institutions. Only in 1910 did King's join the Federal University of London. Before that it had expressed no interest whatsoever in becoming a research institution.[13]

As Professor of Modern History Laughton was a member of the Department of General Literature and Science, which educated boys between the ages of 15 and 18 before they went to Oxford or Cambridge.[14] Other pupils were preparing for Service or Civil Service careers. The Department was split into Arts and Science faculties. In 1888 it provided tuition for twenty-two boys, allowing the staff to give considerable attention to their best pupils, in a university atmosphere. Even so Laughton found 'the work is by no means so interesting' as it had been at Greenwich.[15] Unfortunately the limited number of students and constant pressure to reduce expenditure resulted in major salary cuts in the 1890s, which caused him real financial hardship. In 1889 and 1890 he was forced to compound half of his naval pension for lump sums totalling £1800.[16] This was despite taking over the teaching formerly done by the Lecturer in History. By 1896 Laughton's salary was only £67, so it is little wonder he went to Cambridge in October 1895 to canvas support for his application for the Regius Chair.[17] His only reward was an honorary fellowship of his old college.

Laughton's merits as a teacher were discussed by his most famous King's student, the historian George Peabody Gooch. Gooch went to King's in 1888 aged 15, having left Eton early, and remained for three years. He considered Laughton the 'star turn' of the college, but thought his lectures 'rather uninspiring, for he conceived of history as a record of events rather than a panorama of the many-sided life of humanity'. Yet it was Laughton who encouraged him to study history, and King's

13. Levine, P, *The Amateur and the Professional: Antiquarians, Historians and Archaeologists in Victorian England, 1838-86* (Cambridge 1986), pp144-5.
14. Laughton to Oscar Browning, 6.4.1888, requesting copies of past Cambridge entrance exams, to assist a good student to prepare.
15. Laughton to Luce 11.8.1889. JKL MS.
16. Service Record ADM 196/81.
17. Hearnshaw, salary p364, appointment p367 Gooch, G P, *Under Six Reigns* (London 1958), p11, King's and p42 Regius Chair. Laughton presented copies of some of his books to the library at Caius, where they remain. He chose Trafalgar Day as an auspicious anniversary on which to do so: Laughton to the Librarian 21.10.1895. He was elected an honorary fellow on 15.11.1895. I am indebted to Gordon Hunt, assistant librarian at Caius for assistance on this and other matters relating to Laughton's relations with his old college.

witnessed 'the beginnings of my intellectual life'. While Gooch was not alone in regarding Acton, whom he came to know well, as a better choice for the Regius Chair in 1895, he admitted the merit of Laughton's work, even at the end of his life, when he tended to play down his influence. Gooch's biographer Frank Eyck concluded that it was Laughton, 'who first encouraged Gooch to make history the centre of his studies'.[18] Recognising that he had a 'brilliant'[19] student, Laughton helped Gooch get into Cambridge, probably introduced him to Seeley and remained in touch with him until his death. Curiously Gooch never realised that Laughton was just as much a devotee of the German School and Ranke as he would become. As a result he passed up the one opportunity he had to repay his old teacher's efforts, not even mentioning him in his important survey *History and Historians of the Nineteenth Century* of 1913, an omission that proved fatal for Laughton's reputation. While Mahan is included, Corbett and Laughton are damned by sharing their exclusion with such lightweights as Oscar Browning.[20] In consequence when George Trevelyan assessed the state of historical studies in 1927 he followed Gooch, attributing the revival of naval history to Mahan, and despite wishing to laud Cambridge men, only mentioned Corbett by name.[21] By 1913, after working with Seeley, Acton and a number of French and German scholars, Gooch had developed into a major historian, but his treatment of Laughton, who was still alive, was ungenerous to say the least. Furthermore it did not accord with current thinking. In 1913 the consensus was that Laughton had established his subject at the core of the academic profession. He was recognised as the expert in his field, and a worthy contributor to a new and ambitious crop of historical enterprises.[22] In order to assess the quality of Laughton's output, his methods must be seen in the context of contemporary historical scholarship, and compared with those other British historians practising at the time.

The historical profession that Laughton joined in 1885 was still coming to terms with professionalism, uncertain as to the best methods of study and, fundamentally, still grappling with the question of purpose. Few University historians were original scholars, their written output tending

18. Gooch, G P, *Under Six Reigns* (London 1958), pp11, 42. Eyck, F, *George Peabody Gooch: A Study in History and Politics* (London 1982), pp5-6 and 452 fn11.
19. Laughton to College Secretary 7.10.1891 KA/IC/L70.
20. Gooch, G P, *History and Historians of the Nineteenth Century* (London 1913).
21. Trevelyan, G M, *The Present Position of History* (Cambridge 1927), p15. This was his Inaugural lecture as Regius Professor, and the mention of Corbett was due to Richmond, and the use that Trevelyan was making of Corbett's *England in the Mediterranean* in his *England in the Reign of Queen Anne*.
22. His correspondence with Charles Firth, A W Ward and Harold Temperley among others is conclusive on his status. The point is confirmed by his contribution to such projects as the *English Historical Review* and Acton's *Cambridge Modern History*, together with the support of Alfred Pollard for his naval history department.

to be textbooks in the well-trodden fields of historical examination, rather than fresh studies of modern or controversial subjects. They tended to avoid anything challenging, especially where there was a danger of contact with contemporary politics. They were, as a rule, professional teachers, rather than professional scholars.[23] By contrast the major historians, like Carlyle, Froude and W E H Lecky, worked outside the universities, conducted original research and took themselves very seriously. They were in no doubt that their work had a great contemporary importance, an attitude enhanced by a belief that the 'scientific' history they were writing was the last word on the past.

Only in the 1860s did succeeding governments appoint major historians to posts at Oxford and Cambridge. The first of these, William Stubbs (1825-1901), was selected for the Regius Chair at Oxford by Lord Derby in 1866, even though he had not applied.[24] Between 1866 and his removal to a bishopric in 1884 Stubbs attempted to create a school of history at Oxford, using the latest German scholarship as a model for English practice. Like Laughton, Stubbs was a self-taught historian, having graduated in classics and mathematics, and both men operated in institutions where history was critical to an understanding of present issues. Through his work, his example and his friendships Stubbs established an Oxford history school, which included his friends Edward Augustus Freeman and John Richard Green, and men of another generation like Charles Harding Firth and Alfred Frederick Pollard. Stubbs's outlook was dominated by his solid Conservatism and the work of German medievalists. He regarded Ranke as the greatest modern historian, and shared his rejection of the positivist idea that there could be a predictive science of history. Positivist history had been given a tremendous fillip by Thomas Henry Buckle (1821-62), whose *History of Civilization in England* (1856-61) attempted to develop permanent laws of human development, just in time for Darwin's theory of evolution to render his conclusions obsolete.[25] By contrast Stubbs believed that History became a 'science' when it broke free of other disciplines, and developed its own methodology.[26] Much of the coincidence of outlook between Ranke and Stubbs can be attributed to their shared ambition to found schools of study; University politics ensured that they both needed a distinct discipline. For Stubbs the key lay in the explicit recognition of the distinction between the educational role

23. Soffer, R N, *Discipline and Power: The University, History and the Making of an English Elite, 1870-1930* (Stanford 1994), pp26-35.
24. Hutton, W H (ed), *Letters of William Stubbs, Bishop of Oxford* (London 1904).
25. Marwick, A, *The Nature of History* (London 1970), p43. St Aubyn, G, *A Victorian Eminence* (London 1961). Desmond, A and Moore, J, *Darwin* (London 1991), pp463-4.
26. Goldstein, D S, 'History at Oxford and Cambridge: Professionalization and the influence of Ranke' in Iggers, G G, and Powell, J M, *Leopold von Ranke and the Shaping of the Historical Discipline* (Syracuse, 1990), pp142-5.

of history, as the basis for judgement, and the archive-based methodology of the critical comparison of sources.[27]

Initially Laughton followed Sir John Seeley, Regius Professor at Cambridge 1869-94, treating history as a school for statesmen, even if his target audience included more admirals than ministers. However, responding to the influences of a profession struggling for recognition, and the particular requirements of his own speciality, his methods and approach became more individualistic. Laughton's generation considered that the true significance of history lay in the contemporary lessons that could be drawn from it. While myths served a purpose, only accurate scholarship could provide the basis from which to develop modern doctrine and strategy. Similarly the majority of Laughton's British contemporaries considered a role in present-day politics infinitely preferable to scholarship. Lord Acton used scholarship to attack contemporary Papal policies and solicited posts from Gladstone, who in turn encouraged James Bryce to use his study of the American Constitution to support a Federal solution to the Irish problem.[28] Gladstone's Irish Home Rule policy split the Liberal historical establishment as sharply as it did the parliamentary party.[29] Seeley, Lecky and Laughton became Liberal Imperialists,[30] while Gardiner, Acton, Bryce, Freeman and Oscar Browning remained with Gladstone. Across the political divide Froude accepted colonial missions from the Tory Colonial Secretary Lord Carnarvon, and received the Regius Chair at Oxford from Lord Salisbury, who shared his views on Empire and Race, rather than on historical issues.[31] In fact the great 'debates' of the late nineteenth century, notably that between Lecky and Froude over Ireland, had far more to do with contemporary politics than historical scholarship. Laughton considered Lecky a great historian, while Froude was the last lion of the older literary tradition.

If Laughton adopted a narrower focus for his work than most of his fellow labourers, he was at one with them on the contemporary relevance of history. The role of the historian was well put by Stubbs's friend, and Clements Markham's school-fellow,[32] Edward Augustus Freeman in his inaugural lecture series as Regius Professor at Oxford in 1884. The

---

27. Stubbs, W, *Lectures on Medieval and Modern History* (3rd ed, Oxford 1900), pp23-5.
28. Tulloch, H, *Acton* (London 1988), pp51-4, 89, and Tulloch, H, *James Bryce's American Commonwealth* (London RHS 1988).
29. Harvie, C, *The Lights of Liberalism: University Liberals and the Challenge of Democracy 1860-86* (London 1976), pp174-5, 220-2. Parry, J, *The Rise and Fall of Liberal Government in Victorian Britain* (Yale 1993), pp292-303.
30. Wormell, D, *Sir John Seeley and the Uses of History* (London 1980), pp164-73: McCartney, D *W.E.H. Lecky: Historian and Politician 1838-1903* (Dublin 1994).
31. Thompson, T W, *James Anthony Froude on Nation and Empire: A Study in Victorian Racialism* (New York 1987), pp641-57 at p650.
32. Markham, A H, *Life of Sir Clements Markham* (London 1917), p8.

lectures were published two years later as *Methods of Historical Study*, one of the key texts of the decade. This book contained concepts that were central to Laughton's professional development, starting with an enduringly famous quotation on the purpose of history:

> If I am right in holding that history is past politics and that politics is present history, that which can never be of any use to anybody would seem to quite shut out from our range.[33]

In studying history Freeman called on his fellow professionals to emphasise the 'patient study of contemporary texts' which had more enduring value than, 'the piling together of theories to be upset the next day by some other theory'. The historian:

> must work to lay the foundation; when the foundation is once laid on the rock of original research, a superstructure may be raised on it which may live through a good many blasts and storms of controversy. But he who without a foundation builds on the sands of theory, he who rushes at a difficult and controversial period with no knowledge of the periods that went before it or of the periods that came after it, he who conceives of events, not as they are reported by those who saw them, but as may be convenient for some favourite doctrine, political or theological, philosophical or artistic – against such as these our professor will hardly need to raise his voice of warning. He may spare himself the task; he may leave events to take their course; the house built on sand will presently crumble of itself, without needing any special blasts and storms to sweep it away.[34]

Freeman, like Laughton, considered archive based scholarship 'scientific'.[35] That he did very little work in the archives himself was not the least of his contradictions. An independent scholar who hated working in libraries, and philological pedant of the highest order, Freeman was a curious amalgam of Victorian attitudes. His letters reveal a pathological hatred of Celts, Jews and Negroes, together with Catholicism and Islam, of Teutonic thoroughness, yet he upheld the national rights of the Balkan Slavs against the tyranny of Turkey and Austria. While his circle of friends overlapped with that of Laughton, including Gardiner, Montagu Burrows and Clements Markham, Freeman's death in 1892 limited his contact with Laughton.[36] However, his ideas had an enormous impact.

---

33. Freeman, E A, *The Methods of Historical Study: Eight Lectures on the Office of the Historical Professor* (London 1886), p44. This was Freeman's inaugural course of 1884.
34. Ibid, p17.
35. Ibid, p152.
36. Stephens, W R W, *The Life and Letters of Edward A Freeman* (London 1895) 2 vols. Provides a very revealing portrait from his own correspondence. Bryce, J, *Studies in Contemporary Biography* (London 1903), pp262-92 is a sympathetic summary by a colleague and friend.

Laughton's historical studies matched Freeman's specification, they were directed at the present, they took the form of foundation building from archival sources, and were 'scientific' in their rigour.

Two contemporary historians exercised a particular influence over Laughton; Sir John Seeley and Samuel Rawson Gardiner. Seeley (1834-95), appointed Regius Professor of History at Cambridge by Gladstone in 1869, remained there until his death in 1895. He had been elected a Fellow of Caius in 1882, a matter of no small importance to Laughton. Seeley was a positivist, believing the best approach to truth and reason lay through 'the extension of the *methods* of physical science to the whole domain of knowledge'.[37] His inaugural lecture had stressed that the value of modern history lay in the 'teaching of politics', he believed that 'history is the school for statesmanship'.[38] Unlike Stubbs, Seeley did not recognise the essential dichotomy between the educational role he advocated, and the Rankean ambition to understand the past on its own terms.[39] He saw the historian's first task as being to sweep away the romantic views that held the field, before laying down the lines for new work. He also believed that the 'Oxford' men, notably Edward Freeman, were hostile, despite Freeman's open admiration of the new Historical Tripos and the methods of study that Seeley had introduced at Cambridge. However, the Historical Tripos never matched up to Seeley's hopes, remaining an inferior qualification until after his death. Seeley's great book on British Foreign Policy from the 1550s was never completed. His popular lecture series *The Expansion of England* of 1886, based on research for the larger project, served as an essay in methodology. He tried to understand Britain's rise to greatness, and the rise and fall of nations generally, so that Britain could avoid the fall. His small book became one of the key imperialist texts.[40] It remained a powerful influence on Laughton, explaining the development of an imperial vision in his later work. Seeley became an intellectual leader of the Liberal Imperialists, and was knighted by Lord Rosebery in 1894. *The Expansion of England* persuaded Joseph Chamberlain to send his son Austen to take the History Tripos.[41] A section of Seeley's larger book, covering the period from the accession of Elizabeth I to 1688, was published posthumously. Seeley had consulted Laughton on the Elizabethan naval

37. Wormell, p30.
38. Ibid, p43.
39. Goldstein, p146.
40. Seeley, J R, *The Expansion of England* (London 1886). Wormell, pp94 and 129.
41. Dutton, D, *Austen Chamberlain: Gentleman in Politics* (Bolton 1985), p15. Austen would enter public life as Junior Civil Lord of the Admiralty, and serve on the Council of the Navy Records Society.

wars.[42] Other aspects of Seeley's work to affect Laughton were his dis-
trust of mass democracy, which he shared with Froude, Leslie Stephen,
Lecky and even John Morley, and the Whiggish approach of judging the
past by contemporary standards.[43] It was a refinement of Seeley's message that provided the 'school for the Navy' focus of Laughton's later
work, and the idea that only through the production of better history
could the subject educate better statesmen, and naval officers.

The move to King's witnessed a decisive shift in Laughton's methods
from analytical surveys of the secondary literature to archive-based research. Although his object remained constant, he sought the support of
his new profession to enhance his message. He was heavily influenced by
his friend and predecessor, Samuel Rawson Gardiner (1829-1902).
Gardiner had been at King's since 1872, having been excluded from Oxford by his 'Irvingite' Catholic faith. When he returned to the Church of
England and secured a Fellowship at All Souls' in 1884, he retired from
King's. Gardiner practised the new professional history of Ranke, his
avowed exemplar, and the German School. He accepted Ranke's view
that the critical comparison of primary source materials was the 'scientific' method of writing history, to the exclusion of the work of earlier
historians. For George Gooch he was an unrivalled paragon of professional objectivity:

> No Englishman of his time, or of any time did more to raise the standard of
> responsibility in historical work, and he has left us the most exact and
> impartial account of any period in the history of our race.[44]

Like Ranke Gardiner favoured the publication of critically-edited primary documents.[45] He also considered the constant comparison of the past
with the present 'altogether destructive of historical knowledge'.[46] This
influence is the most obvious explanation for the fact that Laughton's
work became less blatantly didactic in his academic years. In addition
Gardiner was always ready to help and encourage promising scholars.[47]
However, he did not practice the 'impartial' history for which he is best

42. Seeley, J R, *The Growth of British Policy* (London 1895). Laughton to Seeley 8.6.1890
Seeley MS, Special Collection, University of London MSS Dept. Seeley to Laughton
10.6.1890 JKL MS.
43. Von Arx, J, *Progress and Pessimism: Religion, Politics and History in late Nineteenth
Century Britain* (Harvard 1985), pp8, 18, 31-2, 204, 206-7.
44. Gooch, G P, *History and Historians of the Nineteenth Century* (London 1913), p364.
45. Kenyon, J, *The History Men* (London 1993. 2nd edition), pp224-33.
46. Marwick, A, *The Nature of History* (London 1970), p44.
47. Gardiner, S R, *DNB*. The entry was written by his pupil and close friend Professor
Charles H Firth. See also Corbett's Correspondence with Gardiner in 1889, during the
writing of his brief life of George Monck. Corbett MS.

remembered quite as rigorously as he preached.[48] His magisterial, 'objective' histories of the reign of Charles I and the Civil War were just as much products of their day as the work of lesser historians. The point is essential for any assessment of the quality of contemporary historical scholarship. Politically Gardiner was a staunch Gladstonian Liberal, Acton advising the 'Grand Old Man' to reward him with a Civil List pension in 1882. Professionally he was close to Acton, John Morley, Freeman and James Bryce. He saw Gladstone as a 'towering, heroic figure', whom he identified with Cromwell, turning his Civil War history into a parable of 'the Gladstonian liberal as hero'.[49] During the Home Rule split he remained an active and public supporter of Gladstone, and in 1892 his politics cost him the Regius Chair at Oxford, the Tory Prime Minister Lord Salisbury giving it to Froude.[50] A revision of the degree to which Gardiner the man influenced Gardiner the scholar emphasises his humanity, and places him back in the realm of mere mortals, alongside his friends and colleagues. He identified so closely with Gladstone because he, like Seeley and so much of the liberal intelligentsia of the day, distrusted democracy, and relied on a noble character to avoid the tyranny of mere majorities. Because his work was profoundly influenced by the age in which he lived he shared Freeman's opinion that the most important object of historical enquiry was 'statesmanship *looking forward,* and trying to find solutions for difficult problems'. To this end he argued, 'is it not possible to do for history what Darwin has done for science?'[51] Here was man in tune with Laughton's ideas, a thorough scholar who believed that his work had a particular contemporary significance. At the same time Gardiner's austere methodology impressed Laughton, for while his own approach, derived from science, had already been formed, Gardiner's document-based scholarship provided an authoritative stamp of approval. Despite leaving King's College Gardiner, who still lived close to London, accepted the post of Lecturer in History and Ancient History to the separate King's Ladies College. The two men were in regular contact from the mid-1880s until Gardiner's death, his sons were often in Laughton's house, and his widow later moved close to Laughton in Wimbledon.[52]

While Laughton had a critical contemporary agenda for his work, the academic methodology he developed gave him the insight to temper any positivist impulses. There is no evidence that he had read Buckle's book,

48. Adamson, J S A, 'Eminent Victorians: S. R. Gardiner and the Liberal as Hero', *The Historical Journal* Vol 33 (1990), pp641-57 is an essential corrective to older 'idealised' treatments.
49. Ibid, p657.
50. Ibid, pp641-3.
51. Ibid, p650.
52. Laughton-Mathews, V, *Blue Tapestry: The Story of the WRNS* (London 1948), p26.

but he cannot have been unaware of it, and certainly preferred the 'scientific' to the 'literary' historical model. By the early 1890s he had accepted the new professional orthodoxy of the *English Historical Review*. This ensured that he and his subject had a place within the new discipline; a development that would be critical to his ambition to use history as the basis of naval education.

Gardiner had already exerted a powerful influence on Laughton before he moved to King's. They first came into contact while working on the *Dictionary of National Biography* (henceforth *DNB*). The *DNB* project was started in 1882 by George Smith, publisher of *The Cornhill Magazine* and *The Pall Mall Gazette,* in emulation of continental biographical surveys, which were significant elements in the process of creating national consciousness. The *DNB* was organised by Leslie Stephen, hitherto editor of *The Cornhill Magazine,* who selected all the subjects to be written, and commissioned articles.[53] When the project was announced in *The Times* and *The Athenaeum* in late 1882, Laughton wrote to Stephen, offering his services which 'may probably be of some use to you in respect of naval subjects'. He reported that his work, which had the sanction of the Admiralty, was intended to result in a new and accurate naval history and hoped that 'there was a chance of the memories of our naval worthies being cleared of the cobwebs of fiction'.[54] The work was arranged alphabetically, which necessarily complicated research. The first volume appeared in 1885, the sixty-third and last in 1900, whereupon the whole process began again to address the inevitable omissions, and reflect the steady progress of time. Laughton was one of only three men to contribute an article to every single volume. As a liberal blue-water navalist Stephen was well-disposed to the inclusion of naval subjects, while Laughton was an obvious choice; he had the standing provided by Greenwich, was already a contributor to the *Pall Mall Gazette*, and accessible. Gardiner, who was heavily involved in writing and organising the seventeenth-century material, valued Laughton's assistance.[55] Stephen, who revered Gardiner, would have needed no further encouragement.[56]

The dominant concerns in Stephen's writing were the need to recognise progress, and to educate the masses to accept the revision of ethical standards. He used biographical studies of the purveyors of popular culture as a medium for his own intellectual development, and the transmission

53. Glynn, J, *The Prince of Publishers: A Biography of the Great Victorian Publisher George Smith* (London 1986), pp199-207.
54. Laughton to Stephen 10.11.1882 and 24.12.1882: Sidney Lee DNB Files Bodleian Library Oxford.
55. Gardiner to Laughton 10.10.1886 JKL MS. This is the first extant letter from Gardiner in Laughton's archive. No Gardiner archive has yet appeared.
56. Adamson, p642.

of his ideas. He was anxious to get his audience to see the individual in the context of his own time.

> This contribution to modern understanding originated in the need of troubled Victorian Intellectuals like Leslie Stephen to make the past yield the meaning and direction that the present seemed to lack.[57]

The creation of a 'Whig' history by intellectuals claiming a 'scientific' basis for their work was intended to have a powerful effect on popular consciousness.[58] The *DNB* made a major contribution to the process by providing a suitable medium of exchange between the academic scholarship of the new professional historians and the newly literate masses. It would establish a suitable past for those enfranchised by the Reform Act of 1884, about whom so many of the intelligentsia were paranoid. Stephen required contributors to the *DNB* to render the judgement of the age, not their own individual assessment, on the character and claims of the subject covered.

Stephen shared the 'foundation' approach of Freeman, while his esteem for Gardiner was unlimited.[59] Writing in 1896 he recognised that the hardest task of the *DNB* had been the recovery of the lives of 'second rate men', lives that were full of suggestion for the intelligent reader. To illustrate his point he enlarged on Laughton's contribution, which had involved a large amount of this work. He contrasted these lives with the 'literary' perception of the sailor, admiring the industry and skill involved in the production of 'a little Valhalla', which had 'imbedded something like a complete naval history of the country' in the pages of the *DNB*.[60] Laughton composed over 900 entries for the *DNB*, out of a total of 29,120, including almost all of the naval studies. He had been in a unique position to organise and present a major aspect of the national past. Like Stephen his model was essentially progressivist, his judgement based on the contribution of his subjects to the advancement of naval power and national interests. His disdain for Tory officers, from George Rooke to Lord Hood of Avalon, reflected more than just a personal political view. Stephen and his successor, Sidney Lee, recognised Laughton's ability and industry, while the regular additional income was useful.[61] Lee became a personal friend. Alfred Pollard, a Deputy Editor of the *DNB* between 1893 and 1902, a great admirer of Laughton, attributed much of his

---

57. Von Arx, p56.
58. Ibid, p58.
59. Stephen, L, 'National Biography' in *Studies of a Biographer* (London 1907), Vol I, p7.
60. Ibid, pp20 and 25-7.
61. Matthew, Prof H G C, 'The DNB and the New DNB: Leslie Stephen and Sidney Lee a Hundred Years On'; The London Library Lecture 1.12.1994, given at the Royal Geographical Society.

success to the training he received from Lee.[62] Following Pollard, John Kenyon has argued that the *DNB* was the finest historical training available at the time. It undoubtedly advanced Laughton's education, transforming him into the complete modern historian.[63] Laughton was already aware of the advantages of the biographical format, which had been employed by Campbell, Charnock, Marshall and, most recently, O'Byrne.[64] It was doubtless with a view to continuing and improving upon these sources that he offered John Murray a naval biographical dictionary in 1880.[65] His contribution to the *DNB* served the same end. Being a large scale work of national reference, it ensured that the services of the Navy could not be ignored by succeeding generations of historians.

Laughton began work on the *DNB* at a significant stage in the development of his methodology. He had already mastered the critical comparison of sources, and the exploitation of personal contacts. The recent opening of the Public Record Office provided the final piece in the jigsaw that became his standard method, the Service Records of more 'ancient' officers and other public documents. When the opportunity arose, in 1882, he had already written several brief lives, based on critical book reviews. In 1881 he devoted thirteen pages of *Fraser's Magazine* to his first Captain, Henry Codrington. This resulted in an overlong and rather unbalanced *DNB* entry on an officer who had done little to earn the compliment. Codrington was an arrogant, opinionated snob; his conduct as a senior Captain in 1854 had been insubordinate and undistinguished. He had not flown his flag at sea, and without the efforts of a dutiful sister he might have passed unnoticed.[66] Another entry grew out of a forensic review of Hobart Pasha's often imaginative memoirs in 1886. This prompted a correspondence with Admiral Sir Beauchamp Seymour, recently created Lord Alcester, although better known as 'the Ocean Swell'. Alcester shared Laughton's reservations about Hobart's memoirs, with good cause, and had access to his service records.[67] Laughton later composed an entry on Alcester.

Naval contacts were vital to the completion of Laughton's work on nineteenth-century officers, as a glance at those written by other hands

62. Galbraith, V H, 'Albert Frederick Pollard 1869-1948', *Proceedings of the British Academy* Vol XXXV (1949), pp257-74.
63. Kenyon, pp203-4. Annan, N, *Leslie Stephen* (London 1984), pp82-9.
64. Campbell, J, *Lives of the Admirals* (London 1744), 4 vols, later continuations by other authors. Charnock, J, *Biographica Navalis* (London 1794-8), 6 vols; Marshall, J, *Royal Naval Biography* (London 1823-35), 4 vols. In 8 parts and 4 supplementary vols; O'Byrne, W, *Naval Biographical Dictionary* (London 1847).
65. Undated note in JKL MS.
66. Bourchier, Lady, *Selections from the Correspondence of Sir Henry Codrington* (London 1880).
67. Laughton, J K, 'Hobart Pasha', *Longman's Magazine* Vol 9 (Nov 1886), pp32-43. Alcester to Laughton 4 and 8.11.1886: JKL MS.

reveals. The citation 'personal information' among Laughton's sources invariably refers to help provided by family members, old colleagues and followers. These could have been a minefield of misinformation in a service filled with personal factions, political groups and cliques. However, Laughton had the respect of all, and the knowledge to filter out the majority of untruths. He also placed requests for help in the journal *Notes and Queries*, although these provided very few answers.[68] His entry on Sir William 'Pincher' Martin relied heavily on Edward Fanshawe for family details, while Cyprian Bridge provided an assessment of his impact on the service.[69] Hubert Hall made an important contribution to the entry on Frederick Marryat, while Philip Colomb corrected Laughton's assessment of Marryat's mercantile signal code.[70] Perhaps the most revealing correspondence concerned Sir Phipps Hornby, father of Sir Geoffrey. Laughton sent his draft entry to Hornby, who was impressed by the concise, accurate format as well as the content. He reminded Laughton that his father had served on the Admiralty Board in 1852, and suggested that his elder brother, the Provost of Eton, should be named.[71] Hornby's amendments appear in the published version.

Laughton's longest correspondence on a *DNB* entry was, unsurprisingly, with the combative daughter of his first Commander-in-Chief, Sir Charles Napier. Serving aboard Codrington's *Royal George*, Laughton had picked up his Captain's strong bias against Napier, which was garnished with a fund of unpleasant stories dating back over twenty years, and insinuations about his courage and drinking habits. After Napier died in 1860, Fanny Jodrell had devoted the rest of her long life to the establishment of his greatness. That she was struggling against the tide should have been obvious; Napier, the last of the old school of naval warriors, had been too eccentric, vainglorious and boastful for his true merits to be recognised by a more decorous age in which a naval officer was expected, above all, to be a gentleman. Fanny Jodrell had been trying to find a publisher for Napier's papers, but none were interested. Her prospective editor then advised her to make them available to Laughton for the *DNB*, or even a full-length study.[72] He did not take up the offer, having long ago made up his mind about Napier. When the entry appeared he received an apoplectic letter from Fanny Jodrell, by now over 80, and still determined to defend her father from his 'enemies'. Laughton noted that he 'answ'd civilly' and pointed out that it was 'the historian's

---

68. Laughton to Sidney Lee 26.2.1896: MSS Eng. Misc. d.178 f248 Lee MSS Bodleian Library.
69. Fanshawe to Laughton 28.7.1892; Bridge to Laughton 14.3.1893: JKL MS.
70. Hall to Laughton 3.5.1892; Colomb to Laughton 26.7.1892: JKL MS.
71. Hornby to Laughton 12.6.1890.
72. Captain S P, Oliver to Laughton 30.3.1892, Jodrell to Laughton 4.4.1892: JKL MS.

business to hold the balance [between] friends and enemies, sometimes to the annoyance of both'.[73] For all the civility with which he answered an intemperate letter Laughton was in the wrong, and he came close to admitting as much to Lee.[74] This case demonstrates the most important weakness of his work on the *DNB*. The entry on Napier was, in strictly factual terms, a correct record of a naval career, but it missed out important aspects of his life, underplayed his political career and the political aspects of his final and most controversial command, ignored his role in maritime technical development and entirely missed his true significance as the cutting edge of Palmerstonian diplomacy. It imputed weaknesses and failings to Napier solely on the basis of hearsay, and missed important aspects of his career that were detailed in the material offered by Fanny Jodrell. The fault was the more serious because the article was relatively long. Napier's reputation has never recovered.[75]

In dealing with his contemporaries Laughton allowed personal, political and service bias to affect his judgement. This was important because the *DNB* would provide the basic biographical reference for scholars for years to come. His magisterial judgements have exercised a powerful influence on those who have followed. Among the men of his own era he demonstrated a marked aversion for Tory officers, creating hostile images of 'reactionary' admirals, notably Lord Hood of Avalon, who deserved better of his country. Because Laughton's work became the basis of naval scholarship, and of historical appreciation of naval officers, these rather one-dimensional images have been repeated. Because Laughton lived to write entries on so many men of his own time, ranging from the unimpressive Henry Codrington to the commanding figure of Hornby, he found it hard to achieve true detachment. The Liberal political bias reflected his politics, and the politics of the project.

Laughton's strengths as a contributor to the *DNB* were his unique, encyclopaedic, knowledge of British naval history, his self-devised critical approach to published sources, unique access to the leading men of the service and the ability to work quickly. He displayed a marked preference for careers made at sea over those who served ashore, and furthermore his handling of the political careers of senior officers was cursory, although rarely inaccurate. To expect perfection from so prolific a contributor would be churlish, and on balance Laughton's work deserves the highest praise. He ensured that the Navy was at the heart of a great national work of reference. Today some of the minor subjects he suggested would be

---

73. Jodrell to Napier 9.3.1901, and draft answer of 12.3.1901: JKL MS.
74. Laughton to Lee 15.3.1901. Lee MSS f.250.
75. Kemp, P, *The Oxford Companion to Ships and the Sea* (Oxford 1976), p572, is among the better known examples of a work reproducing Laughton's views in a biographical notice.

ignored, while others that he omitted have had to be added. Yet he gave the naval entries a consistency and factual quality that have stood the test of time. In revising the nineteenth-century entries it was necessary to add information on patronage, politics, service at the Admiralty, parentage and money, issues that would have seemed inappropriate at the end of the nineteenth century, particularly when so many of his subjects were scarcely cold in the ground. If we take a more rounded view of the Victorian Navy today, we are still heavily dependent on Laughton's insight, and the information he collected. Among the less obvious men to be preserved for ever in Laughton's spare prose was Michael Howe, 'the last and worst of the Australian bushwhackers', who appeared just before the great Admiral, Richard, Earl Howe!

Even Laughton found it difficult to keep up with the remorseless schedule of the *DNB* over a period of close on twenty years, in addition to his numerous other commitments. In 1895 he fell behind, having devoted more time to the first pair of volumes for the Navy Records Society than he had anticipated.[76] As a result the quality of his work slipped, if only slightly, as he approached the final few letters of the alphabet. The notice of Admiral Sir Baldwin Walker is little more than O'Byrne's *Naval Biographical Dictionary* entry of 1847 with a final sentence added to cover fourteen years as Surveyor and later Controller of the Navy, three years sea service as an Admiral, and a Home Port command. That Walker oversaw the introduction of screw steam warships, and the first ironclads passes without notice, as does his role in the strategy of the Crimean War, and the defeat of the French naval challenge between 1852 and 1862. In a rare case of omission Laughton denied Charles Yorke, Fourth Earl of Hardwicke his final sea-going command, and gave him scant credit for service as a Tory cabinet minister. Elsewhere he has been criticised as dogmatic and, if only occasionally, inaccurate.[77]

These reservations aside, Laughton's *DNB* essays, which totalled over 1000 pages, made a massive contribution to the development of naval history. As Leslie Stephen had intended, they took it out of the age of myths and romances, and into the modern era of careful research and measured analysis. In his 'Laughton Memorial Lecture' Julian Corbett declared that the articles were Laughton's greatest contribution, that they had 're-written our naval history' and should be published as a stand alone work.[78] He doubtless knew that Laughton had approached the publishers more than once with the same idea, but without success.[79]

---

76. Laughton to Corbett 1.2.1895 Corbett MS Box 14.
77. Rodger, N A M, *The Wooden World.* (London 1986), p270.
78. Corbett, J S, 'The Revival of Naval History', *The Contemporary Review* off print p1.
79. Smith, Elder and Co. to Laughton 18.3.1907. JKL MS.

When he joined the mainstream academic community, Laughton was exposed to new methods of study. From the wide range of approaches then in use the one that had the greatest impact on him was the edition of primary source documents. Once again Gardiner provided the catalyst; this time as Director of the Camden Society (1869-97). Founded in 1838 'for the publication of Early Historical or Literary Remains', by 1860 the Society emphasised historical material by 1860, an emphasis it retained this until it amalgamated into the Royal Historical Society in 1897.[80] Gardiner persuaded Laughton to edit the manuscript *Memoirs relating to the Lord Torrington,* which appeared in 1889.[81] The original manuscript covered the career of Admiral Sir George Byng down to January 1705.[82] It had been purchased for the British Museum in 1882. Laughton admired Byng and twenty years later persuaded Herbert Richmond to begin his historical studies with a paper on Byng's victory at Cape Passaro.[83] Editing this volume brought Laughton into the Camden Society, and the Royal Historical Society. It provided him with the experience and many of the academic contacts he used to organise the Navy Records Society. In 1897 Gardiner became a member of the Royal Commission on Historical Manuscripts.[84] Once again he involved Laughton in his work, but the *Report on the Manuscripts of Lady du Cane,* only appeared in 1906, four years after Gardiner's death.[85] The material largely consists of the papers of Vice-Admiral Henry Medley (1687?-1747), for the period 1720 to 1747, at the end of which he was Commander-in-Chief in the Mediterranean. It includes captured material belonging to the French Captain de Caylus. As an example of Laughton's work the report was a solid, scholarly effort, similar in intent, if rather superior in delivery, to *Torrington.* It was restricted to reporting the evidence; there were no lessons, no particular strategic or tactical issues to consider, merely an interesting addition to the store of published literature. The edited volume of documents would remain his preferred format for historical scholarship for the rest of his life.

The foundation of the *English Historical Review* (*EHR*) in 1886 provided a vital focus for the professionalisation of English History. As the second editor, from 1891 until his death in 1902, Gardiner used his

80. Johnson, C, 'The Camden Society' in Humphreys, R A, *The Royal Historical Society 1868-1968* (London 1969), pp52-67, quote at p53.
81. Laughton, J K (ed), *Memoirs Relating to the Lord Torrington* (London, Camden Society Vol XLVI 1889).
82. Not Admiral Sir Arthur Herbert, the previous Lord Torrington, who had been disgraced after the Battle of Beachy Head. They are confused in Schurman's account p90.
83. Laughton to Corbett 19.12.1905 Corbett MS Deed Box C. NMM see Tunstall, W J C (ed. Tracey, N), *Naval Warfare in the Age of Sail* (London 1990), p69.
84. On the origins and work of the Royal Commission see: *Manuscripts and Men: the Centenary of the Royal Commission on Historical Manuscripts 1869-1969* (London 1969).
85. Laughton, J K (ed), *Report on the Manuscripts of Lady Du Cane* (London HMC 1905).

journal to support naval history, and *the* naval historian. Recognition in the leading professional journal ensured that Laughton, and the cause he sought to further, were well received. While Laughton's contributions to the *EHR* were restricted to one article, one notice and eight reviews, all of which were published between 1889 and 1898, his work was reviewed on six occasions, between 1888 and 1914. While Laughton could not afford to take a central role in the new enterprise, because it quickly ceased to pay for articles, his standing in the profession was clear from the reviews he received and, even more significantly, from the material he was selected to review. This included Mahan's *Life of Nelson*, Corbett's *Drake and the Tudor Navy* and Gardiner's *History of the Commonwealth and Protectorate*. Laughton's two extended pieces, both published in 1889 under Mandell Creighton's editorship, were typical of his output at the time, built on the *Studies* essays, examining and correcting existing accounts. One provided archival support for a notable incident in the famous memoirs of a Protestant French galley slave, the other demonstrated that the unfortunate Captain Richard Jenkins really did lose his ear to Spanish *guarda costas*.[86] Notices of his work recognised the originality of his *Studies in Naval History*, the quality of his Navy Records Society volumes and the work of the Society generally.[87] Few were in any doubt that the intended audience for his work was the contemporary Royal Navy. The most important contribution of the *EHR* to Laughton's work was Gardiner's notice of the foundation of the Navy Records Society. In July 1893 he described Laughton, with some justification as 'our naval Plutarch' and urged his fellow scholars to support the enterprise.[88] The only reviewer to be openly critical, Major Martin Hume, editor of *The Calendar of Spanish State Papers of Elizabeth I*, considered that his *State Papers on the Defeat of the Spanish Armada* had said little about the origins of the war, and downplayed the religious element. Hume was either ignorant of the object of the volume, or had failed to notice that it was restricted to the year 1588. Never a man to forget a slight, Laughton took his revenge three years later, reviewing Hume's popular life of Raleigh with cutting efficiency: 'For a careful and scholarly biography of Raleigh there was and is still room; but we have had enough of mere popular stories, such as Major Hume has apparently aimed at producing'.[89] Although Laughton would accept advice and criticism from

---

86. Laughton, J.K, 'The Captains of the *Nightingale*', *The English Historical Review (EHR)* Vol IV (1889), pp65-80: Laughton, J K, 'Jenkins's Ear', *EHR* Vol IV (1889) pp741-9.

87. See Mahan's review of Leyland, J (ed), *Documents and Letters relating to the Blockade of Brest 1803-05* (London NRS) 2 vols. 1899 and 1902 at *EHR* (1903) pp185-8, esp. p188 where he commends Laughton's methods.

88. *EHR* (1893), p608.

89. *EHR* (1895), pp365-9; *EHR* (1898), p363. JKL's work appeared in the *EHR* in 1888-90, 1893, 1895, 1897 and 1898.

fellow scholars and naval officers, he had little time for the remarks of those without appropriate standing. Working on the *EHR* with Creighton and Gardiner ensured that Laughton, and more especially his subject, were at the core of English History. The *EHR* was central to the professionalisation of history in England, a process in which it was ably seconded by the foundation of learned publishing societies, notably the Navy Records.[90]

As might be expected of a scholar with a large family and a small income, Laughton's *oeuvre* was characterised by repetition and re-use. He never threw anything away, and was always prepared to re-deploy his learning in a new guise. This reflected financial pressures, which were also evident in a number of unambitious pot-boilers.[91] However, this was not a static process. Laughton's base of knowledge continued to grow, as did the sophistication of his analysis. Dan Baugh has observed: 'Throughout Laughton's career he encouraged Naval Historians to abandon their narrow focus on "the fighting" and attempt to examine naval history within the context of national development'.[92] The sheer scale of his output, particularly in the 1890s, including two books, four edited volumes, two major papers, contributions to the *DNB* and numerous long review articles, ensured that there would be some overlap. Convinced that his educational purpose could only be served by accurate work, he had to re-use and develop a few subjects to meet his needs, until he had a larger *corpus* with which to work. The subjects on which he wrote most often were the Armada, which illustrated the naval role in strategic defence, and Nelson, who was the key to teaching leadership and the development of doctrine.

In 1888, its tercentenary, Laughton lectured on 'The Invincible Armada', at the Royal Institution. The paper reflected his new 'academic' style, using source analysis, primary materials and informed criticism to demythologise the subject. He concluded by pointing out the contemporary lesson, for those in the audience who had been asleep:

> the lesson stands out for our instruction and imitation, that 300 years ago, although our Navy was then starved – pretty much as it is now – still by care ingenuity, and supervision our ships were more handy, more weatherly, more heavily armed than those of our enemy; and, above all, they were ready when wanted. Today neither our ships nor our guns are better than those of our neighbours; and according to official statements many of our largest ships are practically useless for want of guns which are

---

90. Levine, P, *The Amateur and the Professional: Antiquarians, Historians and Archaeologists in Victorian England, 1838-86* (Cambridge 1986).
91. Laughton, J K, etc. *The Story of the Sea* (London 1895-6). Laughton, J K, *Sea Fights and Adventures* (London 1901).
92. Baugh, D, in Higham, R (ed), *British Military History* (London 1971), pp84-97.

not yet made. Money will do a great deal, but the want here shown is not that of money, but of intelligence, care, judgement, and economy.[93]

Two weeks later Bridge drove home the point with a letter to *The Times:*

> So long as a conflict is to be apprehended we should direct all the energies of our defence to becoming supreme on the element on which a maritime, and especially an insular, State is most likely to have its opponents at a disadvantage. Till we have secured undisputed command of the sea, till our trade can pass over it unmolested, we should not think of, much less make preparations for, Continental expeditions.[94]

Laughton's paper was well received. Philip Colomb praised it highly and re-used a large part of it as the relevant section of his book *Naval Warfare,* in what must be one of the longest attributed quotations in the canon.[95] In 1894 Laughton exploited his expertise to edit the first Navy Records Society Volume, *State Papers relating to the Defeat of the Spanish Armada.* The 84-page 'Introduction' demonstrated Laughton's mastery of the archive. His object was demolish the argument that the wind had scattered an otherwise unbroken Armada, instead demonstrating that the navy had defeated the invasion attempt. This was an important contribution to the contemporary defence debate, in which the unequivocal establishment that naval defence was effective had real value. These volumes remain the basis of Armada historiography.[96] The same material, enhanced by a small number of subsequent publications, reappeared in his essay on Lord Howard of Effingham in the textbook *From Howard to Nelson* in 1899, and the chapter 'The Elizabethan Naval War with Spain' in Volume Three of *The Cambridge Modern History,* which appeared in 1907, although it had been commissioned by Lord Acton in the late 1890s. Significantly he did not re-write the material, merely re-editing the earlier version. The *Cambridge Modern History* chapter remains an important study, marred only by Acton's policy of not using footnotes. It provided insights that were subsequently forgotten, to be rediscovered at the quatracentenary. These include the critical impact of Drake's raid of 1587 in destroying the stock of seasoned barrel staves, and the superior calibre and number of English heavy guns. Recent archaeological evidence has supplemented his work, while further examination of the

---

93. *The Times* Monday 7 May 1888, p7. Lecture given on Friday 4 May. I am indebted to my student Robert Mullins for this and the following reference.
94. Bridge, *The Times,* Wednesday 23 May 1888 p6.
95. Laughton, J K, 'The Invincible Armada', *The Royal Institution* (1888). Colomb, P H, *Naval Warfare* (London 1891), pp228-43.
96. Laughton to Corbett 3.1.1895 and 1.2.1895. Knerr, D, 'Through the "Golden Mist": A Brief overview of Armada Historiography', *The American Neptune* Vol XLIX (1988), pp5-13.

Spanish archive has revealed more of the decision-making process of Philip II.[97] Laughton's contribution to Acton's project marked the coming of age of naval history in the academic world. It was an appropriate point at which to end work on the Armada.

Between 1885 and 1896 Laughton published three books on Nelson, establishing himself as the leading English authority. The Nelson he wrote about was the basis for the inculcation of professional education and an enhanced national awareness of the Navy. After the 1886 volume of correspondence he wrote two short biographies, one for MacMillan's 'English Men of Action' series of 1889, and the illustrated *The Nelson Memorial: Nelson and His Companions* of 1896. The biographies were popular works, written to order, for profit. Both were revised and reprinted in cheaper editions and were his most successful books. *The Times* praised the 'direct and vivid style' of his 'Men of Action' study, and noted his reversal of Southey's account of Nelson's actions at Naples.[98] The review was probably written by his friend James Thursfield. In writing the second biography he had the doubtful advantage of advice from Earl Nelson, who did not believe Horatia was Lady Hamilton's daughter, let alone Nelson's.[99] The second biography clearly re-used earlier material, a method revealed by the bibliography and a close reading of the text. However, that should not condemn the book, for Laughton was too well informed and too intelligent to write a bad book on Nelson, even when working to schedule. He stressed that Nelson, if unique, was not the only outstanding officer of his generation and that it took more than one man to win the war at sea. Mahan, upset at being 'scooped' on certain Nelson material, was not an entirely unbiased commentator. He considered it, 'a sketchy – possibly hasty book by a man widely read and thoroughly posted on his subject – but I question whether he has had the time or space to do justice to his knowledge'.[100] It is ironic that Mahan's more ambitious text, which he considered his best book, has become too large for modern tastes.[101]

The speed at which Laughton worked resulted in occasional errors of fact and judgement. Perhaps the most obvious was the frontispiece of the *Memorial*, which purported to be a representation of the Trafalgar Signal, which he gave using the 1808 signal book, rather than the 1799 book that

97. Martin, C, and Parker, G, *The Spanish Armada* (London 1988) esp. p196 for the artillery question.
98. *The Times* 15.8.1895 p6.
99. Nelson to Laughton 25.10 189 ––. Miscellaneous correspondence regarding this and subsequent Nelson projects: JKL MS.
100. Mahan to John M. Brown 15.12.1896 and Mahan to J. Franklin Johnson 16.12.1896: Seager, R, and Maguire, D D (eds), *Letters and Papers of Alfred Thayer Mahan* (Annapolis 1975), Vol II, p477.
101. Mahan, A T, *The Life of Nelson: The Embodiment of the Seapower of Great Britain* (Boston 1899) 2 vols.

Nelson used.[102] Less obviously he put the time of Nelson's withdrawal from before Copenhagen as the evening, which supported his case for Nelson's good faith in his offer of an armistice to the Danes. The error was pointed out by Mahan, who had copies of the log-books.[103] In his review of Mahan's *Nelson* Laughton admitted his error, leaving Nelson's conduct to 'rest on its own merits'![104] Galling as such matters must have been to a man who prided himself on exactness, they were part of the price he had to pay for the sheer scale and variety of his activity, for even as he moved to King's College, and became an academic historian, he was also maturing into a significant critic of contemporary naval policy.

Although he served the Navy loyally for thirty years, Laughton never accepted official policies unthinkingly. For him true loyalty required that he use his talent to further the interests of the service. This was an approach he shared with many of the junior officers that he taught, with the Junior Naval Professional Association of the 1870s, and most notably with Bridge. Both men began by questioning the accepted wisdom in specific areas, tactics and education being the most important, but by the end of the 1870s, after the collapse of the first naval intellectual movement, they were questioning the higher direction of the service. Bridge was a major, if unsigned, contributor to the *Pall Mall Gazette* in the late 1870s. When he was appointed, at very short notice, to a ship on the Australian Station in October 1881 he turned over the position, together with his old essays and other advice, to Laughton. Bridge argued that the Navy was in good order, with a few exceptions. These were the educational system, the lack of an effective reserve drawn from the mercantile marine, and the 'atrociously inefficient' muzzle-loading armament. This last was entirely the fault of the Army Director of Artillery. Bridge criticised over-large battleships like the *Inflexible*, the idea that France was a real naval challenge and the 'denavalisation' of the country.[105] This was a sound, realistic assessment. Curiously there are no letters from Bridge in Laughton's archive between October 1881 and 1886, the period when Laughton replaced Bridge as the leading authority on naval policy in the *Edinburgh Review*. The timing was peculiarly propitious, as in 1884 naval policy suddenly became a topic of widespread interest. Because his contributions were unsigned, his naval policy debate has been ignored. However, his close friends were always privy to the secret, while any intelligent reader would have unlocked the anonymity with ease.

---

102. Bridge to Laughton 21.12.1897 JKL MS. which predates the correction offered in: White, C (ed), *The Nelson Companion* (Gloucester 1995), p190.
103. Mahan to Laughton 28.8.1895 JKL MS.
104. Laughton, *EHR* (1897) pp801-5, at p805.
105. Bridge to Laughton 23.10.1881 JKL MS. Bridge, C A G, *Some Recollections* (London 1918), pp226-7.

The emergence of the Navy as a major topic of public concern coincided with the Home Rule crisis. After 1886 the *Edinburgh* was a Whig/Liberal Imperialist journal, and doubted the possibility of a Liberal reunion under Gladstone.[106] Over the next decade the politics of the journal, and the shift in Laughton's own politics, were closely aligned. His strategic ideas were subject to less change. In 1882 he reviewed the first two volumes of Sir Thomas Brassey's monumental five-volume *The British Navy* and Lord Henry Lennox's alarmist *Forewarned, Forearmed*. He opened by linking the piece to Bridge's last (unsigned) contribution, and praised Brassey's liberality in publishing the book at his own expense. The comment suggests why Laughton produced so little in book form. By contrast Lennox, the erstwhile Tory minister, received short shrift for his party-political attack on the Liberal government. Lord Henry based his argument on an erroneous calculation of French strength in First Class battleships. In Parliament he had claimed there were thirty-eight, in print he cut this figure to fifteen, but Laughton settled on ten, of which six were old ships with wooden hulls. The Royal Navy had twenty-three equivalent ships. He then despatched the strategic argument that in a war with France 60 per cent of the Royal Navy would be required to defend the colonies.

> The fact is that in any such war our colonies would be mainly protected in European seas, in the Bay of Biscay, or in the Mediterranean: it is there that any hostile expedition ought to be crushed; it is there that our ironclad fleet would be massed, detaching only individual members of it for special service, or to arrange for those already detached by the enemy. In their own waters, against mere predatory attacks, the colonies must largely trust to local armaments, to floating batteries or torpedoes, to the light cruisers, and above all to a well-devised system of intelligence.[107]

The primacy of the Home, Grand or Channel Fleet was, and remained, the basis of British strategy. Tirpitz would have benefited from reading this passage. Laughton doubted that 'the real strength of a navy is to be estimated solely, or even chiefly, by its armoured ships', citing the views of Admiral Aube, founder of the *Jeune Ecole*, that in future the role of ironclads would be limited, while commerce destroyers roamed the sea at will. For, Laughton observed, 'To prey on commerce is easier than to protect it', citing John Colomb on the role of trade routes and strategic crossings, which, the Hydrographer Captain Hull argued, would be the scene of future naval battles. In this he supported John Colomb, a fellow

106. Clive, J, 'The Edinburgh Review' in Briggs, A (ed), *Essays in the History of Publishing: Longmans* (London 1974), pp115-140.
107. 'Sir Thomas Brassey on the British Navy' *The Edinburgh Review* (April 1882), pp477-504 at pp486-7.

'scientific' analyst, in creating the fallacy that there were 'Sea Lines of Communication'. While it was relatively easy to calculate departures, and mark out the approved routes on a chart, there was nothing sacrosanct about any specific course. Despite this unnecessarily focused concern he saw grounds for comfort. British cruiser and armed merchant cruiser strength was even greater in proportion than her ironclad fleet. Only the guns, returning to Bridge's line, were inferior, although improvements were in hand. He praised Brassey for considering the men, 'the very soul of the machine', who were ignored by other commentators.[108] Brassey had cited Xavier Raymond's 1863 essay comparing Britain and France as naval powers, in which he concluded that Britain had an overwhelming advantage in the scale and skill of her maritime labour force, as well as the other two constituents of seapower, material wealth and a dynamic industry. Laughton argued, on the basis of his earlier 'Studies' papers, that the Royal Navy was:

> unequivocally the most powerful navy in the world – behind our navy we have, as a second line of defence, a maritime force whose strength is not the less real because it has none of the pomp or circumstance of war, and is hidden from public consideration in the pursuit of its daily industry.

The real naval balance between Britain and France remained much as it had been when Raymond wrote. The Navy was a national issue, and the alarm that the opposition was trying to excite was no more real than those of the 1850s and 1860s. It was a party-political manoeuvre that had nothing to do with the underlying continuity and wisdom of naval policy. That a Liberal navalist should say this in a Liberal journal, repudiating Tory cries of alarm, on the evidence of the Liberal Naval Civil Lord of the Admiralty was hardly surprising. The skill with which he assembled his evidence, the breadth of his understanding, and the coherence of his case were altogether more impressive.[109] The essentially moderate naval policy he advocated was close to that of the Admiralty Board under his old friend Key. Although Key was rapidly forgotten once he had left the Admiralty in mid-1885, he had made real progress during his administration in ship-building and gun design at a time when few bothered to think about the Navy.[110]

After 1880 the administration of the Navy was subject to increasing criticism. In 1884 H O Arnold-Foster persuaded the editor of the ostensibly liberal *Pall Mall Gazette*, W T Stead to complete the task, already largely carried through in the popular press, of getting up a scare with his

108. Ibid, p502.
109. Ibid, p504.
110. Mackay, R F, *Fisher of Kilverstone* (Oxford 1973) pp178-9.

articles 'The Truth about the Navy'. Stead consulted Fisher, through Admiral Hoskins, although Hornby, to whom Fisher was now closely linked, was manipulating the move.[111] The alarm was raised in September 1884, exploited by Key and largely silenced by the 'Northbrook' construction programme, named for the absentee First Lord, in early December.[112] The scare was premature; neither the foreign threat, nor the naval technology of the day warranted a sudden increase in construction. The 'Northbrook' ships were the last ironclads, including the ill-fated *Victoria*. They were rapidly outmoded, unlike those built for the Naval Defence Act of 1889, which were altogether better balanced and remained effective far longer.

In 1885 Laughton had two opportunities to reflect on the scare. He concentrated on the criticisms of those whose careers and experience gave them some claim to expertise. The scare had raised a vital question. Was the Navy adequate? If it was then the latest outburst was a deliberate falsehood, and should be exposed, if not 'it is impossible to . . . find language strong enough to condemn the torpor or the parsimony of the Government which has permitted a blight so deadly to fall upon us'.[113] He quickly disposed of the eighteenth-century Two Power standard, which he argued had been based on keeping old hulks on the Navy list, and did not reflect on the very real Two Power standard that was adopted in 1817 and sustained thereafter.[114] In all probability he was unaware of it. In fact the Admiralty response to the Franco-Spanish challenge of 1763-93 was remarkably like a true 'Two Power Standard' and the rotten hulks were largely imagined by critics of the Admiralty. Laughton concluded that 'so far as its capital ships are concerned, our Navy has never, in time of peace, been relatively stronger than it is at the present day'.[115] He singled out Admiral Sir Thomas Symonds and his one-time collaborator Sir Edward Reed for particular censure; the former for failing to understand the issue, the latter for dishonesty.[116] He recognised that the Navy would need to be reconstructed within a few years, and deprecated wasting money on ironclads.

We have therefore no hesitation in saying that the outcry of urgency which has been raised is entirely uncalled for, is mischievous and dangerous. Panic

---

111. Ibid, pp180-5.
112. Marder, A J, *The Anatomy of British Sea Power* (London 1940), pp121-3.
113. 'Past and Present State of the Navy', *The Edinburgh Review* (April 1885), pp492-513 at p493.
114. Lambert, A D, *The Last Sailing Battlefleet: Maintaining Naval Mastery 1815-1850* (London 1991), p5.
115. 'Past and Present State . . . p499.
116. **Symonds**, Admiral of the Fleet Sir Thomas Matthew Charles (1813-94). C-in-C Channel 1868-70, Devonport 1875-78. Brilliant ship handler, later a significant tactical thinker and amateur ship designer.

and wild expenditures are fatal to the permanent efficiency of the navy, and few things could be more injurious than that we should be weighted with a large number of ships, unnecessary now, and likely to become obsolete almost before they are launched. The increase which the Admiralty, yielding to some extent to popular clamour, has now asked the House of Commons to provide for, is not sufficient to bring this evil on us; and the laying down of four ironclads instead of two is but a forestalment of the necessary work of providing against deterioration and decay.[117]

He went on to repeat his argument that the real problem would be the defence of trade, for the great prizes in any future sea war would not be Spanish treasure ships but British vessels carrying Australian gold and Cape diamonds. To defend British commerce would require fast 'cruiser-destroyers' capable of at least 18 knots. These would be provided by that great liberal gun-founder and shipbuilder, Sir William Armstrong of Tyneside, whose famous Chilean cruiser *Esmeralda* was held up as an ideal. They should be built in lieu of the two extra ironclads. He also called for a considerable increase in the number of torpedo boats, both to serve with the fleet and as an alternative to land-based harbour and coast defence systems. In concluding he attributed the alarm of 1884 to 'ignorance of the facts', for 'panic is the child of darkness and ignorance; with light and knowledge comes a return of steadfast courage and sober judgement'.[118] In July he discussed naval tactics, the impact of torpedo boats and the *Jeune Ecole*. He recognised that war at sea would change. As Whitehead torpedoes could now range out to 400 yards they had replaced the ram, but they would not revolutionise war at sea. Similarly he observed that the French were still searching for a system of war at sea to circumvent the innate superiority of Britain in seamanship and seafaring population. This was doomed to fail, for the end of masts and yards had only introduced a new kind of seamanship, the sort so sadly wanting in the recent disastrous ramming accidents.[119]

The three reviews were consistent, coherent and persuasive. They provided a powerful alternative to the party-political, opportunistic outpourings that dominated the 1884 scare. Laughton was an inside reformer. He deprecated appeals to 'popular' opinion as necessarily exaggerated, simplistic and transitory. That the alarmists spent their time childishly making up more or less inaccurate lists of First Class battleships when the real danger would come from a direct attack on merchant shipping was indicative of the intellectual level of the so-called 'debate'. As Laughton made clear in his references the key to naval security lay in understanding the nature of the threat, and developing the intellectual apparatus to

117. 'Past and Present State', p508.
118. Ibid, p513.
119. 'Naval Warfare', *The Edinburgh Review* (July 1885), pp234-64.

control the response. He supported John Colomb's efforts, and would have approved the work of the Carnarvon Committee, had it ever come into the public domain.[120]

Not only did Laughton's discussion of naval policy comprise a significantly smaller proportion of his output than was the case with the other historian/strategists of the pre-1914 period, it was also essentially reactive. Being confined to the review format meant that he was dependant on the availability of literature, and the interest of the editor. In the latter case he was well served by Henry Reeve, but it is noteworthy that after 1885 his next discussion of contemporary naval policy came in 1890, following another year of panic and response. Despite that he exercised significant influence.

One important result of the growing public interest in naval and defence issues was the close co-operation between Laughton and Philip Colomb. Both men had been significant contributors to the tactical debate of the 1860s and 1870s, from distinct standpoints in technology and history. Now their interests had shifted to strategy, and there was a growing meeting of minds, a trend reinforced by regular contact at the RUSI. Colomb had been influenced by Laughton's 'Scientific Study' paper, with clear references in his work from 1878. His decisive switch to an historical methodology came in the late 1880s.[121] Having completed his work on the signal book in 1886 Colomb replaced Laughton at Greenwich in 1887, lecturing on Naval Strategy and Tactics. The content of Colomb's course was closely reflected in his 1891 book *Naval Warfare*, which was written at the same time. History provided the evidence for discussions of principles and concepts.[122] When Colomb devoted his intellectual energies to the 'larger questions of Imperial Defence' he did so using a history-based methodology derived from Laughton. *Naval Warfare* was 'an attempt to show how naval warfare was as strictly governed and limited by rule, as warfare on land, though no previous writer had attempted to show it'.[123] There are striking parallels between the ambition of Colomb's book and the almost exactly contemporaneous work of Mahan. Both were seeking principles to guide the conduct of naval operations, and looked to military examples for inspiration.

In March 1889 Colomb defended the use of history as the basis for strategic studies in a heated debate at the RUSI, strongly supported by

---

120. For the debate on the defence of trade at this time see: Ranft, B McL, 'The Protection of British Seaborne Trade and the Development of Systematic Planning for War, 1860-1906' in Ranft (ed), *Technical Change and British Naval Policy 1860-1939* (London 1977), pp1-23.
121. Schurman, pp40-1.
122. Copy of Colomb's 1887-88 Course Exam Paper: Hornby MS PHI/120c/part 8. I am indebted to my student Robert Mullins for locating this paper.
123. 'Memoir of Vice-Admiral Philip Howard Colomb' unpub. MS in private hands.

Laughton in the audience. Colomb's object had been to demolish the case for a further round of fortifications, which were to be paid for by cutting the naval budget. While the strategic principles were those of his brother, the argument and the evidence were Laughton's. Laughton knew that only an officer could make this case to a service audience.[124] His efforts were crowned with success. Colomb was among the most important strategic thinkers of the period; in combination with his brother John, he pioneered the use of strategic studies to develop a national strategy. His principle defect, which Laughton recognised, was a lack of precision. When he became an historically-based strategist Colomb exploited Laughton's work, using several pages on the Armada verbatim, while Laughton's 1892 essay on Beachy Head required him to rewrite his own account for the second edition of his book. Colomb remained an important figure in the service, even after his retirement, with many followers among the intellectuals. His support for Laughton's work was unreserved, and on occasion, very important.

The next round of alarm culminated in the Naval Defence Act of 1889, a five-year programme to build ten battleships, nine large and twenty-nine small cruisers and other vessels. It was linked to a re-assertion of the Two Power Standard, necessitated by the increasingly tense state of European politics. Laughton made a powerful contribution to this debate with his 'Armada' lecture. For his review considered the true function of the Navy in national strategy, and attacked the defeatist arguments that underpinned the construction of costly and unnecessary forts. He adopted Philip Colomb's maxim that 'the frontier of our Empire is the enemy's coast' and attacked Admiral Hood for denying the possibility of defending Britain's burgeoning maritime commerce, because this would encourage those who wanted to restrict defences to the British isles alone, and transfer the shipping to a neutral flag. This last, a fatuous proposal, had already been exploded by a French declaration that such transfers would not be respected. History demonstrated that while absolute security could not be provided for maritime commerce a relative, and advantageous balance of captures would result once Britain had defeated the enemy fleet.[125] In 1890 Mahan made this point with a comparison of commerce-destroying by *guerre de course* and by command of the sea.[126] The latter was, as Laughton argued, critical for insular security. To secure it Britain required a battlefleet, with the minimum standard being

---

124. Gough, B, introduction to his edition of *Naval Warfare* (Annapolis 1991), pxx, quoting from Schurman *Education*, p42.
125. 'Naval Supremacy and Naval Tactics', *The Edinburgh Review* (January 1890), pp146-78 at p148.
126. Mahan, A T, *The Influence of Sea Power Upon History 1660-1782* (Boston 1890), pp132-3.

Colomb's 'Fleet in Being', for to abandon command of the Channel was national suicide.

> This is not to be considered as, in any sense, a question of rival services: it is a question of the integrity and even of the existence of the Empire. No-one pretends that the most stupendous fortifications can defend anything but the one spot where they are placed. They can do absolutely nothing to prevent an enemy landing on any convenient beach; nothing to preserve intact our commerce, or the communications with our remote dependencies. But those who know the power of a fleet, contend that it can, at one and the same time, secure our commerce, our communications, our shores and our arsenals; and that the same strength which can secure the first, can secure all the others. But there must be the sufficient strength, and that necessarily involves a sufficient outlay, and therefore a rigorous economy.[127]

He also intervened in the debate between Spenser Wilkinson and Colomb as to the definition of a 'Fleet in Being'.[128] He supported Colomb, arguing that the term only applied to a fleet capable of coming out to engage the enemy. It did not cover a mere collection of ships, or a fleet like the Russians at Cronstadt in 1854, too weak to be a threat. When Lord Torrington coined the phrase, after the defeat at Beachy Head, he was confident that he could sortie out and stop any French attempt to invade England.[129]

Laughton adopted the wisdom of the old wars, and of more recent authorities, among whom he named Hornby, Key and Fanshawe, that the first stage of this defence would be to blockade the enemy's harbours. He adopted Colomb's argument that there were several distinct types of blockade, only some of which remained appropriate to modern conditions. With suitable forces, fortified harbours could be blockaded by a superior fleet, and until that fleet had been beaten there was no danger of an invasion. Consequently heavy local defences were a waste of effort, an opinion in which the late Inspector General of Fortifications, Sir Andrew Clarke, concurred, having long recognised that the Navy was critical to British Imperial power and diplomatic weight. His letter to *The Times* in 1889 had been a powerful reinforcement for the naval cause.[130] Overseas fortresses were equally futile, because while Britain had command of the sea they were unnecessary, and if it was lost they were indefensible. He considered that the role of the fortress in the Russian War was quite

---

127. 'Naval Supremacy' pp151-2.
128. **Wilkinson**, Henry Spenser (1853-1937). Defence correspondent, Military Historian and Chichele Professor of the History of War at Oxford.
129. *The Times* 23.10.1894 p4: Laughton letter of 20.10.1894.
130. Vetch, R H, *Life of Lieutenant General Sir A. Clarke* (London 1905), pp289-90. Clarke served on the Council of the Navy Records Society between 1893 and 1898.

E.G - SINGAPORE

inapplicable to the case of Britain. Russia could not be starved, therefore Cronstadt was a useful strongpoint. But holding Portsmouth or Gravesend would not feed the people; 'to us, and to us alone among nations, the strength of the Navy is the very life of the Empire; that on it our being depends; and that its welfare is, to the Government, a trust of transcendent importance'.[131] As modern wars began so suddenly, and often ended quickly, it was no longer realistic to wait for the imminent outbreak of war to build the necessary ships. Because Europe was already resting on, 'a powder magazine', something had been done in 1889.

Laughton was less happy with the eight *Royal Sovereign* class battleships that lay at the heart of the Naval Defence Act. He preferred ships of 9-10,000 tons to these 14,000-ton giants, and reckoned their 6in quickfiring guns would be the real main armament. The putative main armament, four 67-ton 13.5in pieces, were altogether too clumsy for his taste, he preferred the 22-ton 10in gun in this role. The 'hail of shot and shell' produced by small guns would quickly disable the heavier guns. He preferred the two Second Class battleships provided in the programme, the *Centurion* and *Barfleur*, which were markedly inferior in every respect except shallow draft, having been designed to navigate the Suez Canal and the Yangtze. Yet, under the influence of Laughton, and Bridge, they were widely accepted as the acme of excellence, and provided Reginald Custance with his pen-name. Laughton was also critical of the armoured or belted cruiser, which 'according to all the principles of naval strategy . . . are an anomaly', being unable to contend with capital ships. He suggested their tonnage would be far better spread over a larger number of 3000-ton ships without armour.[132] Here he was on more reliable historical ground.   YES

The need for additional cruisers reflected his conviction that the Declaration of Paris would not be adhered to in the event of war. In the Channel naval defence would require an almost omnipresent system of patrolling cruisers to deal with a swarm of light raiders. Further out he was inclined to fall into the 'sea lanes of communication' fallacy that has exercised so baleful an influence over twentieth-century naval strategy. Matthew Fontaine Maury's ideal sailing ship routes effectively channelled American sailing ships into areas where Confederate States' steam cruisers captured them with ease. Laughton, who had studied Maury's work in the 1860s, and adopted John Colomb's ideas, was an easy convert to this thesis. These 'sea-lanes' he suggested, were known, and the points where they intersected should be patrolled. This strategy would have very quickly dealt with the *Alabama*, as her captain testified. That it would be

131. 'Naval Supremacy', p166.
132. Ibid, p171-2.

THIS IS A RIDICULOUS STATEMENT! IT IGNORES THE MUCH LONGER RANGE OF A BIG GUN expensive to acquire the necessary warships he did not doubt, but looked on the cost as 'a fair insurance premium'.[133] The warships would be supported by the fastest mercantile steamers, left under their own officers, as Royal Naval Reserve commands going about their regular business, but well armed to keep the routes clear. This system was preferable to existing arrangements because it avoided the disruption occasioned by moving the officers and men into warships. With an adequate force of cruisers, well deployed, 'there can be no serious cause for apprehension'.[134] Against the very limited threat posed by the national cruiser fleets of France and Russia, even if reinforced by their ocean-going liners, this was entirely correct.

This essay marked a significant shift from the papers of 1882 and 1885. It advocated a significant increase in naval preparedness, because the state of Europe was now more threatening. To suggest that Laughton was more critical because the ministers were Tory would be an injustice, but only partially. The politics of the *Edinburgh Review* had changed, and Laughton knew Reeve too well not to reflect the fact in his work. Naval defence had become a major issue, and would remain at the forefront of popular attention for the next thirty years. While Laughton was responding to this phenomenon he was doing so from a uniquely well-informed standpoint.

His next contribution addressed the more specific question of fortification, but rapidly moved onto a higher level of analysis.[135] The paper began as a review of Major George Sydenham Clarke RE's *Fortification*. Bridge, impressed by Clarke's iconoclastic opinions, made Laughton promise to review it in the Conservative *Quarterly Review*. He wanted 'to keep the noticing of the book out of the hands of these mere bricklaying passive defence engineers who have got a foot hold in nearly every newspaper and periodical in London'.[136]

Clarke argued that costly permanent systems of fortification rarely gave any better results than the most hastily thrown-up earthworks, provided the latter were designed from first principles. Therefore the British Empire should not waste money and effort on large-scale permanent works, particularly not at the expense of the fleet, which alone could guarantee Imperial Security.[137] Laughton's influence on the book was, large, if unacknowledged.[138] Clarke committed some cardinal errors of

---

133. Ibid, p177.
134. Ibid, p178.
135. Bridge persuaded Laughton to write this review, stressing Clarke's astonishing breadth of view 'for a Sapper'. Bridge to Custance 15.11.1890 BRI/18 NMM.
136. Bridge to Custance 15.11.1890 BRI 18.
137. Clarke, G S, *Fortification* (London 1890, 2nd Ed. 1907).
138. Clarke based his discussion of Thurot at p172 on Laughton's essay, although he did not cite his source.

historical scholarship, both in the selection and use of evidence. While much of the book concerned works for land warfare, and Laughton was only interested in coast defence, he could not resist correcting the Colonel on details of land operations during the Franco-Prussian War. This helped to establish his credentials, and his methodology:

> the key to the problem seems to us to lie in the experience of the past, and in the study of our history; not history carefully selected and manipulated, but history, as recorded in full, minute and exact detail.[139]

Clarke argued that offensive operations against the coast would only be undertaken by a force with absolute command of the sea, Laughton added the rider that this did not include the situation when the defending fleet was 'in being', a point developed by Philip Colomb. In 1690 and 1779 the French did nothing because they were held in check by a smaller fleet. In 1667 the Dutch raided the Medway because there was no fleet. Laughton considered it was unnecessary to erect any considerable fortification for the British dockyards, and drew strong support from St Vincent's condemnation of the 1785 plan to fortify the dockyards after the experience of 1779.[140] Indeed, any money spent on coastal fortification was 'utterly wasted'.[141] Forts had been necessary in Henry VIII's time, when the navy was weak, but this was no longer the case. For Laughton coast defence was required by

> the belligerent who is, and who contemplates being, the weaker at sea. For Russia, for Germany, for France, for Spain, for Italy, to defend their ports by batteries of the most scientific, and if necessary, the most costly construction, is imperatively demanded; for each of them may be engaged in a war with an enemy having a distinct naval superiority.[142]

Fortifications were useful to weaker powers, as Cronstadt had been for Russia in 1854-55. But the defences of the British dockyards had been pathetic throughout the Napoleonic Wars, with no ill effect. He also joined Philip Colomb in attacking the 1859 Royal Commission, which had set out the need for the fixed defences of the dockyards to be upgraded, even though they were told that the real need was to maintain command of the Channel.[143] Colomb had set out the key argument of the

---

139. 'Forts and Fleets', *The Quarterly Review* (April 1891), pp351-79 at p358.
140. Ehrman, J, *The Younger Pitt: Vol 1* (London 1969), pp518-9 for the 1785 fortification debate. Earl Howe, First Lord of the Admiralty also opposed the plan.
141. 'Forts and Fleets', p361.
142. Ibid.
143. Colomb, P H, 'The Naval Defences of the United Kingdom', *JRUSI* (1888) and 'The Relation between Local Fortifications and a Moving Navy', *JRUSI* (1889). Laughton was in the audience for the postponed debate on this epochal paper, which launched the 'Blue-Water' strategy.

'Blue-Water' navalists in 1888-89, and Laughton agreed with him, on the issue of forts at least. In this both were a little hard on the men of 1859, who had to make their decision at a time of profound uncertainty about the future balance of advantage between ships and forts. They seemed to have forgotten the sudden alarming dominance armoured warships had acquired over old fixed defences in 1855.[144]

Laughton was dismissive of the argument that the British fleet might be destroyed, or decoyed away. He reminded his readers that the so-called 'decoying' of Nelson by Villeneuve was the move of only a small portion of the British fleet, and did not give the French a chance to invade. In essence the level of fortification required for the home ports was entirely dependent upon the nature of the Navy that the nation intended to maintain. If the Navy remained dominant then he agreed with Clarke that there was little need for any local defences. He was also in agreement with the idea that ships would not in future engage batteries, but would land troops to capture them, as they had always done. He even managed to say a kind word for Sir Charles Napier, now that the lessons of 1854 supported his case.[145] Clarke's account of the use of converted muzzle-loading rifled guns as howitzers was particularly noted. It allowed Laughton to show that very little money need be spent on forts in order to hold off the latest battleships. Further afield the colonies were in no serious danger while Britain retained command of the sea, which he defined as:

> the power of conducting operations of naval war, such as territorial attack, the passage of troops, or the maintenance of communications, without the probability of being interfered with by the enemy; conversely, also, the power of interfering with or preventing such operations on the part of the enemy.[146]

This required the 'Grand Fleet' to mask the enemy fleet in its bases. He concluded that.

> We wish it to be recognised that, as our Empire has grown by our sea power, so by our sea power alone can it be maintained; and that the true problem of coast defence for us is not to find the minimum of naval strength needed to support the works on shore, but to ascertain the minimum of such works necessary to support the power of the navy . . . reliance on forts, harbour defences, submarine mines, is a first step towards relinquishing the command of the sea, on which our commerce, our Empire, and our national existence depend.[147]

---

144. For a discussion of the issues see Lambert, A D, 'Politics, Technology and Policy-Making 1859-65: Palmerston, Gladstone and the Management of the Ironclad Naval Race', *The Northern Mariner* (August 1998).
145. 'Forts and Fleets', p368.
146. Ibid, p374.
147. Ibid, pp378-9.

The coherence of Laughton's arguments, the linkage with his important early paper of 1877 on Thurot and the new 'historical' output of Philip Colomb, made 'Forts and Fleets' a paper of particular importance. It was flawed by an analytical sleight of hand that marred much of the navalist case. In arguing against the need for forts Laughton and others exaggerated their power to resist a direct attack by ships. It is one of the surpassing ironies of the navalist lobby of the 1890s that they made, and accepted, this case when three of their leading lights, Laughton, Mahan and Philip Colomb, had served in campaigns which had demonstrated the exact opposite. It is to their writings on this subject that we can trace much of the negative image of the strategic role of navies that has exercised such a distorting influence on the study of war in the twentieth century. The most obvious explanation for their accounts, which were mutually supportive and closely connected, was that their anxiety to make the case outweighed their scholarly scruples. Mahan's target was the 'Endicott' Programme of forts, which competed with the battlefleet for the American tax dollar, while Bridge's object in getting Laughton to make the case in a Tory journal during an important debate on the national defence were obvious. The Tories were always more favourable to a 'military' argument than the 'navalist' Liberals. In 1893 Laughton wrote another major review combining history and naval policy for the *Quarterly*.[148] More significantly Clarke quickly became one of Laughton's inner circle and a long-term supporter of the naval case, and naval history.

---

148. 'The Battle of La Hogue and Maritime War', *The Quarterly Review* (April 1893), pp484-518.

CHAPTER 5

Navalism 1890-1895

————— · —————

Laughton's efforts to enhance the national awareness of the Navy reached their widest audience with the highly successful Royal Naval Exhibition of 1891. He served on the organising committee, assembled by the First Lord, Lord George Hamilton, with the publicists Commander Charles Napier Robinson and William Laird Clowes. Financial support was provided by a number of Laughton's friends, including Beresford, Brassey, Colomb, Hornby, Clements Markham and First Sea Lord Sir Richard Vesey-Hamilton. Under Royal patronage the exhibition met Laughton's underlying requirement, raising interest in every aspect of the history and current development of the service. It did so by exploiting the past in a popular form, and paved the way for the success of Mahan, the Navy Records Society and the Navy League. Over two million people visited the exhibition over a period of 151 days, many of them taking away a catalogue that had been written to make the naval case, a 'considerable share' of it by Laughton.[1] They entered under an arch bearing a paraphrase of the preamble to the 1866 Articles of War, the motto of the event. 'It is on the *Navy* under the good providence of God, that our wealth, prosperity and peace depend'.[2] This had been Laughton's epitome of the naval case since the 1860s, and it was doubtless adopted for the exhibition on his advice.[3]

The 1891 Exhibition was Laughton's only significant contribution to the rise of popular navalism. His one public utterance on the subject was a characteristically choleric letter to *The Times*, condemning the 'Trafalgar Panorama', which had been made in Germany, as utterly unrealistic,

1. Laughton, J K, 'The Naval Exhibition at the Hague', *The Monthly Review* (November 1900), pp67-82 at p69.
2. Hamilton, W M, *The Nation and the Navy* (Unpub. London Ph.D. 1977), pp94-6. For the actual wording see fn 3 below. Marder, A J, *The Anatomy of British Seapower: A History of British Naval Policy in the Pre-Dreadnought Era 1880-1905* (London 1940), p45, based on Clowes, W L, *The Royal Navy*: Vol. VII (London 1904), pp82-3. Morriss, A J A, *The Scaremongers: Advocacy of War and Rearmament 1896-1914* (London 1984).
3. The motto was a paraphrase of the 1866 Articles of War. The actual wording of the Articles reads, 'the Navy, whereon, under the good Providence of God, the Wealth, Safety, and strength of the Kingdom Chiefly depend.' Rodger, N A M, *Articles of War* (Havant 1982), p35.

along with many of the paintings.[4] If the past was going to be called in support of the present it had to be an accurate version, not a well-intentioned but absurd pastiche. Although he joined the Navy League, founded in 1894, this may well have been out of loyalty to Hornby, the First President of the League, rather than from any deep interest. Even so there was a considerable overlap of senior membership between the League and the Records Society, but the League had 14,000 members by 1900 and over 100,000 at the outbreak of war.[5] In 1914 the Records Society had 536 subscribers, almost exactly the same number as twenty years before, a bank balance in excess of £1000 and a healthy publications list.[6] This was hardly surprising, middle-class public agitation not being to Laughton's taste. He preferred to engage the intellect of policy-makers, as an insider, valuing contacts and connections above newspaper pressure. By 1900 he was openly critical of the League's alarmist message. He had been a trenchant critic of alarmism in the early 1880s, and his views had not changed, objecting to the League's attempt to hijack naval administration and force its commercial interests on the Admiralty. In part he could take this rather detached view because the 1891 Exhibition, Mahan and the Navy Records Society had defeated the 'little navy' element of the Liberal party. In 1900 the Conservative government was committed to a Two Power Standard, maintaining a dominant sea-control fleet and using his arguments to support their policy. Nine years before leading Liberal politicians, from the 'little navy' Harcourt and Labouchere to Charles Dilke, who was otherwise pro-navy, had stated in the House of Commons that they considered the true role of the Navy was coast defence, and that the protection of ocean-going commerce was unnecessary.[7] Dilke would come round, under the influence of Spenser Wilkinson, to become a major supporter of the naval case.[8] The City of London and other commercial interests responded to the rise of global navalism by taking control of the Navy League, and using it as a popular front. Through a well-funded campaign they secured a massive programme of cruiser construction, adequate to protect British commerce. It was cruisers rather than battleships that inflated the Estimates in the late 1890s.[9] In pursuing enlarged Naval Estimates the League abandoned any criticism of the Admiralty, although it had been set up to press for a

---

4. *The Times* 17.7.1891 p4 letter from Laughton dated 14.7.1891. as fn1 p69.

5. Hamilton, pp360, 119, 123-4, 166-7.

6. Navy Records Society: Report of the Council 30.6.1914.

7. Hamilton, p275-7.

8. Dilke, C, and Wilkinson, H S, *Imperial Defence* (London 1891). Colomb, P, to Dilke 22.2.1892. Thanking Dilke for a copy of *Imperial Defence* and concurring in his views. Vol 13 Wilkinson MS NAM 9011.

9. Sumida, J T, *In Defence of Naval Supremacy: Finance, Technology and British Naval Policy 1889-1914* (London 1989), pp20-1.

Naval Staff and administrative reform at the Admiralty.[10] Following the change of purpose Wilkinson left. As H W Wilson lamented, the League had, 'sold Spenser Wilkinson for Thursfield, and Thursfield has never lifted a hand to help us'.[11] Thursfield, the *Times* naval correspondent, was an blue-water navalist, but hardly of Wilkinson's stature. The secession of Wilkinson and the shift of focus, compounded by the sudden death of Hornby, weakened the League before it had ever really got going.[12] It also destroyed what little appeal it had ever held for Laughton, who had altogether more sophisticated ideas on the best method of influencing policy.

Laughton's work, in combination with that of Mahan and Colomb, provided the new navalism of the 1890s with an intellectual base. Yet he was never an alarmist, disliking the cycle of complacency, retrenchment, scare and panic that set in after 1884. He preferred a steady effort to sustain naval mastery, and approved of the Naval Defence Act, which gave naval programmes three years' freedom from political interference. He never allowed the popular cry to dictate his views. When addressing the invasion debate of the late 1890s he marshalled a range of examples to prove the position he had supported all along, that the presence of an adequate fleet precluded an invasion. In this he agreed whole-heartedly with Philip Colomb. He found the Navy League's call for a navy equal to those of Russia, Germany, France and the United States , as well, perhaps, as Austria and Japan, foolish. 'I conceive' he lamented 'the Navy League does not strengthen its arguments by the suggestion of impossible contingencies'. In support of his case he quoted Mahan on the relative weakness of allied fleets, as opposed to those made up by one nation, and deployed his own observations on the 'want of unity' that marked Anglo-French Baltic operations during the Russian War. He concluded that a Two Power Standard was a sound insurance, and that anything more would be unreasonable.[13]

Despite his indifference to popular alarmism Laughton realised that the Navy had to retain the support of the country and in consequence he was always prepared to enter the public arena to defend the service. One of his most effective collaborators in this cause, and many of the others that he advanced, was Commander Charles Napier Robinson (1849-1936) who served as assistant editor of William Howard Russell's *Army and Navy*

---

10. Wilkinson, H S, *The Command of the Sea* (London 1894) and *The Brain of the Navy* (London 1895) are the key texts. There is a convenient 1992 reprint of both books in one volume.
11. H W Wilson to Laird Clowes 12.12.1896, Clowes MS NMM.
12. W T Ainslie to Wilkinson 26.5.1919 Vol 22. Wilkinson MS NAM 9011.
13. Laughton, J K, 'The National Study of Naval History', *Transactions of the Royal Historical Society* (1898), pp81-93 at p92.

Gazette, and joined *The Times* in 1895.[14] Laughton worked closely with Robinson, and often reviewed for the *Army and Navy Gazette*, usually shorter pieces on works he would examine in depth for the *Edinburgh Review*. In 1892 he began a series of twelve short studies 'Our Naval Literature', offering access to his experience and insight for those who wished to study the naval past.[15] The series was part of the build-up to the Navy Records Society. Laughton and Robinson were developing a constituency for the Society, while *The Army and Navy Gazette* would be a stout advocate once it had been founded. The series provided the Navy with an opportunity to demonstrate its appreciation of his work.

In the final instalment, published on 2 September 1893, Laughton discussed 'scurrilous' literature, to warn his readers of the dangers of such books. He began with a recent example, the anonymously published *The Navy in the Present Year of Grace*, which had appeared in three slim volumes in 1885. The author, ex-paymaster RN Henry James Boyle Montgomery, had been court-martialled twice, imprisoned for two years and dismissed the service with dishonour for theft in 1887.[16] While amusing and not without insight, Montgomery's book was a scathing indictment of the officer corps, the Royal Naval College, Naval Instructors, the influence of Freemasonry, the Admiralty and patronage. Some of the attacks were on individuals, and were only very thinly disguised. Only the seamen, warrant and petty officers came out well. One example of the wit and venom of the book will have to suffice. Montgomery declared that there were only two officers on the list of captains and admirals with any reputation, Frederick Richards and John Fisher. Of these, one was greatly over-rated, while the other was not a gentleman. Laughton could not allow the book to pass unchallenged. The scope and ferocity of the satire united Laughton and the officer corps in their hostility, while at least three aspects touched him personally.

The *Army and Navy Gazette* had reviewed the book when it first appeared, and largely accepted the charges. Laughton disagreed: his brief summary was forthright, damning and effective. The book combined insight with malice and a talent to deceive. It was 'a mass of impudent and scurrilous falsehood' intended to denigrate the officers and institutions of the service.[17] Montgomery decided to sue for libel, and the *Gazette* was

---

14. Hankinson, A, *Man of Wars: William Howard Russell of The Times* (London 1982), pp147-9 for the *Army & Navy*, which Russell founded in 1859. For Robinson see *Who Was Who*.

15. *The Army and Navy Gazette* (1892), pp70, 119, 198, 291-2, 479, 679, 840 and 986: (1893), pp131, 275, 459 and 732.

16. *The Times* 30.5.1887, p6, 31.5.1887, p5, 2.6.1887, p9.

17. Laughton, J K, 'Our Naval Literature XII', *The Army and Navy Gazette* (2.9.1893), p732.

not anxious to be involved.[18] In danger of a heavy fine, which he could not afford, Laughton wrote to Hornby, Admiral Sir Richard Vesey-Hamilton, Admiral Sir Thomas Brandreth, the last two Chaplains of the Fleet and the Director of Naval Hospitals for support. Sir Geoffrey replied that under the old 'Articles of War' he was bound 'to assist a known friend in view to the utmost of his power'. He was unimpressed by Montgomery's 'silly scurrility'.[19] Vesey-Hamilton used the same expression, and went to the Admiralty to discover exactly when Montgomery had been court-martialled and dismissed the service.[20] After a period when it appeared that the case would be dropped, Montgomery decided to press his suit for damages of £2000 against Laughton, as the author of the libel, Russell as the editor and Eyre & Spottiswoode as the publishers. Hornby agreed to act as a character witness.

The hearing, on 11 and 12 June 1894 was a triumph for Laughton. The defence admitted the libel, but denied Montgomery was being libelled, being unaware that he was the author. In addition they argued that the words were written *bona fides*, without malice and were fair comment, being true. Montgomery was well represented, having secured Rufus Isaacs QC, later Lord Reading, but the defendants were on an equal standing, with Sir Henry James QC and another QC. Isaacs opened his case by drawing attention to Montgomery's earlier 'problems', claiming he had not taken the money. Montgomery complained of the altered tone of the *Army and Navy Gazette* between 1885 and 1893. On the second day Laughton entered the witness box. Claiming that he had been unaware of the author's identity, he described how he came to review the book in his series. He had spoken out so strongly to warn others not to rely on it. He claimed not to have noticed the attacks on Greenwich and Naval Instructors, but this prompted some laughter in court. Hornby was the next to take the stand. He refuted the charges made in the book against the Board of Admiralty, flag lieutenants, Chaplains, Doctors and two individuals who were not named, but were sufficiently clearly described as to be notorious. Isaacs, recognising the case was hopeless, refused to cross-examine Hornby. The jury took little time to find for the defendants. The judge, awarding costs to the Defence as well, remarked that the 'language of the defendant was most moderate, for a more scurrilous production than the plaintiff's he had never heard'. The press was entirely sympathetic to Laughton and his fellow defendants, Russell and Eyre & Spottiswoode.[21]

---

18. Louis J Amos (Solicitor) to Laughton 28.11.1893 JKL MS.
19. Hornby to Laughton 29.12.1893 and 4.1.1893 JKL MS. Laughton to Hornby 31.12.1893 Hornby MSS NMM PHI/120d.
20. Vesey-Hamilton to Laughton 14.1.1894 JKL MS.
21. *The Times* Reports of 12 and 13.6.1894 pp3-4, and p3. See: *The Army and Navy Gazette* (16.6.1894), 'Montogomery v. Laughton and others' pp489-90 for a discussion of the case and a review of the press response.

Sidney Lee congratulated him on:

> your admirable action in resisting the impudence of the person who had the
> audacity to bring the action against you . . . Both by your original article and
> by your conduct of the case you did very good service to many interests.[22]

Hornby took the occasion to reflect on the need for legal reform, to
prevent such a 'worthless scoundrel' levying blackmail. In his patrician
way he blamed John Bright, cheap newspapers and lying politicians for
the nation's ills.[23] Little wonder he agreed to act as President of the Navy
League.

Despite his victory Laughton still faced the prospect of legal bills totalling over £100, for Montgomery, a man of straw, had no money. To make
a public demonstration of the esteem in which he was held by the service,
Hornby, Vesey-Hamilton Bridge, Reginald Custance and Prince Louis of
Battenberg, among others, set up the 'Laughton Guarantee Fund' to secure donations from the Navy to cover any costs. Their object was use the
sheer number of donations to demonstrate their appreciation of the 'public spirit which characterised the criticism'. Battenberg circulated the
printed handbill around the Mediterranean fleet (see overleaf).[24]

A claim against W H Russell having been dismissed as frivolous,
Montgomery protested to Hornby, claiming that he would be bank-
rupted by the case, but he dismissed him with a cutting reference to the
findings of the trial judge on him, his backer Thomas Gibson-Bowles and
'low class newspapers generally'.[25]

The fund was wound up in May 1896, having paid off the solicitor.[26]
Three years later Laughton discovered that Montgomery, already in trouble for domestic violence, had been sent to prison for five years for
stealing almost £1000 from a company which had appointed him as secretary. He noted the occurrence with a pleasure that was genuine, vindictive
and characteristic.[27] That the events of 1894 had been a strain became
obvious with the beginnings of the eye trouble that would plague him for
the rest of his life. Among his correspondents Bridge, who knew him best,
Lee and Mahan all asked about his sight. The problem, attributed to
'gout' (this may have been iritis), eventually cost him the sight of one eye.
The affliction must have been hard to bear for a man who lived in print.

---

22. Lee to Laughton 13.6.1894 JKL MS.
23. Hornby to Laughton 16.6.1894 JKL MS.
24. Laughton to Hornby 31.12.1893, 13.4.1894. Cmdr B H Chevalier (Secretary of the
Fund) to Hornby 6.12.1894. Printed Handbill of the 'Laughton Guarantee Fund December
1894'.
25. *The Times* 14.12.1894 p14. HJB Montgomery to Hornby 25.12.1894, and draft reply.
Hornby MSS PHI/120d NMM. Naylor, L E, *The Irrepressible Victorian: The Story of
Thomas Gibson Bowles* (London 1965).
26. Chevalier to Laughton 17.5.1896 JKL MS.
27. *Morning Post* 11.1.1899 JKL MS.

LAUGHTON GUARANTEE FUND

December, 1894.

It has been brought to the notice of certain Naval Officers that Professor JOHN KNOX LAUGHTON, the well-known Naval Historian, is liable for a sum of about £120, as his share of the costs incurred in an action recently brought against him by the Author of a book entitled "*The British Navy in the Present Year of Grace*."

The action was decided in Professor Laughton's favour, and the remarks of the Judge who presided at the trial, shew how justifiable was the criticism on the book which led to the action being brought.

It is considered that, under such circumstances, it would be very regrettable were Professor Laughton allowed to be out of pocket in consequence of the course he has taken in this matter, and a Committee, consisting of the undermentioned officers has, therefore, been formed for the purpose of raising sufficient funds to guarantee him against any pecuniary loss.

The large number of Naval Officers to whom Professor Laughton is known personally, as well as the larger number to whom he is known by reason of his valuable and instructive writings, will, the Committee feel certain, ensure a generous response to this appeal to their brother officers to shew their appreciation of the public spirit which characterised the criticism referred to.

The Committee are specially anxious that this fund should be made up of a large number of small subscriptions, rather than of a small number of large ones, as the value of the gift will thereby be greatly enhanced.

Subscriptions should be forwarded to Messrs. WOODHEAD & Co., 44, Charing Cross, London, S.W., for "Laughton Guarantee Fund," and any balance which may be in hand, after carrying out the object for which the Fund is raised, will, at the discretion of the Committee, be applied to some Naval charitable object, except in the case of those subscribers who may inform the Secretary that they wish some other course to be followed.

> Admiral of the Fleet, SIR GEOFFREY PHIPPS HORNBY, G.C.B.
> Admiral SIR R. VESEY HAMILTON, K.C.B.
> Vice-Admiral H. F. NICHOLSON, C.B.
> Rear-Admiral CYPRIAN A. BRIDGE.
> Rear-Admiral ARTHUR H. ALINGTON.
> Captain REGINALD N. CUSTANCE, R.N.
> Captain R. W. STOPFORD, R.N
> Captain H.S.H. PRINCE LOUIS OF BATTENBURG, G.C.B., R.N.
> Captain HENRY D. BARRY, R.N.

Secretary :—

Commander B. H. CHEVALLIER, R.N.,
1, Victoria Road,
Old Charlton, Kent.

Handbill circulated by Prince Louis of Battenberg to the Mediterranean Fleet for the Laughton Guarantee Fund, December 1894.

His second family continued to grow, and in the end there were five more children, the last arriving close to his 70th birthday. However, despite the hard work of founding the Navy Records Society, dealing with Montgomery, keeping up his usual schedule of work on the *Dictionary of National Biography* and the *Edinburgh Review*, teaching and other tasks, he found the time to develop one of the most significant intellectual relationships of his life. Shortly before the Montgomery trial he had taken an official part in the grand banquet for the officers of the USS *Chicago* at St James's Hall. The object of the evening was to laud the ship's Captain, Alfred Thayer Mahan USN, a reluctant mariner who had long before fallen out of love with the sea.[28]

In many ways Mahan carried Laughton's work on to the next phase. He took the existing literature, analysed it, presented it in a coherent narrative form, and used the results to teach leadership and strategy to naval officers.[29] As a writer of large-scale history, with a powerful didactic purpose, he was by far the most effective naval author. Where he and Laughton differed was in the relative weight they gave to scholarship and message. Laughton, and later Corbett, always considered Mahan's synthesis a great achievement, but flawed by premature delivery. For them the historical flaws were a serious impediment. Mahan, a teacher, strategist and analyst, was never wholly persuaded that the quality of the evidence was crucial, although his 1897 Nelson biography provided a belated education. In essence Mahan did what Laughton believed would be the work of the next generation, the development of a strategic system. The fact that they recognised, and accepted, their differences is vital to any understanding of their relationship. Because they shared so many objectives, and acknowledged each other as pre-eminent in their own fields, they sustained a productive working relationship for twenty-one years. That Mahan became an international celebrity in a matter of three years, while Laughton remained relatively unknown largely reflected the divergent nature of their ambitions.

Through his relationship with Stephen Luce, Laughton was already familiar with the growing intellectual output of the United States Navy. Luce and Laughton shared many interests related to naval service and sea life, and if Luce did not possess an original mind, in the sense that Corbett did, he was, like Laughton, a profoundly practical man. He sought

---

28. Souvenir of the USS *Chicago* banquet, 28.5.1894. Corbett MSS NMM Box 2, added by Brian Tunstall.
29. Sumida, J T, *Inventing Grand Strategy and Teaching Command: The Classic Works of Alfred Thayer Mahan Reconsidered* (Washington 1997). A powerful new analysis of Mahan's thought that demonstrates its underlying coherence, and reveals much more of the intellectual sophistication that made it so effective. Unfortunately it does not address Mahan's relationship with Laughton.

knowledge from the past for the enlightenment it could cast on the problems of the present and the education of officers to meet an uncertain future. His work was heavily influenced by Laughton's pivotal papers of 1873 and 1874, especially their central argument, that history was the prime medium from which to develop the study of tactics and strategy, leading to the development of modern naval doctrine and national strategies. These papers were still at the core of his thought when he led the campaign to establish the United States Naval War College, his greatest contribution to the United States Navy.[30] The importance of this relationship was enhanced by Luce's role in Mahan's career.

Luce selected Mahan as Professor of Naval Warfare, after his first choice for the post had turned it down.[31] He also planned the College syllabus, including the role of naval history, and directed Mahan to create a 'science [Laughton's favourite word] of naval warfare under steam . . . and do for it what Jomini has done for the military science'.[32] Mahan would transcend this instruction, but the original impulse was critical. Laughton had first encountered Mahan when he reviewed his book *The Gulf and Inland Waters,* as part of a large study of the Civil War, in 1883. He praised the moderation of Mahan's language and his detached analysis, in contrast to other American accounts of the war.[33] When Luce told Laughton of the forthcoming publication of Mahan's War College lectures, he remembered having been impressed, 'with a high opinion of his ability and clearness'.[34] Although Luce had exploited military intellectual models Laughton's work had been a major influence on the desire for;

> a philosophic study of naval history . . . to recognise where the principles of science have been illustrated . . . Such studies might well occupy the very best thoughts of the naval officer, for they belong to the highest branch of his profession.[35]

This was the lesson of Laughton's essay on Tegetthoff. Although Luce directed Mahan's attention to Laughton's essays, he was already familiar with most of them. Mahan's letters at this time reveal a wide and sophisticated appreciation of British naval history.[36] As his first *Sea Power* book neared completion Mahan was struck by the similarity of his arguments

---

30. Hayes, J and Hattendorf, J (eds), *The Writings of Stephen B Luce* (Newport R.I. 1975), pp31 and 71.
31. Spector, R, *Professors of War: The Naval War College and the Development of the Naval Profession* (Newport R.I. 1977), pp29-30.
32. Hayes and Hattendorf, p68 (A lecture of 1885). Gleaves, A, *Life and Letters of Stephen B Luce* (New York 1925), pp181, 312-4: Mahan to Luce 22.1.1886.
33. 'Vicksburg and Gettysburg' *Edinburgh Review* (October 1883), pp510-47 at p511.
34. Laughton to Luce 11.8.1889 Luce MS LoC.
35. Luce in the *Naval Institute Proceedings* (April 1883) ibid. p171.
36. Mahan to Luce 19.11.1885 & 31.5.1886. Seager & Macguire, *Letters* Vol I p619, 633-4.

with those advanced by Seeley.[37] This was only to be expected given the close intellectual links between Seeley and Laughton.

When Laughton received Luce's unsigned review of *The Influence of Sea Power upon History, 1660-1783* he reported that he had already read the book, and apart from some trifling mistakes of detail, thought it 'quite the most important contribution to naval literature which has appeared for very many years'. In a second letter he attributed the errors to details; 'taken too exclusively from French sources, and many of them certainly inaccurate'.[38] At the end of the year, having written his own review, he noted that 'the book has excited much interest here'.[39] Not the least significant was the response of the First Sea Lord, Admiral Sir Richard Vesey-Hamilton, who stopped Laughton as he walked through St James's Park to discuss the book.[40]

Laughton's own review of *The Influence of Sea Power Upon History*, which appeared in the October 1890 number of the *Edinburgh Review*, played a major role in introducing the book to a British audience. He got to the heart of the matter at once. After four lines on Mahan and the War College origins of the book, he declared:

> It is thus to be considered, primarily, at least not so much as a contribution to history as an exposition of the principles of naval strategy and tactics, and of the aims and methods of the science of naval war.[41]

He was generous in his praise of the book, for good reason. He stressed that not only was it was a timely contribution to the defence debate, but that Mahan was a detached commentator. This was an important qualification, because Laughton was going to use Mahan's work to argue a British case. Mahan had accepted Laughton's basic premise, that the lessons of the past were vital, especially for strategy. Where Laughton diverged from Mahan, reflecting British strategy rather than a strategy for Hemispheric defence, was in stressing the offensive dynamic in British seapower. While Mahan noted that Cherbourg had in part rectified the advantage of physical conformation that had given Britain command of the Channel, Laughton observed:

> It may, however, be questioned whether, under modern conditions, Cherbourg would be a safe port, and whether the arsenal would long continue to be one if, in time of war, its destruction was attempted, say with the equivalent of such a force was brought against Sweaborg in 1855.[42]

37. Mahan to Luce 7.10.1889 ibid. p713.
38. Laughton to Luce 3 & 12.8.1890 NWC MS. Coll. 10 Folder 2.
39. Laughton to Luce 7.12.1890. Luce MS LoC.
40. Laughton, Draft Obituary of Mahan: JKL MS.
41. 'Captain Mahan on Maritime Power', *Edinburgh Review* (October 1890), pp420-53 at p420.
42. Ibid, p427.

This was particularly significant as Admiral Aube had recently observed that there would be no naval battles in the future, inferior fleets would stay in harbour, with all that that implied for the role of coastal attack.[43] This analysis calls into question the sincerity of his review of George Sydenham Clarke's *Fortification*, where he downgraded the ability of naval forces to engage forts, let alone first-class fortresses.[44] During the Fashoda Crisis of 1898 the French were convinced that the Royal Navy would attack Cherbourg, their most powerful fortress, and were equally certain that they could not hope to resist.[45] He also doubted Mahan's argument that it was the relative poverty of the land that forced men to go to sea. In the process he observed a clear statement by Mahan of the argument that Frederick Jackson Turner would make into his famous 'Frontier' thesis of 1893, that America had turned her back on the sea because of the attractions of the internal frontier.[46] Mahan hoped she would return to the sea when that phase of her history passed. For his own audience Laughton noted Mahan's concern that democratic Britain was losing her will to sustain naval mastery, an opinion which he advised should be carefully weighed. The result of weakness, if it were short of defeat in war, would be ruinous losses to merchant shipping from the enemy's fleets, rather than his cruisers. Laughton supported Mahan's thesis that the *guerre de course* was an inferior and secondary form of war, and used it to criticise recent alarmists at home.

> In this country, commercial sensitiveness has led many to believe in and to dread the application of what may be called the French theory of commerce-destroying, or, in more modern phrase, of swarms of *Alabamas*; but that the Government has never, since that fatal 1667, attempted to put it into practice is, in itself, a sufficient proof that our Admiralty has all along recognised the truths which Captain Mahan has so clearly and forcibly stated. The fact is that our Admiralty, though often the victim, and sometimes the tool, of jobbery and corruption, is and always has been largely composed of naval officers of ability and experience, and has generally been abreast of the situation, so far as the restrictions of the Treasury have permitted. And although it has always been perhaps the best abused body of men in England, and though proposals to reform it out of existence are continually cropping up, it is well to remember that it was under the government of such a board that, during the last two hundred years, our navy has grown to be the splendid service which

43. Ibid, pp427, 442.
44. Laughton, review of *Fortification* in *The Quarterly Review*. For a discussion of this review and its purpose see pp110-113.
45. Lambert, A D, 'Deterrence' in Duffy, M (ed), *The Parameters of British Naval Power 1856-1945* (Exeter 1999).
46. Billington, R A, *Frederick Jackson Turner* (New York 1973).

it actually is, and has won for the country that gigantic sea-power which our foreign critics admire and envy.[47]

He agreed with Mahan that the destruction of the enemy fleet was the true object, despite the fact that command of the sea could be held by a superior fleet without a decisive victory. The point was critical to his attack on the novelty urged for Admiral Aube's *Jeune Ecole*. Laughton recognised that inferior fleets had always sheltered in harbour. This had nothing to do with the introduction of new technology. The ability to destroy fleets sheltering in fortified harbours was the pinnacle of Laughton's concept of what he termed sea-power, in a conscious distinction from Mahan's Sea Power.

On a critical note he complained that Mahan had relied too much on Troude's *Batailles Navales de la France,* without access to the mass of printed materials and records available in Britain. He provided a list of errors, mostly irrelevant to the purpose of the work, and set out Colomb's version of the battle of Beachy Head, which he considered much superior to the one Mahan had developed from Macaulay's *History* and the French sources. In addition Mahan had not developed the strategic principle of a 'Fleet in Being' that Colomb urged as part of his 'Blue-Water' strategy. In giving great praise to the work Laughton recognised that:

> He has, of course, had the circumstances of his own country definitely in view; and it is allowable to suppose that in publishing these lectures he has hoped to rekindle in the hearts of his fellow-citizens some desire to contest the supremacy of the seas, in so far, at any rate, as the necessities of home defence render it advisable and geographical conditions may render it feasible. The great preponderance of sea power is at present ours. To predict the future is impossible; but the light of history's lamp shows us that we have enormous advantages to assist us in maintaining that sea power which is the life of the empire; it also shows us that these advantages will not maintain it of themselves; that care, forethought, and vigilance are their necessary complements.[48]

If there was nothing new in the content of Mahan's book, as Laughton, Vesey-Hamilton and others observed, the fault was excused by the intellectual power of the argument and the skilful synthesis of existing elements. If he was too well informed to shower uncritical adulation on Mahan, Laughton recognised that the American had, in attempting to advance the cause of his own service, provided a powerful weapon for all those in Britain who favoured a maritime strategy. This did not obscure

---

47. 'Captain Mahan', p441. The 1667 reference is to Charles II's decision not to fit out the battlefleet for the last year of the Second Dutch War, which allowed De Ruyter to stage his raid on the Medway.
48. Ibid, p453

errors of fact and faulty analysis, but the superior concept and execution of the work made it unique. For the rest of his life Laughton would acknowledge Mahan's pre-eminence as a strategic analyst. He would also work hard to develop Mahan's historical methodology, acting as guide, critic, research co-ordinator and publicist. This relationship was already forming in Mahan's mind in 1890. When he ran into problems locating commercial statistics for the 1793-1812 book Mahan wrote to Luce, who passed the query to Laughton.[49]

When Luce passed on Laughton's high opinion of the first *Influence* volume, in the thirty-page *Edinburgh Review* article Mahan, although stung by some of Laughton's reflections on the accuracy of his sources, was so pleased with the review that his studied prose momentarily slipped:

> I . . . considered myself fortunate to come off so easy at his hands, for he probably knows more naval history than any English speaking man living. Pity he don't produce a great work instead of piddling about in the byways of naval history. If he had, I need not have fallen into my mistakes and yet all that is best in my book would still have been worth writing.

It would be some years more before he understood the limitations of the method he had employed. At this stage he considered writing to Laughton for further assistance with the statistics of British mercantile losses, but the need passed.[50]

Mahan always recognised that his career had been made by Luce, for Luce had provided him with the post and the intellectual stimulus that led to the *Influence* series.[51] Mahan read Laughton's work long before he was appointed to the Naval War College, and always acknowledged the impact of his essays, particularly the 'Scientific Study' of 1874.[52]

Laughton reviewed *The Influence of Sea Power Upon the French Revolution and Empire, 1793-1812* for the *Edinburgh Review* in 1893, together with Philip Colomb's *Essays on Naval Defence*. He began by contrasting the different value accorded to the study of history at the colleges with which the authors were connected, Colomb having taken over from Laughton as lecturer in Naval Strategy and Tactics at Greenwich. At Greenwich 'history is wholly neglected, while the cognate subjects of strategy and tactics are illustrated each year by one short course of six lectures'. In consequence Colomb could not reproduce a coherent,

---

49. Mahan to Luce 4 and 9.4.1890 and 27.10.1890. *Letters Vol* II pp1-3 & 29-30.
Luce to Laughton 10.11.1890 JKL MS and Laughton to Luce 7.12.1890. Luce MS LoC.
50. Mahan to Luce 20. and 31.12.1890. *Letters* Vol II, pp34, 37.
51. Mahan, A T, *The Influence of Sea Power upon the French Revolution and Empire: 1793-1812* (London 1892), ppv-vi. Hayes & Hattendorf, p17.
52. Mahan, A T, *From Sail to Steam*, (London 1907), p280. Corbett, J S, 'The Revival of Naval History', p1 where Corbett refers to a letter from Mahan to Laughton that Laughton had placed in his hands shortly before his death.

structured Greenwich course, just a group of diverse lectures from RUSI; 'collectively the work is on a lower level than that which we have from the United States Naval War College'. He held up Mahan's role at Newport, and his recent elevation to the post of President as an example to be followed.[53] This was a rather forced contrast, as he must have known that Colomb's *Naval Warfare* was the equivalent Naval College text. Laughton considered Mahan's second book more important than the first, because it was addressed to all who had an interest in the sea – statesmen, merchants and ship-owners. His argument that the Napoleonic Wars were a commercial struggle, and that Britain won, would be invaluable in promoting a maritime strategy. Laughton stressed that the book had to be treated on its merits:

> In the highest and best sense Captain Mahan's book is a treatise on the philosophy of history, of history teaching by examples. It is not in itself a history, nor does it make any pretence at original research. But the mere acts are seldom in dispute. Accepting them, for the most part, as he finds them recorded in the standard histories and contemporary memoirs and correspondence, Captain Mahan's very great merit is that he has so arranged them that their significance now shines forth, projected like an electric beam on the clouds of heaven, so as to compel the notice of all who come within its comprehensive sphere.[54]

Mahan demonstrated that it was fear of the British fleet that had imprisoned the French fleet in Brest after 1795, and discussed the strategic effect of Admiral Hotham's inconclusive actions with the French Mediterranean Fleet of 1795, following Nelson's contention that had these been decisive victories they would have prevented the French invasion of Italy. On a more obvious contemporary note Laughton quoted, with approval, Mahan's assessment of Napoleon's attempts to attack British trade. Although her commerce was exposed it could only be stopped by addressing the heart of the problem:

> To command the sea approaches to the British Islands will be to destroy the power of the State. As a preliminary thereto the British Navy must be neutralised by superior numbers or by superior skill.[55]

This struck Laughton as 'more scientific and correct' than Colomb's fatalistic argument that the Empire might be destroyed by the loss of a single colony or trade. Indeed, British commerce had always grown in wartime, despite the French *guerre de course*. He was doubtless aware of

53. 'Captain Mahan on Maritime Power', *The Edinburgh Review* (April 1893), pp484-518, at p484.
54. Ibid, p485.
55. Ibid, p499.

the reasons why the two men took such diametrically opposed views, but was not going to make a blatant reference to the contemporary political value of their work. The remaining chapters of Mahan's book continued the agreeable theme that British strategy, in competent hands, was invulnerable to all pressures, short of the loss of command of the sea. In this respect both men lauded St Vincent for his refusal to waste resources on gunboats, a lesson of obvious significance for those grappling with the current torpedo-boat obsession on both sides of the Atlantic. Laughton criticised Mahan for failing to discuss the massive effort launched by Bonaparte in 1807 to build a battlefleet capable of beating the British. This, Laughton argued, demonstrated the continuity of the struggle better than any other aspect.[56] However, the discussion of the post-Trafalgar period as a commercial war was lauded, for demonstrating that 'the principles on which (the destruction or protection of commerce) depend are the same as they were a hundred years ago, or as they will be a hundred years hence.'[57] He agreed with Mahan that concentration of effort made hunting for individual marauders like looking for a needle in haystack, but added that

> properly arranged convoys can sail over a controlled sea with a minimum of risk. In 1782 when Suffren disputed our command of the Indian Ocean, the (insurance) premium of insurance on ships in the China and India trade was fifteen per cent. During the Revolutionary War it did not exceed half that rate.[58]

After 1805 the rate for ships in convoy was only 5 per cent, although those not convoyed were at risk. Mahan did not trouble to argue for convoy, merely demonstrated that it was a 'concentration of effort' and took it for granted that it would adopted. Colomb reached practically the same conclusion. Where Mahan added a new dimension was in stressing the wisdom of the British after 1805 in capturing France's overseas cruiser bases, for without them no campaign could be sustained. This was critical in a war that was 'literally one of endurance', in which Napoleon tried to humble that sea power, 'before which his empire crumbled into ruin'.[59] It was at this time that Laughton wrote his important paper 'On Convoy', published in 1894, which set out his case that convoy was the key, so long

---

56. Corbett, J S, 'Napoleon and the British Navy after Trafalgar', *The Quarterly Review* (1922) addressed these issues. See Glover, R, 'The French Fleet, 1807-1814: Britain's problem and Madison's opportunity', *The Historical Journal* (1967). Glete, J, *Navies and Nations: Warships, Navies and State Building in Europe and America, 1500-1850* (Stockholm 1993) provides a more thorough analysis.
57. 'Captain Mahan' (1893), p509.
58. Ibid.
59. Ibid, p518.

Mahan found this, or another contemporary portrait of Laughton, 'like, but exaggeratedly sedate'. This one shows a man at the peak of his powers, Professor of Modern History at King's College, London and Secretary of the Navy Records Society. (King's College Archives)

The Battle of Fatsham Creek, 1 June 1857. John Knox Laughton's gallantry during this bloody boat action was noticed in the London Gazette. (Chatham collection)

Laughton's last ship, the ironclad frigate HMS *Prince Consort*. (National Maritime Museum: A2884)

The Royal Naval College, Portsmouth. Laughton worked in this 'draughty. cramped, illsmelling' building between 1866 and 1873. Conditions inside have improved somewhat in the past 120 years! (Courtesy of Jonathan Coad)

The Staff of the Royal Naval College at Greenwich, outside the Chapel, *circa* 1878. The Admiral President Sir Edward Gennys Fanshawe is seated, with arms folded, in the centre. Laughton is the second man on his left, with the top hat. (Royal Naval College, Greenwich)

The baroque splendour of the Royal Naval College, Greenwich, with the Royal Naval School, now the National Maritime Museum, to the right. The drill ship *Fame is* prominent in the School grounds, in front of the Queen's House. This aerial photograph was taken in the early 1920s, only a decade after Laughton's death. (Royal Naval College, Greenwich)

Samuel Rawson Gardiner, Laughton's closest friend and colleague in the English historical profession. Gardiner, the model scholarly historian, recruited Laughton to the profession, encouraged him to edit documentary sources, ensured he had a place in the *Dictionary of National Biography* project, and supported the Navy Records Society. He was also his predecessor as Professor of Modern History at King's College, London. (King's College Archives)

King's College, London. The Main Building and quadrangle at the turn of the century. (King's College Archives)

Admiral Stephen Bleecker Luce USN. One of Laughton's most important contacts outside Britain. Between 1870 and 1900 Luce used Laughton's work as part of his campaign to modernise the United States Navy. Critically he provided the early conduit through which Mahan came into contact with Laughton, helping to create modern naval history. (United States Naval War College).

Captain Alfred Thayer Mahan USN. The relationship between Mahan, the analyst and theorist, and Laughton, the archival scholar, created modern naval history. Their shared ambition to use the subject to educate their services led them to create a body of work that has remained at the heart of naval thought to this day. (United States Naval War College)

Admiral of the Fleet Sir Geoffrey Thomas Phipps Hornby, seen here in his other incarnation, every inch the Hampshire country squire. Between 1875 and his death in 1895 Hornby was the embodiment of the service, an example and inspiration to every officer. His support for Laughton's work both at Greenwich, and later when he helped to establish the Records Society, ensured it reached the target audience. Although recognised as a master of fleet tactics Hornby has yet to receive due credit for his part in reviving the Navy. (Author)

as the convoying navy had command of the sea.[60] Contemporary British strategy had a strong focus on the neutralisation of the Franco-Russian Dual Alliance's overseas cruiser bases.

Mahan's new book demonstrated the relevance, vitality and continuity of British strategy even better than its predecessor. Here was the 'Great War' being won by sea power, properly applied by men of skill and insight, and continued by their less gifted successors. Little wonder Laughton trumpeted its merits, for despite the odd weakness it was a key text. It made the case Laughton had been developing for two decades, and did so within the Naval War College environment, prompting Laughton to lament the inferior situation of history at Greenwich. Having finished his review Laughton wrote to Mahan for the first time. Here was a major contributor to the cause of naval history, and Laughton set out to recruit him. His object in approaching Mahan was revealed by the way he described the impact of the book:

> It is a great work, and ought to open the eyes of many on this side who are obstinately blind to many of the truths you have so clearly put forward.

He linked Mahan's work with that of Colomb, which was more pessimistic about the defence of the Empire, a view which he believed to be more widely supported in Britain. His excuse for writing had been to ask Mahan how he pronounced his name, in time for a forthcoming lecture. He ended by admitting responsibility for the *Edinburgh Review* notice of 1890 and another due in April 1893 and asked that his regards be passed on to Luce.[61]

Mahan was delighted with the letter, and hastened to reply. Luce had already told him that Laughton had written the 1890 *Edinburgh Review* notice, and he stressed the importance of seeing both sides of any issue, intending to contrast his own views with Colomb's more dogmatic pronouncements. As to his name his revealed:

> we put the accent on the last syllable. I fancy this arose from a mistake – my father having been a child of Irish parents, though born in this country – but the usage with us is well settled . . .

Mahan always recognised Laughton as *the* naval historian, an assessment he acknowledged, in his own self-absorbed way, with a compliment that combined praise, disclosure and encouragement:

> Before closing, may I express the hope uttered by Prof. Burrows in his *Life of Hawke*, that we are some day to have from you a history of the British

---

60. Laughton, J K, 'On Convoy' in Robinson, C N (ed), *Brassey's Naval Annual 1894* (London 1894), pp225-41.
61. Laughton to Mahan 11.3.1893: Mahan MS LoC.

Navy. I had occasion to realise the need of it during many painful hunts for details – and you must, with your particular and intimate knowledge, have seen that I have practically given up in many ceased, accepting ignorance of details as not material to the broad lines I wished to draw. Still, without Nelson's *Dispatches* and Napoleon's *Correspondence* I should have been in a bad way. It was upon them, not upon any published naval history that I built my work. Immense as is the task I hope you have undertaken it.[62]

This opening exchange of letters set the tone for two decades of correspondence. From the start they recognised each other's mastery in their particular fields, the vital contribution that each could make to the other's work, and the cause they shared, the importance of history in demonstrating the central role of naval power in national policy.

Laughton put this information to good use when he spoke on 'Recent Naval Literature' at the Royal United Services Institute on 23 June. His task was to outline the important new works for a professional audience, who may have missed the *Edinburgh Review* notices, and he took the opportunity to proselytise for the historical approach that he had pioneered. After all, the Navy Records Society had been founded only ten days before.[63] On this occasion he discussed Mahan's two books and Colomb's *Naval Warfare*. After outlining Mahan's heritage and his strategic and didactic attainments, he concluded that some of the opposition to Colomb's theories reflected the 'imperfection' of his language. Laughton supported both men in stating that while the Royal Navy held command of the sea Britain was safe from invasion. He went on to say that the fleet could not be decoyed away, defeated by surprise or superior foreign cunning, and that any attempt to invade without first defeating the British fleet would end in 'disaster, if not in utter ruin'. In supporting Colomb's contention that Britain had little need for fixed fortifications. Citing Sydenham Clarke's *Fortification* of 1890, he stressed that this was not a general principle, applicable to weaker naval powers, but a particular reflection of the nature of British power: 'any extended outlay on shore defences is a waste of public money, and, as diverting the expenditure from the navy, as the true national defence, is a public danger'.[64] In assessing the danger of invasion Laughton analysed Colomb's 'Fleet in Being' thesis. He stressed that, in his view, Colomb had not intended to set out 'an abstract, general proposition', but was thinking only of the circumstances of 1690, and the fleet under Lord Torrington's command.[65]

---

62. Mahan to Laughton 21.3.1893: J K L MS.
63. See Ch. 7.
64. Laughton, J K, 'Recent Naval Literature', *JRUSI* Vol XXXVII (November 1893), pp1161-82 at p1163. Lecture given on 23.6.1893 with Admiral Sir R. Vesey-Hamilton in the Chair.
65. Ibid, p1165.

Even so he was convinced Tourville could have done more, despite Torrington's best efforts, and so was Mahan. There were any number of examples of the reverse situation, of inferior French fleets being quite unable to affect the operations of the British, and he drew a good one from Colomb's own book.

In demonstrating the role of sea power Laughton stretched far wider than mere naval works alone, recognising that the whole field of history was filled with important examples, and only needed to be studied properly to give up the lessons. That he cited his friend Samuel Rawson Gardiner's *History of the Great Civil War* is not to be wondered at, but the encouragement he offered to his service audience to widen the scope of their studies should not be missed. He stressed that 'in August, 1643, it was the Navy alone that stood in the way of the King's success'.[66] On the subject of blockade Laughton accepted that opinion was divided; some leading officers thought it impossible, some doubtful, but Colomb was adamant that steam had improved the application of blockade, and cited the American Civil War to make his case. Laughton compared these views with the 'Report of the Three Admirals' on the 1888 manoeuvres, which had called for a greater degree of numerical superiority at sea in order to enforce a blockade. This, Laughton argued, was a good reason to stop building 14-15,000 ton battleships and return to the old standard of 9-10,000 tons, claiming the support of both Mahan and Colomb for his contention. He backed up the case with two pages of historical examples, which, however convincing they might have seemed to him as a random sample, had far too many common features to convince a modern analyst.[67] He criticised Mahan's handling of the case of the 110-gun *Revolutionnaire* in the preliminary moves of the battle of the Glorious First of June. These opinions, on a technical subject, reflected Bridge's views. The two men, reluctant to accept the logic of the case, had discussed the subject while Laughton prepared his lecture. Bridge contended that: 'A desire to persuade his countrymen to have huge armour-clads clouds even Mahan's clear historical judgement'.[68] In preference to ships of great size Laughton urged the primacy of numbers of ships, as strategically and tactically more flexible, capable of concentration and dispersion.[69] In wrapping-up, Laughton supported the assessment that convoy, 'is by no means dead', and repeated Mahan's argument that commerce-destroying 'may irritate, but cannot crush an enemy', unlike command of the sea. He ended with a ringing call to action:

---

66. Ibid, p1169.
67. Ibid, pp1171-3.
68. Bridge to Laughton 14 & 15.3.1893 JKL MS. Internal evidence demonstrates that there would have been an intervening letter from Laughton.
69. 'Recent Naval Literature', p1175.

I will, therefore, in conclusion, only say to any of you who may not yet have read Captain Mahan's books, read them: to those who have read them, read them again; read them a third time; for in them you will find the best exposition of the blunders and the glories of our forefathers, the best explanation of the influence of sea power.[70]

Although Vesey-Hamilton tried to direct the discussion onto the size of ships, Bridge immediately improved the quality of proceedings by calling for a clear definition of blockade, contrasting Nelson's open blockade of Toulon, to stop supplies getting in, with a close blockade intended to stop an enemy getting out. These had quite different force requirements, and needed to be distinguished. Recognising that the audience was hardly in the mood for an animated examination of any issues, meeting on the day after the loss of the *Victoria*, Colomb praised Laughton for so clearly explaining the more controversial points that he had been trying to advance, and then, in his inimitable, long-winded way proceeded to dispute many of those interpretations. He set out the need for a level of local defence adequate to force the enemy to come in such strength as would necessarily reveal his movements. Significantly, he concluded that in future blockades would be conducted by 'keeping the fighting forces in a convenient harbour, while only the watching scouts were kept off the port itself', rather than trying to maintain the fighting force off the port. The 'Three Admirals' had accepted this point, as the key to an efficient blockade with a smaller force.[71] Only if the fleet was always at sea would it be necessary to have the five-to-three superiority that they mentioned.[72]

That Laughton used his correspondence with Mahan and Bridge to develop the themes of the lecture should not come as a surprise, in view of the wide range of demands on his time in the period when he was founding the Navy Records Society and preparing to meet Montgomery's libel action. His success, on a particularly melancholy day for the Navy, was important. He had completed the promotion of historically-based naval strategic thought, which had matured in the work of two men who had received their critical impulse from him. Little wonder he was so generous in his praise. The admonition to read and re-read Mahan was followed by many of his audience, for this lecture reached a major part of his target audience. Having addressed the leading men in politics and the services, his final task would be to persuade his fellow historians. Unfortunately one of the most acute minds in the service, an Admiral with the experience, ability and opportunity to revitalise the service from the top, and a

---

70. Ibid, p1176.
71. Marder, A J, *The Anatomy of British Sea Power* (London 1940), pp88, 109, 131-2.
72. 'Recent Naval Literature', pp1178-9.

convert to Mahan's message, had been lost with the *Victoria.* In one of his last conversations Sir George Tryon had described Mahan's books as 'simply great, the best things ever written'.[73] Tryon's untimely death was a tragedy for the modernisers in the service. In the short term it ended his new tactical thinking, but the long-term effects are harder to assess. Had he lived Tryon would almost certainly have taken his place at the head of the service, and begun a more 'intellectual' revolution than the one carried out by Fisher.

Two months later, on 10 August, Mahan dined with Laughton. They were to meet infrequently over the next twenty years, which may well account for a relatively full correspondence. On this occasion they discussed Nelson, a subject on which both were at work.[74] Mahan was delighted with the printed version of Laughton's lecture:

> It will not, I hope, be necessary for me to enlarge upon the gratification I feel at being spoken of in so flattering a manner by a person of your attainments in our particular field.[75]

Flattery can serve many purposes. Laughton was using it, together with a steady diet of historical insight, information and contacts, to secure Mahan's support for his cause.

Laughton recognised that the Royal Naval Exhibition and a general heightened awareness of the Navy made Mahan's two works the books of the decade. By contrast his own *Studies in Naval History* had appeared at a time when there was little public interest in the subject. Although there was a second edition, the first had only been of 1000 copies.[76] It was not only the propitious times that made Mahan's books so successful. He provided a positive and self-satisfying image of the Royal Navy and its glorious past, combining a simple message with straightforward narrative covering the operations of the major fleets. This was no coincidence: Mahan was writing a study of the rise and ascendancy of British sea-power, to educate his own service and persuade his countrymen to build an ocean-going battlefleet. Just as Frederick Jackson Turner was explaining to them that, with the land frontier finally closed, it was possible to see how the frontier had shaped their lives and institutions, Mahan offered them a new frontier on the sea.[77] The success of the book in Britain was incidental to its purpose. It was also greatly assisted by the skilful and positive assessment provided by Laughton in the critical

---

73. Gleaves, *Luce*, p188. Mahan to Mrs Mahan 1.7.1893: *Letters* Vol II, p114.
74. Mahan to Mrs Mahan 11.8.1893: *Letters* Vol II, p134-6.
75. Mahan to Laughton 1.12.1893: JKL MS.
76. Contract for *Studies* 21.8.1885: Longman Archive II 233/104 Reading University Library.
77. Billington, R, *Frederick Jackson Turner* (New York 1973).

journals. That Mahan's simple chronological approach worked better than Laughton's episodic and thematic treatment reflected the popular taste of the age and the impressive, weighty prose style of the American. By contrast Laughton's essays were complex and provocative; they required reflection and were, as he had always intended, more suitable for officers undergoing professional education than popular reading. Michael Oppenheim observed that 'from a naval point of view, Mahan's may be considered one of the great books of the world. I am sorry it was not written by an Englishman'.[78] Laughton would have concurred in the former sentiment, but not in the subsequent lament. He gloried in Mahan's book *because* it had been written by an American officer, a foreigner, and could therefore be put forward as a more 'objective' assessment of British strategy.

Laughton held a high opinion of Mahan's work as a strategic synthesis, especially the second *Sea Power* volume. At the same time he recognised that the American was less of an historian than a political scientist. He also stressed, as few others did at the time, that the ultimate purpose of Mahan's work was to encourage his countrymen to contest the supremacy of the sea with Britain.[79] At the same time he was critical of the American's scholarship. While the limited use of primary sources was excused by the scale of the work and the lack of access, the reliance on inaccurate French sources without cross-checking was a fundamental methodological weakness. Laughton responded by acting as Mahan's research co-ordinator, lending him his extensive notebooks for his chapter on the American War of Independence in Clowes's *The Royal Navy*. This selfless, high-minded approach was normal for Laughton. He remained anxious to advance the great work of producing naval history for doctrine development, national strategy, and historical understanding. Mahan was a major contributor to the task and, with encouragement, could produce really powerful work. Although Mahan, in awe of Laughton's encyclopaedic knowledge, became alarmed that the Englishman's *Nelson Memorial* of 1896 would scoop his larger two-volume study, he gradually came to realise that their shared ambitions and distinct approaches made the closest possible intellectual co-operation the most effective relationship. A more measured reflection of his sense of obligation came in the form of the signed copies of all his books, which he sent Laughton as they appeared.[80]

Mahan combined the 'lessons of history' for naval education approach that Laughton had employed in the 1870s, with an impressive strategic

78. Oppenheim to Laughton, undated fragment: appears to be from 1893-4: JKL MS.
79. Seager, *Mahan*, quoting from the 1890 *Edinburgh Review* essay, p213.
80. Seager and Maguire II letters of 12.1881.

analysis that diverged from the proscriptive model provided by Jomini and the practical drive of Luce to produce both a classic work and a remarkable *corpus*. However, by the time the first *Sea Power* volume appeared, Laughton had moved on from the methods that had sufficed in the 1870s, and even then he had been far more critical of his material than Mahan. By 1890 he had become a professional historian, valuing accuracy above impact, and evidence above analysis. While Mahan's approach to scholarship developed after the turn of the century, he never escaped the trammels of his method. It was left to the most important of Laughton's disciples, Julian Corbett, to produce a truly great work on the role of maritime power in national strategy. In the interval the task of promoting the naval vision of national strategy still required Laughton's assistance.

A year after his examination of Mahan's second 'Sea Power' book Laughton continued his discussion of national defence in the *Edinburgh Review*. Using a collection of Parliamentary Returns, Naval Handbooks and foreign publications he linked the growing intimacy between France and Russia, which had culminated in a secret alliance before the review appeared, with the need to increase the Navy. Before giving way to alarm Laughton cautioned his readers to consider why these two states were spending so lavishly money they had to raise in loans to build up their naval power. He discounted the 'challenge' posed by the Naval Defence Act, on the grounds that: 'For England the navy is a necessity of existence; for France and for Russia it is a mere appendage of power ... Beyond certain easily defined limits, it cannot be other than aggressive'.[81] This was demonstrated by contrasting the 13½ million tons of British merchant shipping with 1½ million tons possessed by France and Russia combined. Their ambitions, he believed, included mastery of the Mediterranean, the recovery of sea-borne trade and the conquest of Turkey. In fact the Dual Alliance was only ever effective as a defensive instrument against Germany, against whom their naval forces offered a real offensive opportunity in the mid-1890s. However, Laughton addressed the core debate on the challenge to Britain's command of the Mediterranean.

> All this, however, is entirely a question of relative force. At present, and still less in the immediate future, we have not that superiority which might be required, not only in the Mediterranean, but everywhere.

In the face of a Franco-Russian combination the Mediterranean was the most obvious cause for concern.[82] But Laughton took a wider view, wanting an adequate reserve of modern battleships to support British

---

81. 'Naval Armaments', *Edinburgh Review* (April 1894), pp447-78 at p448.
82. Marder, A J, *The Anatomy of British Sea Power* (London 1940), pp209-12.

policy.[83] Using official returns he calculated that a bare margin of superiority in 1894, twenty-seven to twenty-five, would turn into a marked inferiority by 1898, thirty-four to forty-nine. These figures prompted a powerful attack on Gladstone:

> how was it possible to believe the interests and the honour of the country safe in the hands of a Minister who, with the figures we have quoted before him, could say that 'the navy was adequate to perform its duties and to meet all contingencies in a manner adequate to the wants of the country.[84]

Such short-term complacency could only lead to a revolt. In truth the revolt was coming from within the Cabinet, with the demands of the Admiralty Lords under the formidable Frederick Richards, being exploited by Lord Rosebery, the Foreign Secretary. Rosebery wanted to restore British dominance of the Mediterranean to secure Britain's balancing position between the Triple Alliance and the Franco-Russian bloc. The ultimate object was to retain British freedom from the European alliance system, from a position of strength. Earl Spencer was a willing agent in a process that brought Gladstone's political career to an end a month before the review appeared.[85] Laughton considered the persistence of naval scares in the last twenty years 'not creditable either to the country, or to the constitution of the navy'. They arose because the Navy was essential to Britain, and yet there was no definite policy to maintain it. This he traced to the disciples of Cobden:

> they have failed to understand the enormous increase to the responsibilities thrown on the navy by the adoption of Free Trade. They are willing to accept the financial and economic advantages of the system; they quail before the outlay which is an integral part of it.[86]

Much of the problem could be traced to the dominance of contemporary politics by financial issues, for low estimates were invariably followed by panic and hasty expenditure. Laughton pointed out that he had exposed politically-motivated alarm in 1885, when the Navy had been in good shape, and praised the Naval Defence Act for attempting, 'to lift the control of the Navy out of the rut of party politics'.[87] By way of contrast the current administration had only belatedly announced a programme that would not sustain the 'Two Power Standard' that had been

---

83. 'Naval Armaments', p457.
84. Ibid, p459.
85. Martel, G, *Imperial Diplomacy: Lord Rosebery and the Failure of Foreign Policy* (Montreal 1986), pp151-7. Gordon, P (ed), *The Red Earl: The Papers of the Fifth Earl Spencer 1835-1910*, Vol II *1885-1910* (Northampton 1986), pp231-43.
86. 'Naval Armaments', pp463-4.
87. Ibid, p465.

re-affirmed in 1889. He offered some hope for the embattled Chancellor of the Exchequer by repeating his call for 9-10,000-ton battleships in lieu of the 14-15,000-ton monsters currently being built. In this argument, one of his longest-running themes, Laughton had allowed strategic and tactical ideas from the past to solidify into dogma. He was completely wrong on this question, while the historical evidence he deployed to support his case was unconvincing. Not only were Sir William White's epochal battleship designs, the *Royal Sovereign* of 1889 and the *Majestic* of 1894, greatly superior to their foreign contemporaries,[88] but they were also far cheaper to build, because the British Royal Dockyards and private shipbuilders were highly efficient.[89] Laughton's attack on the excessive size of cruisers, prompted by the 14,000-ton *Powerful,* was more coherent. He proposed to limit cruisers to 4000 tons, and above them build Second Class battleships. This was in line with the experience of the past.

The security of the Empire rested on the Navy, and he recognised that the Franco-Russian attempt to out-build the Royal Navy was a peculiar form of challenge:

> a financial struggle for the supremacy of the sea. Nor can we avoid it, or shrink from it without sustaining a defeat which would certainly involve us in far more serious losses and a much larger expenditure.

Failure to sustain British dominance in the Mediterranean would upset the European equilibrium, with incalculable results. For Laughton arms races were a key component in the deterrent core of British strategy. A major naval programme, involving very heavy expenditure, might well kill off the embryo naval race before it had even begun.[90] He was also alarmed by the lack of an adequate reserve of officers and men, as it was the men, not the ships, that would win the next war.

The cause of seapower was advanced once more when Laughton analysed the Sino-Japanese War of 1894. He argued that it was illogical to assume that just because all Europe had become a vast armed camp, Britain should follow suit. Her unique situation and requirements made naval strength the only sure defence. Where Mahan had shown that the lessons of sea power could be drawn from the past, the current war provided fresh evidence to support the case. He also took the opportunity to lambaste Rosebery for 'inaction' in an area where British interests were large.[91]

---

88. Burt, R A, *British Battleships 1889-1904* (London 1988), pp 311-16.
89. Manning, F, *Sir William White* (London 1923), pp188-231. Haas, J, *A Management Odyssey: the Royal Dockyards 1701-1914* (New York 1994), pp147-67. Pollard, S, and Robertson, P, *The British Shipbuilding Industry 1870-1914* (Harvard 1979), pp206-7.
90. 'Naval Armaments', pp473 and 474.
91. 'The Naval War in the East', *Edinburgh Review* (Oct 1894), pp497-516 at pp498-9 and 515.

HE CONCEPT of AN ARMOURED CRUISER of 10 TO 14,000 TONS WAS FATALLY FLAWED

Writing in *The Nineteenth Century* in March 1895, the naval journalist William Laird Clowes (1856-1904) had advocated 'scuttling' out of the Mediterranean, and sealing up the exits with new bases. He was widely condemned, most effectively by George Sydenham Clarke, who observed that the loss of national honour and traditions together with the eternal principles of naval strategy opposed such a surrender.[92] James Thursfield in *The Times* was equally trenchant. Clarke's essay was one the two men republished in their collection *The Navy and the Nation* of 1897, in order to deal with the 'dangerous fallacy' that Clarke had exposed.[93] The fact that there were two such powerful, well-placed and effective writers prepared to devote their efforts to supporting the historical case must have pleased Laughton. The task he and Bridge had carried out for nearly thirty years could now be largely left to others. This passing of the torch would leave him more time for the larger task of recovering national strategy from the archives. After the 'scuttle' controversy he did not feel that Clowes's projected *Naval History* would be of much help in this task. He required work of a higher standard.

After 1870 history dominated Laughton's work. He used the experience of the past to instruct and prepare the decision-makers and warriors of the present to meet an uncertain future. He believed that, in addition to taking the central role in the development of modern naval doctrine, history could provide much of the evidence required to build a national strategy.[94] Having recognised the vital importance of professional scholarship through his work with mathematics and contact with Gardiner, Laughton sought archival materials with which to illuminate the strategy of the past. His historical training, however belated, had been sufficiently thorough for him to recognise that there was no purpose in building castles on the sand. Having little worthwhile material with which to work, he devoted the last three decades of his life to the publication of those materials. Both the selection of material and the editorial approach were influenced by the contemporary defence debates. This was the real utility of his work. Hard evidence and realistic analysis were the only antidote to the romantic picture of heroic amateurs that passed for naval history. History would provide both the doctrine to educate the Navy of the future, and the strategic direction which would guide it. Where Mahan imposed his analysis on the broad sweep of history, Laughton sought key events and subjected them to professional study in depth, breadth and context to illuminate the problems of the present. This was a method he had found particularly effective with a naval audience.

---

92. Marder, A J, *The Anatomy of British Sea Power* (London 1940), p211.
93. Clarke, G S and Thursfield, J R, *The Navy and the Nation* (London 1897), p228.
94. Laughton, J K, 'Historians and Naval History', *The Cornhill Magazine* (1913).

From the beginning Laughton recognised the distinction between tactics and strategy, observing how national strategies differed, and the consequences this had for battle tactics. Only a careful examination of the historical record could provide the evidence to develop a national strategy. This was not an academic exercise: the debate on national strategy in the second half of the nineteenth century raised a series of challenges to the accepted wisdom of the preceding two centuries. Steam, armour, heavy artillery, railways and mass armies clearly changed the nature of warfare, and the role of seapower within the overall picture. Laughton examined the major historical examples for the benefit of the contemporary Navy. Initially he did this in essays, reviews and lectures at Greenwich and the RUSI, but after 1885 he came to rely more on the edited collection of documents, convinced that a more sophisticated analysis could only be built when the materials had been exploited. This approach required him to enlist the support of other professional historians, and develop a school to carry on his work. The influence he could exert would increasingly be indirect, and his archival labours would be exploited by others. While he praised Mahan's efforts at synthesis, he deprecated his weak research base and his lack of archival authority. His response was as astonishing as it was selfless. Laughton acted as Mahan's research coordinator in Britain, ensuring that the American had access to the materials required to write better books. He was equally generous with his time and knowledge with other scholars. Their labours would enhance and further the themes and ideas that he had worked at for so long. His selfless approach is most obvious in his reviews, which contained almost all his post-1885 writing on strategy.

Although Laughton never published a work on strategy, he was eminently capable of writing on the subject. In 1895 he contracted to write *Naval Strategy and the Protection of Commerce* in 'The Royal Navy Handbooks' series.[95] Other contributors to the series included Vesey-Hamilton, and the series editor Charles Napier Robinson. Robinson edited *Brassey's Naval Annual* in 1894, which carried Laughton's 'Convoy' essay, which suggests the plan had already been settled.[96] The series required short, largely factual studies. The combination of other demands on his time and the existing strategic work of Mahan, which Laughton considered had already served the purpose, may explain his failure to deliver. Given the pressure of work he was subjecting himself to, with the *DNB* in full spate, the administration and editing requirements of the Navy Records Society, with *Nelson and His Companions* and the *Memoir of Henry Reeve* to compose it is likely that the financial rewards did not

95. George Bell & Sons to Laughton 23.2.1895. JKL MS.
96. Vesey-Hamilton, Admiral Sir R, *Naval Administration* (London 1896). Armstrong, Lt. E, *Torpedoes and Torpedo Vessels* (London 2nd ed. 1901).

justify him setting aside other tasks for a work which would add little or nothing to the existing literature.

The protection of commercial shipping had been a feature of Laughton's work from the early 1870s, with a separate lecture proposed for the Greenwich course. It received fresh emphasis in the 1890s, reflecting contemporary concern with Franco-Russian cruiser squadrons. Laughton had stressed the importance of the strategic picture from his first papers, indeed the ability to comprehend the strategic picture was a critical part of the distinction he made between history and chronicles.[97] Trade and trade defence had been significant themes in his 'scientific' phase, and in *Edinburgh Review* articles on naval policy. Mahan's second *Sea Power* volume and Colomb's *Essays on Naval Defence* persuaded him that convoy was the answer. In contrast to the useless waste of hunting, he recognised convoy as a 'concentration of effort' combining his favourite tactical concept with sound strategy. He also endorsed Mahan's recognition that British strategists had made a major contribution to trade defence by capturing hostile cruiser bases in the later stages of the Napoleonic Wars. He recognised, and here he and Mahan were running against the tide, that Britain's greatest strength had been, and would be, her endurance.[98]

Twelve years later Laughton examined 'Britain's Naval Policy' for the Cambridge summer extension lectures. Here he stressed that naval actions were only the mean to the end of securing sea communications, and repeated the message that history demonstrated that convoy would be the real answer to French attacks on British commerce. With naval superiority the country was safe from invasion, the Empire would be preserved and the commerce that linked them would be secured. Naval warfare was concerned with securing and maintaining that command.[99] In 1910 he observed that the principle concern of the Admiralty during the campaign of 1805 had been the protection of sea-borne commerce, not the visionary *chimera* of an invasion. Nothing had changed in the intervening century.[100]

Despite the role of Ranke in his development as an historian Laughton, unlike his friend Stephen Luce, was not influenced by the continental military strategists. His approach was firmly based on naval experience. As a result he never produced a systematic appreciation of the relationship between politics and grand strategy. However, he understood the issues, and covered this theme in any number of reviews after 1882. It is

---

97. Laughton, J K, 'The Study of Naval History', *JRUSI* (1896), p798.
98. Ibid, April 1893, p511.
99. Laughton, J K, 'Britain's Naval Policy' in Kirkpatrick, F A, *Lectures on History in the Nineteenth Century* (Cambridge 1903), pp79-95.
100. Laughton, J K (ed), *Letters of Lord Barham* Vol III (London, NRS 1910), pxxxii.

noteworthy that his disciple, Corbett, brilliantly combined the empirical British tradition with the system building analysis of Clausewitz, and that he did so in the period 1905-06. Laughton had made a massive contribution to the development of a British strategy, his insistence on the primacy of clear and accurate historical scholarship and the deployment of examples to examine issues, rather than to support preconceived nostrums provided Corbett with the building blocks for *Some Principles of Maritime Strategy* in 1911. In the introduction Corbett deployed a single example to support his theoretical study of war, one that had been used many times by Laughton as the basis of a call for doctrine.[101]

101. Corbett, J S, *Some Principles of Maritime Strategy* (London 1911), p2. The example is Captain Carkett's failure to comprehend the meaning of Admiral Sir George Rodney's signal on 17 April 1780. See Laughton, J K, *Letters and Papers of Charles, Lord Barham* Vol I (London NRS 1907) pxlviii. The example was such a good one that it survived into an early draft of the Royal Navy's first public statement of doctrine BR 1806 of 1996, despite the events of 17 April 1780 being quite unknown to all but a handful of specialist historians!

CHAPTER 6

'You have the satisfaction of looking back upon an unusual amount of solid work accomplished'[1]: The Navy Records Society 1893-1915

———————— · ————————

The marked change in fortune for naval issues that occurred between the passage of the Naval Defence Act of 1889 and the appearance of Mahan's second *Sea Power* volume in 1892, made naval history genuinely 'popular'. To exploit the opportunity to serve the interests of the Navy and the state, Laughton used his pivotal position to marshal the disparate elements that would form the Navy Records Society (NRS). Although the journalists David Hannay and William Laird Clowes were instrumental in raising the debate, the Society was founded by Laughton, with help from Bridge, the Director of Naval Intelligence (DNI). The link with the DNI's department was sustained down to 1914, by a succession of brilliant officers who came under the influence of Bridge and Laughton, including Reginald Custance, Prince Louis of Battenberg, Charles Ottley, Edmond Slade, Henry May and Herbert Richmond. The presence of gifted officers within a stone's throw of the regular meeting place of the Council was, no doubt, an attraction, but there was a deeper import to this link.

Laughton had long been anxious to publish some of the rich archival materials he had located. He discussed the issue with Bridge and Napier Robinson, but doubted there would be sufficient public support. He had no hope of government aid. When Hannay's *National Observer* articles appeared, calling for rare books to be reprinted, Laughton and Bridge decided to act.[2] A decade later Clowes claimed that he had been responsible for the Society.[3] Generously attributing much of its success to, 'the devotion of its secretary and editor, Professor John Knox Laughton', hardly compensated for the sheer audacity of his assertion. Yet Clowes

---

1. Mahan to Laughton 23.7.1912 JKL MS.
2. Laughton, J K, 'The Study of Naval History', *JRUSI* (1896), p808.
3. Clowes, Sir W L, *The Royal Navy: A History* Vol VII (London 1904), p83.

THIS IS LAUGHTONS CONCLUSION: THE PASSAGE CAN BE INTEPRETED DIFFERENTLY

has gone down in the record as the founder of the Society. Arthur Marder accepted Clowes's version and ignored Laughton, who did not even warrant an entry in the index. Given the derivative nature of so much history it is scarcely surprising that this omission, in the only substantial work on the period, should have influenced the literature.[4] That the claim was untrue should have been obvious from Clowes's failure to contribute anything to the Society. Laughton's personal copy of Clowes's book contains the following rebuttal, written on the offending page:

> A very impudent lie. Neither then, nor afterwards had Clowes any knowledge of the Admiralty Records, and his suggestion must have been based on a conversation with me at Chelsea in the spring of '91. I never saw – nor heard of, till long afterwards – the letters he refers to: & the NRS grew out of a conversation between me and Admiral Bridge in the spring of '93. JKL.[5]

The Chelsea Exhibition had been particularly important. Laughton was already thinking how to exploit the success of the event, and had sketched out in his own mind the scheme that he would adopt in 1893. His own contribution was central, as only a professional historian would have proposed publishing volumes of edited documents. Furthermore his relationship with Bridge was critical. The two men had worked together in the interests of the service for over thirty years. Having achieved eminence in their respective careers they had the authority, experience and contacts for a new departure. The first six names in the list of members are revealing; after Laughton and Bridge come Robinson, Admiral Sir Edward Fanshawe, Hornby and *The Times* naval correspondent James Thursfield.[6] Laughton and Bridge had canvassed support before attempting to set up the Society, receiving over fifty pledges. Laughton wrote to his friend Hornby and James Anthony Froude, the Regius Professor at Oxford. Froude was uncertain, hoping the editors would not follow the practice of 'giving us a great deal of themselves with a limited quantity of original matter'.[7] There was some truth in Froude's observations, but he did not live to comment on Laughton's Armada volumes, where he had some expertise.

By the time the founders met there were already fifty-six names on the list, including Joseph Chamberlain, the Duke of Norfolk, George Sydenham Clarke and his friend Captain Caspar Goodrich USN, the American naval attaché, Lord Northbrook and the Bishop of Peterborough. The Society was formed at a meeting in the Royal United

---

4. Marder, A J, *The Anatomy of British Seapower: A History of British Naval Policy in the Pre-Dreadnought Era 1880-1905* (London 1940), p45.
5. Laughton's personal copy of Clowes, Vol VII, Library of King's College, London. Marginalia on p83. (He reviewed the book for the *Athanaeum*.)
6. Navy Records Society Minute Books NRS1 p1.
7. Froude to Laughton 12.6.23 and 29.7.1893 JKL MS. Quote from 29.7.1893.

Services Institute on 13 June 1893, with Bridge in the Chair. The room was filled with Laughton's friends and colleagues; he knew everyone there. He proposed that a Society be established 'for publishing rare works or manuscripts of naval interest'. Sidney Lee seconded the motion. Fanshawe and Prince Louis then proposed the Society, and that the First Lord of Admiralty, Earl Spencer be requested to accept the office of President. Admiral Sir Richard Vesey-Hamilton, First Sea Lord 1889-91 suggested that a provisional committee should draw up a Council list and submit it to a general meeting, seconded by Hubert Hall from the Public Record Office. This was agreed by an audience that included Sir Thomas Brassey, Clarke, Hannay, Admiral Wharton the Hydrographer of the Navy, and Philip Colomb. Much of the discussion centred on finding an appropriate name. Following the precedent of the Hakluyt and Camden Societies, the name of Sir William Monson was thought most suitable. A report in the *Daily Chronicle* stressed that the society was to be historical rather than naval.[8] Bridge found the meeting, 'very encouraging', and urged his friend Custance to secure more supporters.[9] Elected Secretary, Laughton's first task was to write to Earl Spencer, with the Society's request that he become the President.[10] When Spencer agreed Laughton sought his assistance in securing the Duke of Edinburgh to chair the Council in Spencer's absence, as 'it would give us a hoist into public notice that might be worth a great deal.[11]

The membership of Council was agreed at a meeting on 27 June. In the interim Laughton had obtained the written advice of several leading scholars and editors, namely Montagu Burrows, the Tory Chichele Professor at Oxford, Sir John Seeley, Regius Professor at Cambridge, Gardiner, Charles Hadfield Firth, Henry Reeve, Sidney Lee and Thursfield. The scholars contributed their experience of the Camden and other learned publishing societies to the process, which simplified the search for rules and provided support for the scholarly rigour Laughton desired. Reeve, Robinson and Thursfield provided the powerful endorsement and continuing support of the *Edinburgh Review*, the *Army and Navy Gazette* and *The Times*. Thursfield proved to be a stout supporter of the Society, and a great admirer of Laughton. The First Annual General Meeting on 4 July confirmed the work of the Special Committee.[12] In a report that read like a resume of Laughton's agenda, *The Times* observed there was no naval history of the country worthy of the name, despite the abundance of

---

8. *The Army and Navy Gazette* (17.6.1893), p498.
9. Bridge to Custance 14.6.1893. Bridge MSS NMM BRI 18.
10. Laughton to Spencer 13.6.1893, endorsed 'I approve, reply' in Spencer's hand: Althorp MS BL K342.
11. Laughton to Spencer 15.7.1893: ibid.
12. Laughton to Sidney Lee 23.11.1893: MSS Eng. Misc. d.178 Sidney Lee MS Bodleian Library, Oxford. f246.

NAVY RECORDS SOCIETY.

MINUTE FOR THE GUIDANCE OF EDITORS.

At a Meeting of the Council held on 26th July, 1893, it was resolved that :—

In order to provide for uniformity of plan in the Society's publications, the Editor of any work for the Society be requested to observe the following Regulations.

1.—Every publication is to be preceded by introductory matter, briefly setting forth the condition of affairs at the time, and the relation of the persons who form the subject of the book with those times.

2.—Every work is to be illustrated by notes, sufficient ·to make it intelligible and interesting.

3.—Every volume is to have a full index of names (persons, places and ships) and of subjects.

4.—Every work is to be printed *verbatim* from the best available text; and if previously printed, to be compared with the original MS. when practicable.

> [Especial care must be taken to avoid even the suspicion of having garbled the original, in accordance with, or in support of any preconceived notion.   When it is necessary to omit passages on account of excessive length, or otherwise, or in the case of a collection of letters, on account of their having only private or non-naval interest, it is generally desirable that a précis of such passages or omitted letters should be given, sufficient to show clearly the subject of them.]

5.—Modern spelling, use of capitals and punctuation, are as a rule, to be adopted ; but remarkable monstrosities of spelling may be given in notes.   Obsolete words are to be spelt uniformly, according to the best antique usage.

6.— Obsolete names of places are to be spelt uniformly, as far as practicable, with a note of the modern names, or of their locality, if no longer in existence.

7.—The spelling of men's names is to follow, as far as practicable, their own signatures.   Misspellings, apparently phonetic, may be given in a note as a guide to the pronunciation of the time.

documentary sources, consequently 'the object of that Society was to gather those documents together, and to produce from them an adequate naval history of England'.[13] On the 19th a Committee discussed the editorial rules, and produced a set based on Camden practice (see page 145).

> Especial care must be taken to avoid even the suspicion of having garbled the original, in accordance with, or in support of any preconceived notion.[14]

The meeting accepted Laughton's offer to edit the papers on the critical years 1585-88, David Hannay's proposal to edit Lord Hood's correspondence from 1780-82 and Clements Markham's suggestion of the Journal of Stephen Martin.

Before Council met at the end of July Laughton had 12,000 prospectuses printed, placing 5000 each in the *Journal of the Royal Geographical Society* and the *Journal of the Royal United Services Institution*. The membership of these two bodies contained his target audience; statesmen, sailors and soldiers. They had also provided him with experience of Society administration and politics. He had just been recalled to the Council of the Royal Geographical by the new President, Sir Clements Markham, who sought his aid to quash the double-headed revolt of 1892 over the 'women' and 'doctrinnaire' questions.[15] Prince Louis had recruited the Royal Sailor Dukes, Edinburgh and York (later King George V). In an effort to boost recruitment of desirable members, Laughton wrote to 'Mahan, Chevalier and any other foreigners of literary distinction'.[16] The next Council, in November, gave him a blanket permission to admit new members whose social status was not in doubt, reserving only the unknown and 'doubtful' for Council's consideration.[17]

Laughton believed the time was ripe to establish a permanent body to carry on his work in the archives, enlarging the pool of scholars to create a worthwhile database from which to develop doctrine. In 1896 he explained what he hoped the Society would achieve. The opening of national archives to scholars during the past fifty years had revolutionised the opportunities for historical study, but, in the case of the Public Record Office, the old problem of paucity of sources had been replaced by 'an enormous store':

> The principal, and at present insuperable difficulty is in the excessive abundance of material. Life is short, and the task of deciphering

---

13. *The Times* 5.7.1893, p5; almost certainly written by Thursfield.
14. Navy Records Society: Minute for the Guidance of Editors. NRS 1 p55 interleaved.
15. Minute Book of the Royal Geographical Society. Unpublished memoir of the RGS by Sir Clements Markham.
16. NRS1, p60.
17. Council 7.11.1893 NRS1, p64.

manuscripts, often very badly written in ink that has faded or been partly obliterated by damp or dust, is long. What one man can do is relatively nothing; and even when he confines his labours to a very short period, or to one special subject, to be quite sure of having arrived at an exhaustive result is very difficult indeed. And yet without that exhaustive treatment, finality is not to be obtained. Selections – whether made by chance or by judgement – are unsatisfactory and uncertain. There is always a suspicion that the selector has been guided by prejudice rather than by an unbiased search for truth, and that documents which tell against his preconceived notions have been withheld.

As an example he noted that naval dispatches were invariably edited before publication, either for brevity, style or to satisfy more sinister motives. The original papers would reveal much.[18]

As Secretary, Laughton ran the Society; he directed its publishing programme, sought editors, and often advised shifting the focus of volumes. His main resources were his own unrivalled knowledge, the support of the leading members of the Society, and the availability of Society funds to pay for transcripts. This last was of inestimable value, the availability of transcripts persuading busy scholars to take on editorial tasks. They had a major role in Corbett's first volume, funded the acquisition and translation of the Dutch material that Gardiner used, opened archives in Italy and France, and were even considered as a method of securing the archival wealth of Spain. They also allowed naval officers to contribute, despite lacking the time for sustained archival work. Society policy was for such transcripts as were of real interest to be deposited in the British Library, notably the Dutch material used by Gardiner. The Society never owned manuscripts, or even the facilities to store them, relying on friendly archives and libraries to act as custodians of material on loan. Any archival materials that were presented were deposited at the British Library, whose Director, Frederick Kenyon, was a founder member.[19]

Laughton's approach to the publication programme was revealing. Although anxious to fill in the yawning chasm that lay between Nicolas and James, with particular emphasis on the major wars and campaigns, he recognised that an unrelieved diet of high policy and strategy would not meet his objects. The Council Minutes over the first twenty years demonstrate that Laughton was combining work on the core subjects that were vital for doctrine development, such as his own *Armada* and *Barham* volumes, Oppenheim's *Henry VII* and *Monson*, Gardiner's *First Dutch War*, Corbett's *1585-87* and *Fighting Instructions*, and the Vesey-Hamilton/Leyland *Blockade of Brest*, with the lighter, more human dimension provided by individual memoirs and accounts from less

18. Laughton, J K, 'Our Naval Records', *The Army and Navy Illustrated* (29.5.1896), pp265-6.
19. Council 13.10.1903 NRS 2: p34.

prominent figures. He also strove to produce two volumes on different periods each year; the clear understanding being that the guinea a year entitled subscribers to two volumes. When the First World War threatened to cut production to only one volume per annum Council reduced the subscription to half a guinea.[20]

As a subscription society established to print manuscripts dealing with the history, organisation or social life of the Navy, the Navy Records Society combined Laughton's drive to develop a written doctrine for the Navy with the methodology of the professional historian. The Society, which has recently celebrated its centenary, still bears his imprint. He built it in his own image, bringing together all the strands that made up his hectic life; and assembled his friends and colleagues into the critical membership, including Royal Princes, senior naval officers, professional and amateur historians, statesmen, soldiers, politicians and journalists. His one-time pupils were now admirals, and through them he had access to the First Lord of Admiralty, senior politicians and Royalty.[21] Laughton used the publication of documents to justify naval history to 'professional' historians, and encouraged many to join the Society. They, in turn, lent additional credibility to its work.[22] Hornby summed up the attitude of the service when he declared:

> I hope the Navy Records Society may succeed. I fancy our forefathers were more careful than we are about telling the truth, and therefore the more we can retain of what they recorded, the better.[23]

This must have gratified Laughton. Having introduced history into the naval curriculum he now sought the aid of the academic community in furthering his efforts. He saw naval history as the critical educational tool for the modern Navy, and tried to widen the sources from which materials for this study could be drawn. Without the support of additional civilian scholars he could not hope to provide the range and quality of history needed to support naval doctrine and education. Laughton wanted to involve the academic community in the preparation and interpretation of materials on naval history for the instruction of the contemporary Royal Navy. As he explained to the Secretary of the RUSI, when asking for a reduced charge for the use of a Committee Room, the

---

20. Council 19.11.1915 NRS 3 p35.

21. Sainsbury, A B, *The Centenary of the Navy Records Society 1893-1993* (London 1993) discusses the origins and early days of the Society, together with details of the more prominent members.

22. Schurman, p95 fn.46. The praise heaped on Laughton in the prefaces to NRS volumes has to be taken at face value. Laughton would never have allowed any unwarranted advertisement to pass into print while he ran the Society.

23. Hornby to Laughton 16.6.1894 JKL MS.

Navy Records was 'entirely devoted to objects directly connected with the Royal Navy'.[24] From the outset it was envisaged that the Admiralty would buy a significant number of copies of volumes.[25]

By the end of 1893 Laughton had begun work on the first volume. Originally he had intended to cover the entire war with Spain, but 'the opinion of the Council was decidedly and probably correct, that it would be better to begin with the Armada'. After all, there was still a lively invasion debate to influence, and the role of the Navy in 1588 was just the sort of ammunition the navalists needed. The two-volume *State Papers Relating to the Defeat of the Spanish Armada* appeared in 1894, setting the Society's style. Laughton provided a very full Introduction, developing the strategic issues for a contemporary audience. Bridge asked Reeve, a fellow founder member, if he could review the volumes for the *Edinburgh Review*. Reeve was pleased to 'give a push to the Navy Records'.[26] Robinson and Thursfield ensured that the *Army and Navy Gazette* and *The Times* did the same.

The foundation of the Society was greatly influenced by Bridge's Naval Intelligence Department, which had a major influence on its objects and methods. Although the link was unofficial, it was highly significant. Bridge helped to recruit other 'intellectual' officers, and ensured that the institutional contact was maintained after he left the Department. Bridge served as Director of Naval Intelligence for close on six years and largely created the Department. In late 1892 Battenberg, the Assistant DNI, and Philip Colomb were the naval members of a Joint Service Committee investigating the possibility that Britain might be invaded.[27] They visited various French ports in the course of their work.[28] This Committee, and the whole question of naval primacy in national defence, which was a central theme of both Colomb's and Laughton's work, explain why the Council of the Records Society, which included Battenberg, Bridge and Colomb, insisted that the first volume deal with 1588.

A more obvious example of the intimate relationship between the Society and the service came in the field of tactics. Laughton's tactical writing continued to exert a significant impact on the service. This could be seen not only in the heightened, if eccentric, interest taken in the tactics of Trafalgar at the Centenary, but more specifically in the work of Admiral Custance (1847-1935).[29] Custance, an Assistant DNI under Bridge, also acknowledged his intellectual debt to Philip Colomb. He served as a

---

24. Laughton to RUSI 8.5.1895 NRS 1, p90.
25. Council 15.8.1895 NRS 1, p98.
26. Reeve to Bridge 23.8.1894 Bridge MSS BRI/17 NMM.
27. Kerr, M, *Prince Louis of Battenberg* (London 1934). Marder, *Anatomy*, pp68-78.
28. Battenberg to Colomb 6 & 14.12.1892: Colomb MS in private hands.
29. See Ch 8 for Custance's other work.

Councillor or Vice-President of the Society almost without a break from 1899 until his death. As DNI (1899-1902) Custance issued the fleet with a volume of old 'Fighting Instructions'. They were intended to promote the study of tactical doctrine, by illustrating the underlying principles.[30] Custance may have been advised by Laughton and William Perrin, the Admiralty Librarian. Custance was trying to start a study of war at the Admiralty, as an *alternative* to relying on the results of exercises. He believed the Army's experience in South Africa had demonstrated these to be a profoundly flawed source. Having collaborated to locate and develop the material Laughton and Custance decided that the most effective method of dissemination would be for the Society to publish it, with the clear intention that it should be made more generally available to the Navy. In October 1903 Laughton reported that the Earl of Dartmouth's MS had been loaned to the Record Office, and inspected by himself and Julian Corbett. The Fighting Instructions relating to the Third Dutch War were of particular interest, and Corbett agreed to edit them, with other material, to make a volume.[31] When the volume was published in 1905, Corbett admitted a 'special obligation' to Laughton and Custance:

> for, not only have they been kind enough to read the proofs of the work, but they have been indefatigable in offering suggestions, the one from his high professional knowledge and the other from his unrivalled learning in naval history. Any value indeed the work may be found to possess must in a large measure be attributed to them.[32]

The second volume, *Signals and Instructions*, began life as a small collection of new material. Laughton initially suggested that it be issued in a *Miscellany* volume, but the Council demanded that it be produced separately, clearly for the convenience of the Navy. In the end Corbett found enough new material to produce another full-sized volume, and the Council, while regretting the added cost incurred because the short version had already been set up in type, was anxious to produce the best volume. At the same meeting it was decided not to make a public appeal to secure the funds for a large-scale project to work in the Spanish archives.[33] The contrasting fates of these two projects reflects the intimate link between the Society and the Navy, and a relative dilution of the academic side of Laughton's objectives. By 1908 Corbett and Custance

30. Allen, M, 'Rear-Admiral Reginald Custance: Director of Naval Intelligence 1899-1902', *Mariner's Mirror* Vol 78 No 1 (1992), pp61-75, see p68.
31. Council 13.10.1903 NRS: p37.
32. Corbett, J S (ed), *Fighting Instructions 1530-1816* (London 1905), px. Internal evidence establishes that the only contemporary published authority Corbett used, and indeed used more than he cited, was Laughton's introduction to the *Letters and Dispatches of Lord Nelson*. See p337 on Dundonald and p422 on the 'Trafalgar memorandum'.
33. Council 13.3.1905; 13.10.1908, 9.3.1909: NRS 2: pp77, 126 & 132.

WHY?

had fallen out over Trafalgar, and Custance's name did not appear in the preface, being replaced by Perrin's. Laughton was thanked for locating new material, and other assistance.[34] Despite this Custance continued to work closely with Laughton, sending him copies of his 1910 Naval War College Lectures.[35]

When Corbett's *Fighting Instructions* appeared, Council agreed that it should be made available to officers in both services at the member's price of half a guinea, an offer repeated for the second volume. The Admiralty immediately ordered 100 copies, above and beyond their standing order of a dozen.[36] By 1913 the Admiralty's demands for certain, sadly unidentified, volumes, was such that reprinting had to be considered, and it was agreed that in future such volumes should have a larger initial print run.[37] One such volume may have been Herbert Richmond's *The Loss of Minorca 1756*, which appeared in the same year. Richmond printed the papers collected by the Admiralty to defend its handling of the Byng disaster. It was significant that the subject, the proper level of force to be maintained in the Mediterranean, was being discussed historically just as the contemporary Admiralty was having to deal with the same issue. As Richmond observed, the case 'enunciates some points of fact and strategy which are as true to-day as they were when they were written'.[38] Significantly *The Times* noted that the editor held a high position on the War Staff.[39] Richmond was then Assistant Director of the Operations Division, and the historical dimension of contemporary problems was the key to his output.[40]

Laughton's object in founding the Navy Records Society, and in the process taking on a large amount of unpaid work, was the promotion of naval history as the basis of service education, and the naval case in national defence. By publishing archival material he hoped to build a durable foundation for the subject, so that it could bear the weight of scholarship and service polemic without compromise. He recognised that the 1890s were a propitious time for a Society that would spread the message beyond the service itself. This required him to enlist the widest range of supporters in his cause, tempering his scholastic rigour, if only slightly, in the interest of intellectual appeal. The membership of the Society, although small, more than compensated for this by its distinction

34. Corbett, J S, *Signals and Instructions 1776-94* (London 1908), px.
35. Custance, R, 'The Military Growth of the Capital Ship' and 'Lissa, the Yalu and the Capital Ship': Laughton Pamphlet Collection, Admiralty Library P465, & P462.
36. Council 5.7.1905: 10.10.1905 NRS 2: pp70-2.
37. Council 14.10.1913 & 9.12.1913: NRS 3: pp3-8.
38. Richmond, H W (ed), *Papers Relating to the Loss of Minorca in 1756* (London NRS 1913) Vol XLII, pxxxix.
39. *The Times* 26.6.1913 p9 Review.
40. I am indebted to my friend Professor Dan Baugh for this insight.

and, more significantly, its access to the levers of power (see the Appendix for a list of the Council 1893-1915). It must have gladdened his heart to read out the apologies of the Prime Minister, Lord Rosebery, to the 1894 Annual General Meeting.[41] Other leading figures included the father and son pairing of Joseph and Austen Chamberlain; Austen would serve on the Council.

By contrast to the membership, which was largely out of his hands, the Council, which met regularly at the RUSI to direct the policy of the Society, was renewed by rotation every year; councillors served for four years before standing-down. An analysis of those who served on the Council in the period 1893 to 1915 throws up some interesting individuals, and a number of important trends. When Sir John Seeley died Laughton replaced him with Clements Markham, who was a good chairman for meetings, and had already acted as such.[42] After an initial burst of enthusiasm the Council meetings were attended for most of the 1890s by a hard core of less than ten members. After 1900 the figures went up to the low teens. This was a group which Laughton could influence, he could rely on it to further his aims.

Laughton was among the first to recognise that Mahan's success could be exploited to further the naval cause. Having enlisted Mahan as a member he repeatedly tried to get him to attend the Council, and although events conspired to prevent this occurring, the support of the one truly world-famous naval writer was useful.[43] Mahan was an early convert to the importance of the Society, and an avid reader of its volumes.[44] The third, *Letters of Lord Hood, 1781-1782*, led him to reconsider the influence this remarkable man had exercised on Nelson. The letters were so suggestive that he came to regard Hood as second only to his great protégé.[45] When the controversy over Nelson's conduct at Naples drew to a close, Mahan was delighted by Gardiner's felicitous suggestion that the materials should be published by the Society: 'I can conceive of no worthier use of the Society's means than to gather in one accessible volume the demonstration of Nelson's integrity, & trust it may be feasible to do so.'[46] When he reviewed the resulting volume he took particular care to give the Society, 'some of the credit it deserves'.[47] Later Laughton asked Mahan to check an eighteenth-century Spanish naval manuscript in

41. *The Times* 13.6.1894 p10.
42. Markham, A H, *Life of Sir Clements Markham* (London 1917), p324. Markham's Journal: RGS.
43. Mahan to Laughton 13.6.1894 and 9.6.1904 JKL MS.
44. Mahan, A T, *From Sail to Steam* (Boston 1907), p280.
45. Mahan to Laughton 14.8.1895 JKL MS.
46. Mahan to Laughton 23.11.1899 JKL MS. Gutteridge, H C (ed), *Nelson and the Neapolitan Jacobins* (London NRS 1900).
47. Mahan to Laughton 9.6.1904.

Boston for the Society. Mahan responded, 'Pray make what use you can of me for the N.R.S. I shall still remain a debtor to it, and especially to you personally'.[48] He assessed the importance of the manuscript as an addition to the existing British materials and recommended publication.[49] He also handled the arrangements for obtaining a transcript, which he checked before sending it to Laughton.[50]

It was a mark of Laughton's uniqueness that he served as Secretary and Editorial Director of the Society from 1893, and of his determination that he should hold the reigns for twenty years, before trying to hand the task on to his son Leonard in 1912. Although he was able to sub-contract the most mundane tasks, like stamping envelopes and proof-reading, to the children of his second marriage, the work load remained daunting.[51] It was not made easier by the sheer variety of editors who responded to his request. Even the most competent and 'professional' of these made great demands on his time, for his knowledge of the subject was unique, while he had an unrivalled range of contacts and, as Secretary, invariably wrote to the owners of private collections on behalf of his editors. He also arranged for transcripts to be made, at the Societies' expense,[52] exploiting his knowledge of the archives, and the advice of his friend Hubert Hall at the Public Record Office. From the beginning he was enjoined by Council to 'exercise strict supervision over the editing'.[53]

The sheer scale of his efforts is revealed by the extant correspondence, the well-earned thanks that even he had to leave in the Introductions to the Society's volumes and unsolicited payments. By early 1897 the Councillors, prompted by Vesey-Hamilton and Marquis of Lothian, decided that he should receive an honorarium of £50 'in view of the services rendered to the Society . . . As a small token of their appreciation'. In accepting Laughton stressed that he had taken on the work, 'without expectation of reward, and purely as a labour of love'.[54] The following day Vesey-Hamilton suggested to the President, Earl Spencer, that an appropriate recognition should be made of Laughton's services.[55] In the event Laughton had to wait another decade, until the Liberals were back in power, for public recognition. In 1900 his value to the Society as Secretary and Editorial Director led Vesey-Hamilton and Gardiner to

48. Mahan to Laughton 18.6.1901.
49. Mahan to Laughton 7.10.1901 JKL MS. The paper appeared as 'The Journal of M De Lage de Cueilly, Captain the Spanish Navy' in Laughton, J K (ed), *The Naval Miscellany: Volume II* (London, NRS 1910), pp207-28.
50. Mahan to Laughton 21.1.1902 JKL MS.
51. Laughton-Mathews, V, *The Blue Tapestry* (London 1948), p23.
52. Laughton to Corbett 5.1.1895 Corbett MS Box 14.
53. Council 5.6.1894 NRS 1 p76.
54. Lothian Minute 2.2.1897 NRS 1 p112.
55. Spencer to Vesey-Hamilton 2.2.1897. Vesey-Hamilton MS VH/9.

move that he should receive an annual salary of £100, backdated to the preceding January. In expressing his gratitude Laughton observed that as the Society could afford the sum he accepted it with thanks.[56] Vesey-Hamilton had caused him problems by taking up and then dropping projects, his first proposal, to deal with the Blockade of Brest 1803-1805, had to be given up to a paid editor, John Leyland, who worked under Hamilton's 'supervision' at £25 a volume.[57] Laughton had recruited Leyland, sub-editor of the *Army and Navy Gazette,* who he considered 'a very capable man', for the task.[58] He adopted this otherwise undesirable solution because he was anxious to produce a well-balanced programme.

The editorial policy of the Society reflected the didactic purpose for which it had been created. The more important volumes were provided with lengthy introductions, which covered not only the provenance of the material, and its contemporary significance, but extended to provide 'lessons' for the policy-makers of the day. This was quite distinct from the bare notices that were prefaced to the standard 'Historical Manuscript Commission' volumes. Despite this scholarship took precedence over the message. Laughton saw the NRS volumes as the basis from which teaching texts would be written. These would be much improved by contact with primary sources. They, and not the NRS volumes, would make the more overtly propagandistic points for the Navy. In this respect the presence of navalist journalists and even Kipling on the Council can be seen as a critical part of the Society's ambition. While the editorial treatment may have reflected the political circumstances that had given rise to the Society, the selection of subjects addressed the needs of naval historical scholarship. Laughton had long recognised the problems caused by the weak or non-existent coverage of the period between 1417 and 1793. He was anxious to begin with the Dutch Wars, which combined fundamental tactical developments, intense periods of combat and purely 'maritime' wars. He would also use the Society's resources to address controversial themes and subjects, notably the Neapolitan material relating to Nelson.[59] He persuaded the Council to provide £20 for Gutteridge to 'support' his efforts to persuade the Neapolitan archivists to be more forthcoming with their treasures.[60] In general the editors who worked for the Society performed their allotted tasks well. This reflected Laughton's selection policy, and his careful supervision. Only one editor failed to meet his high standards and, unfortunately, the resulting volume managed to get into print, where it has remained as a salutary example of how not to edit documents.

OSCAR
BROWNING

---

56. Council 22.5.1900 NRS 1 p149.
57. Council 11.12.1895 NRS 1 p100.
58. Laughton to Sidney Lee 26.2.1896. Lee MSS, f248.
59. Council 1.12.1899 NRS 1 p147.
60. Council 19.11.1901 NRS 2 p11.

Laughton recognised that the Society would only make progress when it had something to show, and in consequence took on the task of producing the first volume himself.[61] He also recruited some important editors. Within days Michael Oppenheim (1853-1927) had offered to edit a series of Elizabethan pamphlets.[62] Oppenheim produced six volumes for the Society, among other important contributions to the subject, and was an unusual historian. The son of a Jewish East End furniture maker, he qualified as a surgeon and briefly served at sea in that capacity in the 1880s with the Royal Mail Steamship Company. But by 1888 he had acquired enough money, either by marriage or inheritance, to take up the life of a gentleman scholar, and began to publish on the Elizabethan Navy in the *English Historical Review* from 1891. These articles led to his major work, *The Administration of the Royal Navy: Vol. I 1509-1660* of 1896. An avowed republican,[63] he seems to have suffered from hypochondria and depression, abandoning work on the manuscript of the second and third volumes of his *Administration* book after problems with his publisher.[64] Typically, after consulting Laughton his original plans changed and the first volume he produced, the eighth to appear, examined the naval accounts of the reign of Henry VII.[65] This was an important contribution to a long-term project that was attempting to 'fill in' the period between the work of Nicolas and James. In November 1897 the Society accepted Oppenheim's offer to edit the naval tracts of Sir William Monson, the Elizabethan and early Stuart naval commander. There were already a number of published versions of these texts in existence, so Oppenheim and Laughton had to track down the originals, and collate. These appeared in five volumes between 1902 and 1914. Oppenheim's works reveal an overriding concern for accuracy. His *Administration* was the first major study of this aspect of the subject, and remains a work of real significance.[66]

Oppenheim shared Laughton's contemporary concerns, writing of an early review of Laughton's *Armada* volumes 'anything that bangs into the Electoral head what the Navy is to England is yeoman's service'.[67] He

---

61. Laughton to Earl Spencer 15.7.1893 Althorp MS BL. K.342.
62. Oppenheim to Laughton 24.7.1893 JKL MS.
63. Oppenheim to Laughton 26.7.1895 JKL MS.
64. Oppenheim to Charles Napier Robinson 23.10.1910: *MM* 1978 p326.
For biographical details see Minchinton, W, 'Michael Oppenheim, 1853-1927: A Memoir' in Oppenheim, M A, *The Maritime History of Devon* (Exeter 1968), ppxiii-xxii.
65. Oppenheim, M A (ed), *The Naval Accounts of the Reign of Henry VII, 1485-8 and 1495-7* (London NRS 1896).
66. Andrews, K R, unpaginated 'Introduction' to Oppenheim, M A, *A History of the Administration of the Royal Navy and of Merchant Shipping in relation to the Navy from 1509 to 1660 with an Introduction treating of the Preceding Period* (new ed Aldershot 1988, first 1896).
67. Oppenheim to Laughton 26.7.1895 JKL MS.

was among the first to join the Society, initially serving as an auditor, and possessed undoubted skill as an historian and editor, but he never served on the Council. This may reflect his extensive travelling, residence abroad and his characteristic anti-social habits, or the fact that a man of his origins and political opinions would be *persona non grata* with the greater part of the membership.

While Oppenheim needed little help editing the material, he relied on Laughton to secure access to manuscripts, and arrange for him to attend a destroyer's speed trials.[68] Both William White and Alfred Yarrow offered an experience at sea, Oppenheim spending a day aboard the Thorneycroft-built HMS *Ariel*. The Marquess of Bath was happy to send his Monson material to the British Library, but Lord Salisbury insisted that his collection must be consulted at Hatfield.[69] After the turn of the century Oppenheim slowed down, the final Monson volume only appearing in 1914.

An altogether more effective recruit to the cause was Julian Corbett (1854-1922).[70] Corbett's first historical work had been a brief life of Monck in 1889, for the 'English Men of Action' series in which Laughton's first Nelson biography had appeared. He followed this with a volume on Drake in 1890, which came to Laughton's attention. When Corbett applied to join the Society Laughton had just read his article on Thomas Doughty, and asked his opinion of Froude's recent work on Elizabethan seamen, which he did not rate very highly.[71] After discussing the Medway raid of 1667 Corbett finally agreed to Laughton's suggestion that he work on the Spanish War 1585-87. Laughton had already secured Gardiner to work on the First Dutch War, and still hoped to carry out some work in this area himself.[72] When the Council accepted Corbett's proposal Laughton cautioned him that:

> it was felt that great care would be necessary not to give the members too much of any one period . . . We must distribute them so as to give our members a taste of all . . .[so that] it may possibly be three or four years before it can publish it.

---

68. Oppenheim to Laughton 5.11.1897 *re* Lord Leconfield's MS & 15. & 31.7.1898 *re* destroyer: JKL.
69. Bath to Laughton 22.9. & 2.10.1898 JKL MS. H T Gunton (for Lord Salisbury) to Laughton 16.11.1898 JKL MS.
70. Schurman, D M, *Julian S. Corbett, 1854-1922: Historian of British Maritime Policy from Drake to Jellicoe* (London 1981). The foundation of any study of this seminal thinker, from a master of the subject.
71. Corbett, J S, 'Tragedy of Thomas Doughty; his relations with Sir Francis Drake', *MacMillan's Magazine* 68 (August 1893), pp258-68. Corbett to Laughton 8.8.1893 Corbett MS Box 14.
72. Corbett to Laughton 28.9.1893 and 3.1.1895 Corbett MS Box 14.

Laughton sent Corbett the 'Instructions to Editors' and helped to organise the transcripts at the Record Office while his *Armada* provided an example of excellent editorial work and of how to combine scholarship with the strategic objectives that lay behind the Society's work. The NRS was the key to Corbett's development into a modern, archive-based historian.[73] Corbett's volume appeared in 1898, as the Society's eleventh volume.[74] In the interval he and Laughton discussed such subjects as the use of the term 'galley' to describe low-built flush decked sailing ships, which also involved Oppenheim, and whether Drake had discovered Cape Horn.[75] When Corbett was thinking about his next major project he consulted Laughton, who responded: 'I am very glad to find that you are meditating the Navy of the Commonwealth. Why not take Blake as the central figure, as you have done with Drake ?'[76] With Gardiner at work on the documents Laughton saw an opportunity to obtain a first-class history from the best 'literary' naval historian. When he considered his options Corbett saw that if he started a new book in 1603 he had two themes open to him. The Dutch Wars were a self-contained episode, but the rise of British power in the Mediterranean was the main line of advance for national naval power. The inspiration came from Clarke, whose concern for the maintenance of British power in that sea was of long standing. This theme provided a strong contemporary focus; it also enabled Corbett to deal with the wider aspects of policy, which he would need to address in his forthcoming Naval War Course Lectures. Corbett set out the reasons for his choice in the Preface to the new book primarily, it would seem, to persuade Laughton.[77] Under Laughton's influence Corbett had developed a more sophisticated appreciation of the subject, and of the didactic opportunities it provided. After 1900 he began to stretch his work out onto the strategic level, to meet the Navy's educational requirements.[78]

The two men remained close personal friends. Corbett tried to lighten the load on Laughton, and ensure that the Council recognised his contribution: 'You have done quite enough for the Society without that' he declared when Laughton had to largely re-edit Vesey-Hamilton's first volume of *The Letters of Admiral Sir Thomas Byam Martin*.[79] Corbett was among the leading figures of the Society in the new century, a position he owed to the

73. Professor Schurman at p19 attributes the key influence to Gardiner, but their only surviving correspondence concerns Corbett's 1889 study of Monck.
74. Laughton to Corbett 1.2.1895 Corbett MS Box 14. Corbett, J S (ed), *Papers relating to the Navy during the Spanish War, 1585-1587* (London, NRS 1898).
75. Laughton to Corbett 20.5. & 4.10.1895 Corbett MS Box 14.
76. Laughton to Corbett 11.11.1900 Corbett MS Box 14.
77. Corbett, J S, *England in the Mediterranean: A Study of the Rise, and Influence of British Power within the Straits* (London 1903), ppv-vii.
78. Schurman, pp18-27.
79. Corbett to Laughton 7.5.1903 JKL MS.

merits of his work, his unfailing patience and a fine record of attendance. He edited four more volumes for the Society. The recruitment of Corbett proved to be critical to the Records Society's work with the Admiralty in the next century. Laughton's agenda, to develop history *for* the Royal Navy, was fundamental to the foundation of the Society, and to the sustained interest of the Naval Intelligence Department.

In contrast to this happy and effective intellectual and personal relationship stands the case of Oscar Browning (1837-1923).[80] Laughton had known Browning since the mid-1880s, and as one of the few historians working at Cambridge, his was a name of some weight. After Seeley's death Browning kept up the Cambridge representation, vetted manuscripts and even chaired the Council on one occasion. His offer to edit Admiral Rooke's Journal was accepted, and a provisional publication date of 1897 suggested.[81] Laughton handled the indexing, he had a man 'who works for the Hydrographic Office' to draw the maps, and passed on some notes on the situation of the batteries at Vigo, and the Council's request that Browning modernise the spelling as they were not interested in the vagaries of Rooke's secretary.[82] When the proof sheets arrived Laughton was so busy that he could only read them on the train. The editorial process dragged on for three painful months, Browning resisting all Laughton's requests to standardise spelling, or even attend to the most basic editorial tasks.[83]

The first reviews to come in were favourable, but they were the calm before the worst storm that was to beset the Society in Laughton's lifetime.[84] The first to see the problem was Clarke, who found the new edition made a poor showing against an old *printed* edition in his library. The language of the old version was so much more like Rooke, he argued; nor did he like 'Mr Browning's editing, which leaves much to be desired'.[85] More seriously James Frederick Chance uncovered damning evidence of Browning's slipshod, careless and incompetent work in a notice for the *English Historical Review*. The volume was 'not a success', he declared with pardonable finality. While Browning had introduced the material reasonably, 'he has not, unfortunately, considered it part of his editorial duty to provide a correct text, and the book teems with errors'. Chance found over 250 departures from the MS, 100 of which affected the comprehension of the text. Browning had also incorporated a much later document that was clearly an addition to the original. Chance was not

80. Anstruther, I, *Oscar Browning* (London 1983).
81. Laughton to Browning 16.11.1895 Browning MS OB/iA King's College, Cambridge.
82. Ibid, 24.1.1896.
83. Ibid, 11.2; 18.2, 28.2; 10.3; 5.5; 6.5; 9.5; 10.5; 18.5; 17.6.1897.
84. Laughton to Browning 10.10.1897 ibid.
85. GS Clarke to Laughton 8.8.1897 JKL MS.

impressed by the editing or indexing.[86] Given advanced warning before Chance's notice appeared in the *English Historical Review*, doubtless by Gardiner, a furious Laughton hastily produced an errata slip to deal with the worst offences. It was eight pages long, and incomplete at that. It was not enough. Chance was not impressed: 'it can never be satisfactory, nor obviate the real want, that of a new edition'.[87] Little wonder Laughton hesitated to issue the errata slip, fearing the embarrassment would kill the Society. Henry Yorke, the Treasurer, hoped that few members would see the *English Historical Review*, but that was little comfort. Browning had edited an unreliable and incomplete transcript without troubling to check its provenance, or even the existing *published* literature. He had compounded the problem by 'omissions and transpositions'. Struggling to keep his letter polite, Laughton stressed that he had no desire to quarrel with Browning, but would have to act in the best interests of the Society. He printed the following disclaimer:

> The Council regrets that owing to an unfortunate misconception, the text of the *Journal of Sir George Rooke* (Vol. IX) was printed from an uncorrected transcript. Since the volume was published several errata have been discovered, a list of which is now issued to the members.[88]

In the end Laughton left the errata slip and disclaimer to stand alone. In view of the 'defective editing of Volume IX, and in order to prevent any similar misconceptions in future', Council amended the instructions to editors, enjoining them to check the proof sheets against the original source at least once, and emphasising that the editor alone was responsible for the final result.[89] Browning left Council six months later, at the Annual General Meeting.[90] Oppenheim had the best suggestion for the volume, advising Laughton, 'you can use it as the gamekeepers do vermin'.[91] It had taken Laughton a little time to get the measure of Browning, which was hardy surprising in view of the myriad other demands on his time, but when the failings of an individual editor threatened the Society that he had created, his response was decisive. Although Browning attended one Council meeting after the publication of *Rooke*, when the main item was the errata slip, it is unlikely that even his thick skin would have been impervious to the withering glance of a disgusted Secretary. Apart from a note of congratulation from Browning on his knighthood there would be no more correspondence between them.[92] Laughton did not preserve any

---

86. J F Chance review in *EHR* (Jan 1898), pp171-4.
87. Ibid, p174.
88. Laughton to Browning 5.12.1897 OB/Ia.
89. Council 4.11.1897 NRS 1 p119.
90. Council 10.12.1897 and 5th AGM 16.6.1898: NRS 1 pp123, 129.
91. Oppenheim to Laughton 5.11.1897 JKL MS.
92. Laughton to Browning 29.6.1907 ibid.

of Browning's letters. Curiously enough this event was the occasion for his only recorded foray in the world of verse:

> This is the volume that Jack dammed
> These are the faults that lay in the volume . . .
> These are the errata that eked out the faults that
> This is the Editor OB that passed the Errata and committed the faults . . .
> This is the Chance that exposed the Editor OB
> This is the Poole that floated the Chance
> This is the Gardiner, a long way from a fool
> Directed a rake, hoe and shovel that stirred up the Poole
> This is *The English Historical Review*
> Which is bound to distinguish the false from the true . . .
> Now arranged by the Gardiner . . .
>
> This is the firm of Longmans & Co
> At the sign of the Ship, the South side of the Row
> who publish *The English Historical Review*
>
> These are the members of the N.R. Society
> Gasping for words that don't savour of pity
> all cursing at once the *Review* and reviewers
> And condemning OB to cesspools and sewers[93]

The problem was that Browning was not a scholar; dates, places and even the original text were relatively unimportant, and he rarely bothered to check them. In this he was entirely out of step with his contemporaries, who found his elevation of form and simplicity over accuracy as shocking as his overt and promiscuous relationships with handsome boys. That he had already been heavily criticised in the press for 'grotesque and slip-shod' work, and was widely regarded as a lightweight by those at Cambridge must have escaped Laughton's notice.[94] His friend Seeley, who knew OB only too well, might have warned him. So might Hornby, his brother having dismissed Browning from Eton.[95] Sadly both were dead. Laughton did not try to suppress Chance's review, despite the fact that it appeared in the journal edited by his friend Gardiner. While he would argue with Gardiner to the last for Nelson's good name, Laughton was not going to raise a finger for Browning. The exposure of sloppy scholarship was the very stuff on which the *EHR* had been built.[96]

Of all the editors who worked for the NRS in Laughton's day the most eminent, beyond doubt, was Samuel Rawson Gardiner. His standing in

---

93. Verse composition in Laughton's hand: JKL MS.
94. Anstruther, pp103-6.
95. Ibid, pp67-9.
96. This embarrassing failure is in process of being rectified. Professor John Hattendorf is working on the replacement edition that Chance recommended in 1898!

the profession and his mastery of his subject, the First Dutch War, were unrivalled. To secure his services Laughton promised the Society would pay for Dutch transcripts, and their translation. Laughton was determined that the Dutch Wars should be covered, and if Gardiner was unable to help he promised the Council that he would do the work himself.[97] The potential benefit of Gardiner's work for the credibility of the Society, not least in attracting other scholars, was immense. Unlike Seeley and Froude, the two Regius Professors, Gardiner lived long enough to contribute more than just his name to the success of his friend's venture. He served on the Council, took his turn as a Vice-President and by April 1895 was at work on the English and Dutch records. In 1897-98 he sent Laughton almost one hundred short queries on naval and technical issues.[98] Answering them was the real cost of Gardiner's work for the Society. The correspondence offers a unique insight into Gardiner's methods. He worked on the sources a year at a time, rather than succumbing to the temptation of ranging ahead. Consequently each query was vital, because it held up the completion of the text, which he liked to send to the printer in small sections as soon as it was finished. As a result he worked in the archives with a pile of pre-stamped postcards at his elbow, ready to scribble down his problems and send them off to Laughton. Occasionally, when they were both at work in the British Library, he would simply drop a note on Laughton's desk. Although Gardiner did not live to complete *Letters and Papers relating to the First Dutch War, 1652-1654* – he died in 1901 – he did produce two volumes, and left the material well in hand for the third. The sixth and final volume, edited by Charles Atkinson, appeared in 1930.[99] It was a mark of the sheer scale of the task that even with Laughton's help, Gardiner and Atkinson left a number of Dutch technical and geographical terms uncertain or unresolved. At the request of the then Secretary, W G Perrin, and Charles Atkinson, A C Dewar produced a thirty two page 'Corrigenda', with help from Dutch officers and historians in 1931.[100] Gardiner lent his prestige to the Society and provided an introduction to other scholars; some, like Charles Firth served on the Council and produced a volume, J R Tanner produced two volumes, others served on the Council and a number were only members, but they included major figures like W E H Lecky.

Among the other editors were journalists like David Hannay and John Leyland; Sir Clements Markham, President of the Royal Geographical

97. Council 29.1.1895 NRS 1 p87.
98. Samuel Rawson Gardiner's Correspondence with John Knox Laughton: JKL.
99. Gardiner, S R (ed), *Letters and Papers relating to the First Dutch War* (London, NRS 1899-1930), Vol 13, 17, 30, 37, 41 and 66. The later volumes by C T Atkinson.
100. Dewar, A C (ed), *Corrigenda to Letters and Papers Relating to the First Dutch War 1652-54* (London NRS 1931).

Society; the French historian, Alfred Spont; and naval officers, Vesey-Hamilton, Sturges-Jackson, and Herbert Richmond. While Cyprian Bridge produced a volume dealing with work of a British secret agent in the navy of Peter the Great, a particularly timely and appropriate contribution, his main contribution lay in the general running of the Society.[101] Whenever Bridge was in England he was effectively ever-present on Council. He led discussions, supported Laughton and provided a Trafalgar Centenary lecture in an effort to boost recruitment and secure further royal patronage. After agreeing that Mahan would be an appropriate speaker, and promising to approach the King and Prince of Wales, Lord Spencer advised that 'the address should not include anything which might wound the susceptibilities of France or any other foreign nation'.[102] The Entente had already changed the environment in which naval policy was being formed, and this affected the Society. Laughton had 600 copies of Bridge's lecture printed, on his own initiative, for the members, along with the same number of copies of Philip Colomb's posthumous paper on the same subject, which had appeared in the *JRUSI* in September. While Council agreed to cover all the costs and distribute Bridge's paper they would not send Colomb's controversial piece.[103]

By 1914 the Society had produced forty-eight volumes, Laughton's contribution of eight being the largest. He had also recruited most of the other editors and assisted their work with his encyclopaedic knowledge. Laughton largely defined the subject and established the areas where work was needed. Many of the suggestions he raised, such as a volume on the social life of the eighteenth-century navy, are only now being realised. Today the fruit of his labour, combined with the efforts of his colleagues and successors stands at over 130 volumes. It is the single greatest contribution yet made to the study of naval history, and is all the more creditable in that the Society has always been entirely financed by members' subscriptions, and still relies on the voluntary efforts of editors and officers.

Having established the Society, and launched its publication programme, Laughton had to persuade his target audience, those who framed national strategy and consequently the policy of the Royal Navy, to adopt the Society's work as the basis for doctrinal development. He was

---

101. Bridge, C A G (ed), *History of the Russian Fleet during the Reign of Peter the Great, by a Contemporary Englishman* (London 1899), *The Art of Naval Warfare* (London 1907) (the dedication is long and fulsome), *Seapower and Other Studies* (London 1910) and *Some Recollections* (London 1918). Unfortunately Bridge's memoirs dealt only with his sea service, having little to say about his time as DNI. His archive is similarly reticent, and contains no letters from Laughton.
102. Council 11.10.1904; 13.12.1904; 3.1.1905; 14.3.1905: NRS 2 pp55–63. Graham-Greene to Laughton 18.12.1904, conveying Spencer's opinions. In NRS 2 at p60. Annual General Meeting 5.7.1905 NRS 1 p164.
103. Council 10.10.1905: NRS 2 p72. For Laughton's view of these papers see Ch 8.

also anxious to recruit more historians, and this could only be done if he ensured that the Society's publications were considered respectable. While he could have waited on results, this was not Laughton's style. He devoted two major lectures to the task. These were based on his long-term historiographical interests, and specifically targeted directed at the service and academic audiences.

Laughton spoke on 'The Study of Naval History' at the RUSI in March 1896 with the Marquis of Lothian in the Chair. Lothian was an admirable choice: he was an active Vice President of the Society, and as a Colonel in the Scots Guards stressed the wider ramifications of the Society's work. Laughton had already persuaded the Council to print and circulate 500 copies of the lecture, to aid recruitment.[104] He began by noting the increased interest in 'Naval History'.

> It is now realised that it is the past which must lead us in the future, and that the study of naval strategy and of naval tactics is linked in the closest possible manner with the study of our history; that to know what the men of old did, and why and how they did it; to know what they failed in doing, and why and how they failed, is the best of all guides for achieving success or avoiding failure.[105]

This was an improvement over the situation only twenty years before, when many thought that new technology had rendered the past irrelevant. He then read a 'lesson' on the threat apparently posed by French torpedo-boats in the Channel, citing St. Vincent's opinion that the French gunboats of 1803-05 were no match for battleships and frigates. He attributed the rise of naval history to the efforts of a few, singling out his friend Admiral Key, the first President at Greenwich, for special credit. Key had given him the opportunity to speak at the RUSI, in a semi-official character, and had responded to his call for naval history to be taught. While six or ten lectures a year was inadequate, it was a start, and one which gave an impetus to Mahan's work. He sustained his argument that the 1891 Exhibition had made naval matters popular, by observing that before it few had bought Mahan's book. After 1891 the public would buy any sort of naval history, even if it was 'not always from the best sources'.[106] The problem with this sentimental stuff was, he reminded his audience, that the naval case had to be based on facts, and the facts were provided by history. However, the historians had not done their job properly.

> They have wished to give us the fighting and nothing else, with the result that their descriptions – even of the fighting – are, for the most part, unintelligible. As a mere chronicle of battles, James's *'Naval History'* is a

---

104. Council 11.12.1895 NRS 1 p100.
105. Laughton, J K, 'The Study of Naval History', *JRUSI* (1896), pp795-820 at p795.
106. Ibid, p797.

work of great merit; but as a history, it is almost worthless. From it no-one can make out what it all means; ships roam the ocean, without any why or wherefore, like a black retriever on the rampage; and, when in sight of an enemy's ship, fight her from pure devilry. We know that this was not the case; that the approximate position of every ship as carefully ordered in its relation to some concerted plan of action; but a man might study James from youth to old age without finding this out.[107]

The rest of the old books were little better, being inaccurate and often careless.[108] His own interest in accuracy had been stimulated by Bridge, who had asked him to look into the case of an ancestor who had been shot for cowardice in 1745.[109] In the absence of a satisfactory published account he had asked at the Admiralty for the Court Martial records. He discovered they were at the Public Record Office, and could only be seen by special permission. Key had secured him unrestricted access to early materials, and then in 1885 they were thrown open to everyone down to 1800, the date moving up to 1815 in 1887. For later material specific clearance was still required, but he had never been refused. He lamented that very few naval officers went to the Record Office, despite their curiosity about the past. As an example of the real wealth of material available he demonstrated that the much vaunted 'seamanship' of the eighteenth century was not a matter of 'securing the weather gauge' but the more prosaic business of keeping fleets together in good order, while the enemy were suffering from poor station-keeping and collisions. The records of other Departments also contained important naval materials. It was to exploit these, and the private holdings, that he and Bridge had founded the Records Society, with the support of leading officers, statesmen, historians and journalists.[110]

Laughton then set out what the Society had achieved, Brassey's index to James was a great aid, but Hannay's edition of Lord Hood's correspondence was a revelation, both of his bitter character, and his tactical genius. Laughton had no doubt that Hood's reflections on the battle of the Saintes had a profound influence on Nelson, helping to form his own standard of victory, that of annihilation. With over 500 members, five volumes in print and many more in hand the Society had made a great start:

> supposing subscriptions to come in to the same or greater amount, by the end of ten years, the history of our navy will stand on a very different footing from what it does now. Those of you who are here fifty years hence

---

107. Ibid, p798.
108. Laughton returned to these historigraphical reflections at greater length in 1913 in 'Historians and Naval History', *The Cornhill Magazine* (1913).
109. Bridge to Laughton 21.4.1896 JKL MS, correcting a detail of Laughton's account of Baker-Phillips case.
110. 'The Study of Naval History', pp808-9.

may say to our grandsons or great grandsons that what they know of the art of naval war and of the glories of our country they owe to the Navy Records Society.[111]

Admiral Sir Edward Fanshawe opened the discussion by comparing the happy position of the present with the sad state of ignorance that had led Lord Palmerston to build forts and not ships. 'I do not recollect that the voice of the Navy was much heard in that discussion'.[112] Now, thanks to Laughton, Colomb and Mahan the principles of naval power were illustrated by history. Dr Thomas Miller Maguire added that as little British history was taught at school it was hardly surprising that naval officers did not know their own naval history. Instead they had been crammed with the details of the Peloponnesian War. He, like Laughton, recognised that the greatest value of Mahan's work stemmed from its apparent impartiality, being, as he put it, the work of 'an American Republican Officer'.[113] Colomb was, for once, more positive: 'My strong impression is that the advent of steam has doubled the possible naval power of this country. It has made naval warfare a certainty where it was before greatly a matter of chance, and I do not see any changes in prospect that are likely in the slightest degree to disturb that position'. He went on to say that Key, whose biography he was then writing, had always intended to have a Professor of Naval History at Greenwich, similar to the position subsequently occupied by Mahan in America, which may have given rise to similar results. He ended by suggesting that the army would find better employment for its historical studies in understanding how the empire had been won, by the two services acting in unison, rather than examining great battles that had occurred on the continent.[114] Lothian ended the meeting by hoping that the membership of the Society would

increase very largely . . . Because it is natural that when people subscribe to a society like this, they will read its publications, so the more members there are in the society, the more will the knowledge of the naval history of this country be improved.[115]

In this respect Lothian's hopes have not been met by the Society. Having recruited 500 members by 1897, it had mobilised no more before the Great War broke out. But the size of the membership mattered less than its influence, and here Laughton had secured the select body he sought. If those who served on the Council between 1893 and 1915 read

---

111. Ibid, p812.
112. Fanshawe, p812.
113. Miller Maguire, p814.
114. Colomb, pp816-7.
115. Lothian, p820.

the volumes and understood the message, he would have deemed the effort entirely justified. His success in securing general acceptance of the methods, approach and, of particular importance, the message of the Society ensured that it fulfilled the ambitions of its founders.

In order to continue to educate the service Laughton needed to recruit professional educators, as they alone could maintain the high standards he had set, and ensure continuity of effort. His second major lecture, 'The National Study of Naval History', was addressed to the Royal Historical Society in December 1898, Laughton sharing the platform with his friend Hubert Hall. He defined his subject as 'the lessons of national importance which are to be sought for in the history of our navy'.[116] When he addressed an audience of naval officers, they were encouraged to treat the study of naval history as 'one of the best, if not the very best, the most vital of all the preparations for the conduct of a naval campaign'.[117]

> In addressing a general audience, my task is different. I have to speak of the peculiar interest of the study of naval history to the statesman, the politician, the elector, the taxpayer, to all of whom it is of absolutely no importance to know how any particular operation has been carried on, but to whom it may be of the very highest importance to know and understand the meaning of it . . . Clearly, it is of importance for us all to understand . . . that the navy is the nation's right arm with which she wards off the enemy's blows and administers the severest punishment . . . The study of our history shows us . . . that it is to the navy, and the navy alone, that we owe our immunity from invasion, our extended commerce, and our vast colonial and Indian Empire.[118]

He went on to consider the wider implications:

> Financiers, political economists, statisticians – I leave humanitarians alone – have written of the ruinous cost of our wars, and have totted up the vast sums added to the national debt. They have overlooked the fact that the national debt has been the capital of the greatest commercial enterprise the world has ever seen, and that the interest payable on it is but a small percentage on the profit derived from it. It is worth stopping to ask why this is? It is that in every war – with one exception – we have swept the enemy's commerce off the sea; and thus in 1748, in 1763, and above all in 1815, we had secured an absolute monopoly of the world's trade.[119]

In this paper Laughton established the strong link between naval mastery and the growth of Empire, a concept that would be developed throughout his remaining years. He reflected at length on the loss of America, which

---

116. Laughton, J K, 'The National Study of Naval History', *Transactions of the Royal Historical Society* Vol XII (London 1898), pp81-93.
117. Ibid, p81.
118. Ibid, p82.
119. Ibid, p83.

he argued resulted from the failure to secure command of the sea. He cited Graves' strategic defeat off Cape Henry as the key battle, using Hood's correspondence to argue that the war had been a 'close run thing', and blaming Lord Sandwich for the weakness of the fleet. Reading across to the current state of naval affairs he concluded that the only way to avoid defeat was 'for the country, that is, for the collective electors and taxpayers, to see that in time of peace, as a preparation for war, the navy is kept at an adequate strength'.[120] This meant real strength, not filling up large lists with useless and rotten ships, which he still believed to have been the case in the eighteenth century. Yet this was not a council of despair, for he did not think any allied fleet equal to the same number of British ships, a Two Power Standard was, for him at least, an effective superiority. He noted that Mahan agreed, and concluded by citing him as a proponent of preparedness. Hubert Hall followed, speaking on 'New Methods of Research' to celebrate the fact that 'Naval history is at length recognised as a subject of special study'. This was largely because it now had 'a large and powerful society' to represent its interests and direct its development.[121] He believed that the days of general history were over, increasing specialisation was the trend, and, as befits a curator, wanted to list and digest everything as an aid to scholarship.

Laughton must have realised that his case, already generally accepted by the service, and the statesmen, was still far from established with the historians.[122] This audience would need further encouragement. Without a recognised speciality, including a chair and a number of posts, he could not hope to secure the long-term commitment of professional academics. Ultimately his ambitions would extend to the establishment of a Department of Naval History at King's College London, to provide trained academics for the Navy and the nation.

Over the years that he served the Society Laughton offered to edit far more volumes than he completed. This was not a reflection of inadequacy or failure: rather it demonstrated the degree to which the interests of the Society, and the Navy, took precedence over his own inclinations. His editorial contribution was dominated by the major themes he wanted the society to examine, and the random appearance of material. In October 1903 he noted the deposit of the papers of the 1st and 2nd Earls of Chatham, and William Pitt the Younger, at the Public Record Office.

---

120. Ibid, p88.
121. Hall, H, 'The National Study of Naval History: II New Methods of Research', *Transactions of the Royal Historical Society* Vol XII (London 1898), pp95-101 at p95.
122. The message would be adopted by A F Pollard, one of the major figures in the professionalisation of English History early in the next century. Pollard, A F, 'The University of London and the Study of History', *The National Review* (December 1904), pp650-63 at pp658-9.

Recognising their importance, Laughton offered to edit the naval material for the Society.[123] In December his old friend Admiral Sir Gerard Noel provided access to the papers of Lord Barham, his great-grandfather, which were then owned by his cousin Lord Gainsborough. Laughton agreed to go to Lincolnshire to inspect them, and to edit them for the Society if they proved suitable. In March the Council accepted his offer to edit the Barham material.[124] He took up the task because he considered the opportunity unique, and largely due to his relationship with Noel. He did so in lieu of the Pitt/Chatham material, which he used to support the Barham collection. The three-volume *Letters and Papers of Charles, Lord Barham*, Laughton's final editorial effort for the Society, were outstanding. They provided new insight into naval administration and strategic planning. In their introductions Laughton set down his views on a number of important historical and contemporary issues. Barham's career gave him the opportunity to draw particular lessons for the makers of national policy. Having passed through a period in which the basis of democratic politics had undergone a profound change, one with which he, like the great majority of his intellectual contemporaries, was not in tune, Laughton considered the petty squabbles of parliamentary politics dangerous:

> One of the doubtful advantages of that system of party government which its admirers acclaim as the palladium of our political liberties, is that – whichever party may be in office – the treasury is unwilling to spend money on our armaments, knowing that, at the next election, it will be denounced as a flock of vultures who have been battening on the very vitals of the poor. It follows that, when need arises, when an enemy, seeing our unprepared state, proposes to take advantage of it, we have to arm in a hurry, imperfectly, and at lavish cost; spending in a few months many times the amount which, if invested year by year, on business principles, might have obviated all need for war, by making it too clearly dangerous; and if not that, would at least have placed the country in a state to meet the enemy's assault without apprehension, and above all without panic.[125]

As a statement of the deterrent core of British strategy this required little elaboration. It goes far beyond Mahan in providing a specific example of why the failure of democracies to prepare adequately in peacetime was so important. In the second volume he reinforced this point with a brief discussion of the Dutch Armament of 1787, 'a very marked instance of the silent working of sea-power; but as the end was gained without any breach of the peace, it has passed unnoticed in our popular histories'.[126]

---

123. Council 13.10.1903 NRS 2 p34.
124. Council 8.12.1903; 8.3.1904: NRS 2 pp41-6.
125. Laughton, J K (ed), *Letters and Papers of Charles, Lord Barham* Vol I (London 1907) (issued on the 1906 subscription), ppxxv-xxvi.
126. *Barham*, Vol II (London 1910), on the 1909 subscription pxii.

The lessons of the American War of Independence remained relevant, and Laughton took care that no-one should miss them. It was not mere historical analysis that lead him to excoriate the North Ministry for failing to fit out the fleet in adequate time; to this neglect he attributed the loss of the American Colonies, grave damage to Britain's standing in Europe and the addition of £100 million to the National Debt. Nor were these all the evils that politics could inflict. When he considered the Keppel and Palliser court martials, which had split the Navy in 1779, he reflected ruefully, and with the sight of his remaining good eye squarely on current affairs; 'Where politics come in, considerations of strategy and the art of war are laid on one side'.[127] In one sense the political insight that the *Barham Papers* provided was a major addition to the existing literature, notably Mahan's section of the Clowes *History*. He also took the opportunity to lambaste the re-introduction of the nucleus crew system as 'a deception to parliament and the nation, and a real danger in time of need'. He also deprecated the contemporary

> dogma that every English ship must be of force not less than any possible antagonist; and that the strength of a fleet depends on the displacement, weight of broadside and number of men of each individual ship; that a fleet is, in fact, an aggregation, not a consolidation of units.[128]

He did not bother to mention Fisher by name. It was not necessary. Of equal relevance was his declaration; 'No one with any competent knowledge of the history of naval war can possibly accept the proposal to neutralise private property'.[129] Here he was at one with Fisher.

He considered strategic alternatives, providing a powerful critique of the indecisive French naval doctrine which ignored the attempt to secure command of the sea in favour of 'ulterior objects'. While this might lead to the occasional strategic success, such as the battle off Cape Henry in 1781, it left the British fleet at liberty to secure a decisive victory less than a year later. In this analysis he had come to be supported by Colomb and Mahan. He also pointed out the irony that while Napoleon abandoned such nonsense on land he persisted with it at sea, doubtless under the influence of French naval officers.[130] This subject received rather more attention in the third volume, which was largely concerned with the campaign of 1805. He began by reminding his readers that the much-vaunted danger of 1805 was not taken seriously by naval officers, a point of great importance in 1910, while the most striking feature of Barham's correspondence was:

---

127. *Barham*, Vol I ppxxxii, xxix.
128. Ibid, pxix, *Barham* Vol III (London 1911) on the 1910 subscription ppxxxi-ii.
129. Ibid, pliv.
130. Ibid, ppxxx-xxxi.

that the main anxiety of the admiralty, and by it imparted to the commanders-in-chief, especially those in the North Sea and off Brest, was not the danger of invasion, which our historians have represented as paramount, but the possibility of danger to the trade.[131]

The production of the *Barham* volumes was Laughton's last great contribution to the subject that he had devoted his life to promoting. He was over eighty, and to his intense annoyance his physical powers were failing. He had to hand on the core task of running the Society, and editing volumes. All of his volumes have stood the test of time sufficiently well to require reprinting, and remain basic texts to this day. That they were produced in a short space of time by a busy man past retiring age was remarkable.

As the Society entered its third decade Laughton was faced by a succession of issues that required action. The President, Earl Spencer, died after a long period of ill-health. Lord George Hamilton, a founder member, ex-First Lord and active Vice-President was an obvious and willing replacement. He was duly elected at the 1911 Annual General Meeting.[132] Then the printers, Spottiswoode's, complained about the increasing size of the back stock, then held as unbound sheets. After sending out 70 sets of sheets to Public Libraries without charge, Laughton reduced the print run from 1000 copies to 800, and pulped up to 200 sets of sheets of the less-popular works.[133] Having settled the back-stock Laughton had to report that the publication of volumes was in arrears. He had been depressed by ill-health and his consequent inability to complete the editorial work on *The Naval Miscellany Volume Two* and *The Barham Papers: Volume Three*, as quickly as he had planned. This

> had forced on him the consideration of his advancing age, and though the issue of the volumes and the Secretaryship of the Society were not by any means the same, the consideration had brought him to the melancholy conclusion that he ought to lay his resignation before the Society, and he proposed to do so at the Annual General Meeting in June.

He resigned from his Chair at King's College at the same time. It was appropriate that Bridge and Corbett should express the Society's high sense of his work, for Bridge had been his lifelong co-adjutor, while Corbett was carrying his work onto fresh ground at the Naval War Course and in his books.[134] At the following Council it was agree that Leonard Carr-Laughton should be offered the Secretaryship, which still included an honorarium of £100.[135] Laughton retired at the nineteenth

---

131. *Barham*, Vol III, ppxv, xxxiv.
132. Council 9.5.1911: NRS 2 p162.
133. Council 10.11.1911, 12.12.1911; 12.3.1912: NRS 2 pp165-73.
134. Council 10.11.1911: NRS 2 pp173-6.
135. Council 14.5.1912 NRS 2 p178.

Annual General Meeting. His decision was accepted with regret by the Society, it being noted that 'he was the founder of the Society'. Mahan reflected, 'you have the satisfaction of looking back upon an unusual amount of solid work accomplished'.[136] Laughton moved onto Council, and in 1915 became a Vice-President. Leonard took over as Secretary, but an editorial committee, comprising Bridge, Erskine Childers and Albert Gray, was required to replace his other work.[137] The new arrangement did not last long. Leonard was more interested in the Society for Nautical Research that he had been largely responsible for founding. After neglecting the day-to-day business of the Society Leonard resigned in 1913, claiming ill-health. Laughton doubted his sanity. The next Secretary, the Admiralty Librarian William G Perrin, was an altogether more suitable candidate. From a combination of ill-health and embarrassment Laughton did not attended Council in 1913, although he was involved in managing Society affairs until a new secretary could be found.[138] Thereafter Laughton became a distant elder statesman; the only meeting he attended after 1912 was the 1914 AGM. His last letter, written to King's College, was a request to use of the Lecture Theatre for the 1915 AGM.[139]

After 1912 the Society was run by Corbett, Custance and Graham-Greene, an unlikely and, at least on the surface, far from harmonious, triumvirate. In fact they were all committed to the cause that the Society served, and did not allow differences of opinion on isolated issues to interfere with the Society's business. In Laughton's absence the Council sent their condolences to Mahan's family, reflecting the 'loss to the British Empire by the termination of the career of one who so generously appreciated the real work of the Royal Navy'.[140] A year later it was Laughton's death the Council had to regret. Corbett and Graham-Greene drafted the letter of condolence, while Bridge and Custance secured Council's consent to send a Memorial calling for Lady Laughton to receive a Civil List Pension. When this was awarded the Council left on record their sense that Laughton's 'devoted labours on behalf of the Society from its foundation secure for him a lasting place in the memory of its members'. He was, it was noted in 1918, the 'founder and Secretary of the Society'.[141] His 'solid work' had laid the foundations for the study of naval history, provided a

---

136. Mahan to Laughton 23.7.1912 JKL MS.
137. Annual General Meeting 28.6.1912. NRS 1 p180.
138. Laughton to W. Graham-Greene 20.7.1913. NRS 2. Annual General Meeting 30.6.1913.
139. Laughton to College Secretary 16.6.1915. KA/IC/L77. The letter was in the hand of his daughter Grace.
140. Council 8.12.1914 NRS 3 p24.
141. Council 19.11.1915; Annual General Meeting 11.7.1916; Council 1.11.1918 NRS 3 pp35-42, 56.

1critical input into the development of naval doctrine, strategy and national policy, built up a powerful interest group to support the Navy, and left a critical mass of scholars in the field who would be led by Corbett and then Richmond, both of whom owed their initial impulse, higher education, methodology and much more to Sir John Knox Laughton.

CHAPTER 7

Nelson, Mahan and Naval Education: 1895-1900

————— · —————

The career of the greatest of all Admirals, Horatio, Lord Nelson, exerted a powerful grip on Laughton's work. His 1886 edition of Nelson's correspondence had developed the tactical and doctrinal aspects of the great man's career for a professional audience, and begun the process of restoring the lustre of his name by removing the slurs of his contemporaries and the slanders of Southey.[1] However, this was only the beginning of the process. Nelson's name had to be returned, untarnished, to the core of national culture if he was to fulfil Laughton's fondest hopes. In this respect his short popular life in the 'English Men of Action' series of 1889 was a key opportunity. In the 1890s his efforts received powerful support from Mahan, and they both began work on biographies of Nelson.[2] They believed the great naval hero should be developed as the basis for naval education, a case study in professional development, leadership, sound doctrine and the exemplar of all that they valued about the Royal Navy. Despite Mahan's concern that his sales might be affected by Laughton's book, the two works were largely complementary and led to their closest intellectual co-operation.

Both men had to face the central dilemma that Nelson, for all his transcendent abilities, posed serious problems as an example to set before young officers and gentlemen at the end of the nineteenth century. The keys issues concerned the time he spent off Naples in 1798-99; his relationship with Emma, Lady Hamilton, the treatment of the Neapolitan Jacobins, especially Commodore Caracciolo, and his disobedience of the orders of Admiral Lord Keith. All three issues were well known. Robert Southey's brilliant portrait had dominated the literature since it first appeared in 1813, particularly after the one-volume edition was published in 1825. Southey produced much critical comment on Nelson's conduct, notably his relationship with Lady Hamilton, and considered that the

1. Laughton, J K, *Letters and Despatches of Horatio, Viscount Nelson* (London 1886). See pp76-8 for a discussion of this book.
2. Sumida, J T, *Mahan* (Washington 1997), pp36-9, for Mahan's concept.

annulment of Cardinal Ruffo's armistice, together with the hasty trial and execution of Carraciolo, constituted 'a deplorable transaction' that could only be recorded with 'sorrow and shame'.[3] More noteworthy as a literary masterpiece than a reliable account, Southey's often hostile book was largely responsible for Nelson's profound unpopularity in the Victorian era.[4] Southey's opinions would have to be overturned if Nelson was going to be cited as the naval commander *par excellence*. In his 1889 biography Laughton attributed most of these problems to the serious head wound Nelson had suffered at the Nile.[5] He stressed that Nelson, although 'the slave of a beautiful and voluptuous woman, did not cease to be a great commander', and did not neglect his duty while at Naples and Palermo. The treatment of the rebels he considered perfectly justified, and pointed out that Caracciolo never objected to the court martial which condemned him. Nelson, with the authority of the King of Naples, acted exactly as he would had the rebels been taken in arms against the King of England. With his usual scrupulous attention to the historiography, Laughton discovered that the slanders on Nelson's good name originated with disappointed Jacobins and malicious English gossips. They had been introduced into the literature by Southey. After four years of heated controversy, Mahan agreed that Southey was responsible for the 'ancient bias'.[6] Laughton was more critical of Nelson's disobedience of Lord Keith, a matter of discipline, however much hindsight had confirmed Nelson's wisdom.[7]

    With new material on Nelson and Emma becoming available in the late 1880s, Laughton developed his understanding. Aware that Emma was 'a key to the composite character of Nelson', he examined the Foreign Office records in 1889. His transcripts, published in the *United Service Magazine*, demonstrated that Emma's claims that she had aided the state by gaining early intelligence of the Spanish decision to change sides in 1796, and securing water for Nelson's squadron before the Nile, were exaggerated versions of her useful, but hardly vital, role as confidante of Queen Maria Carolina. That Nelson believed her claims was no reason for taking them seriously.[8] In 1896 he reviewed the extant literature on Emma for the *Edinburgh Review*. Having established her origins, detailed her career and weighed her abilities, he summed her up as:

> beautiful, sweet voiced, and tender; of a kindly nature and a soft heart, yet capable and energetic; but withal excessively vain, boastful, and an unblushing, irresponsible, perhaps unconscious liar.

---

3. Southey, R, *Life of Nelson* (London 1886 edn), pp162-6.
4. Simmons, J, *Southey* (London 1945), pp142-3 and 226-9.
5. Laughton, J K, *Nelson* (London 1889), p128.
6. Mahan to Laughton 12.7.1901 JKL MS.
7. *Nelson* (1889), pp129-42.
8. Laughton, J K, 'Nelson's Last Codicil', *Colburn's United Service Magazine* (1889), Part II pp647-62, and Part III, pp10-23.

He agreed with Lord Minto, a contemporary observer, who gave her credit for having 'art enough to make fools of many wiser than an admiral'.[9] As he noted 'Nelson had all his life shown himself susceptible to woman's influence' and was, withal, 'still suffering the effects of the wound received in the battle of the Nile'.[10] Even so most of the malicious stories told of Nelson and Emma at Palermo were palpably untrue. The business in the Bay of Naples was passed over in less than a page, pausing only to note Nelson's prior pronouncements on mutiny and treason. It was an approach that Mahan might have followed with profit.

Mahan's biography largely concurred in Laughton's judgements, his only reservation was that Nelson had been too hasty in confirming Caracciolo's sentence, and in ordering his immediate execution. Yet even here he found extenuation in the example of Earl St. Vincent's treatment of English mutineers and, like Laughton, in Nelson's characteristic severity towards officers who betrayed their country or their king. Laughton's *Edinburgh Review* article on Mahan's biography was largely positive, but he stressed, as he had in his own *Memorial*, that orders from home kept Nelson at Naples, not infatuation. Indeed, Emma was often credited with greater influence over Nelson than the facts would support. For example, Nelson's insubordinate conduct towards Keith stemmed from professional jealousy, but it was easier to blame the lady.[11]

Mahan had criticised Captain Foote for mixing up attacks on Nelson's relationship with Lady Hamilton and the whole question of mercy for the Jacobins with a defence of his own conduct in his printed *Vindication*.[12] This was a serious tactical error, for on 15 May 1897 Francis Pritchett Badham took up the cudgels for Foote, his grandfather, publishing a paper on Nelson's conduct at Naples in June and July 1799 in *The Saturday Review*. Badham argued that Nelson had no legal authority to set aside the armistice, or to execute Caracciolo. He then took both Laughton and Mahan to task 'very magisterially' for failing to present all the evidence. Laughton was singled out for having 'patriotically misinterpreted or mutilated the documents'. The attack brought Laughton and Mahan into close concert. While they were individually concerned by the challenge to their personal veracity, the threat to Nelson's good name was altogether more serious. If it was accepted that Nelson had behaved

9. Laughton, J K; 'Emma, Lady Hamilton', *The Edinburgh Review* (April 1896), pp380-407 at pp402-3. This material was largely re-used in Chapter IV of *The Nelson Memorial* of 1896.

10. Laughton, J K, *The Nelson Memorial* (London 1896), p145.

11. Laughton, J K, 'Captain Mahan's *Life of Nelson*', *The Edinburgh Review* (July 1897), pp84-113 at pp105, 107. *The Nelson Memorial* p147.

12. Mahan, A T, *The Life of Nelson: The Embodiment of the Sea Power of Great Britain* (London 1897), Vol I, pp372-443, esp. p437 re Foote, pp439-40 re Caracciolo. Foote, E J, *Vindication of his Conduct when Captain of HMS Seahorse etc. 1799* (London 1807).

improperly in countermanding Cardinal Ruffo's armistice with the rebels, arranging the surrender of the Neapolitan castles and, more seriously, in the trial and execution of Admiral Carraciolo, then Laughton and Mahan could not use him to teach leadership to young officers.

Mahan immediately ordered a search for the correspondence that Badham had 'quoted' but not referenced. When the search drew a blank he asked for Laughton's help.[13] Mahan quickly realised that Badham was guilty of garbling his evidence, and that the issue would only be resolved by examining all the sources, British and Italian. He accepted Laughton's original idea, that Nelson had been given full authority to act in the King's name before he left Palermo with the written confirmation to follow.[14] Badham's piece had appeared too late to be dealt with in his *Edinburgh Review* notice of Mahan's book, so Laughton took his time, conducted some research on his antagonist, and found a second opportunity to review. Hubert Hall reported that Badham had been at Exeter College, Oxford, that he had not been to the Record Office and should have known better 'than write such rot as I saw in the *Saturday Review*'. Hall also advised asking Oscar Browning if he had given Badham any help.[15] Laughton passed the query on to Browning, but struck a blank.[16] When he submitted a strong attack on Badham as the centrepiece of a second review of Mahan's *Nelson*, this time for the *EHR*, Gardiner advised him to be more cautious in his language, and in referring to the fact that Hall had told him Badham had never been in the Record Office.[17] Even so the published version retains some of the original fire, and reveals the objective:

> Not one of his statements, not one of his references, will bear examination. Such slipshod writing is beneath criticism . . . but . . . I have felt bound to place a direct contradiction of them on record.[18]

The tension in his review reflected contrasting desires. While he would have preferred to ignore Badham's rubbish, he had to counter the threat it

---

10. Laughton, J K, *The Nelson Memorial* (London 1896), p145.
11. Laughton, J K, 'Captain Mahan's *Life of Nelson*', *The Edinburgh Review* (July 1897), pp84-113 at pp105, 107. *The Nelson Memorial* p147.
12. Mahan, A T, *The Life of Nelson: The Embodiment of the Sea Power of Great Britain* (London 1897), Vol I, pp372-443, esp. p437 re Foote, pp439-40 re Caracciolo. Foote, E J, *Vindication of his Conduct when Captain of HMS Seahorse etc. 1799* (London 1807).
13. Mahan to Laughton 28.6.1897: JKL. What follows is based on Laughton's correspondence with Mahan and Gardiner. It provides a very different perspective on Mahan's view of the affair than Mahan's letters in Seager and Maguire. See Vol II, pp619, 630, 637, Vol III, pp48 and 118.
14. Mahan to Laughton 3.8.1897 JKL MS.
15. Hall to Laughton 4.8.1897 JKL MS.
16. Laughton to Oscar Browning 6.8.1897 Browning MS King's College, Cambridge.
17. Gardiner to Laughton 10.9.1897 JKL MS.
18. Laughton, J K, Review of Mahan's *Nelson: EHR* (October 1897), p804.

posed to the Nelson he was developing for naval education. Mahan also replied to Badham, countering his charges, and received an evasive response, which he judged to be the work 'of a man of *meagre intellectual morality*, who expects to escape detection like a cuttle-fish, under a cloud of ink'.[19]

When Badham submitted an article for the *EHR*, Gardiner realised that he had landed in the middle of a first-class historical controversy. When he considered the evidence, he was predisposed to favour his old friend, and the famous American. Initially he thought Badham 'a duffer'; but when he looked up his secondary references he concluded that Nelson had 'condescended to a trick to get the men in the two forts into his power' and regretted that Mahan had not seen the letters that Badham had used. Badham's 'evidence' came from garbled and partial Italian and French accounts, with ludicrous translations of Sir William Hamilton's correspondence. Yet Laughton's efforts to save the hero proved in vain. Despite Badham's scholarly weaknesses, he had made his case.[20] Nelson was effectively convicted of 'conduct unbecoming' by the editor of the leading scholarly historical journal on little better evidence than a garbled Italian translation of a letter by Sir William Hamilton.[21] Badham's critique was given the stamp of academic approval by the leading British academic historian. This was a heavy blow for Laughton and Mahan.

The impact of this defeat was fundamental. When Badham's article appeared in the *EHR* Mahan felt obliged to revise his account for a second edition of the *Life*, and to prepare two articles to refute Badham's claims.[22] Having examined the material in more detail during the intervening year, he was now convinced that Badham was guilty of 'false deductions, misstatements, and garbled quotations, not to speak of a phenomenal capacity for overlooking the bearing of different things'. He hoped to pile up enough evidence of these offences to have Badham excluded from the pages of the *EHR*.[23] For the first time in his literary career he launched into a thorough survey of the secondary literature. He uncovered a trail of scribblers who had gradually garbled the far from perfect translations of the documents provided by Alexandre Dumas.[24] He admitted the first article for the *EHR* 'has given me more trouble than any equal amount of result I have ever produced'.[25] As an education in

19. Mahan to Laughton 29.11.1897 JKL MS.
20. Gardiner to Laughton 13.& 14.12.1897 JKL MS.
21. Gardiner to Laughton 21.12.1897 JKL MS.
22. Badham, F P, 'Nelson', *EHR* April 1898. Mahan to John M Brown 17.1.1899: Seager & Maguire, II pp623-4.
23. Mahan to Laughton 9.1.1899 JKL MS.
24. Mahan to Laughton 18.5.1899 JKL MS.
25. Mahan's *EHR* articles appeared in July 1899 and October 1900. Mahan to J R Thursfield 17.6.1899. Seager & Maguire, II p637.

historical method and the importance of primary sources, the experience could hardly have been bettered. While the full fruit of this experience would be seen in his *War of 1812*, Mahan's first serious scholarly work was on Nelson at Naples.

In public Mahan put on a bold front. In the Preface to the Second Edition of the *Life* he declared that he saw 'no cause to change to opinion first expressed'. However, the rider was revealing. He had included the materials and references to 'enable the studious reader to rebut the accusations' if they were ever renewed.[26] The alterations to Chapter XI went little further than expanding a few quotes to render Lady Hamilton's influence, implicit in the first edition, explicit for the second.[27] In Chapter XII the alterations went much further, the whole section from Nelson's return to Naples to the execution of Carraciolo was effectively doubled in length, with an unprecedented (for Mahan) foundation of footnotes referring to the full range of literature.[28] Even if Mahan did not alter the sense of his work, he had transformed its basic method from literary to scholarly.

When Badham published another letter, this time in *The Athenaeum*, he received a speedier reply. Mahan believed he had the upper hand, and resolved to press home his advantage.[29] Badham then wrote to the *Speaker*, a short-lived liberal journal which was used as a forum for a number of defence-related debates, claiming that Mahan had described Laughton as his 'agent', which he had not. Mahan refuted this calumny, and noted that Badham had not met the challenge to print an important letter that he said had been overlooked. In the interval a suitably chastened Gardiner had come up with the ideal solution to a problem with which he, as editor of the *EHR*, must have been heartily sick. All the relevant documents should be published by the Navy Records Society. This was greeted with enthusiasm by Mahan, accepted by the Council of the Society and acted upon by Laughton.[30] The object was to demonstrate that Badham was unreliable; nothing else would suffice to close the press to his dishonest outpourings.[31] By 1900 Badham was reduced to publishing his own pamphlets, as he had run out of willing journals.[32] At the end of the year Gardiner admitted that Mahan need pay no further attention to Badham.[33] This left the field clear for H C Gutteridge, who

26. Mahan, A T, *Nelson* (2nd Ed London 1899), Preface to Second edition pv.
27. Ibid, p342, see Vol I p398 of the 1st edition.
28. Ibid, pp366-400.
29. Mahan to Laughton 4.7.1899 JKL MS.
30. Mahan to Laughton 23.11.1899 JKL MS. Council of the Navy Records Society 1.12.1899. NRS 1 p147.
31. Mahan to Laughton 28.8.1900 JKL MS.
32. Badham, F P, *Nelson at Naples: A Journal for June 10-30, 1799* (London 1900).
33. Mahan to Laughton 25.12.1900 JKL MS.

Laughton had recruited from Cambridge, 'to put Nelson's fame beyond future challenge' in the NRS volume.[34] Years later Mahan admitted that Badham had 'thrown me off my balance', and considered the controversy had affected his later work.[35] This was not entirely to his detriment.

In the next major biography of Nelson, Carola Oman devoted six pages to the Caracciolo affair, and the subsequent attacks on Nelson. After going over much of the same ground as Laughton she reached very similar conclusions. Every one of the hostile contemporary British witnesses was demonstrably inaccurate, or worse, and their motives did not stand up to close scrutiny. Southey was criticised for repeating their falsehoods, and adding a few of his own.[36] Mahan, Laughton and Badham were, perhaps rightly, ignored: their debate was of its time, and left an enduring landmark in Gutteridge's NRS volume. Oman's Nelson was not a naval educational tool, he was a national figure in the struggle for survival against continental tyranny. That there remains a slur on Nelson's reputation, despite the best efforts of the past two hundred years, is testimony to the enduring power of myth. Robert Seager II's examination of the Badham debate, in his critical biography of Mahan, was heavily slanted against Mahan, and Laughton, by a strongly coloured and largely inaccurate version of what actually happened at Naples.[37] Unaware of the role of Gardiner, or the work of Gutteridge, he did not recognise the degree to which Mahan and Laughton had triumphed, let alone the cause for which they had fought.

Neapolitan and modern Italian histories have almost invariably adopted a hostile view of Nelson's proceedings, which is hardly surprising in view of the reputation of the monarch he was serving and the 'liberal' credentials of the rebels.[38] In 1996 leading Italian naval officers and historians were still sufficiently interested in the question to demand a public apology from Britain for Nelson's conduct when the County of Norfolk proposed to make the hero their emblem.[39]

While the Badham case provided an important insight into Laughton's approach to a specific issue, he was equally concerned to uphold standards in the wider field of naval history. The opportunity that Laughton had exploited to found the Navy Records Society and widen the national appreciation of naval history had been recognised by others, and although they often drew on his work, little of their output met his high standards.

34. Mahan to Laughton 12.7.1901 JKL MS. Gutteridge, H C (ed), *Nelson and the Neapolitan Jacobins* (London NRS 1900).
35. Mahan to Laughton 6.3.1908.
36. Oman, C, *Nelson* (London 1947), pp358-64.
37. Seager, R II, *Alfred Thayer Mahan: His Life and Letters* (Annapolis 1977), pp343-8. Seager repeats most of the old myths, and adds some novelties of his own. He has Nelson, a slave to Emma and Queen Maria Carolina, arresting Caracciolo, and the execution delayed for two days.
38. Acton, H, *The Bourbons of Naples* (London 1956) is a good example.
39. *The Eastern Daily Press* 24.7.1996 and generally for July 1996.

Because naval history was vital for the development of naval doctrine and national strategy, Laughton felt compelled to adopt a magisterial approach to reviewing, making heavy use of such favourite adjectives 'slipshod', and 'gross' to get his point across. No-one was safe from correction and criticism, although he was equally forthcoming with praise. His relationship with the most ambitious contemporary project, William Laird Clowes's *History of the Royal Navy*, is particularly revealing.[40] Originally commissioned as a five-volume work, this great enterprise finally ran to seven majestic, weighty books. Clowes was the principle author, but he had expected Laughton and Oppenheim to contribute a large percentage of the work, at a guinea a thousand words. Clowes proposed the project to the publisher Roy Marston, who handled Mahan's books in Britain with Sampson, Low & Co. in early 1896. Marston recognised that 'there has certainly been a wonderful revival of national interest in the navy, but will it last?'.[41] He hoped it would, and was interested in the list of proposed authors; 'I presume, if he could be got, you would give Captain Mahan as much as he cared to do?'. He also stressed that 'its sole object would be to place before the British people a true and worthy history of their Fleet, not written on party lines, or for the object of advancing any particular school of thought respecting naval affairs'.[42] Having settled on five volumes, rather than the ten that Clowes proposed, as the limit to which he was prepared to risk his capital, Marston then added Laughton to the list of named authors in the next letter.[43] Laughton declined Clowes's invitation, claiming to dislike the 'joint-stock' approach, and because he had no time to spare.[44] He also disliked Clowes, which probably reflected a quarrel between Clowes and his friend Robinson.[45] Furthermore he was contemptuous of Clowes' 1895 argument that Britain should 'scuttle' out of the Mediterranean. Along with Colomb and Brassey, Laughton preferred the 'Channel' argument that the Channel fleet should be ready to reinforce the Mediterranean in the event of war.[46] Oppenheim claimed ill-health and over-work,[47] but he was not a man to write anything for anyone, let alone to a deadline.

40. **Clowes** (1856-1905) was educated at King's College, London, joined the *Army & Navy Gazette* in 1882, and was naval correspondent of *The Times* 1890-95. Here he exploited his close contacts with leading naval and political figures. Knighted in 1902, he died of tuberculosis in 1905.
41. R B Marston to Clowes 31.1.1896 NMM MS 93/001.
42. R B Marston to Clowes 10.2.1896 NMM MS 93/001.
43. Ibid, 22 and 27.2.1896.
44. Laughton to Clowes 31.3.1896 ibid.
45. Edward Fraser to Clowes 5.4.1897. Hopes he will make up his quarrel with Robinson. MS 93/001.
46. See Marder, A J, *The Anatomy of British Sea Power* (London 1940), pp210-11, where Laughton's important *Edinburgh* article of 1894 is cited, but his authorship is not recognised.
47. Oppenheim to Clowes 6.4.1896 MS 93/001.

Laughton's abstention was a serious problem for Marston, not least because Mahan more than once asked why Laughton was not involved. 'What can I say?' he lamented.[48] In the end Laughton made a major contribution to the project, helping Mahan with his section on the American War of Independence. He sent book lists, transcripts and even his own notebooks,[49] but he never changed his mind about Clowes's book, repeatedly urging his friend to disinter the material from 'a work of reference' and publish it as a separate volume.[50] Marston's successors finally granted permission for the separate edition *Major Operations of the Navies of the War of American Independence* in 1913.[51]

Early reviews of Volume I justified Laughton's dislike of the multi-author approach and revealed an early example of the mainstream academic historian's disdain of the large illustrated format. Frederick York Powell, Regius Professor of History at Oxford, savaged the work in the *EHR* as 'a fine opportunity thrown away in such a hopeless muddle' and 'this big showy volume'.[52] Although Marston believed that most of York Powell's points were petty printer's errors, he was so worried by the review that he tried to take out a full-page advert in the relevant issue of the *EHR*, replete with approving quotes from other reviews.[53] Laughton's son Leonard joined the project to replace Edward Fraser, who had failed to deliver his section on 'Naval Operations 1603-1660' for Volume II. His selection was justified by Clowes solely on the grounds of his parentage.[54] When the later volumes appeared Laughton's opposition to the project took a more tangible form, Marston reported to Clowes:

> Doubtless you saw Laughton's attack on you in *The Speaker*? Doubtless he did *The Athenaeum* notice also. Mahan has written very strongly about your charging Nelson with conduct 'not quite that of a man of scrupulous honour' p.394. I trust you have not been misled by Badham.[55]

Clowes had committed a cardinal sin; he had allowed the calumnies of Badham to pass into a standard work of reference. Both Mahan and Laughton had devoted a major part of their lives over three years to refuting these allegations, and pursued them wherever they surfaced.[56] Clowes wrote on Naples in 1899, after Mahan and Laughton had exposed

48. Marston to Clowes 3.11.1896 ibid.
49. Mahan to Laughton 1 & 21.5.1897 JKL MS.
50. Laughton to Mahan 21.4.1897; 23.1.1899; 12.10.1903: Mahan MS LoC.
51. Mahan to Laughton 17.6.1912 JKL MS.
52. Laughton's own copy is in the Library of King's' College London. Review of Vol 1 in *The English Historical Review* (April 1898) by Frederick York Powell pp342-4.
53. Marston to Clowes 10.3.1898 MS 93/001.
54. Clowes, W L, *The History of the Royal Navy* (London Vol II Intro. p v dated December 1897). This put Laughton's name on the spine of the series.
55. Marston to Clowes 17.11.1899. See Mahan to Marston 13.4.1900 also in MS 93/001.
56. Mahan wrote to Clowes on 21.3.1904 in his effort to change the text at this point.

the groundless claims of Francis Badham. Despite the complaints of Laughton, Mahan and Marston the damage had been done. Clowes had resuscitated the 'black legend' of Nelson at Naples, and given it a place in the standard history. In a book written to define the image of a service this sort of unsubstantiated calumny was not only out of place but positively dangerous.

Although Clowes recruited Mahan and Theodore Roosevelt, and Sir Clements Markham agreed to provide close on 100,000 words dealing with 'Exploration and Discovery', only Mahan delivered a truly impressive contribution; Markham's was unduly polemical, and Roosevelt's largely irrelevant to the purpose of the book. H W Wilson fell behind and delivered in haste, unlike Leonard Carr-Laughton, who was discarded as inadequate. These failings ensured that most of the book was written by Clowes, but fortunately he had a direct and easy style, making the somewhat repetitive and occasionally plain tedious recounting of detail pass without undue strain. Given the relentless schedule of publication, seven massive volumes between 1897 and 1903, and the fact that Clowes wrote an increasing amount of the work towards the end, the survival of his style is remarkable. Perhaps there is an insight into the man and his methods in a complaint from the typesetters. They wished he would write a little larger and not quite so close together. Marston had never seen so many words on a page!

For most of the period in which he was writing this book, Clowes was living in Switzerland, trying to stave off the ravages of the tuberculosis that would kill him shortly after he finished the project. He conducted some primary source research, or more usually had the research conducted on his behalf, mostly on specific points of detail that he wished to clarify, drawing the greater part of the narrative from existing published accounts of all ages and unequal quality. The publishers helped with specific queries, much as they helped Mahan, being right next door to the Public Record Office. Clowes wrote the final volume almost single-handed, calling on his friends in the service for advice. His files contain numerous letters from officers of all ranks, dealing with everything from the Second China War to the Boxer Rebellion. In consequence the analysis is often reinforced by insight and understanding of a type that is not found in the earlier volumes. His main themes for the volume were the growing harmony between Britain and America, symbolised in the co-operation of their navies, and the inadequacy of the army for Imperial tasks, as evidenced by the ubiquitous presence of naval brigades ashore.

Mahan's section on the major operations of the American War of Independence was not only the best of the book, but also one of the best historical studies he ever wrote. It was the only section to appear as a stand-alone volume. As might be expected Mahan developed a clear

strategic narrative, livened with analytical insight, making the chapter a
key teaching aid for naval staff colleges, and it was for this purpose that
Laughton had long advocated the reprinting. By contrast Theodore Roosevelt's chapter on the War of 1812 was the weakest of the book. Doubtless busy with his political career Roosevelt produced a re-hashed version
of his earlier study *The Naval War of 1812* which appeared in 1882,
largely based on American sources, and directed at an American audience.
He stressed, over and over again, how much the Americans had suffered
for the lack of an adequate fleet to defend their coast and their interests,
without analysing how the Royal Navy had been used to further British
war aims. It would be too much to contend that the contrasting levels of
interest in the two 'American' wars were solely based on the merits of the
relevant chapters in Clowes's book, but Roosevelt did nothing to stimu-
late further study with his dull offering. Clowes seems to have recognised
the weakness, giving his most famous author, by then President of the
United States, the type of puff that would not disgrace a cheap thriller.

Clowes's chapters are not without problems. He was given to making
sweeping strategic judgements without introducing any evidence to support the criticism, for the books lack a sustained strategic narrative, and
are generally weak on the higher direction of war, military affairs, politics
and the strategic relationship between land and sea power. This reflects
the state of contemporary scholarship, and the lack of time for reflection
and analysis. He also took a harsh view of certain individuals, notably
Admiral Duckworth, who could do no right.

For modern tastes the lack of strategic analysis, Mahan aside, and the
excessively detailed coverage of minor and single-ship actions are significant faults, while the potentially ground-breaking civil histories of the
Navy, inspired by Michael Oppenheim's work, are constrained, overly
factual and of limited value. Giving Markham free reign with the entire
history of Voyages and Discoveries was an invitation to repetition that
the great promoter of exploration could not resist. Each chapter reads as a
ringing endorsement of exploration, stressing the naval qualities of endeavour, leadership and fortitude in adversity that such hardship brings
out. These polemical efforts played a part in helping Markham start
Antarctic exploration, providing the Edwardian era with a new Sir John
Franklin in Captain Robert Falcon Scott RN.

Clowes's work has a key place in naval historiography. It was written
to exploit the new popular interest in the naval past, only three years after
the foundation of the Navy Records Society. In time the NRS would
provide the evidence for a better insight, but while Clowes was writing it
could do no more than offer occasional searchlight beams to illuminate
isolated aspects of the past. Clowes had access to the first volume of

the *Papers on the Blockade of Brest, 1803-1805*, but not the second. Consequently much of the coverage is old-fashioned. Produced at the beginning of a new wave of interest it was, by any standards, a remarkable achievement. But it was premature, and was rapidly overtaken by the development of specialist literature. Little wonder Marston was nervous for his investment. He did not make a profit.[57]

Aside from slow or weak contributors Clowes's main problem was scale. He, and his team, consistently over-ran their allotted word length, every volume being longer than planned. The inevitable result was that Marston was forced, reluctantly, to go to six and then seven volumes. He did so in the certain knowledge that his hopes of profit had vanished. His letters to Clowes are filled with injunctions to hasten the volumes along, to meet his publishing schedule, keep costs down and keep to word limits. Yet he, as the publisher, was responsible for the very fate he had most feared. The book was simply too large to be read outside a library. The massive scale of the text, allied to art-quality paper and the unusual page size make this a magnificent achievement of late Victorian publishing, but sales were hampered by the cost and size of the volumes. This denied Clowes the benefit of his greatest contribution, the readability of the text.

The book contains a fair share of myths, both old and of new creation. Clowes gives too much credence to isolated reports of poor gunnery in the post-Trafalgar fleet, while the idea that the Royal Navy was technologically conservative in the nineteenth century can be traced directly back to his declaration that 'with regard to nearly all new inventions bearing upon naval warfare, Great Britain showed herself intensely conservative' (VII p58). This bald assertion, based on the public complaints of disappointed inventors and engineers, is contradicted by all modern research, and often by Clowes's own efforts.

As a pre-modern popular history on the grand scale the book was a unique statement of the naval case at the end of the Victorian age. In meeting the needs of the Navy and the nation at the turn of the century, Clowes earned the knighthood conferred on him in 1902. Tragically he did not live to enjoy his title or the freedom offered by the completion of Volume VII. He died on 14 August 1905 at St Leonard's on Sea aged only forty-nine. The value of his work becomes obvious when one wants to examine the minor activities of the service in the years after 1900. Clowes's book remains an important starting-point for any study of the pre-1900 naval past. We await a modern synthesis to complement Clowes, to build on his achievement, remedy his omissions and oversights, and widen his concept of 'naval' history into an understanding of

---

57. The work is now available in an economic and portable reprint by Chatham Publishing, making it accessible to readers for the first time.

the role of the Royal Navy in the history of Britain. The process had already begun when Clowes was writing, but it remains incomplete.[58]

Laughton was not alone in his efforts to comprehend the nature of national strategy, or even of the particular the role of naval power within that strategy. His views were influenced by a number of contemporaries, notably Hornby, Henry Reeve, Bridge, the Colombs and Mahan. However, apart from Bridge, the earliest, and perhaps the most important influence, was that of Henry Reeve, the long-serving editor of the liberal *Edinburgh Review*. Reeve provided him with a major platform for his work, supported his application to King's College and promoted the Navy Records Society. Laughton repaid his debt with a typical Victorian two-decker tombstone biography, *The Memoirs of the Life of Henry Reeve*, which relied on large sections of correspondence. Reeve was the only British civilian to have any significant influence on Laughton's naval views before the turn of the century. Reeve had recognised the importance of 'maritime power' after observing the influence of naval forces on the Syrian campaign of 1840 and the advantages the allies obtained from their overwhelming naval superiority in the Russian War. This led him to open the *Edinburgh Review* to naval writers and naval subjects, beginning with Bridge in 1872, and Laughton in 1875. In the thirty years that preceded the publication of Mahan's *Influence of Seapower* in 1890 Laughton argued that much of the groundwork had been laid in the *Edinburgh Review*. The subjects ranged from the immediately contemporary to historical studies and reviews, but underlying all was the drive for contemporary understanding, based on the most complete information. Unfortunately Laughton did not discuss his intellectual debt to Reeve in any detail, and there is no surviving correspondence to help reconstruct their relationship. Laughton was a sympathetic biographer. He shared the relatively humble origins of his subject and both had made their careers on merit. Furthermore the Whig/Liberal politics of the *Edinburgh Review* were Laughton's politics, and they coloured his perception of both the modern world, and the recent past. The Irish Home Rule crisis of 1885 finally broke Reeve's wavering attachment to Gladstonian Liberalism, and along with the remaining Whig elements of the old party he moved into the Unionist camp.[59] The *Memoirs* have been described as a poor biography, and inasmuch as anyone would wish to understand Reeve the assessment is fair; W E H Lecky's brilliant six-page obituary

---

58. See Tedder, A W, *The Navy of the Restoration* (Cambridge 1916), ppv and 218 for a reflection of Laughton's views of the book. Rodger, *Safeguard*, the first of a projected three volume work, addresses this need.
59. Clive, J, 'The *Edinburgh Review*' in Briggs, A (ed), *Essays in the History of Publishing* (London 1974), p137.

does that job far more effectively.[60] Yet as a contribution to our understanding of the society in which the decision-makers of the mid-nineteenth century moved, and the relations between individuals the book is invaluable. In many respects it is similar to the famous journals of Charles Greville, which Reeve had edited. Reeve lacked the social rank and private wealth for a political career but, like Macaulay, his ability secured the patronage of Lord Lansdowne, who obtained a post for him at the Council Office, under Greville. Later Reeve wrote most of the *Times* leaders on European politics for ten years, before moving to the more exalted world of the leading quarterly. His literary and intellectual abilities, and his wide range of British and European political correspondents made him a valuable witness, and minor actor between 1845 and 1890. The book is typically self-effacing, it does not even carry Laughton's name on the cover. *The Times*, while adding a few comments on their one-time leader writer, wished the book had been abbreviated.[61]

One of Laughton's greatest strengths as a naval educator was his ability to introduce new and important ideas to a service audience, without alienating them by insisting on his intellectual superiority. His message was always to the point, agreeably packaged and easily digested. In the mid-1890s he and Philip Colomb recognised the need for a naval history textbook, as the essential precursor of any worthwhile study of history at Greenwich, or at any other stage in the career of a naval officer.[62] As ever his purpose was wider than the initial remit might suggest.

It could be argued that the lack of any systematic historical education was the single greatest impediment to the formation of a workable naval staff before the First World War. Until the service produced an adequate body of trained, and more especially educated, officers capable of assessing evidence and of producing analytical papers on strategy and policy, the manpower of any naval staff would depend on those with a predisposition to such work and the benefit of private study. There were invariably too few such men, and they included too high a proportion of 'mavericks' for an effective staff system. The close link between Laughton and the officers who served in the Naval Intelligence Department (NID), especially its Directors, is scarcely surprising. He had been in a position to recognise such talents and foster their studies.

When Fisher faced the Beresford enquiry in 1909 he found, to his disgust, that two of senior members of the NID had been feeding Lord

---

60. Lecky, W E H, 'Henry Reeve' in *Historical and Political Essays* (London 1910), pp221-6.
61. *The Times* 3.10.1898, Review p5.
62. There is no explicit evidence of the intended audience for the book, but as neither Laughton nor Colomb had ever been involved with Dartmouth, while both taught at Greenwich, it is likely that Greenwich was intended.

Charles with references to vital documents.[63] Little wonder he was unwilling to set up a staff until he had more, and better trained, men. For these he looked to the new Naval War Course, where three of Laughton's friends, Captain Henry May, Julian Corbett and Captain Edmond Slade led the way. But it would be some time before the new system produced the necessary officers, as Churchill's weak Admiralty Staff demonstrated in 1912-14. Even the presence of first-rate minds like George Ballard and Herbert Richmond could do little in a system set up to meet ignorant criticism, and staffed by second-rate officers chosen for obedience rather than ability.

Laughton had long argued that officers would benefit from a historical education. He did not suggest this as an alternative to the necessary technical and seamanship training, but instead history would dominate the secondary, truly 'educational' phase of their careers. He also recognised that the basics had to be inculcated early. To smooth the way for a serious study of history at a later stage young officers had to be introduced to the subject in a relevant and intelligible way at the beginning of their careers.[64] To meet this need Laughton used a group of his old friends, Admirals all, to write chapter-length biographies of a dozen famous sailors, keeping to himself the opening piece on Lord Howard, and adopting an unusually interventionist editorial role in the remaining chapters. His touch was sure, avoiding the twin dangers of tedious pedantry and patronising blandness. Some of his asides, marked out in square brackets, notably one on Samuel Hood's opinion of Sir Augustus Keppel, were as sharp as anything he ever wrote.[65]

The project began in mid-1896 as a collaboration between Laughton and Philip Colomb, who would write the lives of St Vincent and Nelson.[66] Colomb suggested approaching Penrose Fitzgerald, then in the throes of trying to get his life of George Tryon into print. 'Rough' Fitzgerald agreed to deal with Rooke, although he asked for help, and warned Laughton to expect more queries.[67] Montagu Burrows, the other naval man to make the transition to a historical chair, handled Blake, and confessed to being heavily dependant on Laughton's *DNB* entry.[68] When Vesey-Hamilton, as usual, ran late with Rodney and Hood, Laughton ended up doing rather more of those chapters than he had intended.[69] The other contributors were Frederick Bedford, Albert Markham, Edmund

---

63. Marder, A J, *From the Dreadnought to Scapa Flow* (Oxford 1961), Vol 1, pp192-204.
64. See his Tegetthoff and *Nelson Correspondence*.
65. Laughton, J K (ed), *From Howard to Nelson: Twelve Sailors* (London 1899), pp316-7.
66. Colomb to Laughton 7.9.1896 JKL MS.
67. Fitzgerald to Laughton 28.9.1896 ibid.
68. Burrows to Laughton 26.9.1896 ibid.
69. Vesey-Hamilton to Laughton 15.12.1896 JKL MS. Laughton, J K (ed), *From Howard to Nelson: Twelve Sailors* (London 1899), Intro. pvii.

Fremantle and Thomas Sturges-Jackson. All were friends of long standing, and all were Councillors of the Navy Records Society.[70] *From
Howard to Nelson: Twelve Sailors*, appeared in 1899, with a uniform
edition of twelve soldiers, edited by Spenser Wilkinson for the Sandhurst
market, although the two volumes were not otherwise connected. In his
introduction Laughton addressed the rationale of the Navy, and used the
question of its origins to make his case. It was impossible, he argued, to
assign a date for the beginning of the English navy, for 'when English
history begins, the navy was already an English institution'. In consequence the work of Alfred and Henry VIII, much like that of 1832 and
the 1860s was 'of reconstruction, of re-organisation'. Henry had the
credit of beginning the modern organisation, which was linked to the
development of ships capable of sustained operations at sea, with ship-
killing weapons and the embryo of tactical thought. The twelve heroes
were also given a role beyond mere fighting, being 'fittingly denominated
the Builders of the Empire', revealing Laughton's parallel development of
the naval role in Imperial History at King's College. The object was not
new research, although Laughton contributed a few insights, but the
exploitation of existing materials, notably Laughton's own *DNB* entries,
for naval education.

> What has been chiefly aimed at is to show how the work and methods of
> the great sailors of the past strike the sailors of the present; and for that, the
> Editor may justly congratulate himself on having secured the co-operation
> of the very distinguished officers who have contributed the several chapters.

To render the result more useful as a textbook Laughton added extensive
notes to broaden the coverage.[71]

The book stressed that these great officers had all been thoroughly
professional, even Blake, whose 'singular preparation for the work' was
stressed by Burrows.[72] Edmund Fremantle used Boscawen to support his
opinion that late entry into the service was no bar to excellence, citing the
careers of Cochrane and Tryon as further evidence.[73] The Admirals were
all written up as Victorians, men who sacrificed their private interests to
the service of the state, even such buccaneers as Drake and Rodney, while
Anson's undisputed wealth was excused by being 'hard-earned'. By contrast politicians were seen a fallible, fickle and, in the case of Laughton's

---

70. **Bedford**, F G H, *The Life and Letters of Admiral Sir Frederick Bedford* (Newcastle
1961). Bedford had been on the staff of HMS *Excellent* 1872-75, Captain of Greenwich
1880-83, served on the Chelsea Exhibition Committee in 1891 and at the Admiralty 1889-92
and 1895-8.
71. Laughton ed. ppv-viii.
72. Ibid, p122.
73. Ibid, p244.

particular *bête noire* Lord Sandwich, responsible for reducing the dockyards to 'sinks of iniquity'.[74] This one-dimensional treatment of politicians was dangerous for junior officers, especially when there was nothing in their later careers to introduce them to the realities of civil-military relations and party politics. Although tactical skill was the acme of excellence, with high praise going to Hawke, Rodney and Howe, Hood and Nelson were the brightest stars. Leadership and moral courage were characteristics these men shared. Professionalism was extended to cover administration, with Howard, Anson and St Vincent being praised for their work ashore.

Nothing so marked the work as a textbook for junior officers as Colomb's handling of Nelson's affair with Emma Hamilton, and his work at Naples. While Nelson's name was now 'pretty well' free of the charges relating to the Neapolitan Jacobins and Carraciolo, the affair with Emma had made the last years of his life 'wretched' and made his death at Trafalgar an 'unclouded mercy'.[75] Despite this rather forced analysis Colomb's two chapters are the best in the book, and among his best work. Not only do they exhibit 'a terseness not always characteristic of his style',[76] but they also combine a depth of insight and clarity of expression that make them a fitting finale to his literary career. Both St Vincent and Nelson emerge as more rounded, human, and sympathetic figures. St Vincent is portrayed as the party admiral, combining influence with sound strategic views and a clear sense of duty. Colomb stressed that he created the image of a stern, unbending commander to discipline the lower deck and dismiss the incompetent officers; it was not the true character of a man who took pleasure in playing practical jokes. Colomb's St Vincent would have been perfectly comprehensible to his Greenwich audience, if a touch too sophisticated a portrait for the callow youths entering *Britannia*. When he came to Nelson, the flawed genius, Colomb excelled himself, demonstrating that Nelson had risen despite his circum-stances, and how his character and career were built on emotion. The influence of Lord Hood, stressed by Vesey-Hamilton, gave him the tacti-cal awareness and standards of success that recur throughout his career, but only because Hood was a man he could love. It was this emotional relationship, rather than the rules of the service, that secured his loyalty. He was only ever loyal to superiors he could love, like Hood and St Vincent; at the same time he often gave unmerited praise to his subordi-nates and remained desperate for love and admiration all his life. This was the key to the business of Lady Hamilton. As a commander Nelson demonstrated his essential greatness when in contact with the enemy,

74. Ibid, p370. The comments are by Laughton.
75. Ibid, pp464-8.
76. *The Times* 8.7.1899 review, p6.

having the most simple and effective tactical system of all, the concentration of force that Laughton had been advocating since the early 1870s. For
Colomb it was summed up in his report on the Nile: 'By attacking the
enemy's van and centre, the wind blowing directly along their line, I was
enabled to throw what force I pleased on a few ships'.[77] The very
simplicity of Nelson's tactics had, Colomb argued, confused Mahan's
analysis of Cape St Vincent and Trafalgar. Colomb summed up this most
complex of commanders by observing that his, 'weakness is but a foil to
the sublime'.[78]

From Howard to Nelson was a good textbook. The careers of the great
commanders were placed in context, linked by lines of professional patronage and used to illustrate key issues. They were not simple stories of
heroism and innate British superiority. By addressing leadership, administration, strategy, professionalism, character and the service ethic Laughton, Colomb and their co-authors provided the officers of the new
century with the 'Victorian' values that underpinned their service, and the
basis to study history as the basis from which to derive tactics, strategy
and doctrine. If a tithe of those who read this book as junior officers had
joined the NRS, Laughton would have been delighted. It is hard to understand why this impressive text, which had the virtue of being a single
volume, the attraction of being written by Admirals, and the benefit of
Laughton's editing, was replaced at Dartmouth by Geoffrey Callender's
'atrocious' *The Sea-Kings of Britain*.[79] Whatever the educational limits of
the cadets at Dartmouth, surely they deserved a better grounding in the
service they had joined.

Historians of the defence debates around the turn of the century have
consistently ignored Laughton. This can be attributed to his limited output of signed papers on contemporary subjects, most of his work appearing unsigned, a failure to consider the nature and purpose of the naval
historical revival, and a tendency to equate volume and sensation with
influence. Laughton had developed history as the basis for naval education, doctrine development and the re-establishment of a sound national
strategy. Having demonstrated the validity of this method by 1894, with
his first volumes for the NRS, Laughton could observe the defence debates of the next decade with some satisfaction. His cause was now being
advanced by men who had developed their methods and ideas from his
writings. They led national opinion back from the abyss of 'little
England', increased fortifications and the inviolability of private property
at sea, an extension of the principle of 'free ships – free goods' established
at the 1856 Declaration of Paris. In effect Laughton had turned over

---

77. *From Howard to Nelson*, p456.
78. Ibid, p468.
79. Richmond to Corbett 1907 Corbett MSS Box 4.

polemical writing to others, who were either better qualified to speak by service or rank, or better positioned, writing in key newspapers and journals. There would be no benefit in his echoing the work of Philip Colomb, George Sydenham Clarke and James Thursfield. Once they had entered the lists the champion of naval history could retire to the sidelines, his preferred position, making an occasional contribution and supporting his fellow labourers with his tireless work on the foundations.

An examination of the contemporary literature demonstrates the universal acceptance of the historical method by those who adopted Laughton's views. Those who favoured alternative strategies were forced to refute the validity of the exercise. When Philip Colomb launched the 'Blue-Water' case at the RUSI in 1889 he relied on historical evidence. His opponents, military men, declared the method was invalid and was not applicable to 'scientific' cases.[80] The original debate became so involved that it had to be held over for another day. When battle resumed Laughton spoke in support of his friend, and accepted the arguments advanced by Sir John Colomb.[81] The strategic triumph of the Colomb brothers must have given Laughton real pleasure. After the success of Mahan's work, which owed so much to Laughton, the 'eternal principles' were rarely questioned.

The most unlikely convert to the naval cause was Sir George Sydenham Clarke RE. Shortly after joining the Fortifications Branch of the War Office in 1883, he secured the addition of a naval officer to the staff. That officer, Captain Thomas Sturges-Jackson, had studied under Laughton afloat and ashore. He became a close friend of Clarke's, serving with him on the Colonial Defence Committee of 1885. Clarke noted that after 1884 he 'began to make a special study of naval questions, to buy all the naval histories that I could afford, and get in touch with the best naval opinion'.[82] Given Laughton's status and his connection with Sturges-Jackson, it is scarcely surprising that Clarke's views were heavily influenced by *the* naval historian.[83] Clarke believed that the Navy 'alone could hold the Imperial Structure together', making a major contribution to the public discussion that culminated in the 1889 Naval Defence Act. He began writing for the *Edinburgh Review* in 1888, and later wrote the original charter of the Navy League.[84] His book *Fortification* of 1890 codified the theme that no amount of fixed shore defences could secure the British

---

80. Schurman, *Education*, p50. Colomb, P, 'The Relations between Local Fortifications and a Moving Navy', *JRUSI* (1889), pp150-202.
81. Ibid, pp197-8.
82. Clarke, G S (Lord Sydenham of Combe), *My Working Life* (London 1927), pp41-7, 69-70, quote p142.
83. However, Clarke did not give Laughton the credit he deserved, he is not mentioned in his memoirs.
84. Clarke, *My Working Life*, pp136 and 104.

Empire, if command of the sea were lost; and that while Britain had a superior fleet the money spent on anything beyond limited local defence against raids was simply thrown away. While Laughton was not mentioned his influence was all-pervasive, Clarke using the example of Thurot from *Studies in Naval History*, but without attribution.[85] Clarke's subsequent writings on strategy echoed the central argument of his book, and used more of Laughton's work.[86] Being in London on leave in June 1893 Clarke was present at the foundation of the NRS, and he continued to take a leading role in its work whenever he was in London, serving as a Councillor or Vice-President for more than ten years between 1893 and 1915.[87] As the First Secretary of the Committee of Imperial Defence, between 1904 and 1907, he exercised considerable influence over the development of British strategy.[88]

Clarke's most significant articles were collected, with the work of James Thursfield (1840-1922) the naval correspondent of *The Times* and another important former of public opinion, in *The Navy and the Nation* of 1897. Thursfield was also a follower of Laughton and a founding member of the NRS. He recognised what Laughton was doing, and gave the Society a push in the *Quarterly Review* with a discussion of the Armada volumes. He considered Laughton's performance 'admirable', although he feared it might be 'almost impertinent' to praise the man who had contributed the 'masterly series of naval biographies' to the *DNB* and demonstrated a firm grasp of the 'philosophy' of naval history.[89] Clarke also used the Armada volumes to support his contention that England could not be invaded while she held command of the sea.[90] When Thursfield discussed naval education, national awareness of the service and the principle of concentration, he was echoing Laughton's work. Yet he, and Clarke, did him scant justice in later years. Perhaps Clarke associated Laughton with the defensive naval views, of which he was so critical after Jutland, which he associated with Corbett,[91] and he did not even mention Laughton or the NRS in his memoirs. Clarke and Thursfield subsequently attributed all the credit for

85. Clarke, Sir G S, *Fortification: Its Past Achievement, Recent Development, and Future Progress* (London 2nd ed 1907), p172. The first edition appeared in 1890, and was reviewed by Laughton in the *Edinburgh*. See Ch4.
86. Clarke, G S, and Thursfield, J R, *The Navy and the Nation; or Naval Warfare and Imperial Defence* (London 1897). Clarke 'Can England be Invaded', ibid, p318 citing Jean de Vienne.
87. Clarke, *My Working Life*, pp124-5.
88. Offer, A, *The First World War: An Agrarian Interpretation* (Oxford 1989), for Clarke at CID.
89. *The Navy and the Nation*; Thursfield 'The Armada' at p156.
90. Clarke, 'Can England be Invaded' ibid p322.
91. Clarke, *My Working Life* pp330-4. Thursfield, J R, *Naval Warfare* (Cambridge 1913), does not mention Laughton, or credit his work although Sir Charles Ottley gave him his due in his Introduction.

the naval revival to the popular success of the American, and their assessment has held the field for a century.

That this analysis was both over-simplified and misleading can be seen in Charles Dilke and Henry Spenser Wilkinson's study *Imperial Defence* of 1892. They adopted the work of Philip Colomb and Laughton as the basis for the strategy of Empire, and cited Mahan only to support the wisdom of the modern approach to blockade.[92] Given the relative paucity of serious historical evidence used by Dilke and Wilkinson, the pivotal role given to Colomb's 1889 'Blue-Water' paper, and Laughton's powerful support at the RUSI is important.

In his studies of the Royal Navy between 1885 and 1919, Arthur Marder accepted Clowes's claim to have founded the NRS, and consequently missed the purpose of the Society. Laughton, history and the development of doctrine simply did not fit into Marder's conception of the Navy in the 'Fisher era'. Laughton's work was too subtle, relying on long-term influence and personal contact, rather than polemical output. Laughton was the most influential defence intellectual of the age because he knew everyone who mattered, was the acknowledged master of his profession, and spoke at a level where short-term controversy was irrelevant. He was, in essence, the voice of the past, passing on the wisdom of the ancients, as Hornby had recognised. The tragedy of his career was that this unique influence did not survive his death. This was not for the want of effort. He recognised the need, and devoted much of the last decade of his life to establishing a firm, institutional base for his legacy.

---

92. Dilke, Sir C W and Wilkinson, H Spenser, *Imperial Defence* (2nd ed, London 1897), pp51-3, p62 for Mahan.

CHAPTER 8

The Department of Naval History: 1900-15

At the turn of the century Laughton was advancing the study of naval history on a broad front. Recognised as a man of national significance, his public lectures were invariably reported in *The Times* by his friend Thursfield. The NRS had reached an optimum level, producing a steady stream of edited texts, once the Browning business had been dealt with. However, contact with the service, and especially his continuing relationship with the intellectual elite in the Naval Intelligence Department, had persuaded him that this type of material was not the most effective method of educating the naval mind. Only when it had been worked up into narrative history, with a full measure of 'lessons', could it be set before the officer corps as a whole. This task was altogether more demanding than could be accomplished by many of the editors then working for the NRS, requiring trained historians of real ability, with the time and application to work on large bodies of primary source materials. It could be aided, and even stimulated, by the transcript funding provided by the Society, but there were very few scholars available with the skill, time and inclination to profit from the opportunity. The example of Corbett was one that Laughton would have wished to see emulated by others. Starting as a novelist and lightweight biographer Corbett was encouraged by Laughton to become an editor, and developed into an analytical scholar who could command a teaching position on the new Naval War Course. Having drawn the historians into editing, Laughton recognised that anything more would require a secure grounding in the subject, which could only come from a thorough university-level historical education and training in the methods of historical research, complemented by more specific instruction on naval issues. The chance that had thrown up Corbett would have to be replaced by a system to produce the trained intellects that would continue the work of education for an expanding navy in the new century.

In the interval there was a need to be met, and Laughton would address it. As was ever the case in his literary career, ambition and opportunity coincided and the results turned out far different from the original intention. In contrast to his best known contemporary followers, Mahan and Corbett, he found the study of the Royal Navy in adversity and recovery to be the most effective educational medium, with the War of the Austrian Succession and the War of American Independence as the best examples. His essentially chronological perspective encouraged the selection of the former, a choice reinforced by the task of editing the papers of Admiral Henry Medley, Commander-in-Chief in the Mediterranean at the end of the war, for the Historical Manuscript Commission and the high regard he had for Mahan's section on the American War in Clowes's *History*.[1]

The Austrian War, 1744-48, and the coterminous 'War of Jenkin's Ear' 1739-48, had already featured largely in his output. Subjects already addressed included the diplomacy of the war, English privateering (a strategy most applicable to periods when the command of the sea was uncertain), the battle of Toulon, the strategy of the Western Squadron and the role of Anson. Laughton submitted a book proposal to Longman's in February 1902, which was accepted with alacrity.[2] Typically, he did not produce the book, and so in 1907 the task was passed to a new disciple, Commander (later Admiral Sir) Herbert Richmond,[3] who completed it by the outbreak of the First World War. The internal evidence of Laughton's role in the resulting book, *The Navy in the War of 1739-1748*, is overwhelming, from the opening quote, drawn from Seeley's *Expansion of England* and the acknowledgement of Laughton's help and his 'great store of knowledge'. Even more significant was Laughton's influence on Richmond's first essay, published in 1909. The subject, Admiral Sir George Byng's expedition to Sicily in 1719, was one Laughton may have selected, and he certainly helped with the material.[4] The success of this piece probably persuaded Laughton to offer him the book project. Richmond's methodology and objectives were heavily influenced by Laughton and Corbett.[5] He was, perhaps, the last major scholar to be encouraged by Laughton directly, the depth of his debt becoming clear on reading his first book, and in the intellectual origins of *The Naval Review*, which was dominated by the aims and members of the NRS. It

---

1. Laughton, J K (ed), *Report on the Manuscripts of Lady Du Cane* (London, HMC 1905).
2. Longman, T N, to Laughton 24.2.1902 JKL MS.
3. Richmond, H W, *The Navy in the War of 1739-48* (Cambridge 1920), 3 vols Vol 1, Preface.
4. Richmond, H W, 'The Expedition to Sicily, 1718, Under Sir George Byng', *JRUSI* Vol 53 (September 1909), pp1135-52. Laughton first wrote about Byng in 1873, and continued to do so throughout his life. Laughton to Corbett 19.12.1905: 'if people would only look they would find that George Byng was one of our tactical masters'. Tunstall, B (ed. Tracy, N), *Naval Warfare in the Age of Sail* (London 1990), p69. Richmond, H W (ed), *Papers Relating to the Loss of Minorca 1756* (London NRS 1913), Preface.
5. Schurman, *Education*, p134.

would remain strong for the rest of his life. His 1939 assessment of the role of naval history in *The Naval Review* was closely based on Laughton's work.[6] Richmond was an unusual naval officer, combining great technical competence with the intellectual sophistication and application of a historian; Laughton and Corbett were quick to recognise his talent. His work was, from first to last, driven by the needs of the present, in the mould provided by Laughton. While the book that Richmond had completed by 1914 was own work, the impulse and direction for it had come from Laughton, but unfortunately Laughton's influence on Richmond, as on Mahan, Colomb, Corbett, Sydenham Clarke and others, has passed without notice.[7] Laughton always encouraged others, with the ability, to take up tasks which he had already begun, and provided them with all the help his powerful memory and full notebooks could offer. The case of Richmond is strikingly similar to his role in the production of Mahan's study of the American War. Both made excellent teaching texts, with their 'lessons' developed for the naval mind.

In his efforts to broaden the appeal of naval history within the academic sector, Laughton stressed the role of the Navy in the development of the Empire. His 1902 Lent lecture series 'The Unity of the British Empire' opened with 'The Growth of our Colonies based on our Maritime Power' before considering the American revolt, Canada, India, Australia and contemporary Imperialism. He opened with a quote from Seeley: history 'should not merely gratify curiosity about the past, but give a clearer picture of the present, or forecast of the future'.[8] Having made a comparative study of empires, Laughton believed that there was no special quality that made Englishmen better colonists; for him the key to the growth of the British Empire lay in maritime power. This lecture series laid the foundation for the study of Imperial history, both at King's College, where Sidney Low and then A P Newton took up the task before 1914, and more generally. When he began his 1913 lecture series 'Sea Power and the Empire' the Principal of the College Dr Burrow presided, and spoke of establishing a school of Imperial and Colonial History.[9] This lecture series was the basis for the naval history textbook Laughton had planned.

While the influence of Seeley is obvious, the mood of the time, and the work of more polemical writers like Sir Charles Dilke, was also significant. That Imperial History took shape in the academic world as an

---

6. Hattendorf, J (ed), *Ubi Sumus: The State of Naval and Maritime History* (Newport R.I. 1994), p3.
7. Hunt, B, *Sailor-Scholar; Admiral Sir Herbert Richmond 1871-1946* (Waterloo, Ontario 1982).
8. Laughton, J, Lecture Notes 1902: JKL MS. Quote is from *The Expansion of England*, p1.
9. 'Sea Power and the Empire', *Morning Post* 9.10.1913.

offshoot of naval history should be obvious from the structure of the first landmark text in the field, *The Cambridge History of the British Empire*, the first volume of which was published in 1929, edited by Newton, John Holland Rose, the Vere-Harmsworth Professor of Naval History at Cambridge, and another Cambridge scholar, E A Benians. The first chapter, and one third of the total, are naval or largely naval in content. Laughton's conception of an empire linked by sea power dominates the whole. Laughton himself continued his efforts to secure the position of naval history at King's College, which became all the more important as it joined the federal University of London with courses leading to the award of degrees from 1903, a process only completed in 1910. This revived the lecturing side of Laughton's career, and improved his salary.

As the acknowledged leader of British naval historians, Laughton's breadth of learning, generous scholarship and pivotal role as founder and Secretary of the NRS brought him into contact with everyone who was interested in the subject. He provided a critical and methodological rigour for projects, which were largely concerned to provide historical raw material for current debates on invasion and strategy. As such he was part of the intellectual support called on by 'the Syndicate of Discontent' lead by Lord Charles Beresford and orchestrated by Reginald Custance in opposition to Fisher. He had already helped Beresford with his illustrated book *Nelson and his Times*, and shared many ideas with Custance, the intellectual force of the 'Syndicate'. The other prominent members of this group were also Councillors of the Records Society, Admirals Richards, Kerr, Fremantle, Fanshawe, Seymour, Culme-Seymour, Markham, and Vesey-Hamilton, along with Clements Markham of the Royal Geographic Society and the ex-Chief Constructor Sir William White. Laughton was part of their social world, and his ideas were the common currency of the 'Syndicate's' complaints, notably a preference for more numerous small battleships.[10] However, he was careful not to join the Fisher controversy in too overt a fashion.[11] His loyalty was, above all, to the service and he could hardly have enjoyed the public spectacle provided by Beresford. The approach and the membership of the Society ensured that it was not to Fisher's taste. Even NRS Councillors who were initially in the 'Fishpond', notably Corbett, Edmond Slade, Charles Ottley, Herbert Richmond, Prince Louis and Henry May, were not above suspicion. Even so, when the Admiralty needed an author for the

---

10. For Laughton's views on battleships see *The Edinburgh Review* (April 1882), p483, (January 1890), pp168-70, and (April 1894) pp468-9. Laughton, J K (ed), *The Barham Papers* (London 1912), Vol III, pxxxi.
11. See *The Barham Papers* (London 1907) Vol 1, pxix for a sharp critique of the nucleus crew system.

confidential history of the Russo-Japanese war in 1906 Laughton was the first to be mentioned, and appropriately Corbett wrote it.[12]

When the old Training Ship *Britannia* was finally closed, and the cadets were moved ashore to the grand new College building, it was fitting that every aspect of the College, from the motto over the door to the almost religious reverence for the past, should reflect Laughton's influence. Cadets entered the building under Laughton's epitome of the naval case, the paraphrase of the preamble to the 1866 Articles of War that had been the motto of the 1891 Exhibition: 'It is on the *Navy* under the good providence of God, that our wealth, prosperity and peace depend'.[13] He had been using the quote since the 1860s, and it was doubtless adopted for the exhibition on his advice. The placing of the motto was undoubtedly due to Fisher, who knew his history, and chose his examples well, but the words had been placed in the public domain by Laughton. Unfortunately, while Laughton's books were used at the College, his message and his methods were allowed to atrophy.[14]

Of more significance for Laughton was Fisher's Naval War Course. At first sight this was an unlikely place to find his influence, Fisher being the one senior officer of the era for whom he never expressed any particular enthusiasm. There is no evidence that Fisher was influenced by Laughton's work, and he was never a member of the NRS. However, Fisher, whatever his faults, was a man of large mind and took a broad view of the needs of the service. While Laughton disapproved of his nucleus crews and big battleships he must have taken real satisfaction from the development of the Naval War Course, a pleasure reinforced by the prominent role that Corbett and other NRS Councillors took in its work. Fisher had long recognised that he could not hope to operate a staff system, which was essential, without a large pool of trained staff officers. He had the ability to pick out the best brains of the service, and apply them to the tasks where they were best qualified, but the task was becoming ever more demanding. Admirals had to be educated if they were to be efficient, and Fisher believed that until the new Naval War Course was established this situation would

12. Schurman, *Corbett*, p132 quoting from Captain Ottley, DNI, to Admiralty Board 14.12.1906.
13. Hamilton, W M, *The Nation and the Navy* (Unpub. London Ph.D. 1977), pp94-6. For the actual wording see fn14 below. Marder, A J, *The Anatomy of British Seapower 1880-1905* (London 1940), p45, based on Clowes, W L, *The Royal Navy* (London 1904), Vol VII, pp82-3. Morriss, A J A, *The Scaremongers: Advocacy of War and Rearmament 1896 – 1914* (London 1984).
14. The motto was the same paraphrase of the 1866 Articles of War that had featured so prominently at the 1891 Exhibtition. The actual wording is 'the Navy, whereon, under the good Providence of God, the wealth, Safety, and Strength fo the Kingdom Chiefly depend'. Rodger, N A M, *Articles of War* (Havant 1982), p35. Hughes, E A, *The Royal Naval College Dartmouth* (London 1950). Richmond to Corbett 1907 Corbett MSS Box 4 NMM.

not be improved.[15] He had urged the establishment of the course on the Admiralty Board when it visited Malta in 1901, with immediate results, and it remained a major issue when he took office as First Sea Lord in 1904.[16] Because he was content to leave the development and delivery of the curriculum to others, notably the brilliant Captain Henry May, Fisher has rarely been given credit for the War Course. The link with the American College was intentional. Luce's work was the model being followed, but the fact that Laughton had inspired Luce was not recognised. The War Course combined staff training and education with an active staff function, Fisher using the Course as an embryo naval staff, developing war plans that could be withheld, or dismissed as 'exercises'. With the assistance of Corbett Fisher's intellectual elite – May, Ottley, Slade, Hankey and Ballard – it provided Sir John with his detailed planning. It should be stressed that this 'brains' trust' was entirely separate from the one that was used for technical questions, which included John Jellicoe, Henry Jackson and Reginald Bacon.

When the War Course started it was intended to provide an education in war fighting and related issues to commanders and captains. Initially spread over eight months it was divided into two parts in 1903, to enable more officers to attend. More significantly it was compulsory from the outset, in marked contrast to the half-hearted and ineffective methods of recruitment adopted for senior Naval College courses. This was the first full-time career path course for senior officers. After six years at Greenwich the course transferred to Portsmouth in 1906, where it remained until the outbreak of war. During Fisher's tenure as First Sea Lord the course was also tasked with important staff duties, such as the Ballard Committee of 1906, which planned for war with Germany.[17] In 1912 the Naval Staff Course for lieutenants, lieutenant-commanders and commanders was set up to provide trained staff officers.[18] By securing the course, providing it with the best brains in the service, and access to the able civilians, Fisher had developed an effective system to educate senior officers, and provided the resources for staff work. In a period dominated by the need to win the naval race on a tight budget this was no mean feat, and deserves higher praise than it is generally accorded. The link between Corbett's major texts, *England in the Mediterranean*, *England in the Seven Year's War* and *The Campaign of Trafalgar* with the War Course requires emphasis. They were the published versions of his lecture

15. Marder, A J, *The Anatomy of British Sea Power* (London 1940), p390, quoting Fisher.
16. Mackay, R F, *Fisher of Kilverstone* (Oxford 1973), pp258-9, 306.
17. Ibid, p366.
18. Marder, A J, *From the Dreadnought to Scapa Flow: Volume 1 1904-1914: The Road to War* (Oxford 1961), pp32-3, 265.

courses, and stand as an example of what Laughton thought naval history should be; well researched, well written, didactic and accessible.[19]

Laughton also worked with Custance, the DNI 1899-1902, who thought history would be useful, 'revealing the underlying principles' even if the details had changed. This basic work was necessary, because, as he told Bridge, 'there is so much ignorance of the first principles of war in the Admiralty'. Custance shared Laughton's view that squadrons were the building-block of fleets, that ships should be no larger than necessary, in order to build more, and that speed was relatively unimportant. Custance's strategic views were largely correct, accepting the primacy of battle in British strategy and treating commerce warfare as a secondary issue.[20] While still on active service Custance published under the pen-name 'Barfleur', which reflected his preferences in battleship design. He clashed with Fisher while DNI, and thereafter was 'paranoid' on any issue connected with him. He fell out with Corbett over Fisher's reforms and the Dreadnought policy, although he worked closely with him in running the NRS after Laughton's death. During his period at the Admiralty the War Course was established at Portsmouth by Captain Henry May, as an outgrowth of Laughton's original lecture series, which Colomb had continued down to 1895, when May took over. Custance published several books but he never achieved the intellectual level of Colomb, or the historical merit of Richmond. His books were too clearly didactic in intent, the history was selected and manipulated, in the manner of Mahan, without his intellectual consistency, and in pursuit of doubtful lessons. As Richmond noted in 1916, Custance was not an historian, 'his labours in history have been directed to making history prove what he wants it to prove'.[21] Custance's major weakness was his failure to engage others. A committed bachelor, he was temperamentally cold and suspicious, enamoured of his own opinions, impervious to other arguments, and utterly unwilling to change his view. His most significant work, *Naval Policy; A Plea for the Study of War*, published under his pen-name in 1907, created the image of conflicting historical and material schools of thought that has entranced intellectual naval historians ever since. These 'schools' never had any reality, the argument was too simplistic to stand intelligent analysis, and much of the 'history' deployed in the book was inaccurate, or unscholarly, invalidating the message he was preaching. The dedication was to Philip Colomb, who was at least as much a 'materialist' as Fisher, although a rather less

---

19. Schurman, *Corbett*, on the role of Henry May, and George Clarke, in completing this process.
20. Allen, M, 'Rear Admiral Reginald Custance; Director of Naval Intelligence 1899-1902', *Mariner's Mirror* Vol 78, No 1 (1992), pp61-75.
21. Richmond Diary entry 11.3.1916 in Marder, A J (ed), *Portrait of an Admiral*. (London 1952), p205.

successful one. It can only be concluded that Custance's contact with Laughton came too late. He appreciated much of the message, and grasped the need for a systematic approach, but he lacked the flexibility that characterised Laughton's approach to advancing the cause.

Custance was also involved in the great debate on the tactics of Trafalgar, begun by Corbett in 1905, and developed in *The Campaign of Trafalgar* in 1910. This was finally 'resolved' in 1912 with the Report of the Admiralty Committee, which had been prompted by Captain Mark Kerr, who was particularly close to Prince Louis of Battenberg.[22] The Committee was chaired by Custance, and included Bridge, Perrin and Charles Firth. Despite Corbett's reservations about the naval members, the report accepted his interpretation. He told his friend the poet, editor and some-time historian Henry Newbolt that 'the real point . . . is whether historians are to take their history from sailors, or sailors from historians. It is a revolt of Bridge, Custance & Co. against people like you and me, actively, behind our backs'.[23] By 1912 Corbett was intimately associated by the Navy with aspects of Fisher's reforms, and therefore the 'Syndicate of Discontent' was hardly going to applaud his version of Trafalgar, whatever he said. They were arguing about who should provide the historical basis for modern doctrine, and Custance's real target was Fisher, rather than Corbett. It has to be borne in mind at all times, that the big issue was the modern service, not the historical record. Laughton took care to avoid becoming entangled in this debate. He managed to work with the Navy for sixty years without a single demonstration of ill-feeling, a fact that helps to explain both his success, and the subsequent oblivion that has descended on his work.

Very little is known about Laughton's private life. In mid-1896 the family moved from Manor Road Barnet in North London to No 5, and two years later No 9, Pepys Road, South Wimbledon. The move enabled the three sons of his second marriage to attend King's College School, which would relocate to Wimbledon at Easter 1897.[24] Both houses, now demolished, were large new red-brick suburban dwellings only two minutes walk from Raynes Park railway station, giving Laughton an easy journey into King's College. From his study in the front room upstairs, he would occasionally bellow down to demand that his second family 'stop making this obscene noise'. Despite these interventions, his children regarded him with 'awe and respect'.[25] The children of his first

22. In his biography of Prince Louis Kerr had his revenge on Corbett, ignoring him and Laughton. In view of Prince Louis's close friendship with Laughton over forty years the latter omission is particularly regrettable.
23. Corbett to Newbolt 21.4.1912. Corbett MS Box 3.
24. Hearnshaw, F J C, *The Centenary History of King's College, London* (London 1929), pp375-6.
25. Laughton-Matthews, V, *The Blue Tapestry* (London 1948), p26. This is the only 'human' source.

marriage were welcome visitors, and his wife made the house a social centre for her children's friends, who included Gardiner's sons. As a member of staff at King's College he was able to educate his children well. This was critical, for the family rarely had any money to spare.

All five children of his second marriage served in the armed forces. Both his daughters joined the Wrens, the elder, Vera, rising to be a truly formidable Wren Commandant in the Second World War, while Grace was only a mere Superintendent. After being wounded and gassed on the Western Front his youngest son, Lieutenant Hubert Laughton, still only 21, died of the plague a fortnight after the Armistice in 1918. Lieutenant Commander Jeffrey Knox Laughton RN died from a poisoned mosquito bite while serving aboard the Royal Yacht in 1925, cutting short a promising career as a naval engineer. The eldest son of his second marriage, Francis, rose to the rank of Lieutenant Colonel, winning the Military Cross.[26] Lady Laughton died in 1946.

A tall and handsome man of striking appearance, Laughton's character and opinions come through strongly in his writing. He was not a xenophobe or a bigot, being scrupulously careful to give the other side of Britain's naval history. In politics he was always an Imperialist. His earliest thoughts on the subject were those of a Palmerstonian Liberal, and he remained consistent to the end, joining the Liberal Imperialists in 1886, as his political heritage was divided between two parties. In all this he was 'an Englishman who has never admitted that any good accrued to his country from the policy of Mr Gladstone or Mr Bright'.[27] Along with the majority of his intellectual contemporaries he feared the advance of democracy, and was no happier with the policy of 'Free Trade'.[28] His personal opinions were equally clear cut. When he planned a Records Society volume on the social life of the eighteenth-century Navy he was convinced that his research would demonstrate that most of the crime, brawling, mutiny and tyranny of the era was due to 'the pestilent habit of drunkeness'.[29] When provoked, by ignorant or malicious opposition to his professional work, he was quick-tempered and maintained his grudges for years. The delight he took in Montgomery's five-year prison term was characteristic. Yet he was an outstanding teacher, reflecting the excellent inter-personal skills he had used to maintain harmonious relations with the naval officer corps for sixty years. Above all he took enormous pride in having served in the Royal Navy, retaining RN among his titles to the end.

26. Ibid.
27. Laughton, J K, 'The Naval Exhibition at the Hague', *The Monthly Review* (November 1900), p67.
28. Laughton, J K, 'Britain's Naval Policy', p83.
29. Laughton, J K, 'Our Naval Records', *The Navy and Army Illustrated* (29.5.1896), p296.

Laughton's last years saw little falling-off in intellectual power, despite some hardening of his attitudes. He became increasingly 'naval' in his approach. His disquiet with contemporary politics, and disgust at the revelations of the past, notably those of his old *bête noire* Sandwich, led him to make sweeping generalisations in the introductions to his *Barham Papers* volumes. When age took its toll it attacked his most vulnerable point. In 1901 he lost the sight of one eye, an affliction that he bore with stoicism. Mahan was 'inexpressibly grieved' to hear the news, and hoped that 'a slight cessation of the high pressure at which you have worked may perhaps benefit you'.[30] As Mahan observed five years later, on receiving Laughton's latest photograph, the image was life-like, but 'exaggeratedly sedate'. He was astonished to discover, very belatedly, in 1907, that Laughton was ten years his senior.[31] For their last seven years of life the two men would exchange the tribulations of ageing, as well as the latest naval news and historical debate. Their last meeting, in London in November 1912, took place at King's College in the early afternoon, as Laughton was unwilling to face the evening traffic.[32] In May 1914 he reported to Mahan that his enthusiasm was waning.[33] That he had continued with his demanding editorial and secretarial schedule for the NRS until 1912, and answered the call to carry on at King's until mid-1914, reveals his determination, and suggests that his ambitions went beyond mere work.

Academic, service and social recognition crowded in on Laughton in his last years. In 1904 Oxford awarded him an honorary D.Litt, on the recommendation of the new Chancellor, Lord Goschen, who had served both liberal and conservative ministries as First Lord between 1871 and 1900. He knew that the NRS had been a key element in the naval revival during his second term at the Admiralty, 1895-1900, and he had used Laughton's arguments to support his policies.[34] Laughton's own University took another nine years to follow suit. In June 1907 he was knighted in the King's Birthday Honours List. The honour was conferred by a Liberal Government dominated by Imperialists of his own stamp, and it was belated recognition of his role at the heart of naval policy. In the same year he was made a fellow of University College, London.[35] He was now part of the establishment. He received the Greenwich Hospital pension of £50 in April 1908.[36]

30. Mahan to Laughton 31.5.1901: JKL MS.
31. Mahan to Laughton 22.5.1906, and 6.9.1907: JKL MS.
32. Mahan to Laughton 21.11.1912: JKL MS.
33. Mahan to Laughton 14.5.1914: JKL MS.
34. Colson, P (ed), *Lord Goschen and his friends* (London 1940), pp188-92.
35. Venn, J A, *Biographical History of Gonville and Caius College, Cambridge* (Cambridge 1898).
36. Service Record ADM 196/81.

In 1910 Laughton's eightieth birthday was celebrated in a manner that must have delighted him. He was presented with an address and a cheque by a large gathering at the RUSI, 'a mark of the subscribers appreciation of his work in the revival of interest in naval history'. Among the contributors were the Prince of Wales, Prince Louis of Battenberg (both founder members of the NRS), and many senior Admirals. The political world was represented by Lord George Hamilton, Lord Cawdor, Earl Desart, Austen Chamberlain and Lord Sanderson, while Mahan, Kipling, and Sir Alfred Lyall were among those from other fields. Speaking from the Chair, Lyall declared there was 'no author to whom our literature owed more for the revival of naval tradition, for the illumination of naval history'. Kipling wrote:

> Apart from the value and significance of his work on its national side, my own personal indebtedness to him in connection with the Navy Records Society extends over many years and, I have helped myself gratefully to the treasures that his labour and forethought have made accessible to us.

In a leading article Thursfield, who was well placed to know, declared that Laughton was the true pioneer of naval history, having begun his work long before Mahan. His work with the NRS;

> has, for the first time enabled our naval history to be written as it should be, and it has thereby developed a school of naval history which has no predecessor and no parallel in our national literature . . . It has changed the whole scope and method of that study and brought it under the spell of the modern historical spirit.[37]

It was not without significance that his service record had been updated and typed out on 1 April.[38] The following week the Council of the RUSI awarded him of the Chesney Gold Medal, 'in consideration of his valuable contributions to naval literature'.[39] This was, if anything, an understatement: Laughton had single-handedly devised a modern academic approach to the subject, secured an audience within a Royal Navy dominated by the rapid pace of technological change and enlisted the academic profession to aid his efforts.

In the same year he served as godfather for the Society for Nautical Research, a movement instigated by his son Leonard and Alan Moore. Laughton brought the new Society a distinguished President, any number of patrons and councillors, including Battenberg, Bridge and Custance,

---

37. *The Times* 25.4.1910 p6. 'Sir John Laughton and Naval History' and the leader.
38. Confidential letter of RG Hayes, Asst. Secretary to the Admiralty 1.4.1910. no addressee specified. Service Record ADM 196/81.
39. *The Times* 4.5.1910, p8.

advertised its foundation in an NRS volume and provided a notice for the *Proceedings of the United States Naval Institute.* The new body was clearly a 'junior division' for the NRS, dealing with issues that were not relevant to the development of national strategy, notably archaeology and the details of ships and seafaring, and opening its pages for correspondence and book reviews.[40]

Laughton continued to produce a steady stream of powerful reviews for the *Edinburgh Review* up until the breakdown in his health in 1912. It was the mark of Laughton's eminence, and ability, that he reviewed on a wide front, that his conclusions were often individualistic and he did not hesitate to criticise. His output reveals an unusual breadth of reading, and wide familiarity with European history from 1500 to 1900. His reviews of Julian Corbett's *Drake and the Tudor Navy* and *England in the Mediterranean* demonstrated the high opinion he had already formed of his most important intellectual companion. This was in marked contrast to his treatment of the short life of Drake in 1890, which he dismissed as 'pleasantly written, but . . . more than usually inaccurate'.[41] For the new work he paid Corbett the ultimate compliment, giving him the benefit of a vigorous review, in which his scholarship and ideas were subjected to the closest scrutiny. Laughton disputed the dominant position Corbett gave to Drake, and properly pointed out that the fleets of the sixteenth-century fought in small groups, not in line-ahead. Yet it was the quality of Corbett's research that enabled the subjects to be discussed: 'He deserves and has the warm gratitude of every student of naval history'.[42] His next Corbett review, *England in the Mediterranean*, was more directly addressed to contemporaries. He noted the debate on whether Britain should abandon the Mediterranean, an idea which, although crushed by George Clarke's admirable paper, was still alive. Corbett's book, itself suggested by a conversation with Clarke, provided an important historical contribution to the debate.[43] While Laughton was startled by the revelation that Marlborough was the architect of Mediterranean strategy in the War of the Spanish Succession, he accepted it on the evidence supplied. What was more he praised a book 'which goes far to remove from our literature the reproach of having no naval history'. He concluded by urging Corbett to carry his study of the interrelationship between fleets and foreign policy in the eighteenth century.[44]

40. Moore, A H, 'The Beginnings of the S.N.R.', *Mariner's Mirror* Vol 41 No 4 (1955), pp267-80. Sainsbury, A B, 'The Origins of the Society for Nautical Research', *Mariner's Mirror* Vol 80 No 4 (1994), pp450-8.
41. Laughton, J K, 'Our Naval Literature I', *The Army and Navy Gazette* (23.1.1892), p70.
42. *The Edinburgh Review* (July 1901), pp1-27 quote p27.
43. Corbett, J S, *England in the Mediterranean* (London 1903), pviii.
44. Ibid. July 1904 pp100-130 quote p129.

Laughton's other major naval review 'The Centenary of Trafalgar', was his only piece in the *Quarterly* after 1900. Amid the celebrations he tried to disentangle the reality from the myth, and examined seven contributions, including Corbett's *Fighting Instructions*, Sturges-Jackson's *Logs of the Great Sea-Fights*, essays by Bridge, Colomb and Edward Fremantle, and the correspondence in *The Times*. As for Nelson, he was without a peer among admirals. He, like his colleagues, did not believe a French invasion of England to be possible, but sought the destruction of Villeneuve's fleet to prevent it doing any harm to English interests anywhere. The most controversial subject of the day was the formation in which he bore down to attack. Bridge and Colomb argued that the fleet went into action on a line of bearing, rather than a line ahead. Laughton demolished this theory with the log-books, printed by the Record Society, new evidence, and his own rigorous logic. Mahan agreed with his analysis.[45] The review concluded with Laughton's thoughts on the place of Trafalgar in the downfall of Napoleon.

> Because he could not strike directly at England, Napoleon felt himself 'compelled' to undertake the conquest of Europe. The 'compulsion' was still stronger after Trafalgar had finally destroyed his hopes of invasion. Out of this grew the Continental System and its tremendous strain on France and her allies; the successive annexation of the coast-line of all western Europe; the refusal of Portugal to submit, the Peninsula War, rendered possible only by the assured command of the sea; the defection of Russia, the invasion, the retreat from Moscow; the Leipzig campaign; Elba; Waterloo and St Helena. These were all the consequences of the great battle of which we have been speaking. It is this, the downfall of tyranny and oppression, the saving of Great Britain and the liberation of Europe, that we now celebrate under the name of Trafalgar.[46]

While the chain of causation might be long, and occasionally somewhat tenuous, it achieved the end Laughton desired. The Royal Navy, led by the greatest admiral of all, had brought down the Napoleonic Empire by maintaining command of the sea. At a time when the strategy and diplomacy of the British Empire were tending towards Great Power alignments and a continental army the point was important. That it appeared in a Conservative journal is suggestive. His own opinions were increasingly conservative, and he fully expected Chamberlainite protectionist policies would be adopted.[47]

In mainstream reviews Laughton made his approach to the writing of history clear. Capitan de la Jonquière's documentary history of

45. Mahan to Laughton 31.12.1905 JKL MS.
46. *Quarterly Review* (October 1905), pp611-30 at p630.
47. Mahan to Laughton 20 and 26.1.1906 JKL MS. Mahan is concurring with Laughton on these issues.

Napoleon's Expedition to Egypt was highly praised for the skill and insight with which the material was handled, the superior understanding of the functioning of seapower, and for demonstrating that Bonaparte had lied about ordering Brueys to Corfu, to make his dead colleague the scapegoat for the disaster at the Nile. He also found time to castigate the Admiralty for keeping useless old ships on the Navy List.[48] Typically Laughton built on this review when he tackled John Holland Rose's *Napoleon*. Rose was commended for original research in British archives, but failed to meet Laughton's standards when he examined battles, for which Spenser Wilkinson was used as a corrective. He had not read Jonquière on Egypt and was weak on naval affairs generally. For all Rose's advocacy Laughton remained unimpressed with Napoleon, who was 'not a great general or statesman', and contended that much of his success was due to always facing coalitions, a type of opponent that grows weaker with every additional member. He recalled his own experience of inter-allied friction in 1854-55, in an argument that had a direct contemporary purpose.[49] Another 'current' problem was examined in Archibald Colquhoun's *The Mastery of the Pacific*, a work prompted by the 'Boxer' Rebellion in China. This was a key question for the British Empire, and Colquhoun did not address this issue, arguing that America and Japan would dominate. Laughton argued that while sea-power was crucial Britain could not be discounted 'until, indeed, an awakened China claims its own'.[50]

The almost simultaneous appearance of John Leyland's NRS volumes on *The Blockade of Brest, 1803-1805* and Edouard Desbrière's *Projets et Tentatives de Debarquement aux Isles Britanniques* prompted further reflection on contemporary strategy. In 1803 the 'actual and efficient defence of the country was entrusted to the navy. Within a few days of the declaration of war, the whole coast of France was blockaded'. As all the French plans discussed relied on evasion for any hope of success they could only lead to disaster, and were curiously at variance with Napoleon's direct strategy on land. Desbrière's inability to recognise Napoleon's limits was the only real weakness of his book. Laughton then passed on to consider the key question 'Is Blockade now possible?' He admitted that fleets would no longer anchor off enemy ports, but they had never done so off Brest or Toulon anyway.

> But, under way and in the offing, it is difficult to believe that, with proper care, torpedo-boats could be any serious danger and, as yet, submarines have not emerged from the realm of the sensation novelist. The difficulty of

---

48. *The Edinburgh Review* (Oct 1901), pp245-75.
49. Ibid (April 1902), pp522-50, quote p549.
50. Ibid (July 1902), pp210-35 at p235.

the blockade under modern conditions, does not lie in any danger of the kind indicated, but in the inability to prevent the enemy's ships, no longer dependant on the wind, escaping from the port.

He believed that a fleet based at Torbay could still blockade Brest, relying on destroyers for the inshore watch. Mines and torpedoes were a mixed blessing. Mines would help to seal the enemy inside the harbour, while torpedo attacks would be made if their ships came out into the open roadstead: 'All history suggests the possibility of such an attempt being made.'[51] Within two years the Japanese would demonstrate the point at Port Arthur.

While Laughton had a strong preference for edited documents, he was as exacting a critic of editors as he was of authors. G W Parmalee's six volumes on *The Siege of Quebec* were spoiled by a lack of large-scale maps, and hero-worship of Montcalm and Wolfe, while he found the comparison of the latter with Nelson 'grotesque'. Sir John Maurice's *Diary of Sir John Moore* was always going to receive a rough ride from Laughton, Moore's criticism of Nelson and Hood during the Corsican campaign being well-known, but Maurice compounded the problem by editing carelessly and without discretion from a copy of the diary. As presented the work would destroy Moore's reputation.[52] The importance of context was stressed in a review of Auriol's *Naples and Napoleon*, without a wider understanding of contemporary events isolated case studies were of little value.[53] Far better were the second pair of volumes from Capitan de la Jonquière's study of the Egyptian Campaign, which prompted fresh thoughts. He observed that Napoleon was invariably defeated by the elements, such as distance, heat, drought and the sea, rather than military rivals.[54] A new edition of *The Paston Letters* was less fortunate, the editor being lambasted for failing to check the original manuscript and repeating the notes of his predecessor.[55] Charles Firth's *The Last Years of the Protectorate* led Laughton to lament Gardiner's death, and praise his pupil for a book that 'excels even our anticipations'. Noting that Carlyle had been the first to show that Cromwell was an honest Englishman, and had sent his work to Sir Robert Peel as a guide for a modern statesman, he commended this new work to Peel's successors.[56] This was the real value of history.

By contrast he condemned the second volume of George Otto Trevelyan's *American Revolution*, published in 1903, as a simplistic,

51. Ibid (January 1903), pp1-33 at pp1, 30 and 31.
52. Ibid (July 1904), pp29-58.
53. Ibid (Oct. 1905), pp450-73.
54. Ibid (July 1908), pp179-208, see p200 *re* Napoleon.
55. Ibid (Oct. 1908), pp390-414.
56. Ibid (April 1910), pp480-510.

belated, party-political polemic which glorified treason. Trevelyan was censured for not consulting Lecky's brilliant eighteenth-century history, and for taking too rosy a view of the Revolution. Laughton took the opportunity to emphasise his own view, that the prime cause of the Revolution was not the vague notion of liberty, but the effect of the rigorous application of the Navigation Acts, which prohibited trade with French colonies, after 1763.[57] Although the thrust of the review was directed at contemporary debates on the relationship between the Dominions and the metropolis, Laughton could not resist retelling the old legend that the bottom of the *Royal George* fell out, to attack a government he despised, and the minister he termed 'the greatest administrative criminal of our modern history'.[58] He also predicted the book would be more popular in the United States.[59] This review demonstrated how far Laughton had developed as an historian in the thirty years since he reviewed Trevelyan's *Early Life of Charles James Fox*.[60] While Trevelyan had remained an inspired amateur, much like his uncle Macaulay, Laughton had become a professional historian.

Never one to be overawed by reputations, Laughton examined Lord Acton's posthumously-published *Lectures on Modern History* with his clear eye. He was disgusted by the introductory essay, which claimed that Acton was the greatest modern historian, which struck him as a 'vulgar puff'. The 'lectures' were full notes rather than complete texts, being too short, and lacking the final polish of a finished composition. While much of it was good, surprisingly so, and such as only Acton could have written, there were too many errors. Acton was at his best on the sixteenth-century Wars of Religion, but less effective on more recent events, where he ascribed too much to religious causes. His discussion of Gustavus Adolphus's German campaigns was weak, and more generally he was careless of the practical facts of finance, administration and military and naval power, preferring abstract and philosophical reflections to the concrete lessons of history. In essence Acton's seventeenth and eighteenth century lectures lacked authority and were unduly reliant on such tainted sources as Macaulay's account of Beachy Head.[61] It would be hard to better this review well-informed, judicious, in both senses, powerful and persuasive review. As a reviewer Laughton had the admirable ability to match his writing to the importance of the subject.

---

57. Laughton, J K, 'The American Revolution', *The National Review* No 253 (March 1904), pp63-76. Stout, N R, *The Royal Navy in America, 1760-1775* (Annapolis 1973) reaches similar conclusions.
58. Ibid, p76. The Minster was, of course, Sandwich.
59. For a more sympathetic, if not uncritical, view of Trevelyan, see Trevelyan, G M, *Sir George Otto Trevelyan* (London 1932), pp137-9.
60. *Edinburgh Review* (October 1880), pp540-77.
61. Ibid (Apr. 1907), pp273-98.

An altogether different task was provided by William Hardman's *History of Malta*, which had been written to examine the Maltese claim that they had given their island to the British, and therefore deserved some share in its administration. As Malta was one of the key strategic positions of the British Empire, to admit the claim would create a national danger. Laughton argued that the Maltese, a racial amalgam of many invaders, had never owned the island, and therefore had no claim to national status and furthermore, as the French garrison of Valletta had surrendered to the British the local populace had no rights over the island.[62] His judgement reflected strategic factors rather than conservatism or a failure to recognise the national aspirations of subject peoples.[63] Consequently he condemned the use of Italian as the official language of Malta, as giving rise to the misleading idea that the island somehow belonged to Italy.

Recent works on Henry VII and Henry VIII by H A L Fisher and A F Pollard were criticised for undervaluing the Navy and, more seriously, ignoring the important NRS volume on the War of 1512-13 by Alfred Spont.[64] His career almost came full circle in October 1911 with a review of T W Fulton's book *The Sovereignty of the Sea*, in which a Scottish expert on fisheries had confused himself by treating the English concept as a fishery question. This was, as Laughton pointed out, a Scots concept introduced to England by James I. In consequence he had an opportunity to reprise much of what he had said back in 1867.[65] John Holland Rose's *Life of William Pitt the Younger* was acclaimed as the new standard, and Laughton pointed out that central importance of the Scheldt, Belgium and Holland in the decision to go to war. By contrast the criticisms contained in John Fortescue's *British Statesmen of the Great War* were considered over-done and often inaccurate.[66] Lord Holland's *Further Memoirs of the Whig Party* provided him with an opportunity to attack Holland for being too favourable to France, and Napoleon, and dominated by party.[67] For his last *Edinburgh* review Laughton examined a new life of the First Earl of Sandwich, written at the behest of the then Earl. He considered the book over-rated Sandwich, too often contending for his genius when there was a more commonplace explanation, and being rather cavalier with the events of the Second Dutch War. Although 'biography ought to be literature', the book was too careless to meet the needs of historians.[68]

62. Ibid (July 1910), pp211-35.
63. See Schurman 'Laughton' p102 for a more critical view.
43. Corbett, J S, *England in the Mediterranean* (London 1903), pviii.
64. *The Edinburgh Review* (Jan. 1911), pp229-54.
65. Ibid (Oct. 1911), pp357-78. It is surprising that Fulton's book is still treated seriously by otherwise well-informed scholars.
66. Ibid (Jan. 1912), pp158-89.
67. Ibid (July 1906), pp133-56.
68. Ibid (Oct. 1912), pp340-54 at p354.

Through his work as a reviewer Laughton kept abreast of the latest literature and tried to impose his own high standards on the writing of history. His reviews continued to be an important building block for his writing, notably his last book. His contributions were invariably well-informed, his judgements sound, if not always fair, and his eye for detail impressive. For the readers of the great reviews he took care to bring out the 'lessons' in a way that was subtle and yet effective. When he stressed that any attempt to invade Britain without command of the sea would always fail, in reviews dealing with 1588 and 1805, his audience would have recognised a contribution to the current debate. He was always looking for work that fitted his own sense of how history should be presented. Skilfully-edited documents were the basic building block, to be developed into analytical studies which would convey larger messages to a wider audience. If he considered Corbett's work outstanding in the latter respect, the passage of time has confirmed the correctness of his assessment. The time was now ripe to build up from the foundations he had so diligently laid; he could complete the development of naval history.

When the new century opened naval history was a recognised branch of the profession, while Laughton's personal standing as a historian was high. His close connection with Gardiner and the support of other professionals for his Society were clear evidence of his success. His contribution to the *DNB*, to the *EHR* and other mainstream projects gave him a standing that was enhanced by the growing importance of King's College. After 1900 he chaired the University of London History Board, examined the Cambridge fellowship thesis of Henry Gutteridge,[69] contributed to Lord Acton's *Cambridge Modern History*, and protested to his successors when H W Wilson repeated the Badham version of Nelson's conduct at Naples.[70] The development of the *Cambridge Naval and Military* Series in 1913 was a further testimony to the success of his subject. It would provide a vehicle for Arthur Tedder's study of the Restoration Navy,[71] Richmond's book, Perrin's study of flags, and his own 1913 historiographical essay, delivered to the International Historical Congress of that year, along with pieces by Corbett, Richmond and Hubert Hall.[72] Battenberg, the First Sea Lord, chaired the naval section of the Congress, held at the RUSI, demonstrating Admiralty support for the subject, and called for a naval history textbook to teach young officers.[73]

---

69. Laughton to Rev. A Austen-Leigh, Provost of King's College 18.12.1901, Cambridge. King's College COLL 42.
70. A W Ward, to Laughton 18.10.1904. JKL MS.
71. Tedder, A W, *The Navy of the Restoration* (Cambridge 1916).
72. H W Temperley to Laughton 15.3.1913: JKL MS. Corbett, J S and Edwards, H J (eds), *Naval and Military Essays* (Cambridge 1914).
73. Undated newspaper cutting in the MS of Admiral Sir Watkin Owen Pell, placed there by his daughter forty years after his death. NMM PLL/88.

This status reflected both a lifetime of achievement, and the constant activity of the moment. Laughton never rested on his laurels. His life was consumed by large themes and driving ambitions. He would not outlive the last of them.

Laughton's last great cause was an attempt to found a Department of Naval History at King's College, a project that occupied the last five years of his life. In this he was attempting to improve upon the opportunity provided by the creation of the University of London, and the new interest King's took in the federal system. His Royal Historical Society Lecture of 1898 had persuaded some of his fellow academics that naval history was a mature element in the modern academic discipline, but even so he must have been delighted by the response of Albert Frederick Pollard (1869-1943). Pollard had taken a First in History at Oxford in 1891, and completed his scholarly education as an assistant editor of the *DNB* between 1893 and 1902. Here he worked under Sidney Lee, and met Laughton. Appointed to a part-time Chair in English Constitutional History at University College in 1903 he became the driving force in the creation of a professional history school in the University, and after the war established the Institute of Historical Research.[74] In his inaugural lecture, given in September 1904, Pollard called for a University School of History, including a postgraduate school.[75] This school should address certain subjects that cried out for serious work. In the published version he declared:

> first and foremost among these I place the study of naval history. For considering that this Empire is the greatest the world has ever known; considering it has had the longest and most glorious naval history on re-cord; considering further that it has been built up and rests upon sea power, that its very existence therefore depends to a large extent upon the true interpretation and appreciation of the lessons of naval history, it is surely an astounding fact that there is not, and never has been, a professorship, or a lectureship, or a readership in naval history in any university whatever within the extensive British dominions. Fortunately there has been of late years no great naval war to test how much the nation may have risked by this neglect; but it is not a fact of which we can be proud that we even know indebted to the individual enterprise and researches of a distinguished American author for the best exposition of the influence of sea power upon history. In London alone can this need be adequately supplied, for here in the Record Office we have, in enormous masses, materials of every descrip-tion, hundreds of volumes of despatches from admirals in command on the

---

74. Galbraith, V H, 'Albert Frederick Pollard', *Proceedings of the British Academy* Vol XXXV (1949), pp257-74. Kenyon, J, *The History Men* (London 2nd ed 1993), pp204-5.
75. Pollard, A F, 'The University of London and the Study of History', *The National Review* (December 1904), pp650-63. Reprinted in *Factors in Modern History* (London 1907) and later editions.

various stations, letters to them from the home government, proceedings of court-martials, and logs of ships recording the individual history of most of the vessels of which the British Navy has from time to time been composed.[76]

His emphasis was partly a recognition of need, partly a response to the availability of expertise, for the original lecture continued:

Nor do we lack the human material; we are fortunate in having among the history teachers of London University, and Chairman of the History Board, a naval expert of the highest practical and theoretical qualification, an expert who, as Secretary of the Navy Records Society, has already done much to further the study of Naval History, and whose services have just been appropriately recognised by the grant of an honorary degree on the nomination of the Chancellor of a sister university, who happens to be an ex-First Lord of the Admiralty. Yet instead of setting this expert to do the work for which he is best fitted by taste and attainments, and the work which would be most useful to his country, we set him to teach the elementary facts of general history.[77]

The excision of this second section from the printed version of the lecture, the largest cut in the entire book, can only be attributed to Pollard's Victorian reluctance to discuss the merits of the living in print. He had no doubt that Laughton was a distinguished historian. Only in the third edition of *Factors in Modern History*, which appeared in 1932, did Pollard provided a key to the numerous inferences which littered the original text.[78] The references to Mahan and the Record Office demonstrated that he had drawn his text from Laughton and Hall's Royal Historical Lectures, which he may have attended. Pollard agreed with Laughton that history had to be relevant.[79] For him naval history was vital, while Laughton was a national asset that was being wasted. The lack of serious study of the naval past at any British University remains as lamentable as it was when Pollard wrote. It stood as an 'astounding' permanent barrier to the development of historical scholarship and naval thought. Pollard's interest in naval history survived the war, and he found further cause to lament the lack of a strong history school.

As a University colleague and fellow contributor to the *National Review*, Laughton saw the published version of Pollard's lecture, if he was not present when it was delivered. Recognising that Pollard had the drive and ability to set up a school, having established himself at the head of the Board of Studies by 1910, Laughton hoped the man and the

76. Ibid, pp658-9.
77. MS. copy of the above. Pollard MS: University of London Paeleography Dept.
78. Pollard, A F, *Factors in Modern History* (London 3rd ed 1932), pp299-312.
79. Parker, C, *The English Historical Tradition Since 1850* (Edinburgh 1990), p136.

moment would suffice for naval history. He wanted to create a department that would train the naval historians needed to educate the growing numbers of naval officers required to man the new fleet, a task for
which he was uniquely qualified. Although he officially retired from his
post at King's College in 1912, he remained a Professor of the University, and in 1913 and 1914 he gave, in line with college policy, public
lecture courses, the first on 'English Naval History', then 'Seapower and
the Empire' and the third on 'The Influence of the English Navy in the
Eighteenth Century', in addition to his regular teaching.[80] His theme
was constant. Because Britain was an island, unlike the continental
states of Europe, the Navy was central to the history of the nation, and
explained the unique political and military institutions of the country.
Furthermore, the Navy was far older, and far more important, than was
generally recognised.[81] Despite resigning his chair in 1912, he was
pressed to continue lecturing.[82] He agreed, continuing until Christmas
1914, struggling on in the gathering gloom of failing eyesight. His only
reason for continuing was to establish a Department of Naval History.
In 1913 he produced a significant historiographical paper, dealing with
the period down to the mid-nineteenth century, for the International
History Congress in London, designed to guide future scholars through
the secondary literature. The themes were already being used in the
1870s, but the detail was of interest. He was critical of the romantic
history of Macaulay, praised Ranke, and considered Sir Harris Nicolas's
unfinished study the best work produced before the recent upsurge of
interest.[83] Arthur Tedder's *The Navy of the Restoration* opened with a
quote from this paper, stressing the width and ambition of Laughton's
'modern' naval history, in contrast to the old-fashioned and fallacious
'battle history' of Clowes. Tedder, a student at Cambridge, stressed the
importance of original sources and of separating what the men of the
day knew from the wisdom of hindsight.[84]

When he wrote the historiographical paper Laughton was also trying to
write the textbook for the Department, with the working title of 'The
Navy's Place in the History of England' but he was hampered by increasing infirmity and the continuing demand for lectures. The book was based
on the lifetime of learning and insight to be found in his collected output
of articles, reviews and *DNB* entries. To facilitate the work, he collected,

80. College Calendar, King's College, London 1913-14 and 1914-15. Hearnshaw F J, *The
Centenary History of King's College, London* (London 1929), p459. Cuttings from *The
Times*.
81. Lecture Notes 8.10.1913. JKL MS.
82. Laughton to Charles Napier Robinson 10.12.1912: Napier Robinson MS NMM.
83. Temperley to Laughton 15.3.1913: JKL. Laughton, J K, 'Historians and Naval History'
in Corbett, J S (ed), *Naval and Military Essays* (Cambridge 1913).
84. Tedder, ppv-viii.

catalogued and bound his articles and reviews into three heavy volumes.[85] In June 1914 he prepared his manuscript and notes so that the book could be completed by Leonard, who was directed to use specific papers from the bound collection.[86] Laughton only completed two draft chapters, and the fragment of a third, covering the period from 1066 to the death of Henry VIII, in 15,000 words. The text reflects its origins in the lectures, reviews, articles and introductions of the past forty years, lending further credence to his repeated claims to be preparing a history of the Navy. The manuscript stresses the role of naval success, and naval failure, in the history of England. The major theme was naval defence against invasions, and he took care to explain the link between naval success, as opposed to mere stress of weather, and the failure of hostile efforts. The final section examines the lengths to which Henry VIII went to build his fleet, and the intimate link between the fleet and England's international standing. The whole is peppered with Laughton's characteristic insight and humour. The manuscript still reads well, and would, if completed, have made a major contribution to the promotion of naval history in the University sector. Unfortunately Leonard once again proved incapable of completing his father's work.[87]

A life-long writer of textbooks, Laughton believed he could achieve far more to promote the study of naval history with a good textbook than narrow monographs, which would only be read by those already interested. He was equally certain that first impressions counted, lambasting school textbooks that were inaccurate, or undervalued the work of the Navy in national history. In consequence when he began his own textbook he took pains to point out the weaknesses of others. His friend Kipling had collaborated with the Oxford tutor C R F Fletcher on *A School History of England* in 1911, a liberal imperialist text that made all the right points about the Navy, considering the monarchy a bulwark against a radical House of Commons trying to reduced the fleet to a level that threatened the security of the Empire, and held up Nelson, all infidelities forgiven, as 'the prototype of the Christian warrior'.[88]

Despite his efforts, the College, which was expanding the range of its interests and departments throughout this period, did not carry his work to completion.[89] Within a decade of his death the subject had effectively

---

85. These are now in the Library of the Royal Military College, Kingston Ontario, having been purchased in London in the 1960s by Professor Schurman.
86. MS Note of 2.6.1914 with the manuscript chapters of the projected book. JKL.
87. The Navy's Place in the History of England MS: JKL. Milford to Leonard G C Laughton 29.5.1925: JKL.
88. Fletcher, C R F and Kipling, R, *A School History of England* (Oxford 1911), p228. Chancellor, V E, *History for their Masters: Opinion in the English History Textbook, 1800-1914* (London 1970), pp44, 59, 74-5, 114, 118 and 129.
89. Hearnshaw, p469.

died out in British universities, and has never recovered the status it held in 1914. However, in his efforts to broaden the appeal of his subject in the University sector Laughton had laid the foundations of another historical specialisation, one that proved more successful than naval history, to the extent that it would annex both his own work at King's, and the best efforts of others to establish a chair at Cambridge. However, the Imperial/ Commonwealth route would provide fresh impetus to naval studies in later years. When this occurred Laughton would be given his due.

The integration of King's College in the University of London enabled Laughton to give specialist lecture courses on the role of the Navy in the creation and maintenance of the Empire. Although these lectures were part of his campaign for a naval history department they actually laid the foundations for the study of Imperial History, both at King's, and more generally. When Laughton retired in 1912 Sidney Low was appointed part-time lecturer on Imperial and Colonial History, and was replaced the following year by A P Newton, who took the post full-time in 1914. Newton established the new specialisation at King's, and made a career for himself in the process. In 1919 the Rhodes Chair in Imperial History was established, and Newton held it until 1938. Having the opportunity to develop post-graduate studies, Newton was able to influence the development of the subject, much as Laughton had hoped a naval chair would. He combined the roles of academic leader with spreading the Imperial message,[90] in line with College policy.[91] It was one of Newton's pupils, Gerald Graham, who reconnected Laughton's work with Imperial History. When he became Rhodes Professor of Imperial History nearly forty years later, Graham noted that Laughton had 'introduced the methods of modern research into the study of naval records and applied them to the history of the empire'.[92] Graham concluded: 'Before 1815 the Royal Navy was the determining force in the establishment of the Empire; after 1815 and until the dissolution of Pax Britannica in the twentieth century, the Royal Navy was the guarantee of its security and further expansion.'[93]

Although King's College bought a few of Laughton's books, and invited Prince Louis and Julian Corbett to open a 'library', the subject remained dormant. Corbett raised the issue for the last time in his

---

90. Spector, M M, 'A P Newton' in Ausubel, A (ed), *Some Modern Historians of Britain* (New York 1951), pp286-305.
91. Newton, A P (ed), *The Sea Commonwealth* (London 1919) with a contribution from Corbett, records the 1917 public access lecture programme, wholly concerned with the Imperial dimension of the Great War.
92. Graham, G S, 'The Maritime Foundations of Imperial History', *Canadian Historical Review* Vol XXXI No 2 (June 1950), pp113-24. The quotation comes from the introductory remarks, which were not published, of which a typescript is included with the copy in the Library of King's College. Hearnshaw, p469.
93. Graham (1950), p122.

Creighton Lecture of 1922, and his death removed the last link with Laughton's work. The failure to create a Department of Naval History inflicted severe damage on the study of the naval dimension of the past. Without a base inside a University the subject became increasingly eccentric to the profession and lost the linkages Laughton had created for it with Imperial, political and other branches of the discipline. Without a fully-funded professorial chair it lacked the status that was vital to sustain academic careers. The width, depth and context that all historians seek in furthering our understanding of the past can only come from strong, well-supported branches of the discipline, where practitioners do not feel the need to apologise for studying their subject and, because they have institutional backing in the form of established professorial chairs, are taken seriously by those working in other branches. Laughton knew this. His career had propelled the subject into a position where it could reasonably expect to join the other specialist branches of historical study. It only required the creation of an institutional framework to make his achievement permanent. Regrettably even his long and full life was not quite long or full enough to encompass so much.

By the outbreak of war in 1914 Laughton had effectively given up work. He did not cease to be interested, as shown by a note among his papers comparing the depredations of the German cruiser *Emden* in the Indian Ocean with Matthew Flinders' observations of French attacks from Mauritius, but he lacked the strength for any sustained effort. On the day that he heard of Mahan's death he was roused to write an obituary, on torn-up strips of College Examination Paper. After recalling the effect of his friend's book he stressed that, despite its impact on Germany, Mahan's work had been written for his own service and his own countrymen.[94] In 1915 *The Times* noted his eighty-fifth birthday in a short article. He died on 14 September 1915 leaving a widow, nine children and effects to the value of £470. His last two projects, the Department of Naval History and the book-length study of the impact of sea power on British history, the 'textbook' for the Department, died with him. The loss was tragic, for as Thursfield noted:

> he was not a student of naval history in any narrow sense. He understood and never overlooked its relation to general history, of which he had a comprehensive grasp, and it is largely through his influence and example that the study of naval history in this country has been taken out of the hands of mere specialists or annalists and infused with the larger spirit of modern historical inquiry.

Perceptively Thursfield sensed that this legacy was a wasting asset, for he concluded:

94. Draft Mahan Obituary: JKL MSS.

But perhaps his most lasting work was his foundation of the Navy Records
Society . . . and the decisive share he took in all its enterprises and
proceedings.[95]

In accordance with his wishes Laughton was cremated at Golder's Green
on 17 September, attended by his family, supported by representatives
from his two Colleges and the many learned societies of which he had
been a member, and his friends Sidney Lee and Charles Napier Robinson.[96] Callender claimed that his ashes were taken to sea on board the
dreadnought HMS *Conqueror* and buried in forty fathoms at the mouth of
the Thames 'in the track of the incoming and outgoing ships'.[97] In death,
as in life, he remained a naval man. The College which he had served with
distinction for the last thirty years of his life recorded that a grateful
nation had 'recognised his contribution . . . to the study of naval history'
by awarding his wife a civil list pension.[98] The Delegates did not care to
record that they had done nothing to secure this award, or that they had
failed to respond to his last great campaign.

Throughout his sixty years of service, afloat, ashore and in his new
career Laughton had invariably demonstrated that combination of 'tact,
skill and good humour' of which he spoke in 1870. His appreciation of
service life, his wide experience of conditions afloat and personal contact
with so many admirals, as well as a more direct relationship with every
officer who had passed through the College between 1866 and 1885 secured him a unique position. In his second career he reinforced his influence by drawing in another group of supporters. Yet at no time did he
alienate the service or the officer corps that had given his life a driving
purpose. That he did so without sacrificing his principles reflected an
ability to walk a fine line, and his intellectual successors would be far less
successful in this respect, even those, like Richmond, who were first and
foremost naval officers.

---

95. *The Times* 15.9.1915, p9.
96. Ibid, 18.9.1915 p9.
97. Calender DNB entry. It is not clear when the burial at sea occurred. The *Conqueror* was
at Scapa Flow with the Grand Fleet throughout the relevant period, although she was
commanded by Richmond in 1917-18.
98. Delegacy Minutes, King's College, London KCLA KC/C/M2. Probate Record, Sir John
Knox Laughton

CHAPTER 9

'The foundations of modern naval history were laid broad and deep by the late Sir John Laughton'[1]

———— · ————

Laughton's opinion that the role of history was first and foremost as a vehicle for the development of naval doctrine, and his stated ambition to found a Department of Naval History to train the historians to carry out the necessary research and teaching for this, make his legacy particularly significant. At the same time his careful insider's approach to the propagation of his message, and his antipathy to anything that smacked of vulgar popularism, have seen his name obscured by lesser men with larger public personae. Herbert Richmond spoke for an entire generation when he wrote in the preface to his first book:

> I was the fortunate recipient of help from the late Sir John Laughton, who was always ready to give to others the benefit of his own great store of knowledge.[2]

Laughton's intellectual legacy, the use of history as the basis for naval education, the study of tactics and strategy, and the development of modern naval doctrine and national strategy, when combined with his methodology, the insistence on meticulous accuracy and the use of primary sources in historical studies, was critical. His stimulus and methodology transformed Corbett from a dilettante novelist into a truly great naval historian and strategic analyst. The critical issue was Laughton's insistence on the 'meticulous use of detailed sources', and Corbett always acknowledged his debt, observing that Laughton's *DNB* articles alone had 'practically rewritten the whole of our naval history in a way that few but naval students can adequately appreciate'.[3] In turn Laughton praised Corbett's contribution, believing that *England in the Mediterranean* went

---

1. Holland-Rose, J, *Naval History and National History* (Cambridge 1919), p41.
2. Richmond, H, *The Navy in the War of 1739-48* (Cambridge 1920) 3 vols, Vol I, Preface.
3. Schurman, D, *Julian S. Corbett 1854-1922* (London 1981), p19 and *The Education of a Navy* (London 1965) for Corbett's links with Laughton. Corbett, J S, *England in the Mediterranean* (London 1903), Vol 1, pviii.

'a long way to remove from our literature the reproach of having no naval history'.[4] Corbett, far more than Mahan, wrote the naval history for which Laughton had laid the groundwork. After 1900 his books began life as Naval War Course lectures, serving as a strategic primer for the pre-1914 Navy. He developed a wider view of British strategy than Laughton, recognising the ultimate primacy of land warfare, but he did see that the sea was vital to Britain, because against her, and her alone, it could be decisive.

Corbett also adopted Laughton's approach to the role of history in naval education. In 1900 he began lecturing on the new Naval War Course, which had been created along the lines of its American precursor, itself heavily influenced by Laughton. In ambition and subject matter the original syllabus reflected the interests of one man, combining history, strategy, tactics and the environmental sciences, although the latter were soon dropped as incompatible. Perhaps by 1900 it was no longer possible to take so comprehensive a view of the educational needs of the serving officer. While Laughton worked to establish a Department of Naval History at King's College, Corbett, as late as 1910, deprecated the idea of studying the subject in a University, believing that only the Admiralty could support the spirit of the subject.[5] His later pronouncements on this matter, after a longer experience of the effects on his own 'spirit' of working with the Admiralty, were very different.[6] When Richmond wrote Corbett's obituary for the *Naval Review* he lamented his death in professional terms as:

> a very serious blow to naval history, and as history is the raw material out of which a knowledge of the principles of strategy and tactics is built up, so the study of those arts will suffer.

There can be no clearer demonstration of the degree to which Corbett, and Richmond, were following the methods established by Laughton. Corbett's work as an historian and strategist built on the base provided by Laughton, later supplemented with a careful study of the work of Clausewitz. Even this last point needs clarification. Corbett only turned to Clausewitz to counter-attack the Army General Staff and the 'Continentalist' thinking it espoused. In the event the German philosopher provided him with a powerful intellectual framework within which to deploy his historical understanding, initially as a tool of historical analysis, and later *On War* became the basis for his strategic thought. This is most obvious in his last five books; *England in the Seven Year's War*,

---

4. *Edinburgh Review* (July 1904), p129.
5. Corbett, J S, *The Campaign of Trafalgar* (London 1910), pxii.
6. Corbett, J S, 'The Revival of Naval History', *The Contemporary Review* No 110 (December 1916).

The Campaign of Trafalgar, Some Principles of Maritime Strategy, the hitherto unpublished *Maritime Operations in the Russo-Japanese War, 1904-1905*, written for the Admiralty in 1914, and the *Official History of the War: Naval Operations*, for which he completed three of the five volumes. These books are marked by the breadth of scope, scrupulous use of sources and strategic insight, and like Laughton's work were intended to serve the contemporary Navy. Laughton, the pioneer who had laid the foundations, never grappled with the continental system-building approach, his strategic thought being empirical to the last.

After Corbett's death in 1922 the work of developing doctrine and strategy from historical study fell to Admiral Sir Herbert Richmond. Initially as a serving officer, and later as Harmsworth Professor of Naval History at Cambridge, Richmond built on the work of Laughton and Corbett, using academic study as the foundation for national strategy. After his experience of high command in the First World War Richmond had a greater sense of urgency, having seen at first hand in 1914 how imperfectly the central direction of the Navy functioned, from lack of historical and doctrinal understanding. This quality he believed could only be drawn from a wide and intelligent study of naval history. However, it was not until 1929 that he accepted that his ultimate service ambitions would be frustrated. In the process he missed an opportunity to press for a naval chair, which he could have filled with distinction. After Corbett's death Richmond was increasingly anxious to build a system of strategy for the present. By 1923-24 Richmond had succeeded in his intellectual quest for a 'British Warfare', as Lord Sydenham observed in the introduction to his pivotal collection of essays *National Policy and Naval Strength* of 1928. Where Mahan had spoken of naval strategy, Richmond was careful to stress that naval operations merely formed a part of strategy, and demonstrate how far the three services were interdependent. His aim was made clear in the paper 'Co-operation', written in 1923:

> What I would now ask is, have we, as a whole, a clear picture as to how this country has made war throughout its' modern history – that is since it became a modern trading state under Cromwell? Military histories or naval histories are only too often – there are admirable exceptions – records of military or naval operations, dissociated from one another, written round only one part of the whole. What we need to be clear about is the means whereby we, this nation, set about employing those assets of strength we possess to force the enemy to desist from the policy he was adopting. . . .
>
> Unless the study of the wars of past is made as a whole I venture to say we are not training ourselves to make real preparation for war, however much we may be preparing ourselves to conduct certain operations of war.[7]

7. Richmond, H W, *National Policy and Naval Strength* (London 1928), Chapter 'Co-Operation'.

In 1929 Richmond came into contact with Captain Basil Liddell-Hart, then Defence Correspondent of the *Daily Telegraph*. They may well have been introduced by General Sir George Aston, an intellectual Royal Marine who served on the Council of the Navy Records Society. The two men shared an interest in combining history and contemporary defence analysis. Richmond provided Liddell-Hart with a wide range of ideas, material and advice for his 'British Way in Warfare' theme, not least by introducing him to the work of Corbett. In return Liddell-Hart gave Richmond the support of the *Daily Telegraph* in his struggle with the Admiralty. Liddell-Hart recognised the superiority of Richmond's methodology:

> that thorough investigation and collation of historical data which I feel more and more to be the only sure way of approach to the truth. Doctrinaires of war have been too content to base themselves on pure theory, spiced with a few examples which serve to illustrate it, and ignoring the possibility that more thorough research might reveal many which contradict it . . .
>
> It seems to me a significant coincidence that the more one pursues real research the closer does one come to coincidence of views with those who likewise are never tired of continuing to probe and to test their conclusions by history.[8]

There could hardly be a more complete coincidence with the ideas being put forward by Laughton in 1874. Richmond's support was critical to Liddell Hart's 'British Way in Warfare', which was reflected, as Brian Bond has observed, 'in the extreme and rather one-sided statement of the maritime case'.[9] In this Liddell-Hart demonstrated that he did not have the time and opportunity to employ best practice. He was prepared to go beyond the materials to hand in developing his argument, as Richmond made clear when reviewing Liddell-Hart's *The Revolution in Warfare* in 1946. In the interval Richmond had left the Navy and taken up a new career at Cambridge in 1934. He died shortly after writing the review, but Liddell-Hart survived to inspire another generation of academics to pursue military history, and as such became the godfather of the Department of War Studies at King's College. In a roundabout way, and unknown to the carrier, Laughton's legacy had returned to his old College.

In the field of naval history Richmond, despite his austere character, played a key role. He encouraged several important figures in the recovery of naval history, notably the American Arthur Marder, who would publish his diary in 1952, the Canadian Gerald Graham, later Professor of Imperial History at King's College and the official historian of the Royal Navy in World War Two, Captain Stephen Roskill RN. Roskill would

---

8. Liddell-Hart to Richmond 1.7.1930. Richmond MSS RIC7/4 NMM.
9. Bond, B, *Liddell Hart: A Study of his Military Thought* (London 1976).

benefit from his legacy, both as a strategist and, through Richmond's friendship with Corbett, in his relations with the Admiralty. As an Admiral and an intellectual leader, Richmond was disabled by his personality, not suffering fools gladly and, even if with good reason, doubting that he had many intellectual equals. Only in his final years at Cambridge did he relax. In the process he secured far more influence on the historical record of his own times, through the work of Arthur Marder, than he had been able to exert over the development of historical study.

Laughton's influence had been universal, and as the pioneer in the field it proved impossible for the new navalists of the 1890s to write without quoting him, or to become serious scholars without becoming personal friends. Among the more important individuals to carry the imprint of his work were four Admirals, Bridge, Colomb, Custance and Battenberg, who became strategists, and to a certain extent historians, in emulation of Laughton. Three of them served as Director of Naval Intelligence, while Battenberg went on to become First Sea Lord. Prince Louis was widely read, highly intelligent and a founder member of the NRS. He accepted the Presidency of the new Society for Nautical Research, and led the movement to restore HMS *Victory*. Among the second rank of civilian commentators Laughton was invariably accepted as *the* expert on historical questions. Those who only began their work in the early twentieth century were unaware of his contribution to the development of naval doctrine and strategic thought, and never grasped the real objects of the NRS. One of the most intelligent was Fred Jane, best known today for his annual 'Fighting Ships' volumes, who used Laughton as his source for the Armada and Nelson. Jane's *Heresies of Seapower* of 1904 was designed to provoke a reconsideration of the Mahanian message that he considered had been swallowed in haste. His evidence is drawn from secondary sources, but shows signs of care and thought. The book is far more useful than the great bulk of contemporary navalist writing, being both original and stimulating. Mahan was unimpressed, but then he was never happy with criticism. Jane's last book *The British Battlefleet* was a pioneering attempt to link the history of ship design with policy, strategy and tactics.[10]

Laughton, by a combination of intellect and sheer hard work, defined modern naval history, the manner in which it should be written, and the way in which it could be used to educate the nation, statesmen and the Navy. On 4 October 1916 Julian Corbett gave the Laughton Memorial Lecture at King's College, with Laughton's old friend Admiral Prince Louis of Battenberg in the chair. The occasion was the formal opening of

10. Jane, F T, *The Heresies of Seapower* (London 1906), and *The British Battlefleet; its inception and growth throughout the centuries* (London 1914). Brooks, R, *Fred. T. Jane: An Eccentric Visionary* (Coulsdon, Surrey 1997).

the Laughton Library of Naval History, based around a newly acquired selection from Sir John's library. Prince Louis contrasted the current state of the subject with his own cadet days, when it was indifferently taught and not taken sufficiently seriously to be an examination subject, and he observed that Laughton, having turned his 'great mind' to the study of naval history, left his legacy in the work of the NRS. He ended by stressing that long before the Admiralty War Staff had been founded, the Directors of Naval Intelligence, including Bridge and Custance, 'past masters in the art of naval warfare', had been the Chiefs of the General Staff.[11] He did not spell out the intimate link between the Department and the Society. When Corbett discussed the revival that Laughton had brought about, he stressed that where naval historians had one merely recorded the effects they now sought the causes. This methodological revolution would lead 'naval history to take its due place as part of general history'. Laughton had carried out the archival research needed to develop the subject. Corbett gave particular attention to the *DNB* articles, which he saw as a guide to research, and adopted Laughton's call for a Department of Naval History to train up future historians on the mass of archival material still untouched. One of the aims of the Department was to bring home to the nation the importance of the Navy, but:

> the highest aim of all . . . will be to open more widely to the Royal Navy itself the treasures of its rich experience, to bring naval officers more intimately in touch with the ideas, the work, and the policy of the men who formed their matchless tradition.

This work required trained specialist historians, and Laughton's Department would have provided them. Until then Corbett lamented that general historians would be dominated by the views of politicians and soldiers, which was to be regretted, in Britain especially, because 'Naval History is the main binding link that unifies world history'. If Corbett remained at heart a romantic, a failing that Laughton had observed, he had absorbed much from his mentor. When Corbett read Clausewitz in 1906, he found a theoretical structure that could contain, develop and elucidate the strong strategic and doctrinal framework provided by Laughton. The result of this combination was a 'British Strategy' that would serve as the doctrine of the Royal Navy in the two World Wars, and influence countless thinkers who have never heard of John Knox Laughton.

Earlier the same year Corbett had spoken to the Historical Association on the teaching of naval history. Quoting Colonel G F R Henderson

---

11. 'British Naval History' report in *The Daily Telegraph* 5.10.1916. I am indebted to my friend Dr Richard Harding for a copy of his report. It is interesting that three-quarters of the report is of Prince Louis's preamble, while Laughton, for whom the lecture was a memorial, was a mentioned only once.

(1854-1903),[12] he stressed the primacy of naval questions in British strategy, and consequently that enemy naval forces should be the first target of the military, as well as the naval forces of a maritime power. He then proceeded to discuss combined operations, a rather sore subject for a British audience on 7 January 1916, focusing on the very appropriate case of Walcheren in 1809. He called for a study of the role of the Navy after 1805, work he had already begun, to demonstrate how the supposedly foolish ministers who frittered away their resources on small expeditions 'held their own single-handed against the greatest master of war, with all Europe at his call, and beat him in the end'. The 'lessons' of this lecture were clear enough, as was Corbett's position on the great question of contemporary British strategy.[13]

During the war, the leading professional supporter of a naval history department, Albert Pollard, had seen how the lack of a coherent, structured national history board had forced the Committee of Imperial Defence to improvise their own historical section, rather than taking over an existing structure, as had been the case in the United States. Once again the career of Sir Julian Corbett had provided an inspired amateur solution to a problem that required long-term professional preparation. As soon as the war ended he advised University College to begin work on expanding the provision of history to meet these needs.[14] He remained committed to naval history, and responded with alacrity when the Navy League requested his support for the establishment of a chair in London to 'spread knowledge and understanding' in 1919.[15] Pollard stressed the need to teach the subject alongside military history, the two being 'aspects of the same subject, particularly so far as the British Empire is concerned, and nothing has hampered its understanding more than the habit of treating

---

12. Luvass, J, *The Education of an Army: British Military Thought 1815-1940* (London 1964), pp216-47 for a study of this brilliant soldier.

13. Corbett, J S, 'The Revival of Naval History', *The Contemporary Review* No 110 (December 1916), pp734-40.

The Professorial Board, King's College, London 15.5.1916 noted that Professor Hearnshaw had raised £26.00 to purchase part of the collection, 'a very useful addition to the historical section of the Library'. Because Laughton had only recently started his naval history lectures the library was not well stocked. The Library has long since disappeared, no-one at the College having any idea where it was located. Some of the books originally belonging to Laughton and Corbett are still held. The remainder may have been destroyed, with much of the Arts Collection, by enemy action, while stored in the Great Hall of Bristol University in 1940: Huelin, G, *King's College London* (London 1978), p85. The remainder of Laughton's library was sold by Sotheby's, while assorted pamphlets were given to the Admiralty Library, where Perrin had them neatly bound in volumes with J.K.L. embossed on the spine. Laughton's three-volume binding of his own essays and reviews was purchased in London in the early 1960s by Professor Schurman, and is now in the library of the Royal Military College, Kingston, Ontario.

14. Pollard, A F, 'The Needs of Historical Studies in the University of London: 26.11.1918' in *Factors in Modern History* (3rd Edn London 1932), p315.

15. Duke of Somerset (President of the Navy League) to Pollard 1.7.1919 and Benson (Secretary to Navy League) 8.7.1919 thanking him for his contribution.

each in isolation'.[16] In the mid-1920s Pollard served on the Council of the NRS. Writing in 1931 he lamented that there was still no chair in Naval History, despite the diversity of new posts.[17] At least Pollard's new Institute of Historical Research recognised the existence of the subject, and provided shelf space for the necessary materials. In the struggle to create and locate this vital professional unit Pollard had little time to advance the cause of Laughton's subject, and there was no-one else with the standing, ability and drive to take up the task.

The failure of Laughton's plan for a Department of Naval History, which was still a 'live' issue in 1922 when Corbett gave the Creighton lecture, can be attributed to the post-war pressure on space at King's College and, more fundamentally, a complete lack of interest on the part of the college.[18] Without a powerful advocate within or outside the college, Corbett's Creighton Lecture was the last occasion on which the cause was pressed at King's. When the Military Education Committee of the University of London organised a course of public lectures on 'advanced war studies' in July 1925 it was appropriate and deliberate that Richmond was asked to deliver the two papers on 'Sea Warfare' in the Great Hall at King's. General Sir George Aston RM, then the Lecturer on Military History at University College, hoped he would use the opportunity to spread 'sound doctrine'.[19] But despite the success of Richmond's lectures the College ignored naval history. A defence chair was established in 1927, but it was in 'Military Studies', narrowly defined, and was held, for its brief life, by General Maurice, whose approach was revealed in the subtitle of his most significant book, *British Strategy: A Study in the Application of the Principles of War.*[20]

In late 1918 the University of Cambridge offered the new Vere-Harmsworth Chair in Naval History to John Holland-Rose. Holland Rose declined the honour, hoping Corbett would be considered, 'for you have that touch with the Navy of the present which will make your teaching fresh and powerful, and will contribute towards the building up of a School of Naval Studies of truly national importance'.[21] Corbett, increasingly unwell and tied to the Official History of Naval Operations, was unable to consider the post, and it seems unlikely he would have been able to accept a similar task in London. There were no suitable

16. Pollard, A F, 'London and Historical Research' (1920), p4.
17. Pollard, *Factors* (1931), pp292-3.
18. Hearnshaw, p468, on the postwar space crisis.
19. General Sir George Aston (Chairman of the Committee) to Richmond 26.7.1925. RIC 7/4 Richmond MSS NMM. The lectures were delivered on 18.2. and 4.3.1926. and published in: Aston, Sir G, *The Study of War for Statesmen and Citizen* (London 1927), and as a separate volume, Richmond, Sir H, *Sea Warfare* (London 1930).
20. Maurice, F, *British Strategy: A Study in the Application of the Principles of War* (London 1929).
21. Holland-Rose to Corbett 6.1.1919. Corbett MSS NMM.

alternatives, and Holland-Rose, after his high-minded gesture, became the first incumbent. His inaugural lecture, auspiciously delivered on Trafalgar Day 1919, addressed the value of the past as a guide for new and uncertain times, in which Britain 'cannot forego her great marine insurance, the Navy'. He suggested that studying 'the simpler past' would help those who had to make policy today. Laughton was given full credit for his work. But Holland-Rose was already on the slippery slope, wanting to work on the wider import of naval history, the diplomatic and strategic aspects.[22] This was premature, because the subject had to establish itself and develop a coherent body of literature before it could devote its efforts to the pursuit of further conquests. Nor did his performance live up to the advance notice, Holland-Rose writing very little of merit on naval subjects during his term. He was followed in the next decade by Herbert Richmond. Even that happy event could be largely attributed to Richmond's family connections and friendship with George Macaulay Trevelyan, the Regius Professor.

In 1952 the new Vere-Harmsworth Professor of Imperial and Naval History, while admitting the strong interdependence of the two subjects, recorded his hope that they would be separated, by the creation of a new Imperial Chair. The chair he held had been founded in 1919 for the study of naval history.[23] This did not come to pass, and the 'administrative and financial expediency' that the University adopted to translate a naval chair into an imperial fiefdom has yet to be reversed.[24]

By 1900 naval history had ceased to be a romantic chronicle, Laughton's standards of factual accuracy and his insistence on the primacy of archival evidence ensuring that subjects were studied in detail, rather than plundered for evidence to support preconceived nostrums. As a naval instructor Laughton adopted a conservative approach to the traditions of the service, but he was not afraid to explode myths, or call into question received wisdom. Although his official connection with the Navy ended in 1885 he remained a naval man to the end of his days. He saw his new post as an opportunity to enlist the academic community in support of his object. The ultimate ambition, a University-based Department of Naval History, entirely independent of the Royal Navy, would have provided professional naval historians to educate the Navy, at Osborne, Dartmouth and Greenwich, and to spread the gospel in newspapers, journals and books. His followers, notably Corbett and Richmond, demonstrated how much had been achieved by 1915, but non-appearance of the Department left the subject in a weak and confused condition in the

---

22. Holland-Rose, J, *Naval History and National History* (Cambridge 1919), pp39, 41, 43.
23. Rich, E E, *The Crises of Imperial History: An Inaugural Lecture* (Cambridge 1952), pp1-2.
24. Ibid, p1.

inter-war years, still dependant on personal contact, chance and fortune. In the academic world only Richmond's links with George Trevelyan ensured that Corbett's *England in the Mediterranean* was a major source for Trevelyan's *England Under Queen Anne*, and that Richmond would be strongly supported when he joined the history faculty at Cambridge.[25] When Trevelyan gave his inaugural lecture as Regius Professor in 1927 the only English naval historian to be mentioned was Corbett, despite his theme being the contribution of 'Cambridge men'.[26] A dozen years after his death the founder of the subject had been forgotten at his old University. The omission can doubtless be traced to George Gooch's book. Even Regius Professors are only as good as their sources.

The Navy, as Richmond, the last naval academic of his age, observed in 1920, was not convinced. It allowed history to remain a quiet antiquarian backwater, eccentric to the scientific core of service education. That the Navy selected Geoffrey Callender as the first Professor of History at Greenwich must stand as an enduring reminder of the value it placed on history. The appointment was little less than a complete rejection of everything that Laughton and Corbett had achieved. Little wonder Richmond could not bring himself to be civil to Callender.

That Laughton did not establish his Department in his own lifetime may be attributed to the scale of the task, and the constant diversion of his efforts into profitable trifles. Whatever his ambitions may have been when he took up his post in 1885, he could hardly have been so sanguine as to foresee how much had been achieved by 1914. By exploiting the changing intellectual climate Laughton achieved much more than he could have hoped. It was in his years at King's that he founded the NRS, recruited Corbett, laid the groundwork for British strategic thought and forced naval history into the academic mainstream, no small achievement for a man already once retired, and weighed down by family and financial worries.

Laughton's pioneering role in the development of strategic thought, naval doctrine, and the professionalisation of naval history have rarely been acknowledged. In his lifetime his prestige was unchallenged, even if the doctrinal intent was not always recognised, but the First World War and the low standing of naval history after 1922 led to a startling decline. The process began with Callender's dull obituary notices in *The Times* and the *DNB*. In part this reflected the death of many of Laughton's closest associates, even those, like Corbett, of another generation, along with the extended period in which he had been active. Many who knew him after 1890 as the doyen of naval historians were unaware of his work on tactics, strategy and doctrine, and consequently they mis-

25. Cannadine, D, *G. M. Trevelyan, A Life in History* (London 1992), p215. Trevelyan, G M, *England Under Queen Anne; Blenheim* (London 1930), pvi.
26. Trevelyan, G M, *The Present Position of History* (Cambridge 1927), p15.

understood the purpose of the NRS, and were content to leave naval history to the Navy. This was something that Laughton, who knew the Navy better than any historian, before or since, resolutely opposed. The only inter-war British scholar to continue the tradition established by Laughton and Corbett, of academic history in the naval environment, was Brian Tunstall, Corbett's son-in-law. In 1936 he published *The Realities of Naval History*, which bore all the indications of Laughton's influence.[27] The book scored a number of easy points by exposing the failings of Callender's *The Naval Side of British History,* and ensured that Tunstall did not stay long at Greenwich. However, his iconoclastic efforts were continued in other posts, and his influence on a number of Canadian and American scholars in the 1950s was a vital element in the modern revival of naval history.[28]

The low point of Laughton's fame came in 1940, with the publication of Arthur Marder's *The Anatomy of British Seapower.* In a book dealing with the Royal Navy between 1885 and 1904 Marder ignored Laughton, denying him any credit for the naval intellectual revival. Marder's book was weak on the historical foundations of naval doctrine, indeed it largely ignored doctrine. The particular themes of the book, the role of industry in promoting commercial navalism, the popular alarmism of the Navy League and the rise of John Fisher were areas where Laughton's role was indeed limited, but to suggest that what Marder wrote about was the core of naval policy would be quite inaccurate. His approach was partial, reducing Hornby to a handful of footnotes, and where Laughton was important Marder ignored him, accepting Clowes's claim to have founded the NRS. The one footnote to mention him merely refers to an article at the end of a long section dealing with Mahan, Colomb, Spenser Wilkinson and Lord Sydenham. This approach does not credit the influence of Laughton on Bridge, Custance and Battenberg, the Directors of Naval Intelligence who applied history to their work.[29] Marder repeated this glaring omission in 1952, when he published the Richmond diaries in *Portrait of an Admiral.* Once again the obvious references to Laughton in Richmond's work were ignored, in favour of comparisons with Mahan, who Richmond, as a follower of Laughton and Corbett, did not cite. Unfortunately Barry Hunt's otherwise excellent biography of Richmond,

---

27. Tunstall, W C B, *The Realities of Naval History* (London 1936).
28. Notice by Prof. Schurman in Tunstall, W C B (ed Tracy, N), *Naval Warfare under Sail* (London 1989), pvii. Tunstall's published work included two critical chapters on Imperial Defence between 1850 and 1900 in *The New Cambridge Modern History*, which reflect the views held by Laughton and others when the subject was a pressing current issue.
29. Marder, A J, *The Anatomy of British Seapower 1880-1905* (London 1940), pp45, 56. Marder, A J, *Portrait of an Admiral* (London 1952). It has been suggested by some who knew him that Marder was 'always in too much of a hurry'. This might explain why he missed Laughton.

Sailor-Scholar, also ignored Laughton's influence.[30] In this he was follow-ing Marder who, as *the* historian of the Fisher era, was largely responsible for modern scholarship marginalising or even ignoring Laughton's work for the Royal Navy.

Laughton was restored to something approaching his due in Don Schurman's excellent biographical essay in *The Education of a Navy* of 1965, which argued that Laughton, 'the editor', had provided the material with which his fellow labourers worked, and established the academic credibility of the subject. The intellectual origins of this book were clear, Professor Schurman always acknowledging that he, and other Canadian historians, notably Barry Hunt, had drawn enormous benefit from work-ing with Brian Tunstall.[31] Having been restored to a central role in the development of naval scholarship by Professor Schurman's masterly as-sessment, it remains to establish his contribution to naval doctrine, which this book has contended was the purpose of his historical endeavour.[32] In the same year Professor Gerald Graham, of King's College, London, published his important 1963-64 Wiles Lectures. He acknowledged the pivotal role of Laughton, his distant predecessor and, following Corbett's 1916 Laughton lecture, contrasted Laughton's work with the system building synthesis of Mahan.[33] Stephen Roskill had come close to seeing Laughton's doctrinal role in his 1961 Lees-Knowles Lectures, but he only credited Laughton with inspiring Mahan, and founding the NRS. He praised the Society for publishing Corbett's vital, if ignored, work on Nelson's tactical memoranda *Signals and Instructions*, without realising the extent of Laughton's work on tactical doctrine two decades before, or his role in producing those volumes.[34] In the United States the process of questioning the 'uniqueness' of Mahan led Peter Karsten to consider his British precursors in 1972. He noted that Laughton, among others, had promoted a 'blue-water' strategy long before Mahan, and demonstrated a far superior comprehension of the functions of sea power than the Ameri-can in his 1883 *Edinburgh Review* of *The Gulf and Inland Waters*.[35] By contrast Paul Kennedy, in his pivotal work, *The Rise and Fall of British Naval Mastery* of 1976 ignored Laughton.[36]

---

30. Hunt, B D, *Sailor-Scholar* (Waterloo Ontario 1982).
31. Schurman, D, *The Education of a Navy* (London 1965) esp. pp83-115. Professor Schur-man speaking at the Corbett-Richmond Conference, USNWC 1992. Goldrick, J, and Hat-tendorff, J B (eds), *Mahan is not Enough* (Newport RI 1993), p103.
32. In a discussion with the author at the Royal Military College, Kingston, Ontario on 26 March 1994, Prof. Schurman suggested that Laughton may have been of more significance as a strategist than he had been as an historian.
33. Graham, G S, *The Politics of Naval Supremacy* (Cambridge 1965), pp4-6.
34. Roskill, S W, *The Strategy of Seapower: its development and application* (London 1962), p81.
35. Karsten, P, *The Naval Aristocracy: the Golden Age of Annapolis and the Emergence of Modern American Navalism* (Annapolis 1972), pp231, 314-5.
36. Kennedy, P M, *The Rise and Fall of British Naval Mastery* (London 1976).

The latest examination of the pioneers of naval thought comes in Azar Gat's otherwise impressive study of nineteenth-century strategic thought. He concentrates on Mahan and Corbett, and stresses that they were 'deeply influenced by the leading military theorists of the age'. This analysis is strikingly perverse in the case of Corbett, and is not borne out by an analysis of his published work before 1906. He had become a sophisticated strategic thinker *before* he read G F R Henderson and Clausewitz. Gat correctly lays out Mahan's intellectual debt to Stephen Luce, but ignores that of Luce and Mahan to Laughton. Even Luce's idea of a 'scientific' approach, which he highlights, was taken directly from Laughton's 1874 paper, to which Luce constantly referred. Luce's contribution, reflecting his experience in the American Civil War, and contact with General Emory Upton, was to introduce the idea that military writers had a direct, transferable intellectual role in the absence of naval works. Neither Laughton nor Colomb ever adopted this method. Jomini formed a basis for Mahan, at Luce's insistence, and Clausewitz eventually made a contribution to Corbett's work, but until 1906 Corbett, like his mentor, developed his ideas solely from naval material.

In dealing with Philip Colomb, Gat notes that his work underwent a profound change after his appointment at Greenwich, although he does not appreciate that this reflected the influence of Laughton, his predecessor as history and tactics lecturer. Laughton's influence on Colomb is apparent from a comparison of his work before 1886 with the *Naval Warfare* of 1891, which is dominated by the use of Laughton's methodology in a sustained teaching text. The treatment and the placing of this section, after those on Mahan and Corbett, are curious. Colomb's major works combined the contemporary strategic vision of his brother with the historical methodology of Laughton. A simple comparison of dates establishes that he was not influenced by either Mahan or Corbett.

Yet it is only after dealing at length with three of his followers that Gat notes Laughton's connection with the growth of modern naval historical scholarship. In a passage of striking perversity Gat declares that Laughton was 'disappointing' because he 'propagated the historical and strategic outlook, which Mahan and Colomb were later to make their own and develop into a magnificent edifice'. On the contrary, Laughton was *the* pioneer of naval tactical and strategic thought in the Anglo-Saxon world, and his work influenced three generations, from Luce, Mahan and Colomb, to Corbett and Richmond. He devoted his efforts to laying the foundations of sound doctrine, through the publication of historical materials. Without his work naval strategic thought would have remained in the age of the chronicle for, like Clausewitz, Laughton was convinced that sound doctrine could only be developed from experience. Gat argues that the object of the NRS was simply to publish archival material, when the contemporary literature makes it clear that it would use history as the foundation for naval doctrine in the machine age. In discussing Corbett's work on British naval tactics, Gat ignores Laughton's pioneering work in this field, dating back to 1867 which, even more directly than that of Corbett, was aimed at the Royal Navy and its contemporary problems. Gat also draws parallels between the work of Corbett and Delbrück, without appreciating that Laughton had begun demythologising the naval past in 1866, to ensure a sound basis for new doctrine. Corbett, like Delbrück, was influenced by Ranke, albeit via Gardiner and Laughton, but by the time Corbett became a serious historian Laughton had already redefined the discipline, using the Rankean methodology.[37]

The centenary of the NRS was celebrated with a pamphlet on the history of the Society. Here Laughton received due credit for founding the Society, and his vital role as the link between the service, the scholarly world, journalists and politicians was revealed by a study of the list of founder members.[38]

Sir John Laughton was the finest educator the Royal Navy has ever possessed. An inspirational teacher, powerful lecturer, supportive colleague and leader in his field, he devoted his career to the maintenance of the Royal Navy as the world's most powerful, and most effective, fleet. The task was critical because only a dominant Royal Navy could defend the British Empire and British interests. British security needs were unique, and required further study of the historical record in order to recover the underlying principles upon which they were based. Through his concepts and methodology Laughton played a critical role in the creation of a new doctrine for the machine-age Navy. He demonstrated to his contemporaries why the Royal Navy was important, and to the Navy that it required more than technical expertise and courage to win the next war. His chosen vehicle was history, for history alone could educate the nation and provide the Navy with a realistic substitute for war experience. Once he had established that history could be 'Scientific', he used it to support the development of modern doctrine, a doctrine that covered every aspect of naval service, including strategy, tactics, leadership, personnel, administration and morale. By the mid-1870s, a time when the initial phase of naval intellectual activity had run its course, Laughton had secured a position from which he exerted a significant influence on the development of British naval doctrine. In the following decade his work had a major impact on service thinking in the United States, through Admiral Stephen Luce, founder of the Naval War College, and his colleague Captain Alfred T Mahan.

37. Gat, A, *The Development of Military Thought: the Nineteenth Century* (Oxford 1992), pp173-214.
38. Sainbury, A B, *Navy Records Society: A note on the first hundred years* (London 1993).

Laughton's methodology improved over time. While in the naval service, 'scientific' phase, he relied on the short lecture and article format, extracting the 'lessons of history' from specific case studies. These papers were aimed at a professional audience. This method was enhanced by access to the archives after 1879, developing into an impressive system of critical source analysis. When he joined the academic profession in 1885 he was introduced to the modern 'scientific' methodology, based on the work of Leopold von Ranke, by his friend Samuel Rawson Gardiner, and in consequence he relied on the publication of edited source documents to provide the material from which to develop naval doctrine, national strategy and, ultimately, a new naval history. As Secretary of the NRS he directed its publishing policy, located editors and aided almost every volume. These provided the material from which others could draw their own lessons. This work was supported by his massive contribution to the *DNB* and historiographical articles, which placed his encyclopaedic knowledge at the disposal of others. By the time the NRS was founded, Laughton had become a mainstream professional historian, and used his new colleagues to support the education of the Navy. Here his most important follower, Sir Julian Corbett, built on his foundations and deployed the theoretical structure of Clausewitz to produce the seminal work on strategy in the English language, a book that explained the peculiarities of 'British Strategy' and provided the doctrinal basis of the Royal Navy in the First World War.

By 1900 naval history had ceased to be a romantic chronicle, and the credit for this development belongs to Laughton. His professional standard of factual accuracy and insistence on the primacy of archival evidence ensured that subjects were studied in detail, rather than plundered for evidence to support preconceived nostrums. As a naval instructor Laughton adopted a conservative approach to the traditions of the service, but he was not afraid to explode myths, or call into question received wisdom. Although his official connection with the Navy ended in 1885 he remained a naval man to the end, and used his new post to enlist the academic community in support of his object. His ultimate ambition, a university-based Department of Naval History, entirely independent of the Royal Navy, would have provided professional naval historians to educate the Navy at the Naval Colleges and to publicise the naval role in the written media. His followers, notably Corbett and Richmond, demonstrated how much had been achieved by 1915. The failure to establish the Department left the subject in a weak and confused condition in the inter war years, still dependant on personal contact, chance and fortune. In the academic world it withered for the want of an institutional base. The Navy consistently undervalued history and historians, who were seen as eccentric to the scientific core of service education. The 'foundations' laid broad and deep were largely ignored for two generations. The work of Michael Lewis and Christopher Lloyd at Greenwich did much to keep the subject alive, and developed the quality of staff college teaching far beyond the antiquarian irrelevance of Callender's time.

Fortunately the combined efforts of the Department of History and International Affairs at the Royal Naval College at Greenwich and the Department of War Studies, King's College London revived academic naval history in the 1970s. Once again the process relied on fortunate circumstance and the efforts of individuals, most notably Brian Ranft. Despite that revival the subject is not yet be quite what Laughton had hoped it would become, either in naval education or mainstream history, but his legacy lives on in the NRS, the Joint Services Command and Staff Course, the United States Naval War College, and the Department of War Studies, King's College, London. It must be hoped that naval history will finally achieve a degree of permanence in British academic life. This will only be secured by the establishment of a Chair. There should be little difficulty finding an appropriate title.

The Vice Presidents and Councillors of the Navy Records Society 1893-1915

─────── · ───────

Vice Presidents:

Bridge, Vice-Adm. Sir C A G 1904-08

Clarke, Col. Sir G S (later Lord Sydenham) 1909-11, 1913-24

Corbett, J S 1908-11

Custance, Adm. Sir R N 1909-11, 1913-14

Desart, the Earl of 1906-10

Fanshawe, Adm. the Hon. Sir E G 1901-03

Firth, Prof C H 1905-09

Fremantle, Adm. the Hon. Sir E 1901-03

Gardiner, S R 1900- (died in office 1901)

Gray, A 1912, 1915-

Hamilton, Lord George 1893-96

Hamilton, Adm. Sir R Vesey 1893-96

Hawksbury, Lord 1902-05 (became Lord Liverpool in 1905)

Hoskins, Adm. Sir A H 1899-1900

Kenyon, F G 1910-14

Kerr, Adm. of the Fleet Lord W 1912-14

Laughton, Prof Sir J K 1915 (died in office)

Lothian, the Marquess of 1893-95, 1898-1902

Lyall, Sir A 1898-1902

Markham, Sir C 1895-98

Northbrook, Earl of, 1896-1901

Prothero, G W 1901-04

Sanderson, Lord 1911-

Seeley, Prof Sir J 1893-95 (died in office)

Yorke, Sir H (Treasurer 1893-1902) 1903-06

25 Vice Presidents: including 7 naval officers, 6 academics, 8 politicians, statesmen and colonial governors, 2 civil servants, 1 army officer, 1 President of the Royal Geographical Society.

Councillors:

Acland, R B D 1911-

Atkinson, C T 1903-06, 1909-14

Balfour, Lt. Col. E 1896-98

Battenberg, HSH Prince Louis 1893-95, 1903-04

Beaumont, Adm. Sir L 1903-05, 1909-11, 1912-

Bedford, R-Adm. Sir F 1895-98, 1909-11

Besant, W 1893-96

Blomfield, R-Adm. Sir R M 1911-

Bowden-Smith, Adm. Sir N 1901-04

Boyd, A 1901-02

Brassey, the Hon. T A 1893-96

Bridge, Sir C A G 1893-95,
1898-1900, (VP 1904-08) 1909-14
Brindley, H H 1911-
Browning, O 1895-98
Burrows, Prof. M 1893-96
Butler, Rev. H M 1893-95
Chamberlain, J A (Austen)
1896-1900
Childers, E 1912-
Clarke, Gen. Sir A 1893-99
Clarke, Col. Sir G S (later Lord
Sydenham) 1895-99, 1904-05 (VP
1909-11, 1913-)
Colomb, Vice Adm. P 1893-99
Corbett, J S 1897-1907, (VP
1908-11), 1912-
Cowie, Capt. N RN 1910-13
Cust, R-Adm. H E Purrey 1907-13
Custance, Adm. Sir RN 1900,
1912-13 (VP 1909-11, 1913-14)
Dartmouth, the Earl of 1906-14
Dasent, A I 1902-04
Dasent, J R 1896-99
Davies, Lt. Gen. H F 1901-03
Desart, the Earl of 1904-05 (VP
1906-10) 1911-
Digby, Col. the Hon. E 1902-04
Drury, R-Adm Sir C 1904-07
Edye, Lt. Col. L 1898
Elgar, Dr F 1896-98, 1901-04
Esher, Viscount 1912-
Fanshawe, Adm. the Hon. Sir E G
1900-01 (VP 1901-03)
Fawkes, Adm. Sir W 1914-
Field, Capt. A M RN 1906-10
Firth, Prof. C H 1893-96, 1902-05
(VP 1905-09) 1910-
Fremantle, Adm. the Hon. Sir E
1900 (VP 1901-03)
Gardiner, S R 1899 (VP 1900-died in
office 1901)
Garnett, Dr R 1893-95
Geary, Lt. Gen. R A 1893-95,
1899-1901, 1907-11
Ginsburg, B W 1903-07
Glasgow, the Lord Provost of,
1893-95
Godley, Sir A 1904-08
Gordon, the Hon. G 1905-08

Graham, Cdr. C Cunninghame RN
1908-11, 1913-14
Gray, A. 1906-11, (VP 1912)
1913-14, (VP 1915-
Grenfell, Capt. H H RN 1895-98
Guinness, The Hon. R E C MP
1915-
Hall, R-Adm. H G King- 1910-14
Hamilton, Adm. Sir R Vesey (VP
1893-96) 1896-05
Hannay, D 1893-96
Hawksbury, Lord 1900-01 (VP
1902-05, as Lord Liverpool from
1905) 1906
Hordern, Lt. L RN 1907-12
Hoskins, Adm. Sir AH 1896-98 (VP
1899-1900)
Hudlestone, Capt. R RN 1912-
Kenyon, F G 1908-09 (VP 1910-14)
1915-
Kerr, Adm. of the Fleet Lord W
1909-12 (VP 1912-14) 1915
Kilkbracken, Lord 1912, 1915-
Kipling, R 1902-04
Laughton, Prof Sir J K (Secretary
1892-1911) 1912-14 (VP 1915)
Lee, S 1893-96, 1900-03
Leyland, J 1915-
Lorraine, R-Adm. Sir L 1893-96,
1904-08
Lothian, the Marquess of 1893-97
(VP 1898-1902)
Lyall, Sir A 1893-98 (VP 1898-1902)
1903-09
Markham, Adm. Sir A H 1896-01,
1906-10
Markham, Sir C 1893-95 (VP
1895-98) 1906-10
Marsden, R G 1900-05, 1910-
May, R-Adm. Sir H J 1903
May, Adm. Sir W 1907-08
Meade, Sir R GCB 1896-98
Morris, M 1898-01
Mowatt, Sir F 1907-11
Murray J 1915-
Newbolt, H 1899-1907, 1915-
Northbrook, Earl of (VP 1896-1901)
1902-04
Oliver, Capt. S P RA 1893-96

Overend, W H 1896-98
Parr, R-Adm. A C 1902-05
Payne, E J 1901-03
Poore, Adm. Sir R 1911
Prothero, G W (VP 1901-04)
  1905-09
Richards Adm. of the Fleet Sir F
  1901-02
Richmond, Capt. H W RN 1908,
  1915-
Robinson, Cdr. C N RN 1893-96
Sanderson, Lord 1908-11 (VP
  1911-
Seymour, Adm of the Fleet Sir E
  1905-09
Shippard, Sir S 1896-1900
Sinclair, W F 1898-99
Slade, Capt. E RN 1904-06, 1912-
Stevens, B F 1895-99
Tanner, J R 1898-1905, 1908-14
Tarleton, Lt. A H RN 1906-10,
  1912-
Thursfield, J R 1893-96, 1902-1907,
  1909-

Tracey, Adm. Sir R 1901-04
Troubridge, R-Adm. E 1910-11,
  1913-14
Trower, H S 1896-1900
Walpole, Sir S 1900-1902
Watts, P 1904-09
Wharton, R-Adm. Sir W 1893-1902
White, Cdr. J B RN 1905-09
White, Sir W 1896-1900, 1906-10
Wilmott, Capt. S Eardley- RN
  1893-96
Yorke, Sir H (Treasurer 1893-1902)
  1903-06

108 Councillors. The list includes
senior Admirals, almost all the
Directors of Naval Intelligence of
the period, Hydrographers, young
naval officers, naval constructors,
statesmen, soldiers, academics,
journalists and soldiers.

On the combined list of 110 Vice
Presidents and Councillors there
were 38 naval officers.

Sources

Archives:

Public Record Office, Kew, England.
Admiralty Papers (ADM)
ADM 53 Ship's Logs, various
ADM 196/81 Laughton's Service Record
ADM 203 The Royal Naval College at Greenwich

National Maritime Museum, Greenwich, England.
Laughton MS. Laughton's MS were deposited in 1979 by his grandson. They remain, uncatalogued and unsorted as MS79/067. They are contained in six boxes. One is largely concerned with flags, one contains letters from Mahan. The other four contain what can only have been a sample of his incoming correspondence. There are also some notebooks filed under Laughton in the old MS Catalogue. These were deposited by Leonard Carr Laughton, who had used them extensively.

Other relevant collections:
Cyprian A G Bridge
William Laird Clowes MS93/001
Julian S Corbett
Reginald N Custance
Geoffrey T P Hornby
Gerard Noel
Herbert W Richmond
Charles N Robinson
Richard Vesey-Hamilton

The Archive of the Navy Records Society is held on deposit at the Museum. The early minute books contain much information on the nature and composition of the navalist movement before the First World War.

The Archives of King's College, London
Laughton files, concerning his appointment and correspondence during his time at King's College

Naval Historical Branch, Whitehall, England
The John Laughton Pamphlet Collection: bound up by WG Perrin in 1916

King's College, Cambridge.
The Oscar Browning MS
King's College MS.

The Bodleian Library, Oxford
Sidney Lee MS (including material belonging to Leslie Stephen concerning the DNB)

Bridges MS

The University of London Paeleography Room, Senate House
Sir John Seeley MS
Albert Frederick Pollard MS

The British Library, Manuscript Division
Althorp MS. Papers of the 5th Earl Spencer.
Sir Charles Dilke MS

The National Army Museum, Chelsea.
Henry Spenser Wilkinson MS

The Royal Geographical Society, London
Society Archives, Minute Books etc.
Papers and MS Journal of Sir Clements Markham

In private hands:
Philip Colomb MS.

Library of the Royal Military College, Kingston, Ontario.
Sir John Laughton's personal bound collection of his articles, 3 vols.

Library of Congress, Washington DC
Papers of Alfred Thayer Mahan
Papers of Stephen Bleecker Luce

Bibliography

Works by Sir John Laughton:
Books
Physical Geography in its Relation to the Prevailing Winds and Currents (J D
  Potter, London 1870, 2nd Edition 1873)
An Introduction to the Practical and Theoretical study of Nautical Surveying
  (Longman, Green & Co, London 1872, 2nd Edition London 1882)
Essay on Naval Tactics (Griffin & Co, Portsmouth: 1873 Commonly bound with
  The Gun, Ram, and Torpedo by Commander Gerard U Noel. 2nd Edition
  1885)
At Home and Abroad; or First Lessons in Geography (London 1878)
Studies in Naval History (Longmans, London 1887, 2nd Edition J J Keliher,
  London 1896. Reprint by Conway Maritime Press, London 1970)
Nelson. 'English Men of Action' Series (MacMillan, London and New York 1889,
  reprinted 1904. Illustrated Edition 1900, reprinted 1905)
The Story of Trafalgar (Griffin & Co, Portsmouth 1891)
The Story of the Sea (with W L Clowes, A Quiller-Couch, H O Arnold-Forster
  and H W Wilson) (Cassell, London 1895-96, 2nd Edition 1897-98)
The Nelson Memorial: Nelson and his Companions in Arms (George Allen, Lon-
  don 1896, 2nd Edition 1899)
Nelson and his Companions in Arms (George Allen, London 1905, pocket format
  edition, omits the critical bibliography of 1896 edition)
Memoirs of the Life and Correspondence of Henry Reeve, 2 vols (Longmans,
  Green, and Co, London 1898, 2nd edition, 1898)

From Howard to Nelson: Twelve Sailors (William Heinemann, London 1899, 2nd
 Edition London 1907 , 3rd Edition as *British Sailor Heroes.* Adapted from the
 original edition, with 48 illustrations and maps London 1913. 4th Edition Lon-
 don 1922 *England's Sailor Heroes.* Without attributions of the other authors,
 and with the editor now identified the sole author and named as T Knox
 Laughton)
Sea Fights and Adventures (London 1901, in 'The Young England Library' 2nd
 Edition 1907)
The Pocket Life of Nelson (Reprinted from the *Dictionary of National Biography*
 London 1993 by the 1805 Club)

Contributions to books written by other authors
'Air Temperature, its Distribution and Range' Lecture II in Edward Stanford,
 Modern Meteorology (London 1879)
Hints to Travelers London Royal Geographical Society 5th Edition edited by
 Laughton and D W Freshfield (London 1882)
'Introduction' to Southey, R, *The Life of Lord Nelson* (Cassell & Co, London
 1891)
'On Convoy' in *Brassey's Naval Annual 1894* (London 1894)
'The National Study of Naval History' in *Transactions of the Royal Historical
 Society*, Vol XII (London 1898)
'Britain's Naval Policy' in Kirkpatrick, F A (ed), *Lectures on History in the
 Nineteenth Century* (Cambridge 1903), pp59-78
'The Elizabethan Naval War with Spain' in Ward, A W, Prothero, G W and
 Leathes, S, *The Cambridge Modern History*, Vol 3 (Cambridge 1907)
'Historians and Naval History' *The Cornhill Magazine* (London, July 1913,
 Reprinted in Corbett, Julian S (ed), *Naval and Military Essays* (Cambridge
 1914))

Edited historical documents
Letters and Despatches of Horatio, Viscount Nelson (Longman, Green & Co,
 London 1886)
Memoirs relating to the Lord Torrington, Camden Society Volume XLVI (Lon-
 don 1889)
State Papers Relating to the Defeat of the Spanish Armada (London: NRS 1894. 2
 volumes: 2nd Edition 1895; 3rd Edition Portsmouth Hampshire 1981; 4th Edi-
 tion, in one volume: Temple Smith, Aldershot, Hampshire 1987)
Journal of Rear Admiral Bartholomew James, 1752-1828 (London, NRS 1896 Vol
 VI; with J Y F Sullivan)
The Naval Miscellany Volume One (London: NRS 1902 Vol XX. Reprint Al-
 dershot Hampshire 1982)
Report on the Manuscripts of Florence Victoria, Lady Du Cane (London: HMC
 Vol 61, 1906)
The Recollections of Commander James Anthony Gardner, 1775-1814 (London,
 NRS, Vol XXXI, 1906 with Admiral Sir Richard Vesey-Hamilton)
Letters and Papers of Charles, Lord Barham, 3 Volumes (London: NRS. 1907,
 1910, 1912; Reprint of all three volumes Aldershot, Hampshire 1984)
The Naval Miscellany Volume Two (London: NRS 1912 Vol XL. Reprint
 Aldershot Hampshire 1982)
Manuscripts of and relating to Admiral Lord Nelson (London 1913), pp50

Contributions to periodicals
ST = reprinted in *Studies in Naval History*.

'The Sovereignty of the Sea', *The Fortnightly Review* Vol V (August 1866), pp718-33

'Le Bailli de Suffren', *United Service Magazine* (May and June 1867). ST.

'An Inquiry into the Evidence on which the Theory of the Circulation of the Atmosphere is based', *Philosophical Magazine* XXXIV (November 1867), pp359-65

'On the Natural Forces that produce the Permanent and Periodical Winds' *Philosophical Magazine* XXXIV (December 1867), pp443-9

'Colbert: The birth of a Navy', *St. Paul's Magazine*. December 1868. pp342-357 ST.

'On Atmospheric Currents', *Symonds Meteorological Magazine* Vol V (1870), pp158-60

'On the Great Currents of the Atmosphere', *British Association Report* XL (1870), p170

'Sketches in Naval History', *St. Paul's Magazine* (October 1870), pp51-65

'Ocean Currents', *Journal of the Royal United Service Magazine (JRUSI)* Vol XV (1871)

'Barometric Differences and Fluctuations', *Philosophical Magazine* (May 1871), pp325-63

'Land and Sea Breezes', *The Proceedings of the Junior Naval Professional Association* Part II (Portsmouth 1873), pp75-90

'Land and Sea Breezes', *Quarterly Journal of Meteorology* Pt I (1873), p203

'Nautical Meteorology', Parts I, II, & III in *Naval Science* (London 1874 and 1875). Part IV appeared in *Van Nostrand's Engineering Magazine* Vol 12 (1875), pp72-80

'On Diurnal Variations of the Barometer', *Quarterly Journal of Meteorology* Part II (1874), p155-64

'The Scientific Study of Naval History', *JRUSI* Vol XVIII (1874), pp508-27

'Du Quesne: The French Navy in the Seventeenth Century', *Fraser's Magazine* (November 1874), pp638-53. ST

'Scientific Instruction in the Royal Navy', *JRUSI* Vol XIX (1875), pp217-41

'The Venetian Navy in the Sixteenth Century', *Fraser's Magazine* (October 1875), pp483-500

'Changes of Climate', *British Quarterly Review* (1 October 1876)

'The French Privateers: III Thurot.', *Fraser's Magazine* (January 1878), pp71-88. ST

'Paul Jones. 'The Pirate'', *Fraser's Magazine* (April 1878), pp501-22. ST

'Tegetthoff: Experiences of Steam and Armour', *Fraser's Magazine* (June 1878), pp671-92. ST

'Weather Forecasting', *Fraser's Magazine* (August 1879), pp242-54

'The Heraldry of the Sea:- Ensigns, Colours and Flags', *JRUSI* Vol XXIV (1880), pp116-48

'Naval Promotion, Arithmetically and Historically considered', *JRUSI* Vol XXIV (1880), pp535-60

'On the Several Systems of European Naval Education', *JRUSI* Vol XXIV (1880), pp108-29

'Law of Storms and Heaving-to Tack', *Nautical Magazine* (September 1880), 11pp.

'Jean de Vienne: A Chapter from the Naval History of the Fourteenth Century', *United Service Magazine* (October 1880). ST

'Henry John Codrington, Admiral of the Fleet', *Fraser's Magazine* (January 1881), pp73-86

'Our Winter Storms', *Fraser's Magazine* (June 1881), pp758-70

'Privateers and Privateering: I Fortunatus Wright.', *Fraser's Magazine* (October 1881), pp462-78. ST

'Privateers and Privateering: II George Walker.', *Fraser's Magazine* (November 1881), pp589-623. ST

'The French Privateers: I Jean Bart.', *Fraser's Magazine* (March 1882), pp343-60. ST

'Naval Education', *JRUSI* Vol XXVI (1882), pp339-68

'The French Privateers: II Du Guay-Trouin', *Fraser's Magazine* (April 1882), pp498-518. ST

'The French Privateers: IV Robert Surcouf', *United Service Magazine* (February and March 1883). ST

'Historical Sketch of Anemometry and Anemometers', *Quarterly Journal of the Royal Meteorological Society* Vol 8 (July 1882), pp161-89

'Presidential Address', *Quarterly Journal of the Meteorological Society* Vol 9 (January 1883), pp71-83

'Wind Force and how it is measured', *Longman's Magazine* Vol 1 (April 1883), pp615-27

'Presidential Address', *QJ Royal MS* Vol 10, No 50 (April 1884), pp77-87

'Notes on the Last Great Naval War', *JRUSI* Vol XXIX (1885), pp909-33

'The Invincible Armada', Lecture to the Royal Institution 1888.

'Nelson's last Codicil', *Colburn's United Service Magazine*. Part 1 'The Spanish War' Vol II (November 1888-April 1889), pp647-662, and Part 2 'The Watering of the Fleet' Vol III (May 1889-October 1889), pp10-23

'The Captains of the Nightingale', *The English Historical Review* Vol IV (January 1889), pp65-80

'Jenkins's Ear', *The English Historical Review* Vol IV (October 1889), pp741-9

'The Early Development of Naval War', *Colburn's United Service Magazine*. Part One Sept. 1889 pp523-37. Part Two Oct 1889 pp683-99

'Beachy Head', *Army and Navy Gazette* 1890

'Our Naval Literature' 12 parts in *The Army and Navy Gazette* (1892), pp70, 119, 198, 291-2, 479, 679, 840, 986. Part 2 titled 'New Lights on the Old Navy' (1893), pp1131, 275, 732,

'Barfleur and la Hogue' *The Army and Navy Gazette* (19.5.1892), pp437-8

'Recent Naval Literature' *JRUSI* Vol XXXVII (November 1893), pp1161-82

'Thirty Years Since', *St. Andrews Magazine* (April 1894), pp82-7 Beyrout. May 1894 pp98-102 Naples. June 1894. pp28-36 Corfu. Taken from Laughton's notebooks of 1861-62.

'Sir George Rooke', *JRUSI* Vol XXXIX (April 1895), pp328-32

'The Battle of the Nile: an Anniversary Study', *Cornhill Magazine* Vol 74 (1896), pp147-58

'The Study of Naval History', *JRUSI* Vol XXXX (1896), pp795-820

'Our Navy Records', *Navy and Army Illustrated* (29.5.1896)

'Nelson at Naples', *The Athenaeum* No 3748 (26 August 1899)

'The Naval Exhibition at the Hague', *The Monthly Review* (November 1900), pp67-82

'Nelson's Home at Merton', *Wimbledon and Merton Annual* (1903), pp32-44

'The American Revolution',*The National Review* (1903/4) 14pp

Introductory Notice for the Society for Nautical Research, *United States Naval Institute Proceedings* (1910), Part 2, p636

'Historians and Naval History', *Cornhill Magazine* (1913)

Book reviews

Almost all of Laughton's major book reviews were written for the *Edinburgh Review* (*ER*), with three in the *Quarterly Review* (*QR*). These took the form of long, usually multi-volume notices, with a significant contribution by the reviewer, including source references and substantial argument. The following are Laughton's own short titles, written out in his own hand in the RMA Kingston volumes. A fuller listing will appear in the forthcoming NRS volume of his correspondence.

Arctic Exploration	*ER* Apr 1875	Rodney & the 18th Century Navy	
Lindsay's 'Merchant Shipping'			*ER* Jan. 1892
	ER Apr 1876	Baron de Marbot	*QR* Jan 1892
New Arctic Lands	*ER* Jan 1877	Marshal de Saxe	*ER* Oct 1892
Charles Kingsley	*ER* Apr 1877	Mahan on Maritime Power	
Low's 'Indian Navy'	*ER* Oct 1878		*ER* Apr 1893
The King's Secret	*ER* Apr 1879	Battle of La Hogue and	
Reign of Queen Anne	*ER* Apr 1880	Maritime War	*QR* Apr 1893
Pepys Diary	*ER* Jul 1880	Sir Richard Burton	*ER* Oct 1893
Trevelyan's Charles James Fox		Naval Armaments	*ER* Apr 1894
	ER Oct. 1880	Naval War in the East	*ER* Oct 1894
Gustavus III	*ER* Jul 1881	Weather Prevision	*ER* Apr 1895
The Bonapartes	*ER* Jan 1882	History of Spain	*ER* Oct 1895
Brassey on the British Navy		House of Conde	*ER* Jan 1896
	ER Apr 1882	Emma, Lady Hamilton	*ER* Apr 1896
Baron de Stael	*ER* Jan 1883	Gunpowder Plot	*ER* Jan 1897
Frederic II & Maria Theresa	*ER* Apr 1883	Mahan's Nelson	*ER* Jul 1897
Vicksburg & Gettysburg (Mahan)		Duke of Grafton	*ER* Apr 1899
	ER Oct 1883	Peasant's Rising	*ER* Jan 1900
John de Witt	*ER* Oct 1884	Goldwin Smith's United Kingdom	
The State of the Navy	*ER* Apr 1885		*ER* Jul 1900
Naval Warfare	*ER* Jul 1885	Corbett's 'Drake'	*ER* Jul 1901
Frederic II & Louis XV	*ER* Oct 1885	The French in Eygpt	*ER* Oct 1901
A French Corsair	*ER* Apr 1888	Holland-Rose's Napoleon	
Stratford de Redcliffe	*ER* Jan 1889		*ER* Apr 1902
Maria Theresa	*ER* Jul 1889	Mastery of the Pacific	*ER* Jul 1902
Naval Supremacy & Naval Tactics		Blockade of Brest/Desbriere	
	ER Jan 1890		*ER* Jan 1903
Mahan on Maritime Power		Charles V	*ER* Apr 1903
	ER Oct 1890	Siege of Quebec	*ER* Jul 1903
Forts and Fleets	*QR* Apr 1891	John Moore	*ER* Jul 1904
Austria in 1848-9	*ER* Oct 1891	'The American Revolution'	
		The National Review Mar 1904	

Corbett's England and the
Mediterranean'   ER Jul 1904
Typhoons & Cyclones   ER Jan 1905
Naples and Napoleon   ER Oct 1905
Centenary of Trafalgar   QR Oct 1905
Holland's Whig Party   ER Jul 1906
Acton's Lecture's   ER Apr 1907
Desbriére's 1805   ER Oct 1907

The French in Eygpt II   ER Jul 1908
Paston Letters   ER Oct 1908
Firth's Protectorate   ER Apr 1910
Malta   ER July 1910
Tudor Kings   ER Jan 1911
Sovereignty of the Seas   ER Oct 1911
Holland Rose's   ER Jan 1912
Sandwich   ER Oct 1912

Other attributed reviews:
'Hobart Pasha'   *Longman's Magazine* Vol 9 (Nov 1886), pp32-43

Official Publications:
Parliamentary Papers 1870 Vol. XXV Shadwell Committee
Report of the Select Committee on the Board of Admiralty 1871

Periodicals
The American Neptune
The Athenaeum
The Army and Navy Gazette
Brassey's Naval Annual
Dictionary of National Biography
(DNB)
The Edinburgh Review
The English Historical Review
The Gentleman's Magazine
The Geographical Journal
The Historical Journal
History
Mariner's Mirror (MM)

The Naval Review
Naval Science 1870-74
The Navy List
The Quarterly Review
Journal of the Royal United Services
Institution (JRUSI)
Journal of the Royal Meteorological
Society
The Times
United Stated Naval Institute
Proceedings
Who Was Who?

Books and Articles

Acton, H, *The Bourbons of Naples* (London 1956)

Adamson, J S A, 'Eminent Victorians: S R Gardiner and the Liberal as Hero', *The Historical Journal* (1990)

Allen, M, 'Rear Admiral Reginald Custance: Director of Naval Intelligence 1899-1902', *MM* Vol 78 (1992)

Annan, N, *Leslie Stephen, the Godless Victorian* (London 1984)

Anstruther, I, *Oscar Browning* (London 1983)

Aston, Sir G, *The Study of War for Statesmen and Citizens* (London 1927)

Bacon, R, *The Life of John Rushworth, Earl Jellicoe* (London 1936)

Badham, F P, *Nelson at Naples: A Journal for June 10-30, 1799* (London 1900)

Baer, G W, *One Hundred Years of Sea Power: The United States Navy, 1890 -1990* (Stanford 1994)

Ballard, Admiral Sir G, 'Admiral Ballard's Memoirs', *MM* Vol 62 (1976)

Barnard, H, *Military Schools and Courses of Instruction in the Art and Science of War* (Washington 1872)

Battesti, M, *La marine de Napoléon III* 2 vols (Paris 1997)

Bedford, F G H, *The Life and Letters of Admiral Sir Frederick Bedford* (Newcastle 1961)

Beeler, J F, *British Naval Policy in the Gladstone-Disraeli Era, 1866-1890* (Stanford 1997)

Billington, R, *Frederick Jackson Turner* (New York 1973)

Bond, B, *Liddell-Hart: A Study of his Military Thought* (London 1976)

Bonner-Smith, D & Lumby, E W R, *The Second China War, 1856-1860* (London, NRS 1954)

Bourchier, Lady, *Selections from the Correspondence of Sir Henry Codrington* (London 1880)

Bradford, E E, *Admiral of the Fleet Sir Arthur K Wilson* (London 1922)

Brassey, Sir T, *The British Navy: its Strength, Resources and Administration* 6 vols (London 1883)

Breemer, J, 'The Burden of Trafalgar: Decisive Battle and Naval Strategic expectations on the Eve of World War One', *Journal of Strategic Studies* (1994)

Bridge, C A G, 'On the necessity of forming a Naval Staff' *Naval Science* (1870)

—, 'Fleet Evolutions and Naval Tactics' *JRUSI* (1873)

—, 'Obituary' *The Geographical Journal* (1915)

—, (ed), *History of the Russian Fleet during the Reign of Peter the Great, by a Contemporary Englishman* (London NRS 1899)

—, *The Art of Naval Warfare* (London 1907)

—, *Seapower and Other Studies* (London 1910)

—, *Some Recollections* (London 1918)

Brooks, R, *Fred T Jane: An Eccentric Visionary* (Coulsdon, Surrey 1997)

Brown, A T, *Some Account of the Royal Institution School, Liverpool* (Cambridge 1924)

Bryce, J, *Studies in Contemporary Biography* (London 1903)

Bucholz, A, *Delbrück and the German Military Establishment* (Iowa 1985)

Burt, R, *British Battleships 1889-1904* (London 1988)

Campbell, J, *Lives of the Admirals*, 4 vols (London 1744)

Cannadine, D G, *G M Trevelyan; A Life in History* (London 1992)

Cantwell, J D, *The Public Record Office: 1838-1958* (London 1991)

Chancellor, V, *History for their Masters: Opinion in the English History Textbook, 1800-1914* (London 1970)

Charnock, J, *Biographica Navalis* 6 vols (London 1794-6)

Clarke, G S *Fortification* (London 1890 and 2nd 1907)

—, & Thursfield, J R, *The Navy and the Nation* (London 1897)

Clarke, G S (Lord Sydenham of Combe), *My Working Life* (London 1927)

Clive, J, 'The *Edinburgh Review*: The Life and Death of a Periodical' in Briggs, A (ed), *Essays in the History of Publishing* (London 1974)

Clowes, W L, *A History of the Royal Navy from the Earliest Times* 7 vols (London 1897-1903, reprinted Chatham Publishing, London, 1996-7)

Collister, P, *The Sulivans and the Slave Trade* (London 1980)

Colomb, P, 'The Naval Defence of the United Kingdom' *JRUSI* (1888)

—, 'The Relation between Local Fortification and a Moving Navy' *JRUSI* (1889)

—, *Naval Warfare* (London 1891)

—, *Memoirs of Sir A Cooper Key* (London 1898)

Colson, P (ed), *Lord Goschen and his friends* (London 1940)

Corbett, J S (ed), *Papers relating to the War with Spain, 1585-87* (London NRS 1898)

—, *Drake and the Tudor Navy* 2 vols (London 1898)

—, *England in the Mediterranean: A Study in the Rise and Influence of British Power within the Straits* (London 1903)

—, (ed), *Fighting Instructions: 1530-1816* (London NRS 1905)

—, (ed), *Signals and Instructions; 1776-1794* (London NRS 1909)

—, *The Campaign of Trafalgar* (London 1910)

—, *Some Principles of Maritime Strategy* (London 1911)

—, 'The Revival of Naval History' *The Contemporary Review* (1916)

—, 'The Teaching of Naval and Military History' *History* (1916)

—, 'Napoleon and the British Navy after Trafalgar' *The Quarterly Review* (1922)

Dawson, C M, *The Story of Greenwich* (London 1977)

Day, A, *The Admiralty Hydrographic Service: 1795-1919* (London 1967)

Deacon, M, *Scientists and the Sea: 1650 -1900* (London 1971)

D'Egville, H, *Imperial Defence and Closer Imperial Union* (London 1913)

Desmond, A & Moore, J, *Darwin* (London 1991)

Dickinson, H W, 'Educational Provision for Officers of the Royal Navy; 1857-1877' (unpub University of London Ph D thesis 1994)

Dilke, C & Wilkinson, H S, *Imperial Defence* (London 1891)

Douglas, Sir H, *Naval Warfare Under Steam* (London 1858)

Dunn, W H, *James Anthony Froude: A Biography 1857-1894* (Oxford 1963)

Dutton, D, *Austen Chamberlain: Gentleman in Politics* (Bolton 1985)

Egerton, Mrs F, *Admiral of the Fleet Sir Geoffrey Phipps Hornby* (London 1896)

Ehrman, J, *The Younger Pitt* Vol 1 (London 1969)

Eyck, F, *George Peabody Gooch: A Study in History and Politics* (London 1982)

Fletcher, C R F, and Kipling, R, *A School History of England* (Oxford 1911)

Foote, E J, *Vindication of his conduct when Captain of HMS Seahorse etc, 1799* (London 1807)

Freeman, E A, *The Methods of Historical Study* (London 1886)

Galbraith, V H, 'Albert Frederick Pollard 1869-1948', *Proceedings of the British Academy* Vol XXXV (1949)

Gardiner, S R (ed), *Letters and Papers relating to the First Dutch War* (London NRS 2 vols 1900-1902)

Gat, A, *The Development of Military Thought: The Nineteenth Century* (Oxford 1992)

Gildea, R, *The Past in French History* (New Haven 1994)

Gleaves, A B, *Life and Letters of Rear Admiral Stephen B Luce US Navy, founder of the Naval War College* (New York 1925)

Glete, J, *Navies and Nations: Warships, Navies and State Building in Europe and America: 1500-1850* (Stockholm 1993)

Glover, R 'The French Fleet, 1807-1814: Britain's problem and Madison's opportunity', *The Historical Journal* (1967)

Glynn, J, *The Prince of Publishers, George Smith* (London 1986)

Goldrick, J & Hattendorf, J, *Mahan is not Enough* (Newport RI 1993)

Goldstein, D S 'History at Oxford and Cambridge: Professionalisation and the influence of Ranke' in Iggers, G C, and Powell, J M, *Leopold von Ranke and the shaping of the Historical Discipline* (Syracuse 1990)

Gooch, G P, *History and Historians in the Nineteenth Century* (London 1913)

—, *Under Six Reigns* (London 1958)

Gordon, A, *The Rules of the Game: Jutland and British Naval Command* (London 1996)

Gordon, P, *The Red Earl: The Papers of the Fifth Earl Spencer, 1835-1910* Vol II 1885-1910 (Northamptonshire Record Society 1986)

Graham, G S, 'The Maritime Foundations of Imperial History', *Canadian Historical Review* Vol XXI (1950)

Graham, G S, *The Politics of Naval Supremacy* (Cambridge 1965)

Groves' Liverpool Directory, various editions

Haas, J, *A Management Odyssey: the Royal Dockyards 1701-1914* (New York 1994)

Hall, H, 'The National Study of Naval History; II New Methods of Research', *Transactions of the Royal Historical Society* Vol XII (1898)

Hamilton, C I, *Anglo-French Naval Rivalry; 1840 -1870* (Oxford 1993)

Hamilton, W M, 'The Nation and the Navy: Methods and Organisation of British Navalist Propaganda; 1889-1914' (unpub Univ of London Ph D thesis 1986)

Hankinson, A, *Man of Wars: William Howard Russell of 'The Times'* (London 1982)

Harvie, C, *The Lights of Liberalism: University Liberals and the Challenge of Democracy 1860-1886* (London 1976)

Hattendorf, J and L C, *A Bibliography of he Works of Alfred Thayer Mahan* (Newport RI 1986)

Hattendorf, J (ed), *Ubi Sumus? The State of Naval History* (Newport RI 1994)

—, (ed), *Doing Naval History: Essays towards Improvement* (Newport 1995)

Hayes, J , and Hattendorff, J, *The Writings of Stephen B Luce* (Newport RI 1975)

Hearnshaw, F J C, *The Centenary History of King's College, London; 1828-1928* (London 1929)

Henderson, W, 'The Naval Society and Review and an Historical Abstract of other service periodicals' *The Naval Review* (1922)

Higham, R, (ed), *British Military History: A bibliography* (London 1971)

Holland-Rose, J, *Naval History and National History* (Cambridge 1919)

Houghton, W E, 'Periodical Literature and the Literate Classes' in Shattock, J, and Wolff, M, *The Victorian Periodical Press* (Toronto 1982)

Huelin, G, *King's College, London* (London 1978)

Hughes, E A, *The Royal Naval College, Dartmouth* (London 1950)

Humphreys, R A, *The Royal Historical Society: 1868 -1968* (London 1968)

Hunt, B D, *Sailor-Scholar: Admiral Sir Herbert Richmond 1871-1946* (Waterloo, Ontario 1982)

Hutton, W H (ed), *Letters of William Stubbs, Bishop of Oxford* (London 1904)

James, W, *The Naval History of Great Britain from the Declaration of war by France in 1793 to the Accession of George IV* 5 vols (London 1822-24 & later editions)

Johnson, C, 'The Camden Society' in Humphreys, R A, *The Royal Historical Society: 1868-1968* (London 1968)

Karsten, P, *The Naval Aristocracy; the Golden Age of Annapolis and the Emergence of Modern American Navalism* (Annapolis 1972)

Kemp, P, *The Oxford Companion to Ships and the Sea* (Oxford 1976)

Kennedy, P M, *The Rise and Fall of British Naval Mastery* (London 1976)

Kennedy, Sir W, *Hurrah for the Life of a Sailor !* (London 1900)

Kenyon, J, *The History Men* (2nd edn London 1993)

Kerr, M, *Prince Louis of Battenberg* (London 1934)

King-Hall, L, *Sea Saga* (London 1935)

Knerr, D, 'Through the 'Golden Mist'; A Brief Overview of Armada Historiography', *The American Neptune* (1989)

Lambert, A D, *Battleships in Transition: The Creation of the Steam Battlefleet* (London 1984)

—, *The Crimean War: British Grand Strategy against Russia 1853-1856* (Manchester 1990)

—, *The Last Sailing Battlefleet: Maintaining Naval Mastery 1815-1850* (London 1991)

—, 'Reflections on a History of the Royal Navy', *The Naval Review* (1997)

—, 'Politics, Technology and Policy-making 1859-1865: Palmerston, Gladstone and the management of the Ironclad Naval Race', *The Northern Mariner* (August 1998)

—, 'Portraits of Past Presidents: Sir John Laughton' in *Weather* (1998)

—, 'Deterrence' in Duffy, M (ed), *Parameters of British Naval Power 1856-1945* (Exeter 1999)

Laughton, J B, *An Address to the Students of Sydney College* (Sydney 1845)

—, *Johnson's historical, topographical and parochial illustrated guide to the Isle of Man* (London various editions 1842-59)

Laughton-Matthews, V, *The Blue Tapestry: The Story of the WRNS* (London 1948)

Lecky, W E H, 'Henry Reeve' in *Historical and Political Essays* (London 1910)

Levine, P, *The Amateur and the Professional: Antiquarians, Historians and Archaeologists in Victorian England: 1838-1886* (Cambridge 1986)

Lewis, M, *The Navy in Transition: A Social History 1814-1864* (London 1965)

Lloyd, C, 'The Royal Naval College at Greenwich and Portsmouth' *MM* Vol 52 (1966)

Luvass, J, *The Education of an Army; British Military Thought; 1815-1940* (London 1967)

Mcartney, D, *W E H Lecky; Historian and Politician 1838-1903* (Dublin 1994)

Mackay, R F, *Fisher of Kilverstone* (Oxford 1973)

Mahan, A T, *The Influence of Sea Power Upon History 1660-1783* (Boston 1890)

—, *The Influence of Sea Power Upon the French Revolution and Empire 1793-1812* 2 vols (Boston 1892)

—, *The Life of Nelson: The Embodiment of the Sea Power of Great Britain* 2 vols (Boston 1897, 2nd revised edn, 1899)

—, *Sea Power in its Relation to the War of 1812* 2 vols (Boston 1905)

—, *From Sail to Steam: Recollections of a Naval Life* (Boston 1907)

—, *The Major Operations of the War of American Independence* (Boston 1913)

(see also the full range of titles cited in Hattendorf: *Bibliography*)

Manning, F, *The Life of Sir William White* (London 1923)

Manuscripts and Men: the Centenary of the Royal Commission on Historical Manuscripts; 1869-1969 (London 1969)

Marder, A J, *The Anatomy of British Sea Power 1880-1905* (London 1940)

—, (ed), *Portrait of an Admiral, Sir Herbert Richmond* (London 1952)

—, *From the Dreadnought to Scapa Flow* 5 vols (Oxford 1961-70)

Markham, A H, *Life of Sir Clements Markham* (London 1917)

Marshall, J, *Royal Naval Biography* 4 vols (London 1823-35)

Martel, G, *Imperial Diplomacy: Lord Rosebery and the Failure of Foreign Policy* (Montreal 1986)

Martin, G, and Parker, C, *The Spanish Armada* (London 1988)

Marwick, A, *The Nature of History* (London 1970)

Matthew, H G C, *Gladstone 1809-1874* (Oxford 1984)

Maurice, F, *British Strategy: A Study in the Application of the Principles of War* (London 1929)

Moore, Sir A H, 'The Beginnings of the Society for Nautical Research', *MM* Vol 41 (1955)

Morley, J, *Life of Gladstone* 3 vols (London 1903)

Morriss, A J A, *The Scaremongers: Advocacy of War and Rearmament 1896-1914* (London 1984)

Naylor, L E, *The Irrepressible Victorian: The Story of Thomas Gibson Bowles* (London 1965)

Neilson, K, and Kennedy, G, *Far Flung Lines: Studies in Imperial Defence in Honour of Donald Mackenzie Schurman* (London 1997)

Newton, A P, *The Sea Commonwealth* (London 1919)

Nicolas, Sir N H, *Dispatches and Letters of Horatio, Lord Viscount Nelson* 7 vols (London 1844-46, reprinted Chatham Publishing, London 1997-8)

—, *A History of the Royal Navy from the Earliest Times to the Wars of the French Revolution* 2 vols (incomplete) (London 1847)

Noel, G H U, *The Gun, Ram and Torpedo* (Portsmouth 1873)

O'Byrne, W, *Naval Biographical Dictionary* 2 vols (London 1847)

Offer, A, *The First World War: An Agrarian Interpretation* (Oxford 1989)

Oman, C, *Nelson* (London 1947)

Oppenheim, M, *A History of the Administration of the Royal Navy; 1509-1660* (London 1896)

— (ed), *The Naval Accounts of Henry VII* (London NRS 1896)

—, *A Maritime History of Devon* (Exeter 1968)

Pack, S W C, *Britannia at Dartmouth* (London 1966)

Parker, C, *The English Historical Tradition Since 1850* (Edinburgh 1990)

Parry, J, *The Rise and Fall of Liberal Government in Victorian Britain* (Yale 1993)

Pasley, L, *Life of Sir Thomas Sabine Pasley* (London 1900)

Perrin, W G, *British Flags* (Cambridge 1922)

Pollard, A F, 'The University of London and the Study of History' *The National Review* (1904)

—, *Factors in Modern History* (London 1907)

—, 'The Needs of Historical Studies in the University of London 26 11 1918' in *Factors in Modern History* (London 3rd ed 1932)

—, 'London and Historical Research' (1920 printed lecture in Pollard MS)

Pollard, S and Robertson, P, *The British Shipbuilding Industry, 1870-1914* (Harvard 1979)

Porter, A, *Victorian Shipping, Business and Imperial Policy. Donald Currie, the Castle Line and Southern Africa* (London 1986)

Ranft, B M, 'The Protection of British Seaborne Trade and the Development of Systematic Planning for war; 1860-1906' in Ranft, B M (ed), *Technical Change and British Naval Policy 1860-1939* (London 1977)

Rawson, G, *Life of Admiral Sir Harry Rawson* (London 1914)

Rich, E E, *The Crises of Imperial History: An Inaugural Lecture* (Cambridge 1952)

Richmond, H W, 'The Expedition to Sicily, 1718 under Sir George Byng', *JRUSI* (1909)

— (ed), *Papers Relating to the Loss of Minorca in 1756* (London NRS 1913)

—, *The Navy in the War of 1739-1748* (Cambridge 1920)

—, *National Policy and Naval Strength* (London 1928)

—, *Naval Training* (Oxford 1933)

Rodger, N A M, *The Articles of War* (Havant 1982)

—, *The Wooden World: The Anatomy of the Georgian Navy* (London 1986)

—, *The Insatiable Earl: A Life of John Montagu, 4th Earl of Sandwich* (London 1993)

—, *The Safeguard of the Sea: A Naval History of Britain* Vol 1 *660-1649* (London 1997)

Ropp, T (ed Roberts, S S), *The Development of a Modern Navy* (Annapolis 1987)

Roskill, S W, *The Strategy of Seapower: its development and application* (London 1962)

Rothblatt, S, *The Revolution of the Dons; Cambridge and Society in Victorian England* (London 1968)

St Aubyn, G, *A Victorian Eminence* (London 1961)

Sainsbury, A B, *The Centenary of the Navy Records Society, 1893-1993* (London NRS 1993)

Sainsbury, A B, 'The Origins of the Society for Nautical Research', *MM* Vol 80 (1994)

Sandler, S, *The Emergence of the Modern Capital Ship* (London 1979)

Schurman, D M *The Education of a Navy: The Development of British Naval Strategic Thought 1867-1914* (London 1967)

—, *Julian S Corbett, 1854-1922; Historian of British Maritime Policy from Drake to Jellicoe* (London 1981)

Seager, R II, and Maguire, D D, *Letters and Papers of Alfred Thayer Mahan* 3 vols (Annapolis 1975)

Seager, R II, *Alfred Thayer Mahan; The Man and his Letters* (Annapolis 1977)

Seeley, J, *The Expansion of England* (London 1886)

—, *The Growth of British Policy* (London 1895)

Seymour, E H, *My Naval Career and Travels* (London 1911)

Shulman, M R, *Navalism and the Emergence of American Seapower 1882-1893* (Annapolis 1995)

Simmons, J, *Southey* (London 1945)

Soffer, R N, *Discipline and Power: The University, History and the Making of the English Elite, 1870-1930* (Stanford 1994)

Soley, J R, *Report on Foreign Systems of Naval Education* (Washington 1880)

Southey, R, *Life of Nelson* (London 1825)

Spector, M M, 'A P Newton' in Ausuble, A (ed), *Some Modern Historians of Britain* (New York 1951)

Spector, R, *Professors of War: The Naval War College and the Development of the Naval Profession* (Newport RI 1977)

Stapleton, E J, *Some Official Correspondence of George Canning* 2 vols (London 1887)

Stephen, L, *Studies of a Biographer* Vol 1 (London 1907)

Stephens, W R W, *The Life and Letters of Edward A Freeman* 2 vols (London 1895)

Stout, N R, *The Royal Navy in North America, 1760-1775* (Annapolis 1973)

Stubbs, W *Lectures on Medieval and Modern History* (3rd edn Oxford 1900)

Sumida, J T, *In Defence of Naval Supremacy: Finance, Technology and British Naval Policy 1889-1914* (London 1989)

—, *Inventing Grand Strategy and Teaching Command: the Classic works of Alfred Thayer Mahan Reconsidered* (Washington 1997)

Tedder, A W, *The Navy of the Restoration* (Cambridge 1916)

Thompson, T W, *James Anthony Froude on Nation and Empire: A Study in Victorian Racialism* (New York 1987)

Thursfield, J R, *Naval Warfare* (London 1913)

Thursfield, Sir J, 'The Navy Records Society' *The Naval Review* (1920)

Trevelyan, G M, *The Present Position of History* (Cambridge 1927)

—, *England Under Queen Anne: Blenheim* (London 1930)

—, *Sir George Otto Trevelyan* (London 1932)

Tucker, A, 'Military' in Don Vann, J, and Van Arsdel, R T, *Victorian Periodicals and Victorian Society* (Toronto 1994)

Tulloch, H, *Acton* (London 1988)

—, *James Bryce's American Commonwealth* (London 1988)

Tunstall, W J C, *The Realities of Naval History* (London 1936)

—, 'Imperial Defence 1815-1870' and 'Imperial Defence 1871-1997' and 'Imperial Defence 1897-1914' in Holland Rose, Newton, A, and Benians, E A, *The Cambridge Modern History of the British Empire* Vol III & Vol IV (Cambridge 1940 & 1959)

—, (ed Tracy N), *Naval Warfare in the Age of Sail* (London 1990)

Venn, J A, *A Biographical Dictionary of Gonville and Caius College* (Cambridge 1898)

—, *Early Collegiate Life* (Cambridge 1913)

Vesey-Hamilton, Sir R, *Naval Administration* (London 1896)

Vetch, R H, *Life of Lieutenant General Sir Andrew Clarke* (London 1905)

Von Arx, J *Progress and Pessimism: Religion, Politics and History in late Nineteenth Century Britain* (Harvard 1985)

Warner, A, *William Allingham* (Cambridge 1975)

Wells, J, *Whaley: the Story of HMS Excellent* (Portsmouth 1980)

White, C (ed), *The Nelson Companion* (Gloucester 1995)

Wilkinson, H S, *The Brain of an Army* (London 1891)

—, *The Command of the Sea* (London 1894)

—, *The Brain of the Navy* (London 1895)

Williams, G, *The Liverpool Privateers* (London 1897)

Wormell, D, *Sir John Seeley and the uses of History* (London 1980)

Young, G V C, and Foster, C, *Captain Francois Thurot* (Stockholm 1986)

Lectures

Matthew, H G C 'The DNB and the new DNB: Leslie Stephen and Sidney Lee a Hundred Years on' The London Library Lecture 1994

Index

———— · ————

Abbreviations

Adm. = Admiral; Capt. = Captain; Cdre = Commodore; CSS = Confederate States Ship; DNB = Dictionary of National Biography; Gen = General; HMS = Her Majesty's Ship; JKL = John Knox Laughton; JPNA = Junior Naval Professional Association; NRS = Navy Records Society; Prof. = Professor; RE = Royal Engineers; RM = Royal Marines; RN = Royal Navy; USN = United States Navy